THE
BIGGAR
PICTURE

DAN BIGGAR

WITH ROSS HARRIES

THE
BIGGAR
PICTURE

MACMILLAN

First published 2024 by Macmillan
an imprint of Pan Macmillan
The Smithson, 6 Briset Street, London EC1M 5NR
EU representative: Macmillan Publishers Ireland Ltd, 1st Floor,
The Liffey Trust Centre, 117–126 Sheriff Street Upper,
Dublin 1, D01 YC43
Associated companies throughout the world
www.panmacmillan.com

ISBN 978-1-0350-2805-4 HB
ISBN 978-1-0350-2806-1 TPB

1 3 5 7 9 8 6 4 2

A CIP catalogue record for this book is available from the British Library.

Typeset in Warnock Pro by Jouve (UK), Milton Keynes
Printed and bound by CPI Group (UK) Ltd, Croydon, CR0 4YY

Visit **www.panmacmillan.com** to read more about all our books
and to buy them. You will also find features, author interviews and
news of any author events, and you can sign up for e-newsletters
so that you're always first to hear about our new releases.

To my beloved mum, Liz, who, in her own words,
'was a rugby fan before she became a mother'. Without
your love, support and guidance, there would be no story
to tell. This is for you, Mum.

CONTENTS

CONTENTS

THE
BIGGAR
PICTURE

PROLOGUE

There it was. Hanging on its peg. On the one hand, a lifeless piece of cloth; on the other, a magical garment, capable of imbuing its wearer with superhuman powers. The red jersey of Wales, with the number '10' emblazoned across the back. It wasn't made from the heavy-duty cotton of yesteryear, but there were myths and legends woven into those fibres. As much as it *was* a piece of cloth, it was also a repository of dreams.

Red. The colour of the Welsh dragon, of blood and danger too. I'd bled into that shirt; I'd broken bones wearing it. I'd clutched its badge with pride and ripped it off in despair. In its own way, it contained a roadmap of my journey to this point. The joy, the graft, the despair, and everything in between. One hundred and eleven times I'd pulled that jersey on. This, potentially, could be the last.

Fly half, outside half, stand-off, first five-eighth, pivot. Call it what you want. In Wales, it's the jersey that matters most. Rugby is a team game, but as a 10 you're a solo artist; the frontman, whether you like it or not. No shirt suffers the cold, harsh light of scrutiny more, and when you wear it, you're standing on the shoulders of giants.

Barry John. The King, they called him. Ghosting and gliding past defenders like they weren't there. Phil Bennett. Benny, the hot stepper. Jinking and weaving, making time stand still. Jonathan Davies – Jiffy. The impish genius, turning on the after-burners, leaving scorch marks in his wake.

Wales has always been a land of poets and dreamers, and so many of my predecessors hypnotized the masses with their mesmerizing artistry.

Me? I'd never fit the mould.

Throughout my career, I'd constantly had to confront the critics, to silence the cynics. I was too slow. I stood too deep. I was petulant, aggressive and one-dimensional. I kicked too much and ran too little. I was, in short, not your typical Welsh fly half. Where Barry would paint you a picture, I'd draw you a diagram. Pragmatism over romanticism, that was me.

For many years I'd thought that I'd never emerge from the long shadows cast by Barry, Benny and Jiffy. Yet here I was, holding this jersey for the 112th time, more than any other number 10 in Welsh history.

I looked it over, rubbing its shiny surface between thumb and forefinger. This one had all the usual signifiers: the three feathers, with my cap number '1063' beneath them. The Rugby World Cup logo and 'France 2023' on the opposite breast. On the left sleeve, 'Cymru v Ariannin, 14eg Hydref 2023'. Wales v Argentina, 14 October 2023. And in the bottom left-hand corner, embroidered above the embossed words of the Welsh National Anthem, just to confirm this hadn't all been a dream: 'Dan Biggar, 112th cap'.

As I gripped it in my hand, I reflected on the spiritual regard in which it's held, on the jumble of contradictions it represents. As a young man, all I had was the hunger to wear it, blissfully unaware of the baggage that came with it. How it can simultaneously feel like a suit of armour and a straitjacket. How it can imbue you with Herculean strength or weigh you down with crippling anxiety. But any misery I'd endured had been outweighed by the joy it had brought. And here I was, back on the grandest stage of all – the Rugby World Cup – with one last shot at glory. A quarter-final against Argentina, and beyond that . . . two more games?

Tugging that iconic red jersey over my head, I knew it was

nearly time to hand it over to the next generation. But I had a job to do first. I turned towards the tunnel knowing that, whatever happened today, I'd do what I'd always done. I would head out there and do everything in my power to help Wales win.

1

'IF THAT BOY DOESN'T PLAY FOR WALES, THERE'S SOMETHING WRONG'

Saturday 14 October 1989

My father, John, is tucking into a curry and a pint the Welsh way – arf 'n' arf. Half chips, half rice. His feet are up, and he's watching the live action from the Arms Park. Cardiff are taking on the mighty All Blacks and are ahead courtesy of a Mark Edwards try. It's a cracking game and an upset is on the cards, so Dad is a little peeved when a nurse appears in the doorway.

'Excuse me, Mr Biggar, your wife is going into labour.'

Downing what remains of his pint, Dad races down the corridor to the maternity ward of Morriston Hospital to witness my arrival in the world. It turned out to be a false alarm, and I didn't actually make an appearance until the early hours of Monday morning. Cardiff ended up losing, so at least Dad didn't miss a famous victory.

A little over a year earlier, the weak flame of Welsh rugby had flickered briefly back to life when Wales won the Triple Crown. The revival was to prove a final gulp for air before the game was drowned by the onrushing tsunami of professionalism. Given how much blame is laid at the feet of Welsh fly halves, I'm sure there are those who consider it my fault.

Dan Biggar? Born in 1989? That's about the time it all went pear-shaped, isn't it?

That's an exaggeration, of course, but I have certainly had to develop a rhino skin being a fly half in Wales; tough enough to repel the relentless slings and arrows of a passionate, opinionated rugby public. It hasn't always been easy.

I'm known for my fiery personality and refusal to take a backwards step and, while there's an element of caricature to the way I've been portrayed, there's no doubt there's an anger in me. Not born of tragedy or a dark past; it's just that I have a fierce competitive streak that's run through me since the day I was born.

As a little kid, I was loud, brash and demanding. During one Sunday lunch, when I was strapped into a high chair, exercising my lungs to their limit, Dad calmly stood, carted me and my chair to the far end of our big back garden, and left me there to holler into the ether while the rest of the family enjoyed their meal in peace.

On another occasion, when I was four, Dad got tickets to the panto in Swansea. He seemed unusually keen and had reserved front-row seats. I was overwhelmed by the noise and bright lights and immediately began wailing in protest. Knowing there was no chance of calming me down, Dad gathered our things and trudged reluctantly out of the theatre. I later discovered his enthusiasm for the event was solely down to the fact that the glamour model, Linda Lusardi, had a starring role. Little wonder he looked so despondent as we traipsed out a mere five minutes after the show had started.

As for Mum, she rarely completed a food shop without me kicking off, often having to abandon a half-filled trolley to bundle her wild, raging baby into the car. I was a nightmare, always needing to be held.

My maternal grandparents refused to look after me because I was so difficult to control. Only Dad's parents were ever willing to step in, so I'd end up spending loads of my weekends with them while my older sister, Rachel, hung out with Mum's parents, Betty and Fred. They'd always hand a smiling Rachel back, having had a lovely time, whereas a frazzled Mamo and Dado virtually hurled me back into my parents' car, desperate to restore the peace I'd so utterly destroyed.

Childhood was a pretty idyllic experience, though. I grew up in the tiny village of Llangennith, on the western end of the Gower peninsula; the first place in the UK to be designated an Area of Outstanding Natural Beauty.

The family home was a sprawling labyrinthine place, set in its own grounds, with a steep rolling lawn affording magnificent views out to sea. From the front garden, sand dunes spilled away towards the ocean, dotted year-round with surfers braving the famous Atlantic swells.

From my bedroom, I'd gaze through the salt-encrusted windows to the distant form of Worm's Head; the mile-long headland once referred to by Dylan Thomas as the 'very promontory of depression.' That might have been because he once got trapped there overnight when the tide rushed in. For me, though, it will always symbolize home.

The only artificial sound you'd hear in Llangennith would be the revving of an engine or the tinkling tune from an ice-cream van, if they could be bothered to come that far down. To this day the phone signal is dodgy, and the broadband connection patchy at best. It essentially consisted of a surf shop, a pub, a church, a scattering of houses, and some winding country lanes where sheep assumed right of way over cars. They'd stare you down disdainfully if you dared to beep the horn on the way out.

Llangennith was contradictory: dark, bleak, and lonely in winter; sun-drenched and dreamy during the summer, when hundreds of kids would flock to the pristine beaches and camp under the stars. The tranquillity of the village would be shattered as legions of raucous teenagers stumbled back to Hill End campsite, drunk on cheap cider from the King's Head pub.

I spent my early childhood summers running myself ragged until the sun went down. I was obsessed with sport. We had football goals in the garden, and I'd play full ninety-minute games, assuming the roles of both teams as well as being referee and commentator. Our neighbours would have to endure these end-less, epic battles being played out and narrated by an over-enthusiastic child with energy to burn. Years later, the same neighbours confessed to my mother that they'd nearly gone insane at the repeated, monotonous thwack of my ball against the dividing wall. It wasn't until later that the football goals turned into rugby posts, and I started kicking the ball over them rather into them.

In spring and summer, we'd head for the beach after school to surf, grill sausages, and watch the sun set behind Worm's Head, casting its fiery crimson glow over our little corner of paradise.

I wasn't your stereotyped long-haired, bleached-blond surfer – Llangennith didn't see enough sunshine for me to develop a year-round tan – but I was dedicated enough. We had one of the best surf beaches in Britain within walking distance, and some of the best surfboards money could buy in PJ's surf shop. So although you couldn't buy a pint of milk in Llangennith, you could buy a top-of-the-range Al Merrick Dumpster Diver. The obsessive drive I'd later develop about rugby was in early evi-dence here, as I'd meticulously wax my board for hours on end before plunging into the foaming breakers.

We'd camp among the dunes on the weekends, where the unpredictable weather would occasionally catch us out. On one memorable occasion a biblical downpour turned an idyllic night under the stars into a nightmare of sopping wet sleeping bags and flooded tents. An SOS call to our parents ended with them get-ting their cars stuck in the sludge that had formed amid the flash floods, and we wound up traipsing home through the sticky swamp with all our gear balanced on our heads.

The waves were bigger and gnarlier in winter, and we'd often be thrashing around until after dark, as the chill began to penetrate our wetsuits. One particularly parky January evening, I virtually froze to death on my walk home. It was about a mile back to the house from our favourite surfing spot, and the temperature had plummeted significantly. I was shivering uncontrollably as I picked my way through the dunes, and my teeth were chattering like a cartoon character's. By the time I crunched up the driveway to the warm sanctuary of our house, I had icicles on my eyelids.

Winter nights indoors were golden; we'd light the fire in the hearth, *cwtch* up on the sofa, and watch *A Question of Sport*. Before the days of streaming or catch-up TV, that was the one show I never missed. If you'd told me then, as a scruffy kid living at the arse-end of nowhere, that I'd be an invited guest on it one day, I'd have considered you insane. I might have shown an aptitude for sport at a young age, but the idea of being good enough – and well-known enough – to graduate to the glamorous world of television was inconceivable. My appearance on the programme in 2015 evoked so many golden memories of those dreamy Friday nights in front of the fire out west.

The Gower is a peninsula, but it feels like an island. Growing up on that thin finger of land jutting into the ocean, you felt physically and emotionally separate from the mainland. We were coastal dwellers living on the margins. Later, when I played for Gorseinon Under-14s, the journey there would feel like passing through a portal into a busier, more frantic world. There was a real sense of sanctuary in our little corner of Wales, tucked away at the north-westerly tip of the Gower.

Most Welsh rugby players have a militant national identity; a sense of being Welsh to the core. Without sounding indifferent, I simply didn't have that growing up. While my extended family is all Welsh, I never felt any patriotic stirrings as a child. It's probably because I grew up where I did. Because of its otherness, and sense of isolation, the Gower has an identity all of its own.

Envisaging the Mumbles with its boutique shops and cafés, or the brightly painted beach huts of Langland, some people assume the whole of the Gower is some sort of posh enclave. It's not though. North Gower is wilder, more chiselled, and less manicured. It doesn't have shiny resort towns like the southern side, and it's definitely not posh. But neither is it particularly 'Welsh'. Little, if any, Welsh was spoken. My childhood was shaped by the waves and the dunes, by the rocks and ridges of Cefn Bryn, rather than the Welshness of the soil. Yes, I wanted to play for Wales, but it was a distant, abstract dream. The weight of history didn't press on my shoulders like it did in some families, and the folklore of Welsh rugby didn't permeate our village like it did in other parts of the country.

There was also the reality that kids tend to be drawn to winning teams and throughout the nineties, the Welsh rugby team was not performing well. When the game turned professional in 1995, we were left scrabbling in the dust as the likes of England and France strode purposefully towards the sunlit uplands. Watching the Six Nations – where we were routinely pumped by our bitterest rivals – was a depressing experience. Instead, my head was turned by the Manchester United side of that era, which was dominating British football. It was the round ball that first captured my heart. Rugby would have to wait a while.

In as much as there is a single Biggar place of origin, it's Onllwyn in the Dulais Valley. Coal-mining country. It's only around forty miles east of Llangennith, but it feels like a different world. There, on Wembley Avenue, three generations of my family grew up in the same house. My great-grandparents, my grandparents and my father and Auntie Julie. My grandparents, Albert and Gwyneth (Mamo and Dado to me) live there to this day, on the main road running through the village. Dad's grandfather, Rees Mitchell, bought the house when it was built in 1926, resettling from his hometown of Merthyr Tydfil to work underground. It's a poky, semi-detached 'Coal Board' house, directly opposite the old mine; it used to be permanently shrouded in smoke as the valley reverberated to the clanging of machinery.

The entire male community worked in the mine, and the colliery used to dominate the landscape; now, where the gaping hole used to be, there sits a broad thicket of trees, and beyond that the majestic peaks of the Brecon Beacons. Nature is doing its best to reclaim the land torn apart by industry.

Albert and Gwyneth met in Porthcawl, the glamorous seaside resort that drew amorous teenagers to its ballroom dances. Albert – a Manchester native and Army officer – was stationed at the Seabank Hotel, a distinctive whitewashed building that still dominates the coast road today. At a sprightly ninety-six years of age, Gwyneth still jokes that Albert once promised her a retirement bungalow in Porthcawl, to which he always responds with a chuckle, 'I haven't won the pools yet, love.' Gwyneth and a friend were wandering along the seafront in the summer of 1943 when Albert spotted them, surmising that Gwyneth – on account of her sartorial splendour – 'looked a bit wealthy', and summoned the courage to ask her on a date. Albert repeatedly trod on Gwyneth's toes during their foray on the dance floor, but he had an alluring mop of wavy hair and an exotic-sounding accent that marked him out as different. After seventy-five years of marriage, he's lost every last strand of that voluminous bouffant, but she's never stopped loving him.

During the Second World War, Albert served in Italy and Austria, keeping in touch with Gwyneth by letter. They married in 1948, when Albert persuaded Gwyneth to move to Manchester, but it wasn't the homecoming he'd hoped for. The street that had held so many fond childhood memories now looked unrecognizable, with many buildings – including his beloved chip shop – bombed out. The Nazis had apparently been aiming for Salford Docks, but had ended up levelling an entire community. It was a city ravaged by war and plunged into recession.

They tried to build a life amid the wreckage, but Gwyneth longed for the clean Welsh air. They'd experienced the tragedy of a stillbirth, and had been told they wouldn't be able to have another child, so when she did become pregnant again – with my father – they didn't want to take any chances. The doctor pretty much prescribed a return to Wales and Albert didn't take much persuading. They packed their bags and returned to the relatively clean air of the Dulais Valley. Albert was a Welshman now. They moved into the family home on Wembley Avenue, where Dad was born shortly afterwards.

My great-grandfather Rees Mitchell was a handy boxer in his day, and his cousin, Eddie Thomas, might well have been a world champion. Eddie was a fiery welterweight who won the British, European and 'Empire' titles and, in 1949, was the number one contender to fight Sugar Ray Robinson for the world title. It never came to pass, but he was considered a huge talent with a lightning-fast left jab that he later passed on to his protégés, Howard Winstone and Ken Buchanan, whom he coached to world titles. Like most of my male forebears, he was a miner, who continued to dig for coal even when his professional career got under way.

Eddie was deified by the people of Merthyr, not just for his boxing prowess, but for his humanitarian efforts during one of the darkest episodes in Welsh history. On that grim morning in Aberfan in 1966 when a slag heap collapsed and engulfed the local primary school, he was among the rescuers, risking his own life to recover several of the bodies from the wreckage. He was given the freedom of Merthyr in 1992, and elected mayor two years later. Perhaps unsurprisingly, given his Welsh choral background, he became known as 'The Singing Boxer', and his party piece was to belt out a passionate rendition of 'Bless This House' after every fight. I've definitely inherited a bit of his fighting spirit and am one of the few boys in the Welsh squad able to hold a tune, so perhaps I have Eddie to thank for that as well.

Dad's father Albert was a football boy, growing up less than ten minutes from Maine Road, and he remains a Man City supporter to this day – a source of tension when I developed my affection for Man United. But when I switched my focus to rugby, Albert became one of my most vocal supporters, and his passion for the oval ball began to outweigh his love for the round one.

Mamo and Dado are still in that Wembley Avenue house, and I see them as often as I can. Gwyneth – at ninety-six – remains sharp as a tack. She's incredibly house-proud and wouldn't want to live anywhere else on earth. She dismisses my childhood home in Llangennith as 'showy', and will always prefer the down-home earthiness of Wembley Avenue, staring out on that same mountain she used to watch her father climb as a young girl.

My affection for them runs deep because they helped raise me from a young age. Mum would drop me off at their place on a Sunday evening and pick me up on Friday, and that pretty much continued until I went to school at the age of five. If there had been room for me at the village school (and Albert did ask), I might not ever have gone home!

As I got older, I would spend hours up on Onllwyn's Recreation Ground, and the rugby pitch in Banwen. Dado would wedge a fruit can in the ground for a kicking tee, and I'd spend hours knocking balls over the posts – in all weathers – while he and Mamo dutifully ran back and forth to collect them. The shadows would be lengthening over the mountains, and they'd be panting and wheezing with the effort, but I was never ready to go home. Those clutch kicks I'd later land, under the most intense pressure in some of the world's grandest stadiums, were all indebted in some way to the hours of relentless practice on that small, unremarkable patch of grass in the Dulais Valley. Their neighbours – Meurig and Wyndham – would see me practising, and tell my grandparents, 'If that boy doesn't play for Wales, there's something wrong.'

I loved those weekends at my grandparents' house. Their life had slowed to a gentle pace, and I found it a real sanctuary there. Whenever I think of that place – so much smaller and more cramped than the family home – I think of the warmth and love to be found within, of steaming mugs of tea, and buttery Welsh cakes, and of piping hot roast dinners eaten in front of the telly.

I didn't have as close a relationship with my maternal grand-parents. Mum's mum, Betty, who was originally from Merthyr, died when I was nine, and Grandad passed away in 2016. Betty had been engaged to another man and broke it off to marry Fred, which caused a bit of a stir in the socially conservative South Wales valleys. But they were happily married for fifty-one years, so it was clearly the right decision.

Fred was from Coelbren, just outside the southern boundary of the Brecon Beacons National Park, and a mere mile from Onll-wyn, so both sets of grandparents could be found in the same little corner of Wales. Fred began his career as a miner too, but soon swapped the shafts for the skies when he joined the Royal Air Force. With the outbreak of war, he was sent to the front line and, like Mamo and Dado, he and Betty kept in touch by letter for much of their early courtship.

As a teenager, Dad was already dreaming of a future that involved escaping what he considered the claustrophobic con-fines of the Dulais Valley, with the inevitable move down the mines at the age of fifteen. He was always attracted to money because, in his words, he'd never had any. While convalescing from an aggressive bout of flu at the age of thirteen, he developed an interest in stocks and shares, and mentioned it to one of his teachers, who had helped him set up a 'bank' of his own. His cousin was the bank manager, and they made their own cheque books, persuading all the kids in their class to deposit half a crown a week.

Somewhere in the BBC's dusty archives, there'll be footage of my teenage Dad being interviewed about it on the Welsh evening news. It sparked an interest in him which in some ways has shaped the way he's lived his life. He's always had an active inter-est in the stock market, and has done pretty well out of it generally.

My sporting genes came from both sides of the family. Mum, a Seven Sisters girl, met Dad at Neath Grammar School when they were seventeen, and they studied together at Treforest

Polytechnic where there was a strong sporting pedigree. Mum played hockey, tennis and squash, and Dad played rugby.

Football had been a dirty word at Neath Grammar, where rugby ruled the roost. The kids weren't even allowed to take a football in to play at lunchtime. Albert would take Dad to the Gnoll stadium as a young boy to watch the Neath of Brian Thomas and Morlais Williams – hard men from farming stock who never took a backwards step.

Dad moved out of the family home in Onllwyn aged eighteen, first heading to Beddau, north-west of Cardiff, and then to Cardiff itself, where he and Mum lived on Cathedral Road, the wide, tree-lined boulevard that leads directly into the city and to Cardiff Arms Park. Mum's parents didn't approve of them living together out of wedlock, so they married young, when they were both twenty-one. Mum used to joke that they'd threatened to cut her out of the will if she continued to 'live in sin', but as an only child I don't think she had anything to worry about.

Mum was funny, kind and outspoken. She always told you what she thought – sometimes to an annoying degree – and was never afraid of an argument. She certainly wasn't the type to sit quietly in the corner of a room; she was feisty, fiery, and never tried to hide her emotions. If you asked her for an opinion, you got one, unvarnished and to the point. On the flipside, if you got a compliment from Mum, you knew it was genuine.

It was around the time they were living in the capital that Dad renounced his Neath loyalties and started following Cardiff. He'd been an abrasive flanker in the Welsh Schools Under-19 squad before university, but Mamo and Dado had tried to get him to prioritize his education after he failed his eleven-plus and A-levels, so his rugby became more of a social pursuit. Unlike me, he was a forward, and tells me I haven't taken after him because I 'can't handle the hard stuff'. Though he does like to take credit for my place-kicking prowess, claiming he used to regularly 'knock them over from the touchline' for Old Tauntonians in Cardiff. Unfortunately, or perhaps fortunately for him, he'd hung up his boots by the time I was able to go and watch, so I'll have to take his word for that.

Dad showed a zeal for engineering at university, where he gained a degree in quantity surveying, which eventually led him into the oil industry, specializing in the financial and legal side of building pipelines. It opened up a world of opportunity, and by the age of twenty-six he'd moved to Abu Dhabi. Rachel and I had arrived by then, and they didn't want to move us all to the Middle East, so the decision was made for Dad to head out on his own.

I didn't know it then, but having an absent father was the shape of things to come; by the time I'd turned five, my parents had decided to split up permanently. Dad's work took him to some far-flung places, and he became something of an itinerant father, moving every few years to new postings in Dubai, Korea, Indonesia and France. The further he travelled, the further his presence receded from our lives. In those early days, when we'd see one another, he'd appear initially as a stranger, but it wouldn't take long for the awkwardness to melt away.

Naturally, we missed having Dad around, but because I was so young when it happened, it didn't seem a huge wrench. Three times a week, we'd get up early before school to call him, but for the most part it felt like the three of us – Mum, Rachel and me – against the world, protecting each other in that big old house.

It's only through the passing of time that I've come to realize what an absolute legend Mum was. She deserves a gold medal for raising us both, and I'll be forever grateful for the time she spent indulging my love of sport. Taxiing, ferrying, and waiting for hours on the touchline during the winter gloom is hard enough when you live in an accessible place, but when you're stuck on the western edge of a remote peninsula, it's a genuine ordeal. Every journey was undertaken on winding country lanes, often in the dark and in less than clement weather. Mum was saintlike in her commitment, and I didn't express anywhere near enough gratitude at the time. She's no longer with us, and I only hope she understood how much of my success was because of her.

We didn't have loads of money. Our grand-looking property in Llangennith belied a ramshackle interior that we couldn't afford to fix up. One day the clanking old immersion heater in the loft blew up, and the bathroom ceiling collapsed. From that point onwards, whenever you had a bath, you'd be staring up through a gaping hole in the ceiling at exposed beams and torn strips of insulation foam.

That summed it up really; a sort of worn-in luxury. It was a handsome old home in a beautiful spot, but behind the façade it was creaking and dilapidated. Things regularly broke, malfunctioned or simply stopped working, and were rarely ever fixed, which occasionally drove Mum to the point of distraction.

One afternoon, Rachel and I got off the school bus to see a gleaming 'For Sale' sign on the driveway. Mum, without telling us – or Dad, presumably – had put the house on the market. She'd had enough and wanted to move to Penclawdd, still on the Gower but closer to Swansea and civilization.

Rachel was dead against it and did her utmost to sabotage the move. She'd hover behind the estate agent like a malevolent shadow, quietly pointing out everything that was wrong with the place to prospective buyers: the damp spots, the leaking pipes, the cracked plaster and the creaking floorboards. Eventually the message got through to Mum. We were more attached to the place than she'd realized.

A move to Penclawdd would have suited me, actually, as I'd joined their Under-10s football team as a striker, where my goal-hanging instincts saw me become top scorer in my first season. I loved football, far more so than rugby at that age. Unlike so many of my contemporaries, Welsh rugby culture wasn't ingrained in me. Going to see Wales play at the Millennium Stadium wasn't an annual pilgrimage as it was for so many of my friends. I never even got taken to watch Neath play, even though Mum and Dad both grew up as staunch fans.

Mum was far more into rugby than me. She'd always be up at the crack of dawn, and on weekends she'd be ensconced in front of the TV by 6 a.m., fresh coffee steaming in her mug while she watched the early Super Rugby game from New Zealand. By the time I'd wander bleary-eyed into the lounge with a bowl of cereal, she'd be getting into the game from Australia, which would normally kick off around 10 a.m. our time. I was far more inclined to watch Premier League football later in the day, often while wearing my full Man United kit. Ryan Giggs was a high-profile Welshman, which helped tilt my loyalties towards United, and it was good call as that side swept all before them for most of my childhood.

Ultimately, I had a really happy upbringing. My parents remained on civil terms and Dad would always keep in touch by phone, often having to negotiate inconvenient time zones and crackly phone connections. And, if there was an upside to Dad working overseas, it was that we were able to take exotic holidays to places like Dubai. Every Easter and summer, Rachel and I would board the plane as 'unaccompanied minors' and jet off to see Dad. Looking back, those trips were formative experiences, giving me a glimpse of the big wide world beyond the Gower, and allowing us to spend some quality time with Dad.

2

AN UNLIKELY HERO

It's October 2003, and I'm standing in the lobby of an opulent Brisbane Hotel; a nervous thirteen-year-old clutching an autograph book. The Rugby World Cup is in full swing and I'm with Mum, who's fulfilling a lifelong dream of travelling to the other side of the world to follow her beloved Wales. But I'm not here in search of Welsh players. This is the England team hotel, and I want to meet their golden boy, Jonny Wilkinson. England may be Wales's bitterest rivals, but I'm not bothered by such parochial concerns. Jonny is my hero, the blond-haired maestro whose artful, dead-eyed goal-kicking has elevated England to top of the world rankings.

I see a little of myself in him.

He's not the most naturally gifted of players. He's definitely not a swashbuckling, swivel-hipped magician like Barry John or Jonathan Davies. More a skilful technician with a razor-sharp rugby brain and a willingness to put his body on the line. I don't care what badge he wears on his chest; I want to meet him and see if a little of his magic rubs off.

It's not to be. His near-monastic existence means he's nowhere to be seen. Some of his teammates wander through the lobby in their branded stash, looking like they mean business. Their captain, Martin Johnson – he of the permanently furrowed brow – relaxes slightly in my presence, putting me in a headlock when he hears my accent. Matt Dawson puts his arm around me and poses for a photo. But it's Jonny I wanted. Maybe next time.

I hadn't been overly excited about the trip. Unlike most Welsh fans travelling with the usual mix of blind faith and optimism, I couldn't ignore the facts. Under Steve Hansen we'd lost ten games in a row, and had sunk into a trough. While England fans were talking confidently about winning the thing, I thought we'd be fortunate to reach the knockout stages. But our match against New Zealand became a definitive turning point in Welsh rugby history; an utterly breathless eighty minutes of captivating, harum-scarum rugby. It might have ended in glorious defeat, but not before the All Blacks had been given an almighty scare.

Mum and I were at the Suncorp Stadium a week later when Wales almost pulled off the shock of the tournament. 10–3 up and cruising against England, it took a single moment of magic from Jason Robinson to change the course of history. England scraped through and went on to win the World Cup. I was at the final too, watching from the stands as Jonny Wilkinson calmly nailed the drop goal that sent the crowd into raptures. It was a seminal moment for England – obviously – but also for me. If rugby had been a passing interest until then, that was the moment my ambition crystallized. That is what I wanted to do. *I* wanted to be the guy in the middle, directing the traffic amid the chaos. *I* wanted to kick the winning drop goal in the World Cup final.

Unlike Mum, I hadn't viewed the trip as some significant pil-grimage. Until then, rugby, to be blunt, had been an incidental part of my life. But being immersed among the supporters and witnessing such drama up close opened my eyes to what rugby might offer me. I started to notice that my friends who played rugby seemed to be enjoying a better social life. There was a deeper sense of camaraderie, and more of a brotherhood than in football. You'd wash away the mud stains in the communal shower and troop into the clubhouse with your hair freshly gelled where there'd be a steaming cauldron of curry to greet you. That was where bonds were forged and memories made. It's the bit about rugby I love the most, and that has continued throughout my professional career; I still love going for coffees with the boys and hanging out in the team room talking shit. To this day, I'm one of the last to leave, preferring the buzz of conversation to the solitude of a hotel room. It's ultimately what I got into the game for, and it all stems from those early days when rugby began to overtake football in my affections.

Jonny just sealed the deal.

I went to secondary school at Gowerton Comprehensive, in the middle of a council estate about six miles west of Swansea. After my cosseted upbringing, it felt like a splash of cold water to the face. The noise, the clamour, and the sheer size of everything was disorienting, and I was shocked to witness my first playground fight. One day a friend smuggled in a bottle of Bailey's and a few of us went behind the bike sheds to share it around. The head-teacher caught us in the act and ordered us to his office. The rest of the boys seemed quite blasé about it, but as a wide-eyed country boy, I convinced myself I was going to be expelled at the age of eleven. That's about as rebellious as I got during my secondary school years, though. I largely remained on the right side of the authorities.

Most people can trace their passion for sport back to an inspirational teacher and I'm no exception. Mr Mason couldn't have been further removed from the stereotype of a Welsh PE teacher: he was short, bald, and not particularly athletic, but he had genuine ability to enthuse his pupils. Schools would often employ ex-players to run their rugby teams; military types who'd bark orders, drive standards, and more than likely hurl themselves into rucks and mauls. Mr Mason was more the gentle, encouraging type; a softly spoken fellow who valued relationships over the more technical side of coaching. He organized annual trips for the rugby, hockey and netball teams to far-flung places like Australia, South Africa and New Zealand. Without his enthusiasm and fund-raising efforts, they'd never have progressed beyond a conversation in the staff room.

Gowerton Comp had a big emphasis on sport, but it wasn't steeped in rugby like Ysgol Glantaf in Cardiff or Brynteg in Bridgend. If you were serious about rugby, you needed to find a club. So that's how I had found myself up at the Welfare Ground in Gorseinon on a blustery Tuesday night at the age of thirteen.

A short, stocky ginger fellow by the name of Rob Steele was our coach at Gorseinon. He was a builder by trade and, unlike Mr Mason, he had an abrasive no-nonsense attitude. He had a short fuse and could be terrifying when he lost his rag. Gorseinon was a fairly unfashionable club at the time, and there'd been stories doing the rounds that other promising youngsters like Ashley Beck and Kristian Phillips were being lured to rival club Tonmawr with the promise of free PlayStations and Xboxes. There were no such luxuries on offer at Gorseinon.

On that first day, there were a lot of brutish-looking boys warming up, shouting at each other in their coarse city accents, and I felt young and puny in their presence. I swear some of them already had stubble. Some of these raw-boned teenagers looked downright intimidating, and I was determined not to come across as some soft lad from the Gower. Gorseinon was hardly the Bronx, but it had an urban grittiness and an underlying sense of menace that made me uncomfortable. I wandered towards a more introspective-looking kid who looked similarly out of place. He was smaller than me, painfully shy, and struggled to maintain eye contact, even while introducing himself. His name was Leigh Halfpenny. In a few short years, the club pavilion would be renamed in his honour, and he'd have carved out a reputation as one of the world's best full backs.

Back then he was just a local boy from Penyrheol Comprehensive, a mile down the road. He was nearly a year older than me but didn't look it. The two of us would have to prove ourselves, and quickly. That first Tuesday night was a real eye-opener. Whatever tackling I'd done at school had amounted to little more than jersey pulling. Some of these Gorseinon boys had a nasty edge, and would clatter into contact with their knees pumping like they really wanted to hurt you. I emerged from that first session with a bruised ego to go with my two bruised shoulders.

Playing with and against boys a year older proved a valuable education. My tackle technique improved overnight, and I toughened up pretty quickly.

Leigh and I certainly weren't among the star players, but we did become first-team regulars. We weren't carving up the way future internationals often do. We were more workmanlike figures, chugging away in the engine room. It was our attitude that stood out and we went on a decent run as a team, piecing together a string of notable victories. By the time we played Brynaman away, we felt invincible.

It's only about twenty miles as the crow flies, but the top of the Swansea Valley can feel like a different world, and there was an unsettling vibe from the moment we arrived. The clubhouse looked derelict and abandoned, the pitch was boggy and lumpy, and the corner flags were whipping violently in the wind. The local park overlooked the ground, and gangs of kids on BMXs stared slack-jawed at us as we trooped onto the pitch. The ref was one of their players' dads, and within a few minutes we'd 'conceded' a litany of penalties. Their game plan revolved around giving the ball to their enormous blind-side flanker and encouraging him to bulldoze his way through our defence. The whiff of violence grew stronger by the minute, and it didn't take long for things to boil over. A brawl erupted, punches were thrown, kicks were rained down on prone bodies and ugly threats were issued from spittle-flecked lips. I remember glancing at the sidelines in a mute appeal for the grown-ups to restore some order, only to see them going at it too. My mum briefly abandoned her pacifist principles and unleashed a barrage of verbal abuse at her nearest neighbour. She might have had a middle-class veneer, but there was always a Neath girl bubbling beneath the surface.

The bad vibes continued after the final whistle had blown on our first defeat of the season, and the parents ushered us directly to the cars. We'd gone there with a bit of swagger, eager to play some rugby, but those valley boys clearly wanted to take the 'city slickers' down a peg or two. It was the first time I'd experienced that kind of ugly tribalism.

Later, at an early Sevens tournament down in Felinfoel, where a young Phil Bennett had first tried out that mesmeric sidestep of his, we'd coasted into the final but found ourselves a couple of tries adrift at half-time. I was furious at how lackadaisical the boys had been and lost my temper, bellowing at my teammates that I hadn't come down here to pick up a loser's medal. It wasn't the most eloquent call to arms, but it did enough to shake us out of our torpor and we recovered to win the tournament.

Once rugby had taken its grip, my perfectionist streak kicked in too. I wanted to be the best. You'll have heard about disgusting rugby initiations involving booze, urine and vomit that I'll refrain from going into on the grounds of taste and decency. That wasn't me. I went in the opposite direction, spending my teenage years as a paragon of health and clean-living. The idea of undoing all the hard training by drinking a skinful of cheap lager every week-end seemed moronic. I became obsessed.

I looked unnaturally bulky during my teenage years, not because I'd pumped up my physique with a rigorous weights regime, but because I took to wearing a weighted vest. The idea was that if you got used to wearing it, you'd feel sharper and more agile when you removed it to play. I wore it *everywhere* – to the cinema, at school, in the house, and when I was out for food with the boys. It was on from the minute I stepped out of the shower until the minute I went to bed. Like Jonny Wilkinson, I developed an obsessive, single-minded approach. It was all or nothing. It might have been heavy, sweaty and uncomfortable, but if it made me even 1 per cent better, it was worth it.

So were the early alarm calls. Waking in the inky-dark of a Gower winter morning to the shrill blast of a 5.30 alarm, piling into the car with a half-munched piece of toast in my hand, and trundling through the lanes where the badgers and hedgehogs still roamed. Mum behind the wheel, stopping to pick up Leigh

Halfpenny, who'd be standing silhouetted in the gloom at the side of the road. She'd drop us at Swansea College where the gym opened at 6 a.m. and we'd train furiously for an hour. With my limbs tingling from a heavy session, I'd don my cumbersome vest, ignoring the quizzical sideways glances from the early morning swimmers. I carried a 2-litre bottle of water everywhere too, because we'd been lectured on the importance of staying hydrated. I refused to drink tap water on the grounds it contained excess oestrogen and pollutants. I wanted to do whatever it took to become a professional rugby player.

The highlight of our year was the annual Gorseinon RFC trip to Kiln Park in Tenby. As with all rugby tours, it was an opportunity to spend more time with the boys and in coach Rob O'Kelly's case, an opportunity to let his hair down in a different postcode. Every year, for reasons unknown, he'd end up stripping naked and running through the caravan park, much to the bemusement of the holidaymakers enjoying a sundowner on their terraces. Those trips were like a cross between *Twin Town* and *The Inbetweeners*, with just as many laughs, high jinks and mishaps.

We'd amuse ourselves in the evenings by sneaking around the site, unplugging people's electrics and cackling in the bushes as caravans were plunged into darkness. Watching enraged campers plodding out in their string vests and pyjamas was the height of hilarity to a bunch of hyperactive teenage boys.

I managed to swerve the indignity of a teenage initiation. The gulping-down of urine or lager through the arse crack of a teammate were things I'd heard about but thankfully never witnessed.

A few of my mates played for Penclawdd, where some of the rituals were a little less revolting; new recruits were ejected from the team bus at the CKs supermarket and forced to run the last 500 yards back to the clubhouse. Not the worst punishment imaginable, you might think, until I reveal they had to do it stark bollock naked.

On arrival, their 'reward' was a tray with half pints of lager, cider, bitter, Guinness and a bottle of WKD, which they had to see off before they were allowed to change out of their birthday suit.

By this point, I'd committed to my Jonny Wilkinson-inspired regimen, and managed to steer well clear of such shenanigans.

The longer I played for Gorseinon, the more confident I became, and every so often I'd experience a quantum leap forwards.

One freezing cold night, when our fingers were blue, the ground was rock solid, and we were desperate to escape to the hot showers, I experienced my first rugby epiphany. We'd been experimenting with block play runners, a simple enough concept which is now commonplace, but to us youngsters back then it felt like we'd tapped into some Harry-Potter-level sorcery.

To the uninitiated, it's a backs move that sees one player run a dummy line in front of the ball, while another goes 'out the back'. The idea being that the dummy runner dupes the defence into thinking he's about to receive the ball, giving the actual receiver extra time and space to make a break. We worked on it until we'd nailed the timing, before unleashing it on the non-playing XV. As planned, their eyes were drawn by the dummy runner, and we went out the back and scored a great try in the corner. In that moment it felt like we'd jumped up a level.

The rudiments of the game were locked into our muscle memory, and now we could add layers of sophistication, like a chess player calculating the outcome several moves in advance, or a musician who has endlessly practised chords and scales to the point where they can suddenly improvise, *create*. This realization – that we could use sleight of hand and trickery to evade the flailing arms of defenders – was enormously satisfying. Rugby is increasingly referred to as a collision sport, but for me it remains a game of manipulation and evasion.

That night, in the bone-numbing cold, I was consumed by a

warm feeling. We were playing Under-14s rugby, but it felt like we'd stepped through a portal into a more advanced world.

Because I was comfortable playing alongside older boys for Gorseinon, Mr Mason put me forward for Swansea schoolboys a year early. He recognized that everyone progresses at a different pace and has different levels of ambition, and understood that my future lay at this level. I'm not sure how many teachers would have advocated for that.

Thanks to his guidance, and my apprenticeship at Gorseinon, I was being talked about as a potential pick for Wales Under-16s and, despite being a year young, I knew I was in with a chance. The team was being announced on email and I remember sitting hunched over our home computer with its dodgy dial-up connection, silently praying I'd get the call. The email eventually appeared and there was my name in bold, next to the number 10. I felt a surge of national pride. This was the first time I really *felt* Welsh. I came out trying to suppress a smile and told Mum to go and have a look. She shrieked with pride, hugged me tight and ran downstairs to call Leigh's mum, Estelle, who was also celebrating her son's call-up. There were a few other names you might recognize too: Rhys Webb was at scrum half, Ryan Bevington was the captain, and some fellow called Sam Warburton was in the second row.

Ultimately, my first match in the red jersey of Wales ended in disappointment. We lost 23–6 against a strong England side, packed with meaty forwards, but I wasn't too downhearted. I'd got to pull on the red shirt and it felt good. Mum and Dad had both been on the sidelines to cheer me on.

It was a relief to see Dad for the first time after his terrifying brush with death. We'd heard about it first in a phone call to Mamo from Auntie Julie, on an otherwise unremarkable Thursday morning in September 2004, in which she claimed she'd just seen Dad on TV, standing amid the rubble of a bombed-out building. There had been a deadly car bomb attack on the Australian embassy in Jakarta, which was next door to Dad's office.

Dad's building had borne the brunt of the explosion, which had sent him flying through the air before he'd landed in a crumpled heap by the filing cabinet. Once the building had been evacuated, the grim reality was laid bare, with scenes of utter carnage greeting him and his colleagues at street level. An estimated eleven people lost their lives in the attack and more than 150 were injured.

Dad and his colleagues fled to the hotel where he and his wife Angie were staying, and proceeded to calm their nerves with a few stiff drinks. Suitably oiled, Dad made a round of phone calls, to let family and friends know what had happened. He opted to tell Mamo a white lie, explaining that any bomb she might have heard about had exploded 'on the other side of the city'. Little did he know that the images of him standing amid the rubble had already been beamed across the world and onto Mamo's old cathode-ray TV screen in Onllwyn. Once she'd established he was OK, she laid into him with the full force of a mother's fury, telling him to 'never lie to your mother again!' And so, his traumatic day was rounded off with a proper ear-bashing from our powerful matriarch.

Some things never change.

3

A KING'S RANSOM

My hand is trembling as I knock on the door. It's Sunday afternoon in Swansea, and the Ospreys are preparing to face Leinster in their brand-new home, the Liberty Stadium. Kick-off is two hours away. I'm nearly sixteen years old and have just been offered a development contract with the Ospreys Academy. Suffused with confidence and no little swagger, I've decided to introduce myself to the senior coaches, and the club's money man, Mike Cuddy, to try to wangle a better deal. But now I'm on the threshold of their office, I suddenly feel like the callow teenager I am. I knock with as much confidence as I can muster and am summoned in. There behind the desk are the three unsmiling figures of Mike Cuddy, the head coach Lyn Jones, and the assistant coach, Sean Holley. Unsure whether to sit or stand, I hover uncomfortably before Mike raises an eyebrow and barks, 'How much is this going to cost me then?'

A week earlier, the news had come through from the Ospreys. Five youngsters including Leigh and me had been offered development deals which would see us train with the academy at the club's Llandarcy HQ. It was essentially a season-long audition to see if we had what it took to step up to professional rugby. It came with an annual salary of £2,000, which might have seemed like a fortune to a teenager living at home but, given the commitment we'd be making, and the amount I'd spend on petrol getting to and from training, I could conceivably be losing money by accepting it. The other boys – Leigh, Kristian Phillips, Ashley

Beck, and Tom Williams – had signed up without a moment's hesitation, but I was a little more sceptical.

A few weeks earlier, Mum had received a phone call from someone purporting to be an agent. She'd hung up after the initial 'Am I speaking with Mrs Biggar?', assuming he was a double-glazing salesman. But this Tim Lopez fellow, as he introduced himself, was persistent, calling straight back and insisting, 'It's about your son.' I have no idea how I'd appeared on their radar, but he was claiming that Northampton's academy was interested in me and were willing to pay £30,000. *A wind-up, surely?* Thirty grand was a king's ransom. The call was a massive ego boost, and the start of a relationship that endures to this day, as the man on the end of the line soon became my agent.

But the confidence that counter-offer had given me evaporated when I was in front of Mike Cuddy, a burly, no-nonsense businessman of some renown. Sean has since worked this into an amusing after-dinner anecdote in which he describes me striding up to the desk and saying 'Hi, I'm Dan Biggar and I'm going to be the next Ospreys fly half.' It didn't quite happen that way. Instead, I laughed nervously when Mike asked how much it was going to cost and shuffled obediently into the chair he was gesturing towards. I explained that I'd had a lucrative offer from an English club, but that I wanted to play for the Ospreys. I might have said I thought I was good enough to eventually be their first-choice 10, but I certainly wasn't as brash as Sean has since made me out to be.

I was wittering on, trying to work out how best to ask for more money, when Mike cut across me, snapping, 'How much do you think you're worth then?' My face flushed with embarrassment as he slid a piece of blank paper across the desk. 'Write it down if you don't want to say it out loud, and I'll do the same.'

This was excruciating.

My mind was racing. Write too much and they'll think you're insufferably arrogant, too little and you don't have the courage of your convictions.

With a trembling hand, I scribbled down £10,000 on the piece of paper, folded it over and slid it back across. To go from £2k to £10k felt ballsy. Mike unfolded it, raised an eyebrow and gestured for me to open his. He'd written £12,500. The charade was over, and I flashed a smile. 'Happy with that?' he asked. I nodded enthusiastically.

He waved my piece of paper in front of me.

'Sure you don't want this?'

'No thank you, Mr Cuddy. This one's just fine.'

As the door swung behind me, I let out an enormous sigh of relief. Mum was in reception and gave me a massive hug when I told her what had happened. I'd have a grand landing in my account every month. As a teenager with no outgoings apart from surf wax, CDs and PlayStation games, that made me rich.

The two of us went up to the stand and watched the Ospreys beat Leinster with a last-minute penalty from Matthew Jones. In a few years, I thought, that could be me; running things from 10 on that pristine surface, winning games with dramatic late kicks. It felt like the first day of the rest of my life.

Before their move to the Liberty, a 20,000-seater football stadium, the Ospreys had played their home games at St Helen's, the iconic old ground looking out over Swansea Bay. It had become a little rough around the edges but had history seeping from every pore. It was the venue for Wales's first ever rugby international in 1882, and also where Garfield Sobers famously hit six sixes in a single over, playing for Nottinghamshire against Glamorgan in August 1968. As I've mentioned, I wasn't a diehard rugby fan growing up, but if I was to be found on the terraces anywhere, it was at St Helen's watching the Whites. I'd watch the fly halves, studying their form and technique, and remember being particularly impressed by Diego Dominguez when he was in the visiting Stade Français team. He was the Italian international who famously kicked thirty points in a Heineken Cup final and ended up on the losing side. I also watched Neil Jenkins in zen mode drowning out a chorus of boos to knock over kicks from every corner of the ground. And the hometown hero was Arwel Thomas, the impish, diminutive pivot who'll always be remembered for punching Philippe Carbonneau in the 1997 Five Nations. It was the Llanelli games I remember most vividly; those combustible West Wales derbies that almost always spilled over into violence.

So when I was selected for Swansea Schoolboys and we started training on that same hallowed turf, it awakened the fan within. To change in those dressing rooms and jog onto that pitch was magical. I'd never owned a Swansea replica shirt – indeed I used to train there in the Crusaders ones my Mum had bought me – but training on that bowling-green surface gave me an appreciation for the club and its history that I hadn't had before.

It was through our Swansea Schoolboys connection that we picked up our development deals, and we were immediately given a rigorous schedule which, looking back, was pretty full-on for a bunch of fifteen-year-olds. There'd be weights sessions before we headed off to school, and training with the Ospreys Under-16s straight after. On Wednesdays we'd have dedicated skills sessions, where one of the coaches would put us through our paces during our lunch break. There was an early morning session on Thursdays in addition to the evening session. Then, in the summer holidays, when our school friends were gearing up for six weeks of uninterrupted leisure time, we'd have something scheduled *every day*.

Normally, you'd associate the beach with sunbathing and relaxation, but the beach-based sessions were the worst. We'd head for Aberavon at 8 a.m. on a Saturday, where we were forced to run three lengths of the beach through claggy wet sand as the Port Talbot steelworks pumped sulphurous fumes into the air down the coast. Our fitness coach, Keith Hollifield, would be cycling on the promenade, weaving around pedestrians and bellowing at us to go faster. Worse still were the notorious sand dunes of Merthyr Mawr. They're the stuff of legend in Welsh rugby, and one of its most brutal testing grounds. Many a Welsh international has been emasculated by those unforgiving dunes, reduced to a vomiting, blubbering mess after being forced to scale them repeatedly until their legs turn to jelly. The mere mention of that hellish place is enough for the bile to rise at the back of my throat.

When my first Ospreys pay cheque came through, I felt like a millionaire. As my sister Rachel slaved away at her holiday job, washing dishes for the minimum wage at the Hill End camp site café, she envied me being paid what seemed like eye-watering sums to essentially kick a ball around.

My first car was my biggest investment. It was a fairly uncool-looking Seat Leon, but given the clapped-out bangers my mates were driving, I considered it a Rolls-Royce. The biggest indicator of my new-found wealth was my ability to fill up the tank, a luxury which cost a colossal £35. Gone were the days of dribbling in five pounds' worth of petrol and hoping it would be enough to get you home.

It was during this period that the Welsh national side finally awoke from its long slumber. As a child of the nineties, I was seriously beginning to doubt whether I'd ever witness a Welsh Grand Slam. The chasm that had opened up between England, France and the rest seemed too wide to breach, and we'd become used to ritual thrashings at the hands of the old enemy. Then, seemingly out of nowhere, 2005 happened: a first Six Nations Grand Slam in twenty-seven years, and – in Gavin Henson – a poster boy to rival Jonny Wilkinson. His nerveless fifty-metre kick to sink England was the catalyst for an unlikely clean sweep. Overnight, rugby started to dominate the national conversation again, tapping into the zeitgeist. This generation of players, elevated by the casual insouciance of Gavin Henson and the impish genius of winger Shane Williams, were rock stars. Forget Cool Cymru and the new wave of Welsh bands like the Manics and the Phonics; the rugby guys were now at the vanguard of popular culture. The game against France in Paris – where Wales performed a Lazarus-like recovery in the second half to win 24–18 – was one for the ages. Martyn Williams, who is now Wales's team manager, still goes on about it to this day. His two tries had sparked the unlikeliest of comebacks, but it was Stephen Jones who had impressed me most. His calm authority and ability to manage the game taught me a valuable lesson about fly half play at the highest level. I watched the final game against Ireland at home with Mum and, needless to say, when Tom Shanklin passed to Kevin 'The Rat' Morgan for the clinching try, we were out of our seats and jumping for joy.

To those unacquainted with the Welsh rugby pyramid, each of the four Welsh professional regions has several 'feeder clubs', which play in the semi-professional Welsh Premiership. It's difficult for people of a certain generation to accept that famous old clubs like Swansea, Llanelli, Cardiff and Newport have been supplanted by the 'plastic' regions and their supposedly inauthentic franchises. I could write an entire book about the labyrinthine politics of Welsh rugby; suffice to say, while I was part of the Ospreys Academy, I was effectively loaned out to Swansea to accelerate my development.

It was another collision of worlds as us callow, inexperienced teenagers were thrown into an environment dominated by grizzled, no-nonsense hard nuts who were quite happy to teach a precocious kid a lesson or two about 'real' rugby. They thought we couldn't properly graduate until we'd experienced the frost-laden pitches of Ebbw Vale or the raucous crowds at Pontypridd on a wintry Wednesday, where the ground feels like solid concrete and the tiles are blowing off the clubhouse roof.

We came from different universes – I'd arrive at training from school, whereas most of them were reporting for duty after a hard day's work on the building site or the factory floor. One was a toilet paper salesman who'd always turn up with reams of the stuff to flog at discounted rates. I'm not sure how legitimate a sideline it was, but it opened my eyes to another world I'd not been privy to as a cosseted schoolboy groomed in the academy.

Signing a contract with the Ospreys might have helped me up a couple of rungs on the ladder, but it was no guarantee of success. I only played for Swansea for eight months, but it was a vital stepping stone. The former Llanelli full back, Ian Jones, was my backs coach, and he gave me a valuable piece of advice. He told me I only had one chance of being a professional rugby player. 'You can always go back to do a course to be a leccy or a plumber,' he said, 'but being a pro rugby player is a one-shot game. Miss, and you're out of the running.'

The head coach was the former Wales and Lions flanker, Richard Webster, a proper old-school, teak-tough bloke, with just the right amount of swivel-eyed madness. We trained twice a week, on Tuesdays and Thursdays. The Tuesday sessions were on a school field in Cockett, and Webby introduced a rule whereby if you dropped the ball, under any circumstances, you had to hit the deck and let the forwards run over you like a horde of marauding buffalo. You can just imagine these thirty-year-old forwards with their big studs, pummelling my soft flesh and relishing every moment. Nothing sharpened your senses more than the prospect of a punishment like that. Swansea were a slick ball-handling team, capable of scoring tries, but had often been accused of having a soft underbelly. Being an abrasive, uncompromising player himself, Webby took those kinds of slights personally and vowed to instil a steelier edge.

Though it sounds cruel, there was a good deal of affection between me and the older guys. Any mockery was friendly rather than mean; the equivalent of sending an apprentice out to buy a glass hammer or a tin of tartan paint. They could see that I wasn't flash or arrogant and had a strong work ethic. As a teenager with school and academy commitments to juggle, I could have been given a bit of leeway, but I made sure I never missed a session. Other academy boys would miss a Tuesday or Thursday, especially those with Webby's famous contact drills, but I knew that was a sure way to lose respect from the senior players, as was not turning up to team socials. Even though I wasn't a drinker, I'd always make sure I popped along to show my face. Prima donnas don't survive long in those environments.

My Swansea debut was twenty minutes off the bench up in Bedwas, a traditional working-class mining town in the Gwent valley. Everything about it was hostile. The pitch was boggy, and the grass long enough for rabbits to roam undetected. The stand – with its peeling paint and broken seats – had seen better days, and the changing rooms were – to put it diplomatically – spartan. On the pitch I felt comfortable in terms of the pace and skill level, but physically it was a real baptism of fire. I was a boy who'd barely started shaving, going up against hard men, all of whom were graduates in the dark arts. Things weren't as dirty as they'd been in the amateur era, but no forward worth his salt could resist a dig in the ribs to a prone teenager lying out of sight of the ref. And you wouldn't get any sympathy from the ultra-partisan home fans who considered anyone from Swansea to be a soft city slicker.

The Premiership back then was a decent testing ground for youngsters like me, and it saddens me to see how much standards have declined. In my sole season for Swansea, it was full of prom-ising players who wanted to play rugby, as opposed to just scrap and fight. A lot of talented academy players fed into those teams, and above them you had strong regional sides, stacked with senior pros and quality overseas signings. Several of the so-called golden generation who played under Warren Gatland cut their teeth in that league: Jonathan Davies at Llanelli, Leigh 'Pence' Halfpenny at Cardiff, and Ashley Beck at Aberavon, as well as people like Kristian Phillips at Neath. Yes, it helped you toughen up and build courage, but it also enabled you to sharpen your skills and hone your game management. Combine that with the well-financed regions who could afford to sign foreign stars like Xavier Rush, Marty Holah and Justin Marshall, and it's easy to see why my generation was able to flourish. As a Welsh rugby fan, I do fear that the pyramid is beginning to crumble.

As short-lived as it was, I look back really fondly on that apprenticeship at Swansea, watching the sun sinking into the ocean as we were put through our paces on that famous old ground. It was also during this time that my deep bond with Leigh was cemented. It was a seminal friendship, and the connection between us remains strong. We've done all right for two teenagers doing endless 'hang clean' reps in Swansea College gym at seven in the morning. Watch us run out for Wales together, and you'll note that we always stand next to each other during the anthem, a silent nod to our shared journey. We were lucky to find one another because we were two peas from the same pod, sharing an obsessive gene. We made the same sacrifices – from turning down nights out, to maintaining a strict, healthy diet. For several years, we insisted on only eating organic food, giving up Red Bull which apparently prevented us from gaining weight because of its high caffeine content, and egg yolks because we were told they contained too much cholesterol. Leigh was my wingman in all of this. We did it together. Neither of us was willing to slacken off or look for a shortcut. If one was feeling less motivated, we didn't dare admit it.

It was around this time we started goal-kicking, recognizing that endless practice and repetition was what separated a decent kicker from an excellent one. We'd spend countless hours at Penclawdd RFC, where on the one side you'd usually be kicking into a hurricane, and on the other towards a house bordered by a dense thicket hedge. Most of the rugby injuries I suffered in those early years weren't broken bones, but gashes and scrapes from clambering into that infernal hedge to retrieve my balls. There must be dozens of them still there.

Slowly but surely, Leigh and I were edging towards professional careers together when, in the blink of an eye, the rug was pulled out from under Pence. At the age of eighteen, he was released by the Ospreys for being too small. While rugby likes to claim it's a game for all shapes and sizes, there's no denying the inexorable trend towards bigger, bulkier players as the professional era motors forwards. As much as Leigh could train, eat right, and pile on the muscle mass, he would never be 'big' in the modern sense. In an era in which most three-quarters are more than six feet tall and fifteen stone, Leigh was an anomaly. Naturally, he was devastated.

Given what's happened in his career since, it's easy to pour scorn on the Ospreys for making such a seemingly bone-headed decision – like Decca rejecting the Beatles – but Leigh's is probably a one-in-a-million case. There was no malice or spite, it was just a professional assessment that he probably wasn't going to make the grade. But it hammered home to both of us how precarious things were. Far from being anointed as the next generation of stars, our progress would be subject to the whims and preferences of a small group of coaches. What made it all the more galling was the fact the guys they brought in to replace him weren't anywhere near as good. They felt like imposters, and I kept my distance, thinking it would be disloyal to get too close to them.

Thankfully, Leigh was soon offered a lifeline from Cardiff RFC, the semi-professional side playing in the Welsh Premiership, and we'd later come up against each other when I was wearing Swansea colours. Initially though, his heart wasn't in it. He'd been hit hard by the rejection and was on the verge of jacking it all in and studying dentistry. Can you imagine that? A world in which Leigh Halfpenny was fitting dentures and filling cavities rather than making heroic last-ditch tackles, scoring epic tries, and scorching his way to a Lions Player of the Series award.

My obsession with rugby meant I was largely oblivious to the fairer sex during my teenage years, until that is, at the age of seventeen, I had my head turned by a chic, flame-haired girl from the year above. On the way to the school bus one afternoon, Alex Cummings fell in step with me and asked about my plans for the weekend. I remember thinking how cute she looked in her skinny jeans and Vans trainers and was flattered that an older girl was paying me attention. We swapped numbers and began messaging. It took me weeks to pluck up the courage to invite her on a date to the cinema. I'd like to say I chose some sophisticated, thought-provoking film that would burnish my intellectual credentials, but I picked – wait for it – *Deuce Bigalow: Male Gigolo*, a dreadful comedy about a male prostitute.

Using the time-honoured 'back seats offer the best view' line, we shared our first kiss in the shadows of the Swansea Odeon. Our next date was at my house and involved a bit more effort on my part. I drove to the video rental shop in Llanrhidian – essentially a small grocery shop attached to the petrol station, with some dusty VHS tapes on a shelf – and rented *The Notebook*. I also stocked up on Coke and Maltesers and, considering it the height of sophistication, a box of Ferrero Rocher.

We *cwtched* up in my sister's bedroom where there was a state-of-the-art TV with video player, and watched this weepy romantic drama while Alex gobbled every last morsel of chocolate. I ate nothing, committed as I was to my rugby diet and fortunately, rather than thinking I was a weirdo, she actually considered it sweet that I'd bought all this stuff just for her.

Thankfully, my taste in movies didn't count against me. Alex would eventually, after a prolonged courtship, become my wife.

4

STEPPING UP

My career could have suffered a significant blow had I not escaped unscathed from a nasty car crash when I was seventeen. My relationship with Alex had entered a volatile on/off phase, and one night after a heated argument, I'd stormed off in a huff to drive home. It was bitterly cold, and the roads were icy. Taking a bend near Llanmorlais at speed, I felt the car slide beneath me, and I completely lost control, spinning off the road. I managed to crawl out, but both the car, and the railings that had prevented me tumbling down a ravine, were completely mangled.

My precious Seat Leon was a write-off, and I was trembling with a combination of shock and cold. I was only a mile from my mate Ben Whitehouse's place, so I called him up. Thankfully, he was there in a flash with his police officer dad, Nigel, switching seamlessly into professional mode and radioing in the incident.

I was really shaken up and didn't want to go to school the next day. The story had spread quickly, and through a combination of Chinese whispers and the Gower grapevine, I was apparently either dead or seriously injured in hospital. My presence at school was therefore greeted with amazement and a barrage of questions. Bizarrely, I felt ashamed about the crash, worried that people would think I was a bad driver, so I made up a story about a cat leaping into the road. I persisted with it at home, even though Mum knew it was a tall tale to distract her from the fact I'd been going way too fast.

If there was ever an illustration of my adult and childhood

worlds colliding, it was this. At the same time I was telling lies about how I crashed my car, I was on the cusp of my professional debut.

During international campaigns, when our star players were away, some of the academy boys would get called into the senior squad to make up the numbers. The first time it happened, I found myself getting changed alongside the likes of Jason Spice, Shaun Connor, Justin Marshall, and Stefan Terblanche – serious players. I remember watching in awe as Terblanche removed his shirt to reveal the shredded physique of a bodybuilder. He was in the twilight of his career – well into his thirties – but without an ounce of fat between those rippling abs.

No matter how inexperienced you are, there's an expectation for fly halves to call the shots. It's like being a quarterback in the NFL. But there's no way a baby-faced teenager can stroll into a senior training session and start ordering grizzled veterans around. I wanted to sound and look authoritative without over-stepping the mark. I was desperately worried about screwing up, or making a wrong call.

Ryan Jones – the Wales captain and another Llangennith resident – was good to me in those early years, putting his arm around me as a senior pro. Before I got my replacement car, the club loaned me a Ford Focus plastered with Ospreys branding. For several months I became Ryan's chauffeur, driving us both to work and back because he was too tight to pay for petrol. At six foot five and more than eighteen stone, he preferred to fold his considerable frame into my tiny Ford Focus than waste unnecessary mileage on his brand-new Mercedes.

Wales had a poor Six Nations in 2007, losing every match apart from the last against England. James Hook bagged a 'full house' in that game, scoring a try, a conversion, four penalties and a drop goal. It was a superlative performance, and he became an overnight hero. I was completely starstruck when he strolled into the Ospreys Café the Monday after with the rest of the Welsh internationals. He'd played so well, I assumed he'd be treated like royalty, but there's nothing like a rugby environment to puncture an inflated ego.

Within five minutes of arriving, he was standing forlornly by the till asking if anyone could lend him a fiver because he'd forgotten his wallet. The rest of the boys were ripping the piss while he pleaded with Phillsy to help him out; 'Come on Mike, I'll pay you back butt, honest.' He'd gone from tearing it up on Saturday, and winning Man of the Match against England, to trying to cadge a loan off Mike Phillips for a ham and cheese baguette. Even so, sitting next to him days after I'd watched him weave his magic on the weekend was a real thrill. I told him I thought he'd played brilliantly, and in his usual unassuming way he just said, 'Cheers butt, I appreciate that.'

Prior to the 2008 Six Nations, I was selected in my first Under-20s squad at the age of eighteen. We didn't know it then, but that squad contained a number of rough diamonds that would go on to form the nucleus of the senior side for a generation. Flankers Justin Tipuric, Sam Warburton and centre Jonathan Davies were among them, and we were invited into the senior Wales camp to act as live opposition during a full-contact session.

It was the first time I'd met Warren Gatland's famously abrasive defence coach, Shaun Edwards who – true to his reputation – was snarling and barking aggressively from the sidelines. When he'd first arrived a few months earlier, he'd heard rumours that the squad was divided over their defensive philosophy, with some favouring the 'blitz' up-and-at-'em approach, and others the more passive 'drift' system. It had led to confusion on the field and some abject performances, not least the defeat against Fiji that had seen Wales knocked out of the World Cup. Shaun's first words to the squad – so the legend goes – were: 'From now on we're a blitzing team, and if you don't like it, you can fuck off.'

He oozed aggression and hostility, encouraging us youngsters to get stuck in rather than just acting as cannon fodder. He wanted us to play through multiple phases, carrying hard into contact to try to stress his defensive system. I had other ideas, seeing this as an opportunity to impress with the national coaches watching on. I opened my full box of tricks, mixing delicate chips with audacious banana kicks, fizzing flat passes off both hands and launching hanging up-and-unders. In other words, ignoring Shaun and showing off a bit, which is exactly what he accused me of. 'Stop fookin' showboating and do as you're told, pal,' he yelled belligerently, but it was too late: I was enjoying myself too much. Call it naivety or youthful exuberance, but I chose to defy the world's most feared defence coach and do my own thing. He wasn't technically my boss, and I felt I had nothing to lose. So, instead of helping Wales train, we actually ripped into them, tearing it up and scoring some spectacular tries in the process. I jogged off, avoiding Shaun's steely gaze, and remember thinking, 'This pro rugby's a pretty easy gig.'

A few weeks later, when Wales had won three from three and were preparing for a Triple Crown decider with Ireland, we were invited back. That was the moment the scales fell from my eyes. Coming up against a well-drilled side honed by weeks of brutal Test rugby was an entirely different proposition. Slighted by our impudence a few weeks earlier, they completely battered us. We were getting bumped off, drilled into the ground, and whacked from every angle. Having been on the other side of the divide since, I can totally understand how the senior boys will have felt about the first meeting. They would have been through some exhausting training sessions, and the last thing they'd have wanted would have been a run-out against a bunch of cocky kids desperate to prove a point. If we'd been smug after the first session, we were crestfallen by the end of the second. It was a salutary lesson as to how much work we still had to put in if we ever wanted to be internationals.

New Zealander Warren Gatland had become the new head coach of Wales in December 2007, and within five months had managed to transform Wales from World Cup flops to Six Nations champions. But there was no rest for the triumphant Grand Slam stars, all of whom were drafted straight back into the Ospreys team for our EDF Energy Cup semi-final against Saracens at the Millennium Stadium; the same stadium at which they'd hoisted the Six Nations trophy aloft a week earlier.

Given their return en masse, I was a little surprised when Sean Holley – who was assistant coach at the time – called me aside to tell me I'd been selected on the bench for my professional debut. Given that the Ospreys had provided the bulk of the players to Warren Gatland's squad (thirteen of the first XV that beat England were Ospreys), it felt a little like being selected for Wales. It came far sooner than I could have ever imagined; I was still at school and managing my training regime around my academic commitments. Sean reassured me that I could organize my schedule differently from the other members of the matchday squad. 'You can miss this weights session,' he said, 'as long as you make the walk-through straight after school.' He joked that I wouldn't be required for the Thursday press conference, and I laughed, but a part of me *wanted* to do the press conference. I wanted the world to know I was the coming man and was happy to embrace the glare of the spotlight.

So my professional debut for the Ospreys came, not at the Liberty Stadium, or even St Helen's, but at the Millennium Stadium in Cardiff, in front of forty thousand people. It amounted to two minutes off the bench when the game was comfortably won, but I was still nervous as hell. My contribution pretty much amounted to a solitary kick to touch. So determined was I not to fluff my lines and give it back to the opposition, I barely hit it further than ten metres.

It felt utterly surreal afterwards, getting changed next to the likes of Shane Williams, Gavin Henson and Justin Marshall – the eighty-one-cap All Black – who I used to hero-worship as a young fan watching Super Rugby on the sofa with my mum. If you'd told me that on my professional debut, I'd be coming on at the national stadium with him as my scrum half, I would have told you to get your head checked. I remember thinking, *This is exactly where I want to be*, among this kind of company and basking in the glory of an emphatic win. I wanted to become the kind of player who inspires awe in others, in the same way Marshall did in me. One day I wanted a young academy kid to come into the changing room and think, 'That's Dan Biggar over there.'

Justin had a reputation for arrogance, but he was fantastic with me. Controversy and Marshy are near constant bedfellows, with him getting involved in a number of implausible scrapes both in Wales and back home in New Zealand, but in private he was a top bloke with a heart of gold. He took the time after my debut to ask about my life, and he appeared genuinely interested in the answers. It sounds like such a simple gesture, but it meant the world to me.

Not all senior players would do the same, with several preferring to maintain a strict hierarchy. Mike Phillips – Marshy's on-field nemesis, even when they were teammates – was also brilliant like that. He takes a bit of flak for being prickly and awkward, but he was superb with the youngsters. His outwardly brash demeanour masks a deep insecurity, and I saw little evidence of his supposed monstrous ego. He'd sit and talk to the academy kids at lunchtime, gently taking the piss but making us feel valued. Tellingly, whenever there was a mistake in training, and it was 50/50 whether it was Mike's fault or one of the youngsters', he'd always shoulder the blame, which to me is an admirable trait.

While no one gave me the cold shoulder exactly, others were less welcoming. Shane Williams was one of those whose respect you had to earn; he was a little hard to read initially. Alun Wyn Jones was distant and aloof, but I was to find out that that's just his way – he's no different now. I remember once, really early in my career, after a victory over the Dragons, I said to the team, 'Make sure you enjoy ourselves tonight, we've had a brilliant win,' and Al looked contemptuously at me, replying: 'We've had a *good* win, and nothing more . . . ' He was right, really: we'd expected to beat the Dragons, and he had no truck with exaggeration.

My next taste of first-team action was in a dead rubber against Connacht at the end of the season. We sent a virtual third-string side, and I remember it chiefly for the plane ride home. As is often the case in Galway, the weather was dreadful. We boarded the plane through sideways wind and rain and, once we were airborne, the turbulence was terrifying. None of our superstars had travelled, so the club had hired a cheap charter; one of those tiny crop dusters that get tossed about alarmingly in strong winds. I was gripping the arms of my seat, desperately trying to mask my fear, when Lyn Jones leapt into the aisle, dropped his pants round his ankles and started shouting, 'We're going down boys, we're going down!' I'd heard plenty of stories about Lyn's eccentric behaviour but hadn't yet seen it first-hand. If his intention had been to distract us from what was going on, it worked a treat.

During June of 2008, Wales hosted the Junior World Championship. We beat Italy and Japan comfortably, before taking on France in a group decider with a place in the semi-finals at stake. It was a bad-tempered game that got away from us, and we were ten points adrift approaching the final three minutes. There was a real fighting spirit in that team, though, and we clawed our way back to stun France with a winning try in the fifth minute of injury time.

As we were celebrating the unlikely victory, a mass brawl erupted. It was genuinely ugly, and unlike anything I'd ever witnessed on a rugby pitch. France had some nasty brutes in their side, and I vividly remember a young Mathieu Bastareaud prowling the touchline with clenched fists, just looking for an excuse to throw a punch. Our coaches, Pat Horgan and Rob Appleyard – the latter no stranger to a ruckus in his playing days – did their best to calm things down, but even Rob got knocked to the floor in the mêlée. Sam Warburton's live TV interview was cut short as he was dragged back to the changing room. Things eventually calmed down, but the ill-feeling remained for some time afterwards.

Both teams were staying at the same hotel in Swansea, and the officials were so fearful of things reigniting that they asked us Welsh boys to return home until tempers had cooled. Our winger, Jimmy Norris, asked if he could grab something from his room before leaving, and reappeared moments later looking as white as a sheet. He'd been stuck in a lift with Bastareaud on the way back down, and the future France international had challenged him to a duel, raising his fists, pugilist style, and saying, 'You and me, now.' Truly the stuff of nightmares.

It was a disgraceful way for the match to end, but the comeback showed the character within that team. Ten of us went on to receive international honours, with six representing the Lions. In fact, Leigh Halfpenny would find himself in the Lions squad the very next year. It was a tantalizing glimpse into the future; those same players would form the spine of Warren Gatland's Wales squad for more than a decade. Our reputations would soon be burnished in the senior squad, but there's no doubt a golden generation was forged in the fires of the Under-20 competitions that year.

Whether it was good fortune or a product of the system, I'm not sure, but there was a ridiculous concentration of talent in that group, a bit like that Man United squad containing Gary Neville, Paul Scholes, David Beckham and Ryan Giggs. We were good players, but even better characters. We had a never-say-die spirit that soon translated into the Test arena, where we became one of the most stubborn, hard-to-beat sides in world rugby. We couldn't overcome the eventual champions, New Zealand, in the semis, losing 31–6 to a side that contained a number of future All Blacks, Aaron Smith and Sam Whitelock among them. It was a disappointing finale, but we knew there was more to come from that group of players.

After the tournament, the senior Wales team toured South Africa, and I was invited to train with the Ospreys again. It was the usual pre-season fitness stuff and involved several trips to the nightmare-inducing Merthyr Mawr sand dunes, along with a series of 'Strongman trials', in which we were forced to flip tractor tyres, flip logs and push lorry cabs. For a puny fly half who hated that kind of stuff, the new season couldn't come quickly enough!

A couple of weeks into the new campaign, as we were gathered in the barn ahead of the away game to Glasgow, I was astonished to be named as starting fly half. I'd had no advance warning and was completely taken by surprise. James Hook was picked on the bench, meaning I'd be pulling on the number 10 jersey for my first ever professional start. I felt as if I was floating on air as I left the barn, and was enveloped by Ashley Beck and Kristian Phillips, both offering their congratulations. I was the first among the academy cohort to get a start.

The game was a Friday-night clash at the old Firhill Ground on the outskirts of Glasgow, a far cry from the gleaming purpose-built Scotstoun where they now play. The changing room was so small, we couldn't all fit in at the same time, so boys were queueing in the corridor to get their kit on. This felt far more pressurized than my late cameo against Saracens, even though it was in some soulless outpost miles from home as opposed to the national stadium. I wasn't coming on with the game safely won this time; I was starting, with all the stress and responsibility that came with it.

As I was running through the plays in my mind and visualizing that first kick-off, Mike Cuddy lumbered into the changing room and clambered on the old-fashioned Victorian-era scales. Mike's a big bloke, and it was no surprise when the needle swung violently to the far end and started vibrating. It was always going to happen, but he was my boss, and I couldn't laugh. Stepping off gingerly, he gave me a sideways glance and raised a comedy eyebrow. As trivial as it sounds, that small exchange did more to settle my nerves than any reassuring speech would have done.

I kicked an early penalty from the left-hand side which calmed me down, and the rest of the half unfolded fairly smoothly. During the second half, we were trailing by a point when the ball came back to me in my own half and impulsively, I thought, 'Sod this, I'm going to drop a goal.' I was more than fifty metres away, but it sailed over with room to spare. When the referee's arm went up, I swelled with pride. I've always been a nuts-and-bolts kind of player without much in the way of stardust, but I pride myself on my ability to execute like that. To do it at the age of eighteen on my first start was immensely satisfying. Down there in the depths of the internet, you can still find the drop goal. It's a wobbly ten-second clip, with Welsh language commentary, but it represents my first taste of fame.

I was under no illusions that tougher tests would come. My next big start was the result of circumstance rather than form. Gavin Henson was in the middle of one of his troubled periods, and had been suspended after a players' vote. I forget what his misdemeanour was on that occasion, but he'd had several brushes with the law, and had upset some of his colleagues by prioritizing his TV appearances over his rugby. He'd been summoned to a meeting with the coaches during training, and while the rest of us were tucking into lunch he emerged from their office, strode past us in silence, and calmly got into his car and drove away. Moments later Sean Holley – who was head coach by that point – came dashing in and asked where he was. We explained that he'd just left, which didn't go down too well with Sean, who'd apparently told him to go and get some air after tempers had begun to fray. Gav had clearly had enough and buggered off. That episode cost him his place in the team to face Perpignan in the Heineken Cup on 18 October 2008.

I don't claim to have any great insight into Gav other than to say he was hugely misunderstood. Beneath the bravado and the clashes with authority, he was the ultimate professional. He looked after himself incredibly well, bringing his own food in every day, measured out in precise portions, and neatly packed in Tupperware containers. His superstar status could easily have swelled his ego, but I never saw any evidence of that. For as long as I knew him, he was generous with his guidance and advice. He was unfairly portrayed as a self-centred troublemaker, but in my experience, he was a shy, reserved bloke, even a little insecure. Gav's issue – and he wasn't unique in this regard – was that he changed after a couple of beers. The ultra-chilled bloke from training would transform into an aggressive, antagonistic night-mare, who enjoyed winding people up and spoiling for fights. It was such a stark contrast to his professional self, where he was always the coolest customer on the field. I vividly remember one session when Richard Hibbard was acting like a berserker, hurl-ing himself around and smashing into people, when Gav – who rarely ever seemed to break sweat – wandered over and said, in his trademark laconic drawl, 'Hibs, chill out mun. You're doing my fucking 'ead in.'

I was named on the bench when Perpignan came to town, but then Hooky suffered a back spasm on the day and I was pro-moted to the starting line-up. You're naturally more chilled when you're on the bench as the likelihood is you'll get fifteen minutes at the end if the game's well won or already gone. Starting is a *total* change of mindset. I headed straight to the ground – a good two and a half hours before kick-off – and launched into an exhaustive kicking routine, wanting to feel like I'd kicked from every spot on the ground. Poor old Jonathan Humphreys was roped in as my assistant, and showed the patience of a saint retrieving all my balls, as I repeatedly shouted, 'Just one more.'

Perpignan would go on to become French champions that season and were a seriously good side. This was a golden oppor-tunity to prove my worth in a big European game and the thought of missing a vital kick and letting the team down was unbearable. It was an absolute pig of a game, low on quality and devoid of tries, but I knocked over five penalties which dragged us to an ugly 15–9 win. Sean Holley gave me a huge hug as I came off, which made me feel really special – a part of the team as opposed to some precocious kid banging on the door and hoping to be let in. I'd turned nineteen two days earlier, so it was a perfect birthday present.

I knew then that my career wouldn't be a flash in the pan. As head coach, Sean had had a plan for me, and he was delighted that his instincts were proving correct. The blitz defence was becoming ever more prominent and spooking more traditional playmakers like James Hook and Gavin Henson. He'd seen in me a more modern fly half, in the mould of Johnny Sexton or Ronan O'Gara, who could manipulate defences through tactical kicking. It's a trend he'd clearly anticipated. The truth is, you rarely get maverick 10s at Test level any more. Marcus Smith is the closest of the current generation, and he can't get a run in the England shirt – or not yet, anyway. The Ospreys backline was brimming with x-factor players – Lee Byrne, James Hook, Shane Williams and Tommy Bowe, to name just a few. They needed someone steady and reliable to marshal that backline and wanted to mould me into that player.

Of course, I didn't know this at the time; I was just happy to have elbowed my way into the side. When Hooky pulled up injured, they'd had to recall Henson to the squad, but tellingly, they'd left him on the bench, even when the game was in the balance. Looking back, that felt symbolic. The easiest thing would have been to revoke the suspension, and hand Gav the 10 shirt from the start. I'd have understood that, given the importance of the game; he was a double Grand Slam champion and a proven match-winner after all. But they backed me, and it felt good.

My next big chance came against the Cardiff Blues at the Arms Park. That was a much bigger deal, a Welsh derby against a star-studded capital-city side, in front of their vociferous home support. Until then, I felt like I'd been navigating the undulating waters of professional rugby with relative ease. Sean explained that he wanted to keep Hooky and Phillsy on the bench, as a kind of psychological trick. He wanted to neuter Cardiff's team talk by leaving his stars out of the starting line-up. That way, there could be no 'go and get stuck into their big dogs' fighting talk from the opposition.

The game was the boxing equivalent of being punched squarely in the face. The poise and composure I'd shown against Perpignan deserted me completely, and I fell into a damaging spiral of mistakes. My kicks from hand were rushed or shanked directly into touch, my passes were forced or off-target, and I started falling off tackles. I began to feel hopelessly out of my depth. As I dragged myself to my feet after conceding a turnover, it felt as though my world was caving in. I was subbed off shortly after, as Hooky glided onto the pitch, took full control, and guided us serenely to victory. Sean put his arm around me at the final whistle and said, 'Don't worry mate, you'll have better days than that.' After my debut at the Millennium Stadium, my match-winning drop goal in Glasgow, and my European baptism against Perpignan, I'd thought the transition into professional rugby would be seamless. The Cardiff game was a harsh, and necessary, reality check.

5

CLAIMING THE JERSEY

Achieving a dream usually involves travelling a long road; navigating twists and turns and overcoming obstacles until the promised land hoves into view. From that perspective, my Wales debut arrived way before I'd earned it. I still felt like an apprentice learning his trade when the news arrived that I'd been selected in the squad for the 2008 autumn internationals. I'd turned nineteen just days earlier and had only had three starts for the Ospreys.

Ryan Jones offered to drive me to my first camp. It was fortunate that he was living in Llangennith at the time, and arriving with the Wales captain certainly burnished my street cred. It made me feel like I belonged, rather than like a prize winner who'd won a competition to train with Wales for the day. I strode in alongside Jughead (as he's universally known) feeling pretty pleased with myself, but was immediately cut down to size by the team manager, Alan 'Thumper' Phillips, who told me off for wearing flip-flops.

Given my experiences with the Ospreys and the Under-20s, I wasn't as overawed as I might have been training with the national squad. I wondered whether I'd been picked just for the coaches to have a look at me, so I was both surprised and delighted when I was selected on the bench for the second game against Canada. It was arguably the ideal introduction to Test rugby. Rather than being thrust straight into a burning hot cauldron against world-class opposition, I'd likely get a fifteen-minute cameo against a tier-two nation with the game – hopefully – already won.

As the moment arrived and I was walking down the tunnel into the stadium, the enormity of it hit me, and emotion flooded my system. Listening to the rising crescendo of noise, I looked pleadingly at Alun Wyn Jones and said, 'Please Al, whatever call I make out there, even if it's the wrong one, just back it.'

He's always been a man of few words, but he nodded reassuringly and said, 'Yeah, of course.'

Eighteen minutes in, Hooky went down injured. A message was relayed to the bench: 'Get Biggs on.'

I'd barely stripped out of my tracksuit when my name was being bellowed through the stadium PA and I was jogging purposefully onto the hallowed turf. The scale of everything was just bigger; the noise was louder, the tackles more forceful, and the tempo more frenetic, but I felt comfortable.

Within minutes the Canadians decided to test my mettle, hoisting a high, dangling kick towards me. It was an isolated moment in the game but, right then, it felt like everything to me. I wasn't in Llandarcy now, or on the windblown fields of Gorseinon. I was in the Millennium Stadium playing for Wales, with sixty thousand pairs of eyes boring into me.

I watched it descend from the heavens, and end over end it spiralled, agonizingly slowly, as I planted my feet and steeled myself for a collision. Up above, the ball. Up ahead, a marauding phalanx of Canadian forwards, intent on taking my head off. As the ball plummeted downward, I leapt, and it felt – momentarily – as if the stadium volume had been turned right down.

Everything froze.

Then, *thunk*, the ball landed cleanly in my arms, and the volume surged back to deafening levels. I sidestepped to avoid the onrushing defence and belted the ball back with interest.

Phew. Test passed.

It was a scrappy, error-strewn and disjointed performance from a very different side to the one that had won the Grand Slam. I was gutted to miss two touchline penalty kicks, but we gradually worked our way into a winning position. Then towards the end, with the result safe, I threw a reckless pass in my own half, gifting Canada a consolation try. I was annoyed at myself but philosophical enough, relieved that the error hadn't cost us the game; but the following morning, as I was checking out of the Vale Hotel, Shaun Edwards approached, his eyes radiating with a burning intensity. 'If the ball's won at the front of the lineout, and you're going hard at the line,' he said, in lieu of a greeting, '*never* throw a long pass.' Before I was able to muster a response, he added, 'Bear that in mind for the future, lad', and strode off. Naively, I'd been expecting him to congratulate me on my international debut.

I grew to love Shaun and to understand how good he was at pushing the right buttons, but that encounter in the hotel lobby had left me reeling. Knowing him as I now do, he'd have made a calculation as to how well I would have taken that. He would have noted my self-assurance and reckoned I'd have been mentally tough enough to absorb the criticism.

Winning my first cap was the realization of a dream, but not the all-encompassing experience I'd anticipated. I'd grown up understanding how sacred the scarlet red number 10 shirt was, but I'd worn a canary yellow one with '21' on the back and it just wasn't the same. That little taste had made me hungry for a whole lot more, but I didn't want to be a fringe player, drifting in and out of squads. I wanted to be the main man.

I had my official cap presentation after the match, and Leigh Halfpenny made sure he was there to share it with me. He'd got his after his debut against South Africa the week before. He'd been lined up for some commercial duties after the Canada game – pressing the flesh with some sponsors in a corporate box – but in a very uncharacteristic show of defiance, he had refused to go, insisting he wanted to be there to share that moment with me. It felt twice as special sharing it with him, the crystallization of a dream that had begun all those years earlier on the muddy fields of Gorseinon RFC.

*

Back at the Ospreys, I was emerging from my shell, and some of the senior players mistook my confidence for arrogance. Sean Holley would occasionally tell me to dial down the histrionics; I had a tendency to wave my arms around in frustration if things weren't going to plan. I'd become almost anal in my attention to detail, and would get angry when others weren't on the same page. I was yet to understand that some players play better when they're given a bit of freedom, and, at the time, my attitude was very much, 'If I know how Leinster defend off a left-side scrum, why the hell don't you?' I just couldn't understand why everyone else wasn't as meticulous in their prep.

It certainly got me into trouble with the forwards a few times. During the training week, we'd do separate units sessions, which were markedly different in content; the backs would be on one side of the pitch, playing touch rugby and working on soft skills, while the forwards would be down the other end, doing endless scrums, mauls, and close-quarter contact stuff. To put it another way, we'd be doing the sophisticated, creative stuff, while they'd be smashing heads, clattering into one another, and snarling like wild animals.

Bringing us together was like mixing oil and water. They'd be fired up and angry, fuelled by testosterone and spoiling for a fight. Chuck in a bossy fly half who's been fannying about playing touch, and it's bound to trigger a certain resentment.

And so it did, one overcast afternoon in Llandarcy, when the normally docile Jerry Collins objected to the way I'd bawled him out, flew into a fearful rage and started chasing me around the pitch. It might have looked like an outtake from Benny Hill, but I was genuinely terrified.

Admittedly, my choice of words had been a little coarse – 'Oi Collins, you dozy prick, what the *fuck* are you playing at?' – and he reacted accordingly, sprinting towards me like some kind of Marvel villain; jaw set, legs pumping, and with murder on his mind. Mercifully, some of his fellow forwards intervened and rescued me from a grisly fate.

In those early days, Sean and Scott Johnson – who'd arrived in 2009 as director of rugby – were looking to groom me as a leader. I was far too young and precocious to be considered as captain, but they wanted me to lead the backline. Depending on your interpretation, I was either extremely diligent or borderline obsessive-compulsive. I wanted to forensically analyse the opposition, probing for weaknesses, looking for various patterns, habits and foibles that we could take advantage of. After the Friday team run, I'd head to Sean's office to hand him a piece of paper containing reams of notes that would make little sense to anyone outside of our environment. After watching our next opposition studiously for hours on end, I'd have figured out how they defended off lineouts, right-hand scrums, and starter plays. By doing that, I could come up with cute ways to exploit them.

Other coaches might have seen this as interfering, but Sean valued the extra pair of eyes. The only other player showing this same level of diligence was Gavin Henson.

The coaches would regularly hand out sheets asking us to analyse our own performances, with sections on what we'd done well, what required more work, what we'd like to develop further. The laid-back guys like Shaun Connor and Sonny Parker would scribble a few vague sentences, but Gav's would always be meticulously completed in tiny, neat writing, often spilling over into extra sheets. For someone who was often portrayed as an off-the-cuff maverick, it was fascinating to see how fastidious he actually was, and it definitely rubbed off on me.

I missed out on the 2009 Six Nations, but I was back in the international fold for the summer tour to America and Canada. Thirteen Welsh players – including Stephen Jones and James Hook – had been selected for the Lions in South Africa, so this was a real chance for me. The vibe around the squad was pretty relaxed, as we were confident of victory against both and, unlike subsequent tours, there wasn't a need to be in 'rugby mode' the whole time. As the youngest, I had to look after the ceremonial love spoon. Love spoons are part of a centuries-old tradition in Wales, and used to be exchanged between lovers as a token of their devotion. For some time, Welsh touring teams have carried an enormous one on every trip as a national symbol, and responsibility always falls to the youngest to keep it safe. It won't surprise you to hear that everywhere we went, the boys tried to steal the spoon, and I became increasingly paranoid about losing it.

As it turned out, the only thing that went 'missing' was Mark Jones's passport, before we'd even touched down on Canadian soil. 'Boycie', as Mark is universally known, is a bit of a character, and was among the most enthusiastic pranksters in the squad. He once kidnapped a sheep and hid it in Dwayne Peel's room, where it ran riot, shitting everywhere and destroying – among other things – Peeley's expensive watch. On this occasion, however, Boycie was the victim. Cue panic as he started searching frantically under all the seats and in the overhead lockers. After ten minutes our team manager, Thumper, piped up saying if anyone had hidden it, now was the time to confess. No one said a word.

The search continued until immigration officers boarded the plane to ask, none too patiently, why on earth we hadn't got off. Post 9/11, airport officials in North America were understandably jumpy, and these ones did *not* see the funny side. We were on the plane for a further forty-five minutes before Thumper got desperate and tried to bribe the officials with some Welsh jerseys. To this day, no one has admitted to hiding the passport, but I'm pretty sure it was Richard Hibbard.

The Tests were in Toronto and Chicago, two incredible cities with so much to tickle the senses. I was with a load of mates I'd played at Under-20s level with, as well as experienced internationals like Gareth Cooper, Dwayne Peel, Duncan Jones and Boycie. It was an eclectic mix.

I started against Canada, kicking twenty-two points in a Man-of-the-Match display. It was an honour to wear the jersey again, but it all felt a bit underwhelming. It was the same yellow shirt I'd worn against the same opposition back in November, though this one at least had number 10 on the back. The occasion was fairly subdued as well, with the game taking place at York University in front of a modest crowd of 8,000.

I was craving a start in Chicago the following weekend, when we'd be playing in red at Toyota Park, so you can imagine my disappointment when Neil Jenkins pulled me aside to tell me Nicky Robinson was starting instead. Nicky had been told he was on standby for the Lions, and the coaches had been asked to play him so that he would be match-ready if the call arrived. It pissed me right off. Nicky was twenty-seven and hadn't played international rugby for three years. In my mind, this was a development tour to blood promising youngsters, and I felt, selfishly, that I should have had the shirt for both games.

Despite this disappointment, by the autumn of 2009 I had become the established first-choice 10 at the Ospreys, with Hooky shifting to inside centre. It was a dynamic we stumbled upon almost by accident, but it worked a treat. I was the steadier, nuts-and-bolts type of player, while Hooky was the creative genius. Having me anchoring things at 10 allowed Hooky up to follow his instincts and weave his magic. He could do things others could only dream of.

As we approached the business end of the season in spring 2010, we were still fighting on two fronts, having navigated a tricky pool to reach the knockouts of the Heineken Cup. Our reward was a quarter-final against Biarritz and we travelled to San Sebastian brimming with confidence.

For a number of years, the Ospreys had been referred to, pejoratively, as the 'Galacticos'. There were plenty of Welsh rugby fans who dismissed us as soulless Chequebook Charlies who'd assembled a dream team off the back of Mike Cuddy's wealth, but hadn't had the success to match the ambition. We were the modern-day equivalent of that nasty Neath team of the nineties who thrived on the 'everyone hates us but we don't care' mentality.

The Heineken Cup – club rugby's glamorous European showpiece – was something we coveted, but the past two campaigns had seen us bow out meekly at the quarter-final stage. First, to Saracens, weeks after we'd smashed them 30–3 in the EDF Cup, and then against Munster when Paul Warwick delivered the best individual performance I'd ever seen. I'd not been involved against Saracens and had only had a cameo against Munster, so this match against Biarritz was the first time I'd been entrusted with the shirt in a big knockout game.

Our team against Biarritz was an international side in all but name. Every member of the starting XV had been capped; eight were British and Irish Lions and two were All Blacks. There was a third All Black on the bench in the shape of Filo Tiatia.

The grumblings over our European shortcomings had been growing louder, with pundits wondering how a team festooned with so many international stars could keep stumbling before the final hurdle. So there was a feeling that this had to be our year. If not now, when?

The supporters flew out with us on a packed charter flight. The early April weather in San Sebastian was glorious – thirty degrees and not a cloud in the sky. After I finished my kicking session the day before the game, I returned to the hotel, showered, changed, and went for a wander to take in the surroundings.

After a leisurely stroll around the city's gorgeous old town, I ambled back to find the hotel had been evacuated and dozens of guests were milling around impatiently by the entrance. I found a few of my teammates, who told me some idiot had left a towel over a lampshade and it had caught fire, triggering the alarm. I tutted and shook my head disparagingly, while my roommate Jonathan Thomas gave me a withering look, knowing full well that the dimwit in question was me. He'd apparently got back to the room just in time to stop it going up in flames, but not in time to prevent the alarm going off. As bad as it was, I remain eternally grateful to JT for rescuing me from a much more embarrassing fate.

The day of the game dawned hot and sultry on Spain's northern coast. The shiny modern stadium looked magnificent, and the playing surface was like a carpet. The decision to take the game to Spain meant the crowd was thronged with passionate Basque fans from both sides of the border, and when I glanced across at their side during the warm-up, I realized how big a deal this was. They had a brilliant team. Imanol Harinordoquy, sporting a Hannibal Lecter-style mask to protect a broken cheek, Dimitri Yachvili, Jérôme Thion, Iain Balshaw and Takudzwa Ngwenya were among their superstars, but there was quality everywhere.

Less than thirty seconds had passed before Damien Traille nudged over one of the ugliest drop goals I've ever seen, but it crept over the bar and got the crowd on their feet. Shortly after Ngwenya scored an absolute wonder try, snaffling the ball in his 22 and turning on the after-burners. Shane gave chase, but he absolutely skinned him. Ngwenya was probably the fastest man in rugby at the time, but it was still jaw-dropping to see him out-pace Shane with such ease. We stuck in the fight; a bit of Hooky magic created some space for Ryan Jones to crash over, and some midfield sorcery sent Lee Byrne in at the corner. We were just a point adrift at the break.

In the changing room, we were confronted by the alarming sight of Scott Johnson, splayed on the physio's bed, gasping for breath. His face was beetroot red and his long hair bedraggled and drenched in sweat. He'd been suffering with bad migraines; another painful attack, in conjunction with the searing heat and the stress of the first half, had knocked the stuffing out of him. Johnno was a wordsmith and a philosopher who'd always hit the right notes in his half-time team talks, but he was in no fit state to address us. As such, there were no rousing speeches, and the changing room was a strangely subdued place. We weren't really focusing on what was coming up next.

A sweetly struck forty-five-metre penalty put us in front for the first time, but they were developing a stranglehold up front, squeezing us at the scrum and disrupting our lineout. Some loose discipline let them back into the game, and they soon re-established an eight-point lead.

I was desperate to seize back the initiative but missed a penalty and a drop-goal attempt in quick succession. With the Basque crowd getting increasingly loud and passionate, we were beginning to wonder if it just wasn't our day, when Mike Phillips embarked on one of his trademark breaks and put Nikki Walker in for a timely try. We were back to within a point with five minutes to go.

What followed still rankles to this day.

With the clock in the red, we found ourselves surging forwards in Biarritz's half, when Yachvili strayed offside and deliberately knocked on. The referee, George Clancy, stuck his arm out for a penalty advantage. It was clear and obvious, and we reacted accordingly.

A penalty advantage gives you a 'free hit', a chance to try something safe in the knowledge that – if it doesn't work out – you'll have a shot at goal to follow. I gave Phillsy the nod, dropped back into the pocket, and readied myself for a drop goal. Mike fizzed the pass to me, and while I struck it cleanly, it didn't quite have the distance. No bother, I thought, I just had to steady myself for the penalty to come.

But it never did. George Clancy pressed the whistle to his lips and blew for full time.

It felt like I was in a lift that had suddenly plummeted several floors at once. A feeling of near-ecstasy replaced instantly by one of soul-crushing despair.

Phillsy was incandescent, confronting Clancy like a snarling Premier League footballer, while I was just thinking about how I'd blown the drop goal. Though I knew I should have had a second bite at it, I couldn't help but feel it was my fault. It was a miserable feeling, and the sense of injustice grated badly.

I bumped into Warren Gatland as I was leaving the stadium,

who'd been there on a watching brief, and he told me to remember how they were celebrating. Given the controversy at the final whistle, he thought they'd lacked a bit of grace and told me to bottle that up and hold onto it. 'There'll be bigger and better moments to come for you,' he said. 'And you'll have a chance to turn the tables on those players, whether it's in an Ospreys shirt or a Wales one.'

The bus to the airport was silent as we gazed listlessly out of the window, pondering what might have been. I was pointlessly replaying that missed drop goal over and over in my mind, wondering whether I'd have struck it better if I'd known there was no penalty coming. The Ospreys fans gave us a standing ovation at the airport, clapping us through and saying we'd done them proud, and I can't express how much that lifted our collective mood.

Looking back, it was a huge opportunity gone begging. Refereeing controversy aside, with the squad we had, and the pedigree we shared, a failure to travel deeper than the quarter-finals was a crushing disappointment. Given the parlous financial state of Welsh rugby right now, there is no way in a million years a region will be assembling a team like that again. That was a watershed moment: 2010 was the year we could and should have reached the final. It remains a massive regret, and there's no doubt it was the European loss that hurt the club the most.

But there wasn't much time for navel-gazing; we arrived home on Saturday evening and were back in the airport on Monday morning for a mini-tour of Ireland. We were still in the mix for the Celtic League play-offs, but had to play three of the best four sides during our run-in. Our game against Ulster earlier in the season had been postponed because of heavy snow, so we now had to shoehorn it in on a Tuesday night, before taking on the mighty Leinster on the Friday. Two big games in four days. We needed to get back on the horse.

Sean Holley sensed the mood post-Biarritz and knew he couldn't crack the whip too hard. He told us to treat this as – his words – an 'old school tour'. We were told to loosen the shackles of professionalism and look to finish the season on a high. He gave me another boost by telling me I'd be starting both matches.

We beat Ulster in a high-scoring game at Ravenhill, with Tommy Bowe racing clear for the decisive try against his old club. It was a timely reminder of the character we had in the group; rather than wallowing in self-pity, we'd travelled to Belfast and racked up thirty points.

Sean thanked us for the attitude shown and finished his post-match speech by saying, 'If anyone hasn't got a beer in their hand in the next five minutes, they're never playing for this club again.'

Back at the hotel, the booze was flowing liberally, and the mood quickly turned raucous. For some, too much beer led to soppy sentimentalism, others to aggression, so it wasn't entirely surprising when – in the early hours – Andrew Bishop launched himself across the table and started swinging at Phillsy, knocking him backwards off his chair. Whatever he'd said had touched a nerve, and after a bit of a dust-up, Mike – in a rare show of sense – sloped off to bed before things got ugly.

Ulster actually used that hotel for their training and recovery, and their director of rugby, David Humphreys, was suitably impressed to see Shane and Lee Byrne already up and about when he arrived at 6.30 the next morning to make a head start on his analysis. It was only when he got closer that he realized that they hadn't been to bed at all, and were now washing down breakfast croissants with the dregs of last night's lager.

Only three of us turned up for pool recovery. As I was getting changed afterwards, a message dropped into the players' Whats-App group, instructing us to meet in the bar at 11 a.m., to 'get back on it'. This was Wednesday, and we were playing Leinster on Friday.

A motley crew of bleary-eyed, sleep-deprived rugby players staggered in at around 11. Several were wearing gaudy, Hawaiian-style shirts, and hadn't yet traversed that painful barrier between drunk and hungover. Within minutes, however, the mood had brightened, and everyone was clutching a Malibu and lemonade, with little cocktail umbrellas poking jauntily out of the top, as bemused residents pondered whether they'd stumbled upon the world's biggest stag do.

It was some time later that our forwards coach, Jon Humphreys, stormed into the bar with a face like thunder, loudly demanding to know, 'What the fuck is going on?' Most of us shuffled nervously in our seats, avoiding his gaze as an awkward silence descended. Then Hooky, with as innocent a tone as he could muster, replied, 'Old school tour, isn't it?' looking around forlornly for others to back him up.

It transpired that we'd grossly misinterpreted the 'old school' directive.

A meeting was called, and we were given an almighty bollocking. Those who weren't in the twenty-three for Friday were to be sent home immediately. Sean reverted to schoolteacher mode, telling us the hotel had received a litany of complaints about our conduct, about the fight between Phillsy and Bish, about the noise, the language, and the general anti-social behaviour. Then, without pausing for effect, or even arching an eyebrow, he added, 'And we've had complaints about boys shitting the bed.'

Something about the turn of phrase, and the fact he'd said it with an entirely straight face, sent the room into paroxysms of laughter. Even Sean struggled to keep a straight face. When it eventually died down, Hooky stood up and asked a little despondently, 'So which boys are going home then, Sean?' It sent the room off into a further fit of giggles, at which point the coaches realized they were fighting a losing battle.

We drove to Dublin the next day, endured one pretty shambolic training session, and then slept for the remainder of the afternoon, and a good portion of game day too. Inevitably though, the ravaging effects of the old school tour caught up with us and we finally ran out of gas. They ended up winning 20–16 which, given the circumstances, wasn't a bad result for us. The losing bonus point kept us in second place.

That trip was the perfect antidote to the Biarritz loss, strengthening the bonds between us. Ask any player from that squad about the 'old school tour', and I guarantee the memories will come flooding back. Although we still don't know who shat the bed.

Six days later, we were back in Ireland. In Limerick this time, for the penultimate game of the regular season against Munster. For the second match running, I scored all our points and we dug out a gutsy, 15–11 win. It was the first time I'd played against Ronan O'Gara and I'd steeled myself for a barrage of verbal abuse. He was renowned for using his famously acid tongue to undermine and belittle opponents. When my Ospreys predecessor, Matthew Jones, arrived at Thomond Park a few years earlier, he'd bumped into O'Gara on the way, raising his hand in recognition, only to be asked, 'What are you doing here? The Under-12s are playing tomorrow.'

As it turned out, O'Gara was largely silent. He had a bad day by his standards, missing three or four kicks in blustery conditions, while I nailed five from five and won Man of the Match.

We thrashed the Dragons to reach the play-offs, before beating Glasgow with ease in the semis.

We hardly trained during that run-in; we'd do a bit of recovery and analysis on a Monday and be out the door by midday. There's sometimes an element of panic when big games come around, and coaches feel like they need to raise the intensity, but that can actually be counterproductive at that stage in the season. We wanted to pitch up on match day feeling fresh and energized.

Going up against Johnny Sexton in the final was a big deal. He was a rising star and a few years ahead of me in terms of status and reputation. It was a star-studded Leinster side, the core of which had won the Heineken Cup and the Grand Slam with Ireland the previous year; Rob Kearney, Shane Horgan, Brian O'Driscoll, Gordon D'Arcy, Isa Nacewa and Jamie Heaslip were just some of the names that rolled off the tongue. It was a golden generation of players, playing at their Royal Dublin Showground fortress; a place at which we'd failed to win in our last six attempts. We were massive underdogs, not just in the eyes of the press, but of our own benefactors, who'd booked us on a flight back that same evening, clearly anticipating a chastening defeat.

We'd studied their patterns hard, though, and had noticed that O'Driscoll liked defending in the outside channel; if you attacked his outside shoulder, he was brilliant at reading the play, making a tackle and hustling for a turnover. We planned to isolate him and Gordon D'Arcy, making them defend as individuals rather than a unit. Tommy Bowe really helped us that week, giving us plenty of valuable insights into how they worked as a defensive duo. He said they'd be looking to hunt down me, him and Shane; to 'kill us', in his words.

We practised loads of 'block plays' during the week, with the 9 passing to the 10, the centres running hard to fix the defence, and a winger running a decoy line 'out the back'. We knew O'Driscoll would mark his outside centre, forcing D'Arcy to mark two play- ers at once and have to make a split-second choice about whether to target the guy running straight at him or the one floating behind.

On the day of the game, we knew we couldn't show our hand too early. As we were approaching the end of the first quarter, we called it. Off a lineout, Phillsy passed to me while Bish ran a tight line with Hooky drifting towards the touchline, his hands up, shaping to receive the pass. Meanwhile Tommy ran on an arc behind the two of them. O'Driscoll, as anticipated, man-marked Hooky, leaving D'Arcy with a choice: drop the shoulder on Bish or track Bowe. He chose the latter, seeing his international team- mate as the bigger threat, and Bish played a blinder, keeping his head down until the last second when he arrived on my shoulder, and scorched through the hole unmarked. Tommy surged through behind him, took the pass, and cantered over the try line. We'd executed it to perfection.

In focusing all their attention on our superstars they'd failed to acknowledge the threat of our silent assassin. Bish never sought credit or craved attention but was the glue that held that backline together, the ultimate team player. He might not have produced the eye-catching, showreel moments that Hooky and Shane did, but he did all the dirty work that allowed them to flourish.

In a decade of playing with him, I'm not sure he ever missed a tackle. He was also the first person you'd want by your side in a street fight, a point proved beyond doubt one Christmas, when everyone came to the annual party in superhero fancy dress. Alun Wyn had come as Captain America, and Bish – rather reluctantly – as Batman.

Now, Al can get a little tactile when he's drunk, and he was niggling Bish, wrapping his arm around him, nudging him, and winding him up a treat. Bish asked him politely to back off, which only seemed to encourage Al, who puffed his chest out and asked Bish, 'What the hell are you going to do about it?' Like a scene in a Western, a silence descended as the tension rose.

Captain America had risen to his full six feet seven inches, and was staring down intimidatingly at Batman, over whom he also held a significant weight advantage. Before anyone thought to intervene, Batman unleashed a punch of such force and precision that Captain America was sent tumbling to the ground in a crumpled heap. The lesson we all learned that day was the same one O'Driscoll and company learned during that day in Dublin: don't underestimate the Bish.

Byrney scored a brilliant try after Tommy's, and we could have been out of sight by half-time, had my try not been disallowed for a forward pass. I knocked over a penalty early in the second half, which took us 17–3 ahead, and we basically hung on for the rest of the game, defending manfully for half an hour. By the time the final whistle blew, we'd kept our try line intact, refusing to concede a try against *that* Leinster side away from home. It was an enormous source of pride, and made the trophy lift even sweeter. A first victory in Dublin for five years, when it mattered the most. The San Sebastian failure – so painful at the time – was fast receding in the rear-view mirror.

6

RIDING THE TRAVELATOR

My heart was pounding as I clattered down the corridor in my studs, heading towards New Zealand's changing room. Physically exhausted, and mentally drained, I was wondering what I'd actually say when I knocked on the door and asked Dan Carter to swap shirts. It was one of the most intimidating moments of my career. I was confronted with a team bathing in the afterglow of yet another victory; Richie McCaw striding around with his top off, all battle-scarred and shredded. Mils Muliaina, Kieran Read, Jerome Kaino – familiar titans of the game looking like cartoon versions of their real selves. Recognizable, but otherworldly. It felt like I'd entered a sacred space, and I couldn't quite believe that I'd just been out there mixing it with these granite-carved superheroes.

I scanned the room to find Carter sitting in the corner, chatting to Keven Mealamu.

'Excuse me,' I asked, in a meek voice that sounded strangely unfamiliar amid all these gruff Kiwi accents, 'would you mind if we swapped jerseys?'

He peeled his off, revealing a nauseatingly flawless physique, all chiselled abs and perfect pecs, and I suddenly felt like a little boy from the Gower proffering an autograph book to his childhood hero. He asked me a few polite questions, before I thanked him awkwardly and fled, my face burning, readying myself for the barrage of abuse I'd get from my teammates when I reappeared: 'Oooh, rugby fwend.'

A couple of hours earlier, I'd been staring at my own shirt hanging on the peg in the changing rooms at the Waikato Stadium. Finally, the iconic red shirt with '10' emblazoned on the back. It was everything I'd worked for, and to see it with my name embroidered on it felt incredibly special: *Dan Biggar, New Zealand v Wales, 26/07/2010, 6th cap.*

I finally felt like I belonged. But in truth, the game came too soon for me. Whether it was the emotion of seeing that shirt, of playing against Dan Carter or of facing the haka, it turned out I just wasn't ready. I'd arrived on tour full of confidence after winning the Celtic League, but the jump between club level and international – particularly the All Blacks in New Zealand – was enormous. There weren't any tougher assignments in world rugby.

We hadn't beaten them home or away in fifty-three years. We lost 29–10, which was a marked improvement on the 42–9 drubbing we'd experienced the week before, but I still felt completely out of my depth. It was far from the Roy of The Rovers experience I'd dreamt about.

Slumped in the changing room afterwards, Gats sidled up to me and told me not to be too hard on myself. 'You missed a few tackles and made a few errors,' he said, 'but you had some nice touches too.'

That was rare for Gats. He wasn't normally the type to put an arm around your shoulder, but he read my mood perfectly at that point. After staring listlessly at the floor for several minutes, I had gathered my thoughts, dusted myself down and gone to find Carter.

I put his shirt in a plastic bag and buried it in my rucksack because I didn't want to risk the airline losing my baggage. By the time I got home and showed Mum, it was absolutely rancid. After a thorough go in the washing machine, I got it framed to hang it on the wall as a permanent reminder. One of my mates came round to take a look, and I asked him whether he thought Dan had washed and framed mine too. 'He probably used it to wash his car the next day, mate,' came the less than encouraging reply.

The truth is that my four years with Wales between 2008 and 2012 actually proved immensely frustrating. I was occasionally invited to dine at the top table, but more often than not I felt like an uninvited guest. I didn't think playing for Wales would be like that. I figured it would be like riding the crest of a wave, but the reality was more like my childhood surfing adventures; catching the occasional great swell before being wiped out and washed ashore. All this time, my form at the Ospreys was excellent. We won the league again in 2012, with my clutch conversion sealing a dramatic last-minute win over Leinster. I was the form fly half in Wales, playing for a trophy-winning team, but that never translated into a regular spot in the Wales team.

Sean Holley and Scott 'Johnno' Johnson backed me to the hilt, picking me at 10 from a young age and empowering me to do the job, but it was the other way round with Wales. I felt I was constantly being asked to prove myself. Every time I turned out for the Ospreys, I felt my reputation was enhanced, but it seemed to count for little with Wales. The Ospreys became a sanctuary; the place where I'd rebuild my confidence after yet another false start at Test level. It saddens me to look back at that period and wonder how many caps went begging, but I also wonder whether it helped to mould me into the competitor I became. The constant feeling of not being quite good enough thickened my hide and strengthened my resolve.

There's an old adage that the best coaches are the ones that pick you. At this point, Johnno was doing that and Gatland wasn't. Johnno's approach was all about positive affirmation – pumping your tyres up, and focusing on what you did well, which was exactly what I needed at a difficult time. The boys used to call him 'the Riddler' because of his tendency to talk gibberish, but I always found him open and transparent. There was a suggestion that he'd undermined Mike Ruddock during his time with Wales, but I never saw his devious side. On the contrary, he seemed to inspire an almost cult-like devotion in all those he'd worked with. He could be difficult and argumentative, but never underhand.

He and Gats were like chalk and cheese. Where Gats was dour, brooding and intense, Johnno was smiley, cheerful and relaxed. Gats was impossible to read; some days he'd be talkative and engaging, others distant and aloof. He and Shaun intimidated me in a way Johnno never did. I felt like there was an undue focus on what I *couldn't* do with Wales, which undoubtedly affected my performances because I worried that any mistake I made would be highlighted and held against me. I became risk-averse, anxious about expressing myself. The kind of mistakes I was making could be brushed off by the more senior players who had glittering CVs to fall back on. I didn't have that body of work behind me, and felt unable to build it up due to the stop-start nature of my international career.

It was a frustrating Catch-22. Between my first cap in 2008 and the start of the 2013 Six Nations, I played for Wales just eleven times, with five of those appearances coming off the bench and most of them against tier-two opposition, where we'd invariably field a second-string side. It was difficult to excel in a scenario like that.

A prime example was the game against Fiji in the autumn of 2010. I struggled to get the backline moving all night and was eventually subbed off. We appeared to be heading for an unconvincing victory when Ryan Jones gave away a last-minute penalty that allowed them to salvage a draw.

Warren was apoplectic, channelling most of his anger towards Ryan. He stormed into the changing room and let rip; 'Sit the *fuck* down, the lot of you,' he yelled, his voice trembling with rage.

'Some of you should be ashamed to be taking a match fee today.

'I'll tell you one thing,' he continued, eyeballing Ryan. 'Matthew Rees will be captain next week.'

The silence hung heavily in the air.

For a man who usually preferred subtlety and mind games, he left us in no doubt about the true nature of his feelings that night.

*

It was later that season that I discovered how the Ospreys' reputation for partying could land us in hot water. That Christmas,
we'd arranged to have our party at Taibach rugby club in Port
Talbot. The theme was Santa and his Elves, with the senior players dressing as Santa Claus, and the rest as elves.

After a relatively civilized lunch at the Bagle Brook Beefeater,
we'd made our way to the club. The boys were a little over-excited
on arrival, and the court session quickly turned rowdy.

At one point, Phillsy stood up and declared angrily that we
were losing our Welsh essence because there too many Scottish
and Irish boys in the club. By everyone else's calculations there
were just one of each – Tommy Bowe and Nikki Walker – but
maths had never been Phillsy's strong suit. Any sense of order
soon crumbled, and with the beer gushing from the taps, things
became rowdier still.

Some of the younger boys who'd struggled to keep pace with
the big drinkers, started wrestling one another in the main bar,
where the tab was escalating quickly. By five o'clock, I was already
feeling worse for wear and when a fleet of taxis arrived to take us
into Swansea, I knew I had no more than a couple of hours left
in me. By seven o'clock, when I gazed through the pub window
and saw Shane Williams squaring up to someone on the city's
notorious Wind Street, I took it as my cue to leave.

Two days later, when we were back at training, having only just
shaken off our hangovers, a police car came crawling down the
hill and into the car park of our Llandarcy HQ.

Our phones started to ping simultaneously, and we were all
summoned to an emergency meeting. When we were all assembled a policeman strode in, removed his hat with a theatrical
flourish and started reading out a pretty grim-sounding rap sheet.

We'd been accused of all sorts; threatening the bar staff, abusing committee members, vomiting into buckets and hurling them
across the bar, defecating on the floor, picking fights with teenagers at a sixteenth birthday party next door, taking drugs and
generally trashing the joint. Jerry Collins had been reported for

refusing to pay a taxi driver and threatening to beat him up when he complained. Andrew Bishop was accused of threatening to knock the Taibach chairman out.

The policeman looked almost personally affronted by this last charge and challenged Bish directly: 'You're a quiet lad, Andrew. But you have a few beers and this happens. What were you thinking?'

Bish, looking a little like a sullen schoolboy, shrugged his shoulders and mumbled, 'I can't remember, sorry.' The policeman kept probing, wanting a confession – or at least some sign of contrition – when Bish snapped, 'Look, if I can't remember, I can't fucking remember, what do you want me to say?'

They'd also claimed we'd caused thousands of pounds' worth of damage. Through the fog of memory, an image appeared in my mind of Tommy Bowe dragging a buffing machine across the dance floor. Several glasses had been smashed, and Tommy had decided to get the buffing machine out to polish the wooden floor. He probably thought he was being helpful, but only suc-ceeded in dragging all those broken shards of glass around the wooden floorboards, leaving them scratched beyond repair.

Hibs, Hooky and a few of the local Port Talbot boys went back to apologize profusely and to pay for the damage. They were mortified to have inadvertently caused such offence.

While we didn't cover ourselves in glory that night, most of the things we'd been accused of were absolute nonsense. It was a classic case of Chinese Whispers, with most of the rumours about what happened beginning on online forums and becoming more and more exaggerated with each telling.

I accept that we behaved poorly, and that the episode was a stain on the Ospreys' history, but it was nowhere near as depraved as it was made out to be.

During the four years that followed my first cap, the Wales man-agement preferred Stephen Jones and Hooky at fly half and, when the 2011 World Cup rolled around, I missed out on selection altogether. Naturally, I was devastated. Hooky and Stephen were picked, with Rhys Priestland as backup. He'd impressed during the warm-up matches when a late injury to Stephen had thrust him into the starting line-up against England.

Rhys was older than me, and had been in Stephen's shadow at the Scarlets, but he seized his chance to leapfrog me in the pecking order. His rise was meteoric, and he became first choice during the World Cup. That was bittersweet for me: on the one hand it felt like I'd been swept aside, but on the other it gave me hope, in that someone had come in and broken the Steve–Hooky hegemony.

After the World Cup, with my international career in limbo, I had an unexpected call from Jacky Lorenzetti, the charismatic owner of Racing 92. He was interested in signing me and offered to fly me to Paris for a chat, which I did take him up on. But I knew that, as tempting as it seemed, it would have sounded the death knell for my international ambitions, and my achievements to date would have become a mere pub quiz question. I was heartbroken after being left out of the 2011 World Cup squad, and vowed to channel that disappointment into something constructive.

The 2011–12 league campaign started with a bang. We trounced Leinster 27–3 in the opening game of the season, and went on a six-game winning streak before eventually coming unstuck against Glasgow. Another purple patch followed during the Six Nations when a big chunk of our squad was away on international duty. I hadn't even been named in the wider squad for that campaign, and had to watch from afar as Wales cruised to another Grand Slam.

Even when Hooky picked up an injury ahead of the third game against England – one that has gone down in folklore for Scott Williams's wonder try – I was overlooked. They pulled in Stephen

Jones to fill the gap after he'd pretty much retired from Test rugby. I love Steve, and he was great role model, but it baffled me that they'd pick a thirty-four-year-old, who clearly wasn't in their future plans, over me. It was another kick in the teeth, ramping up my feelings of paranoia.

I struggled to watch any of the games in that Championship. So many of my mates were there, riding the crest of a wave, surfing towards Grand Slam glory, and I couldn't fathom why I wasn't. I watched that England game at Alex's house and felt conflicted; I couldn't shake the feeling that I should have been out there, sweating and grafting with my teammates, not sitting on the sofa at my girlfriend's house.

I was so disillusioned, I vowed to channel all my energy into another successful campaign with the Ospreys and, as the second half of the season got under way, we moved through the gears, completing home-and-away doubles over the defending champions Munster, and Leinster. When the Grand Slammers returned, we started steamrollering teams, racking up bonus-point victories, and gathering an irresistible momentum. It culminated in our demolition of Munster in the semi-final, where we shattered their dream of back-to-back titles with a near-perfect display of high-octane, attacking rugby. I scored twenty-five points in a 45–10 drubbing, and it felt as though we were gliding to the title.

The 2012 Pro 12 final was a repeat of 2010 – Leinster at the Royal Dublin Showground – except this time they were back-to-back Heineken Cup Champions and had an even more fearsome reputation than before. A tightening of the purse strings meant our squad had been shorn of its global superstars, while theirs had been augmented by several more, including the World Cup winning All Black, Brad Thorn.

It was a glorious May day, boiling hot, with blue skies and barely a murmur of wind. Yet despite the conditions, and our blistering form coming into it, we started abysmally. Abandoning our free-flowing style, we were nervy, stilted and horribly error-prone. After twenty minutes, Shane, who was playing his last game for the Ospreys, gathered us in and read us the Riot Act. 'Boys, we've gone away from *everything* that's defined us in the past six or seven weeks. Stop kicking the ball away and let's play some bloody rugby.'

We were 17–9 down at half-time and, as we were heading down the tunnel, I got into a slanging match with their flanker Shane Jennings. A bit of pushing and shoving ensued, and we had to be separated. It felt good to be angry. We needed to inject a bit of aggression into proceedings.

Steve Tandy had taken over as head coach halfway through the season in controversial circumstances; Sean had been relieved of his duties and Johnno had resigned, leaving Steve – our team-mate until recently – holding the reins. He was brilliant at half-time, cutting through the chorus of jabbering voices with characteristic bluntness. 'Sit down, and shut the fuck up,' came his command. 'I don't want to hear a word from anyone. Just take two minutes and calm down.'

When we'd had a drink and settled down, he went on, 'This team won the Heineken Cup by forty points last week, and we've got them on the ropes. They're hanging on in the scrums, and resorting to pushing and shoving in the tunnel. Believe me, they're there for the taking.'

The second half swung back and forth; Ashley Beck scored under the sticks to bring us back within a point, before Johnny Sexton stretched their lead back to 23–16. It seemed that every time we fought our way back, they'd creep further ahead. It was deathly silent under the sticks after that penalty, which is often a sign that you're beaten. I remember thinking, 'Is this it? Have we fired all our shots?'

We clearly hadn't, as Shane soon appeared at the end of a flowing move to touch down in the corner. They struck back to restore a nine-point cushion, but a scrum penalty gave me a chance to claw back three points.

We moved the ball through the hands from the kick-off, realizing that ambition, not conservatism, was what would win this for us. Ashley Beck made a lovely half-break, and offloaded to Shane, who did what he always does, and conjured something from nothing, evading a series of desperate tackles to dive in at the corner. With his last touch, in his last game, had the little maestro scored the try that would take us to within a point, and potentially deliver the title? It was referred to the Television Match Official (TMO), but after a few minutes, the try was given, and it was over to me.

There have been times when the prospect of having to nail a match-defining kick can be too much to bear. But this time I wanted to step into the full glare of the spotlight for Shane, for the team, and for me. I wanted to gild that try with a trophy-winning conversion. It was the most difficult kick imaginable for a right-footed kicker; wide out on the right-hand touchline, and I resolved to take it quickly. I knew that the longer I dwelled on it, the more the doubt would creep in. I glanced at the posts, began my run-up and swung my leg confidently at the ball. I knew it was over from the moment of impact, and I roared to the heavens in a guttural outpouring of elation and relief.

That feeling might just be the best I've ever experienced after a game. Those few precious moments – when everyone is hugging and celebrating – are so intoxicating. It's a rare experience of being entirely present in the moment. The culmination of all the hard work and sacrifice, and the feeling of communion you get from having done it with your mates.

It was a coming-of-age moment for me, a defining episode in my career. To step up and nail that crucial pressure kick against the best team in Europe on their home ground was utterly magical. Winning by a point at the death was better than trouncing them 35–0. If someone were to ask me, 'Why did you become a rugby player?', that half an hour would be close to the perfect answer.

Leinster were gracious enough losers, clapping us during the medal ceremony, but they looked utterly crestfallen. They'd won three of the last four Heineken Cups and had been gunning for the double, anticipating a victory parade in front of a packed Royal Dublin Showground. During our post-match huddle, our Cornish number 8, Joe Bearman said, 'Boys, Brad Thorn has won the NRL, State of Origin, the World Cup, the Heineken Cup, the Tri-Nations, Super Rugby and the Bledisloe Cup. But, thanks to us, he's hasn't won the fucking Pro 12, has he?'

Earlier in the season, I'd been at loggerheads with Andrew Hore, who'd taken over as managing director. He's a cantankerous, antagonistic bloke who loves a good argument, and we'd fallen out when I'd tried to squeeze a pay rise out of him. I'd resorted to a bit of bluff and bluster, claiming Clermont had made me an offer. They'd made casual enquiries, but nothing more, and I think he saw straight through me.

During the months that followed, there'd been a series of conversations between him and my agent and he'd always held his ground, refusing to budge. After the final, Horey ambled over to me with a beer in his hand and, uncharacteristically, a big grin on his face. We clinked glasses and after a short pause, he said, 'Why don't you just fuck off to Clermont?' Now if you don't know Horey, you'll struggle to understand that that was his way of showing affection, and was actually a tacit admission of defeat. He knew my market value would soar after that final, and he'd finally have to stump up the money to keep hold of me. Victory and that shared feeling of success dispelled all the rancour between us. It was a small moment, but a cherished one, nonetheless.

I went straight to Mum's on the way home. She'd already been to Tesco's in Neath and bought five copies each of the *Western Mail* and *South Wales Evening Post* – with its six-page pull-out souvenir – and had laid them out over the kitchen table. There was a massive photo of me clenching my fist in delight on the front cover. I'd never done this before, but I sat there all morning, devouring every word, along with one of Mum's special fry-ups, and basking in the glory of a job well done.

I felt like I was bossing it at regional level. We'd won two titles in three years, and I'd played a major part in both. I was the controlling general in a team of international stars and, with a Wales tour to Australia looming that summer, I was confident my claims could no longer be overlooked. Missing out on the World Cup and the 2012 Six Nations had been difficult to stomach, but I'd surely done everything in my power to make it down under. I was duly selected in the squad, and the team set about preparing for a warm-up game against the Barbarians in June 2012.

Martyn Williams had been promised a place in the 23 to win his hundredth cap, and Shane was set to lead out the Baa-baas on what was proving to be an interminable farewell tour. I'd lost count of how many 'last' games he'd played!

Because the Baa-baas game was just a week before the first Test, the so-called first XV was sent down under in advance to give them time to recover from jet lag. After our last training session, Rob Howley approached and asked if I had two minutes. I was anticipating a positive conversation, along the lines of, 'You've had a brilliant season, and we're looking forward to working with you again', so I was genuinely blindsided when he said: 'I just wanted to give you a heads-up. You'll be playing against the Baa-baas, but you're not coming on tour.'

Without sounding melodramatic, it felt like a bullet in the chest, and I couldn't even summon a reply. My mouth was dry, and the words got stuck in my throat.

That thirty-second conversation felt like a microcosm of the past four years with Wales: you're good, but not good enough. Normally my instinct in situations like that is to fight, but I had none left in me. First the World Cup, then the Six Nations, and now this. There are only so many rejections you can take before your spirit is crushed, and that's how I felt now; defeated and ready to crawl into a hole.

I rarely get choked up, but I did then. The exchange had taken place by the side of the pitch as I'd been preparing to start my kicking practice, but I was no longer in the mood, so I grabbed my boots and drove back to the hotel.

I called my agent and poor old Tim bore the brunt of my outrage. He was angry on my behalf because he knew as much as anyone what I'd been through. I couldn't wallow in my misery for long because we had a backs meeting scheduled, so I dusted myself off and went down to the bar for a strong coffee.

Jenks wandered in and approached, looking a little nervous. 'Don't shoot the messenger,' he offered meekly, with his hands raised, 'but we want Hooky to take the kicks on Saturday.'

Talk about kicking a man when he was down.

I felt myself physically deflate. Jenks could barely make eye contact and I sensed he wasn't on board with the decision. I'd just landed the winning kick from the touchline in the Pro 12 Grand Final. My strike rate was well over 80 per cent.

Rob ambled in, and I confronted him.

His answer was business-like and dispassionate. He said something about wanting a running threat at fly half, but I didn't absorb much else. It occurred to me then that it didn't matter what I did in an Ospreys shirt or in Wales training; they'd made up their minds that I didn't fit the mould.

The irony was that – from the layman's point of view – I seemed like the ideal fly half for a Gatland-coached side. He'd always favoured structure and pragmatism over enterprise and creativity, and that was what I'd given the Ospreys.

I called Mum on the drive home and that's when the tears began to flow. She'd probably been expecting a call to say I'd made the cut; instead, she had to endure forty minutes of me raging about the injustice of it all.

She was surprised to hear what a bad state I was in, as I'd become adept at building walls and keeping my emotions in check. To drop my guard that way was completely out of character. She told me to make them look silly by playing out of my skin on Saturday, but the truth was I couldn't summon any kind of motivation. It was a meaningless game against an invitational side. I could score thirty points and deliver the performance of my life, but I wasn't going to Australia.

Sapped of all energy, I felt like throwing in the towel. It was an unfamiliar feeling. Throughout my career, I've been defined for my dogged, never-say-die attitude, but for once I felt consumed by self-pity. Four years of working myself to the bone, four years of sacrifice, four years of single-minded determination, only to slam my head once more against the glass ceiling. I felt as if I was on a travelator going in the wrong direction. However many strides forwards I thought I'd taken, I'd look up to discover I was in the same place.

7

REDEMPTION

Poland in the depths of winter is a bleak, forbidding place. Dark, icy mornings. Air so cold it burns the back of your throat, temperatures that chill you to the bone.

I'd heard the horror stories about the Polish training camps but had yet to experience them first hand . . . until now. And here I was, doubled over with my hands on my knees, consumed by waves of nausea. My limbs were trembling with lactic acid, my heart was thudding in my chest and, as I inhaled huge draughts of ice-cold air, I wondered whether being picked for Wales was all it was cracked up to be.

This was the autumn of 2012, and Wales had returned to the Olympic training centre in Spała. Buried deep in the forest, miles from civilization, this was the same place Warren had taken the squad before the World Cup, to push them to the very limits of their endurance. We were undergoing a savage, unrelenting beasting, designed to transform us into near-invincible automatons. It was harder than anything I'd experienced before, and there were no home comforts to offset the brutality of the daily routine. The spartan rooms resembled prison cells, and the food was horrendous.

We'd gone there because of the cryotherapy, a revolutionary new concept based on the idea that exposure to extreme cold accelerates recovery, and magically restores aching, damaged limbs. Gats's rationale was that the quicker we recovered, the more we could do, which meant the workload was ramped up significantly.

There were a number of walk-in chambers where the temperature was a staggering *minus* 140 degrees Celsius. I was nervous ahead of my first experience, having heard stories of others freaking out once they were imprisoned inside. The extreme temperatures and sense of confinement could easily provoke psychological trauma, and I was worried about how I'd react.

We were kitted out in shorts, socks, gloves, headbands and chunky white clogs to protect our extremities from frostbite, and had to first sit in a preparatory 'antechamber' to acclimatize. It was when we were ushered into the main chamber that things got real.

It's such a bizarre sensation that it's almost impossible to describe in words. *Freezing* obviously doesn't do it justice. Within seconds, your entire body becomes numb, and every muscle begins to twitch and throb. It's an utterly disorienting experience because, while you know the temperature is 140 degrees below freezing, the tingling sensation feels a little like burning.

There's a digital clock inside, and the two minutes you're in there passes excruciatingly slowly. With our faces slowly turning blue, we'd distract ourselves with word association games. Once the two minutes were up, there'd be a rush for the door, and we'd head straight for the bikes to get the blood circulating again.

I was sceptical about the benefits. Some of the boys claimed it worked really well for them, but I wonder whether it was more psychological than physiological.

We were left in no doubt about the potential dangers, though, when Bradley Davies emerged from one session, howling in pain, having forgotten his socks. He had a line of angry welts running from his heels to halfway up his calf and it ruled him out of training for three days. He was fined £250 for being 'forgetful' and was forced to endure a punishing cardio schedule instead.

As hard as the camp was physically, it was the mental side I found most draining. There was nothing to incentivize you – no down time; no delicious meal at the end of a hard day. The food was absolutely shocking. I lived on sausages and toast for a week because everything else was deep-fried and dripping in fat. We were burning insane amounts of calories but were unable to replenish them. The setting was as uninspiring as the food – a bleak, windblown prison camp with precious little to lighten the gloom.

Obviously this was all part of the plan. Gatland had built his reputation on supreme physical fitness and mental fortitude, and these camps were about pushing yourself well beyond your comfort zone. The knowledge that we'd journeyed to some dark places and survived would undoubtedly benefit us during the forthcoming autumn internationals, when we'd be up against it and needing to dig deep into our reserves.

I understood the logic, but I also sensed that this kind of approach had run its course. Several of the boys were on their third such trip and there were a few grumblings of discontent. Gethin Jenkins argued that we could build our own cryo chamber at the Vale with all the money flowing into the WRU coffers, and it was also pointed out that the dreadful catering was undermining much of our progress. To our astonishment, the message hit home, and in a rare instance of players getting their own way, we packed up and headed home early. We would never train in Spała again.

Warren had been appointed Lions coach ahead of the 2013 tour to Australia, so Rob Howley took over as interim head coach during the autumn of 2012. Wales had lost all three summer tests in Australia, which had rather punctured the optimism that had accompanied the winning of the Six Nations Grand Slam. It turned out worse was to come. We endured an autumn whitewash, losing all four Tests in Cardiff.

The story remained the same for me when it came to selection. Rob called me in to his office the week of the opening game against Argentina to tell me I wasn't in the twenty-three. Rhys was starting, with Hooky on the bench.

Same shit, different day.

We lost convincingly. I was picked to play against Samoa the following week, but got injured before half-time attempting – for reasons that escape me – to jackal the ball. I've only tried to do it twice in my career and ended up in the medical room on both occasions. It was a brutal game, which we also lost, with a significant injury toll. The changing room looked like the aftermath of a military battle. I felt cursed. Even when given a rare start, I ended up getting injured and on the losing side.

We were beaten again by a streetwise New Zealand, and found ourselves on the wrong end of another nerve-shredding climax against Australia. I had to watch Kurtley Beale's last-minute try from the subs bench, where I'd been selected only because Hooky was unavailable. At least I was on the inside in this campaign, but a solitary half against Samoa in a losing cause did my self-esteem no good. I persuaded myself it could have been worse, though: Leigh Halfpenny, whose club, the Cardiff Blues, were enduring a torrid period, went an entire year without tasting victory at any level; and Rob, who'd now been in charge for seven games, had lost them all. He looked like a broken man.

Newspaper headlines abounded about Wales being nothing without Gats, how without his Midas touch we were clueless and floundering. A series of mocking videos did the rounds on social media, with alternative overdubbed versions of Rob's post-match interviews. It must have been a pretty lonely place for him, but we still had faith in him. He was a bright, intelligent coach who just needed to catch a break.

Just prior to the 2013 Six Nations, the Ospreys beat Toulouse in the Heineken Cup, and Rhys Priestland snapped his Achilles playing for the Scarlets on the same weekend. It was devastating for Rhys, who was sidelined for the season, but a genuine opportunity for me.

The backdrop to the tournament was one of tension and apprehension. The knives were out for Rob Howley, and his reputation was on the line. There was a feeling in some quarters that

Wales had been 'found out', that the flat-track-bully approach that had won us the Grand Slam was a busted flush and didn't work against the bigger, shrewder teams from the southern hemisphere. There had been a curious dynamic at work in the Welsh press. As much as they basked in the success Wales had enjoyed, they couldn't resist criticizing the approach.

'Warrenball', as it had been dubbed, might have been effective, but it wasn't pretty. We'd been blessed with a generation of big, physical three-quarters, capable of blasting holes in opposition defences, and Gatland had crafted a game plan to exploit that. It was more bludgeon than rapier, and that offended the sensibilities of certain sections of the media, who craved a return to the free-running rugby of the seventies.

This kind of external pressure could have weighed heavily on the players, but when we assembled for the Six Nations in early 2013, there was no sense of panic. Rob might have looked more crumpled and less relaxed than normal, but he still had the courage of his convictions and, despite rumours to the contrary, no cliques had developed. There were no signs of internal mutiny, just a bunch of players desperate to restore some wounded pride and defend the trophy that still had our name on it.

To my surprise, I was picked ahead of Hooky for the first game against Ireland. It was my first Six Nations start, five years after my debut, and it couldn't have gone any worse. Ireland arrived seeking vengeance after Wales had knocked them out of the World Cup, and beaten them in Dublin the previous year.

They tore into us with fire and fury from the first whistle, carving gaping holes in our defence, and rocking us back on our heels. Their first try was crafted by slick precise handling, while their second was the result of a lazy kick from yours truly. I took far too long to put boot to ball and Rory Best charged me down. The move was kept alive by an outrageous bit of skill from Simon Zebo and, a few phases later, Cian Healy was burrowing his way over the line.

We were 23–3 down at half-time and the changing room was

like a morgue. There were no commanding voices, no rallying cries, just a vague, unsettling silence. The room reeked of defeat. Normally, I'd be the one geeing people up but, given my long absence from the team and my poor first-half performance, I didn't feel I had the right.

Our misery was compounded at the start of the second half, when Brian O'Driscoll squeezed over from short range. We were staring down the barrel of an ugly defeat, but what should have been the final nail in our coffin actually shook us from our death throes. Those would turn out to be the last points they'd score, as we launched the unlikeliest of comebacks.

All of a sudden, passes began to stick, holes began to appear, and a little of our old swagger returned. Tries from Alex Cuthbert and Leigh Halfpenny brought us back into it, and when Craig Mitchell crashed over in the 75th minute, the seemingly impossible was on the cards. In the end, time ran out, but so decisively had the momentum swung in our favour that – had the game gone on five minutes longer – I'm convinced we'd have won. Sure, it was another defeat, but the despair we'd felt at half-time had been replaced by a tentative optimism.

Was this the moment we'd climbed out of the rut?

I was uneasy about my place in the side, and would have understood if Rob had shaken things up a bit, but to his credit he stuck to his guns, making just a few tweaks rather than ripping up the team sheet. He named the team on the Monday after the Ireland review, which was previously unheard of. Gats would always name the team as late as possible to foster competition, but Rob sensed a need for stability. He deserves credit for that; for ignoring the outside noise and the mounting calls for sweeping changes. He gave me another chance.

Training was tense that week, and Rob drove standards high, coming down hard on anyone who messed up. He was particularly hard on Mike Phillips, with whom he'd always had a tetchy, fiery relationship. As a former scrum half of some renown, Rob reserved his harshest judgements for his fellow 9s, and was a constant flea in Phillsy's ear. During one session, Mike gave me an average pass, and I then shovelled a terrible one out to Foxy, but it was Mike who was on the receiving end. 'Sort your fucking passing out, Phillsy!' was the not-so-subtle refrain from the sideline. There was a method to this; Rob knew Phillsy had to be provoked to be at his snarling, angry best.

During the review of the Ireland game, Rob had shown a clip of a lineout, insisting we should have formed a driving maul off the back of it, and Phillsy lost his shit. This was the last straw for him.

'That's the fucking problem,' he bellowed from the back of the room. 'We've got coaches trying to play the game when we're the ones on the field!'

He got right up on his soapbox, accusing Rob of micro-managing and not trusting the players to make the right decisions in the heat of the moment. The longer the losing streak had gone on, the more he'd felt like he was playing in a straitjacket, and he was fed up of being called out in meetings.

Everyone agreed. We were being hamstrung by our lack of confidence and had lost a vital element of spontaneity. When optimism is high, you're naturally more inclined to risk an offload or attempt a sidestep, to spin it wide instead of keeping it tight. But when you're accustomed to losing, you retreat further inwards, and it can be crippling.

A less experienced coach might have risen to the bait, but Howley understood that a soft touch was required. It was his method being questioned, but not his authority. He agreed to loosen his tactical grip. There will always be disagreements in elite sporting environments; it's how you handle them that counts. Rob nipped things in the bud and ensured that any ill-will wasn't allowed to fester. He'd endured some miserable times in the Welsh jersey himself, and knew a thing or two about facing down adversity.

No one gave us a prayer of winning in Paris, and who knows how deep a vortex we'd have spun into had we not ground out a result. Rob could have been forced out, and my Test career might have fizzled out completely. Sam Warburton was injured and out of sorts, so Ryan Jones was recalled as captain for the trip.

Warby had never been the most vocal leader, and Ryan's presence helped re-energize the group; being quiet and retiring is something you could never accuse 'Jughead' of.

Together with Gethin Jenkins and Phillsy, he resolved to drag the team out of the mire. Mike encouraged everyone to adopt a little of his swagger, encouraging us to push our shoulders back and stride into Paris like we expected to win. He was worried that there were too many fragile egos in the group, and that we'd allowed the losing streak to chip away at our confidence.

I've never met anyone with Mike's unshakeable sense of self-belief. There was undoubtedly a degree of bluster involved, but he genuinely thought he was the best scrum half in the world, and it pained him to see so many of his teammates wrestling with an inferiority complex.

The French crowd belted out a frenzied rendition of 'La Marseillaise', and the atmosphere was as hostile as the weather was grim. It was an ugly game of rugby, riddled with mistakes and lacking any sense of flow. The fact that it was 6–6 with eight minutes to go tells you all you need to know about the game as a spectacle. We were like two stags rutting; constantly smashing into one another without landing any meaningful blows.

A penalty inside the last ten minutes gave us a precious lineout near the French 22 from which we settled into our pattern.

As I stood behind the ruck assessing the options, I noted that their full back, Yoann Huget, was quite central, so I began drifting slowly to the left, conscious that George North was hugging the touchline. The ball arrived in my hands, and I shaped to pass, before putting a dainty little chip over the top of the onrushing defence. George locked onto it like a homing missile, it bounced kindly into his arms, and he had the strength to ride François Trinh-Duc's despairing tackle to touch down in the corner.

We erupted with sheer joy and relief, embracing one another as nearly twelve months of bottled-up frustration exploded in the

Paris night. In the midst of all our hugs and high-fives, a moustachioed man emerged from the crowd, wrapping his arms around George in delight. George pushed him away before being mobbed by his teammates at the same time the mysterious intruder was swamped by a bunch of angry stewards. Leigh's touchline conversion crept over the bar, giving us an all-important seven-point cushion, and a final penalty meant we clung on for a 16–6 victory, built on sweat, grind and dogged determination.

After eight straight defeats, it tasted sweeter than ever.

Back in the changing room, there was a glow to Rob Howley. He was standing at the entrance greeting us one by one, the happiness just radiating from him. The beers we shared around were guzzled in an instant, and the whole group was awash with relief. Apart from George North, who was listening intently to a voicemail on his phone with a look of rising alarm on his face. It was from his mother, explaining worriedly that his dad was being held in a police cell after he'd been arrested for a pitch invasion. It turned out the mystery fan – who George had blanked – was in fact his old man.

On the bus afterwards, the unmistakeable West Walian brogue of Mike Phillips rang out from the back, slightly slurred due to the amount of beers he'd glugged. 'Oi, Howlers. Howlers! When are you going to say thanks?'

Rob turned around, and with the look of a weary schoolteacher asked, 'Say thanks for what, Mike?'

There was a beat pause before Mike replied, 'For saving your fucking job, mate!'

Only Mike could have got away with that, and even Rob had it within him to smile. With that one exchange, all the tension of the last eight months dissolved, and the bus collapsed into a chorus of guffaws.

A police escort delivered us to a swanky nightclub near the Champs-Elysées. I was sitting next to Aaron Shingler; it was a sign of the dramatic shift in mood that he was already asking about bonuses for winning the Championship.

The French boys were great company once they'd got over their disappointment, though Dimitri Szarzewski was a little nonplussed at the constant comparisons to Richard Hibbard. Hibs had recently grown his hair and dyed it blond, leading inevitably to Dimitri being branded 'Sexy Hibs'. Locks aside, I don't think the urbane, sophisticated Szarzewski much appreciated being compared to a tubby lad from the rough side of Port Talbot. Andrew Coombs was one of the many who over-indulged, guzzling red wine like it was going out of style and ending up on all fours outside. He'd tried to hide behind the French team bus, but it had driven away just as he retched violently into the bushes.

The next morning at breakfast, Coombsy was to suffer further torture. He'd come down early, hoping some strong coffee would ease his horrendous hangover, and found himself sitting opposite Rob. As they were chatting politely, Phillsy and I arrived, and Phillsy's eyes lit up. With several pints of wine still swilling round his bloodstream, he filled his plate with charred toast and plonked himself down next to Rob.

'Well done, Howlers,' he began, slathering a generous knob of butter over his toast. 'You excelled yourself yesterday, didn't you?'

Rob exhaled wearily, steeling himself for the onslaught. 'You take your best player off the pitch with ten minutes to go when the game's still in the balance. *Great* coaching that.'

I'd seen this ritual played out many times, but Coombsy was new to the squad, and looked utterly mortified. He was reluctant to laugh along with Phillsy, but equally wary of being seen as a teacher's pet.

'Three cheers for Howlers,' Phillsy continued. 'I'd make a better coach than him, wouldn't I, Coombsy? Coombsy? Wouldn't I?'

Poor Coombsy wanted the ground to swallow him up. Rob was just nodding his head in the resigned manner of a parent looking after a wayward child.

The two of them were governed by a bizarre power dynamic, born out of the fact they were both world-class scrum halves.

There's no doubt Rob held Mike to higher standards than he did the rest of us, but he was also more willing to tolerate dissent in his star prodigy.

We had a fortnight before our third game against Italy, but Rob named the team a week in advance, telling the first XV to go and do it again in Rome. Both Sam Warburton and Alun Wyn Jones were back fit, but neither made the cut.

Rarely did those two fail to make the starting line-up, but Coombsy and Ryan had earned their spots. Naming the team early was a psychological masterstroke, because it infused us with confidence and allowed us to train with a sense of clarity you don't always have when you're worrying about selection.

We won comfortably at a rain-lashed Stadio Olimpico, but Rob Howley looked pretty glum afterwards, offering us nothing more than a perfunctory handshake, and I sensed something was up.

Not wanting to dampen the mood, he told us to enjoy the night and said we'd review the game on Monday.

Spirits were high on the bus and there were plenty of chants doing the rounds. Mark 'Boycie' Jones was part of the coaching staff during that campaign, and we were taunting him about being on 'work experience'. In a counteroffensive, he started a chant of his own: 'You're all doing runways, you're all doing runways, all next week, all next week.' We despised runways, a particularly gruelling training exercise.

He was sitting next to our team doctor, Geoff Davies, and we thought right, Boycie's having it. Our retort was taken up swiftly by the entire bus: 'Geoff earns 250, Boycie's getting nothing, na *naa* na na, na *naa* na na.' The boys all fell about laughing and, as it was dying out, Liam 'Sanj' Williams piped up, 'If he's not he should be, if he's not he should be na naa na na.'

Boycie realized he was hopelessly outnumbered and lapsed into silence for the rest of the journey. For the record, I've no idea what Geoff earns; we just plucked a number from thin air.

Like Paris, the night out got a little boisterous, and ended with the referee, Romain Poite, doing topless press-ups in a Rome nightclub while we all clapped in time, raucously chanting his name. Moments later, for reasons I can't remember, Paul James and Richard Hibbard were dangling him over a banister by his ankles. It was a wild night.

We'd put everything on a tab, and when the bill arrived, it was so long it literally had to be unfurled. I was bracing myself for a big hit to the wallet when Phillsy snatched the bill with a flourish and declared, 'I earn more than all you boys put together, so I'll take care of this.' Wallets disappeared swiftly back into our pockets, and we left feeling extremely grateful to our boozy, swaggering benefactor.

Several hours later, as we were groggily emerging from our collective drunken stupor, our phones pinged simultaneously. We'd all had a message from Mike saying we each owed him €200 to cover the bar bill. As the alcohol had drained from his system, so too – it seemed – had his generosity.

Back home, during the review, we found out why Rob had seemed so sullen after the win. He showed us a clip of Hooky kicking the ball out at the end when we were 26–9 ahead and forty metres from their line.

'Why am I pissed off about that?' he asked, jabbing the pause button impatiently. We all shuffled uneasily in our seats. 'I'll tell you why; because the tournament could come down to points difference, and we didn't have the balls to go for the jugular.'

At the time, it felt like an overreaction, but as the tournament progressed it became apparent that he had a point. It showed that he was looking at the bigger picture, and that the arch competitor in him – rather than basking in the glory of two victories – was still thinking about winning the whole thing.

The Scotland game was a dreary affair dominated by kicking. Hibs scored the only try – a collector's item for him – and after that we just settled into a kicking duel that would have had even the most hardened supporters heading for the turnstiles. The conditions were horrendous, some of the worst I've ever played in, and the howling gale played havoc with the flight of the ball. The match set a world record for the number of attempts on goal. Uncharacteristically, Leigh missed three of his first four shots. He hated kicking at Murrayfield; for some reason that ground was his kryptonite.

We prevailed over the Scots, and the ignominy of that eight-game losing streak was fast becoming a distant memory. We were now setting the right kind of records with five consecutive away wins in the Championship, a feat that hadn't been achieved since the seventies.

Not that it ranked as much of an achievement in Shaun Edwards's book; after the game he said, 'I'm not bothered about the record, and neither should you be. This is just what this team does: wins away from home.' He had no truck with fuss or fanfare, and just cared about the bare facts. *This is what we do.* One thing he did draw attention to was our defensive record – three games; three clean sheets. To travel to Paris, Rome and Edinburgh in consecutive rounds and not concede a solitary try was something to be proud of.

After the debauchery of Paris and Rome, we were given a curfew in Edinburgh – midnight – because we had Grand Slam-chasing England in Cardiff a week later. Against all odds, we'd put ourselves in a position to win the Championship. Quite a few of us ended up drinking in the hotel bar, and Jonathan 'Foxy' Davies – losing track of time – went to get a round in at around five to twelve. By the time he returned with an overflowing tray of Peroni, the bar had already been emptied by Alan 'Thumper' Phillips, who'd appeared like a grumpy headmaster, theatrically tapping his watch. A few of the boys felt their celebrations had been cut short, and surreptitiously ordered trays of burgers and more booze to their rooms. Not so surreptitiously, they dumped all the leftovers in the corridor, which were spotted by an eagle-eyed Thumper the following morning.

Rob saw it as a flagrant breach of trust, and it had clearly got under his skin. 'Burger-gate' became an issue during the week, as no one was taking responsibility. Rob got it into his head that Mike was to blame, and wouldn't let it lie. On the plane home, he accused him directly, and Mike was outraged, denying all knowledge. Rob continued to needle Mike about it all week, sighing and tutting as he walked past, muttering things like, 'Fourie de Preez wouldn't be eating burgers and getting smashed the week before a Championship decider. He's what I'd call a world-class scrum half.'

With each passing day, Mike got more and more wound up and Rob continued to twist the dial. By the end of the week, Mike was a pent-up ball of aggressive energy, hurling himself around the training paddock, smashing into anything that moved.

Those training sessions were short, sharp and intense, with Shaun dialling the intensity levels up to eleven. He knew the key to beating England was our defence. After their low-scoring victory against Italy, the maths was now simple: if we beat them by eight points, we'd win the Championship.

It was Shaun who pioneered the 'Wall of Shame'. After every match, he'd write a pithy, one-sentence review of everyone's performance and pin them up on the team room wall. It could be a humbling experience, thinking you'd done OK, only to be on the receiving end of a savage review. We'd all heard the stories of Jonathan Thomas getting 0 out of 10 for getting himself knocked out at Twickenham.

It sounds harsh but we all loved Shaun and understood that it came from a place of affection. He wanted to help us become the best, and he would never settle for anything less than 100 per cent. It may sound like a contradiction, but the more he rated you, the more he laid into you. Being ignored by Shaun was worse than being persecuted by him. Sometimes he'd just leave a blank space next to your name, which cut deeper than barbed criticism.

Shaun was never overly verbose or even particularly eloquent, but he was an excellent communicator. You were never left in any doubt what was expected of you, and that's exactly what players need. He has this intangible quality that makes him the world's best. He makes you think you're invincible. If anyone else came in and did what Shaun did, we'd probably think he was a limited coach, but therein lies his genius: making what's difficult look easy. Ahead of every game, he'd distil his message down to three basic points that you could write on the back of your hand. What was the point, he'd say, of cramming your notebook with reams of information that would clutter your mind and blunt your focus. It's not as though you can stop the game to thumb through your notes.

His economy-of-style is a skill, whether he knows it or not.

The senior players were called to a meeting on the Thursday night before the England game, where we discussed our overall strategy, and how to approach the eight-point margin required. Warby asked the question; 'What do we do if we're a point up and we win a penalty five metres from our line with the clock in the red.'

Rob didn't hesitate. 'Tap it and kick it out,' he said. The probability of us going the length against England in the eightieth minute was low. It was the clarity we needed. Beating England was the priority, winning the Championship was a bonus. It was the less ambitious approach, but the more realistic one.

I love the pre-match ritual before a big Test match. Once the team run is done, you can essentially relax, knowing all the hard work is in the bank. I'm not sure what people think an elite rugby team does the night before an era-defining Test match, but they probably imagine us eating portion-controlled quantities of chicken and boiled rice before retiring to bed early. The reality couldn't be more different. The night before the England game, we were sprawled on beanbags in the team room gorging on battered fish and sweet potato fries, followed by double helpings of sticky toffee pudding drowned in custard.

*

As I've mentioned, I don't indulge in the kind of tub-thumping patriotism that characterizes Welsh rugby, but you'd have to have a heart of stone for it not to flutter a little at the prospect of Wales versus England in Cardiff. It's a match to stir the soul and stoke those embers of national pride. The richest rugby country on earth versus its nearest rival, whose centuries-old culture remains defiantly independent, refusing to be subsumed into its all-powerful neighbour.

Wales v England, in Cardiff, with the Championship on the line.

If we were in any doubt about the enormity of the occasion, it was dispelled by the bus journey in. Once we'd reached Canton on the west side of Cardiff, the crowds had been whipped into a state of near-hysteria. The noise was unbelievable. Usually when the bus appears, an isolated cheer goes up, but this was different; we were driving through a fevered wall of sound. I removed my headphones, wanting to absorb every last second of it, because it felt utterly unique and unforgettable.

At this point, the video screens in the bus dropped down, and Eminem's 'Till I Collapse' started playing loudly. Video clips of English players talking nonchalantly about coming to Cardiff 'to win the Grand Slam' were interspersed with images of us at our brilliant, dominant best: thunderous tackles, barnstorming runs, and spectacular tries. The analysis boys had knocked it out of the park. It was a perfectly pitched juxtaposition: English complacency – dare I say arrogance – versus Welsh *hwyl*.

My heart began to thump in my chest. I looked around. Everyone's expression was one of single-minded determination.

Jaws clenched, eyes narrowed, shoulders back.

Nudging through the hordes of red-shirted supporters on Westgate Street, we turned right through the stadium gates, and down the ramp into the underground car park. It felt like going underwater. The noise and carnage on the streets became muted, and we enjoyed fifteen seconds of calm before getting off the bus. As we walked into the changing room, the Six Nations trophy was standing on its plinth, polished and gleaming, with our name etched into it.

It occurred to us all as we walked past, that was *our* trophy, *we* were the defending champions, and hell would freeze over before we let England walk in here and take it from us.

One of the papers had referred to us as potential party poopers, looking to shove a spoke in the wheel of an English Grand Slam. *Party poopers?* This was *our* house, *our* party, and we intended to be the ones celebrating at the end of it.

There are a handful of moments in life when you think you're the luckiest person in the world, and walking onto the field that day was one of them. The choir was already in full voice; hymns were being sung with gusto, and the stadium was alive with a sense of expectation.

England's anthem was surprisingly loud, and a little unsettling given where we were. 'God Save the Queen' is often dismissed as a flat, uninspiring dirge, but this version was a rousing call to arms. I'd not seen many white shirts lining the streets, but it suddenly felt like we might be outnumbered in our own stadium. But then 'Hen Wlad Fy Nhadau' kicked in, and the very foundations of the stadium seemed to rumble. It was the most impassioned, emotionally driven rendition I'd ever heard. Halfway through, the band cut out and 75,000 people continued to sing in glorious a cappella. Standing next to me, Leigh had tears streaming down his face. If we'd felt confident before, we felt invincible now.

The English conversely looked visibly troubled, like the weight of all that emotion had sapped their spirits. From the kick-off we absolutely tore into them; we were first to everything – quicker, slicker, and sharper of mind. Sometimes that's all you need. It's less about skill, and more about hunger. We weren't perfect though; early on, Foxy over-hinged, stepping in on a play, and Manu Tuilagi would have been clean through had he not dropped the ball.

We were 6–3 up when England were attacking in our 22, and I picked off an ambitious pass from Ben Youngs. We shifted it quickly and George North was away, legs pumping, gobbling up the open savannah. Justin Tipuric was right behind him, calling for the ball, but George didn't hear him over the roar of the crowd, and was eventually scythed down by a lunging Mike Brown. Had he offloaded, Tips would definitely have scored.

At half-time, we realized how ludicrously fast-paced the game had been. Some of the big lads like Ian Evans and Richard Hibbard looked spent already, drenched in sweat and gasping for breath.

'More of the same' was the message, but I don't think anyone had any idea what was about to unfold.

We held onto the ball at the start of the second half for more than twenty phases, until England eventually transgressed and Leigh extended our lead to 12–3. Not long afterwards, Owen Farrell missed a penalty. Leigh and I weren't sure whose ball it was so we let it bounce, which you should never do.

Panic set in as we both scrambled to retrieve it, but I remember looking up to see that there were no England players chasing. In such a big game, with so much on the line, they seemed to have lost all urgency and desire. It was a small moment, but a telling one.

I took my time, looking to eke out an extra fifteen seconds, when Dylan Hartley eventually arrived shouting, 'Just play the fucking game, mate.'

I grinned at him. 'We're in no fucking rush, mate,' I replied, before casually dotting the ball down and walking to the 22.

There was no doubt we felt in control of the game but then, around the 55-minute mark, we stepped into another dimension.

Ken Owens, keen and hungry off the bench, ripped the ball from Tom Wood in contact, and we snapped into attack mode. Tips was first receiver, and we shipped it on fluently, crisp passes from Phillsy and Foxy freeing Alex Cuthbert on the outside. Mike Brown was tracking across, but he was no match for Cuthy, who accelerated through the gears and swatted him away with a brutal hand-off. It was a sensational finish; a devastating display of pace and power from one of the best in the business. It put us 17–3 up.

From the kick-off we spent another extended period in their 22, hurling bodies into the breakdown, battering into their defensive wall in search of a dent or a chink. Normally, with a lead like that, and their try line in sight, I wouldn't think of dropping a goal, but that eight-point winning margin crept into my head and I realized that three points would take us three scores clear.

Phillsy obviously read my mind, as he gave me the nod to drop into the pocket. Seconds later the ball was sailing through the posts. It was my first drop goal for Wales. If England's Grand Slam hopes had been dangling by a thread, that had sent them tumbling into the abyss. The coup de grâce came moments later.

Had the roof been shut, it would surely have blown off. Taulupe 'Toby' Faletau set the move in motion with some trademark fancy footwork, dancing his way out of danger in our half. From the ruck Sam Warburton – less inclined to sidestep – took the Roman road, scooping up the ball and galloping to their 22 like a charging rhino. Farrell just about managed to slow his progress, but the support was already there – Phillsy to me, me to Jamie, Halfpenny into the line from full back, and then a bit of trademark wizardry from Tips. With the vision and skill level of a world-class back, he turned a promising counterattack into a try for the ages. Tips's brain is wired differently to the rest of us; like a chess grandmaster, always thinking several moves ahead, he can bend defences to his will. With Cuthy on the wing, he sold Mike Brown the sweetest of dummies before cutting inside to create extra space down the tramlines. He then had the presence of mind to lure Brown into the tackle before offloading to Cuthy for the easiest try he's ever scored.

That game propelled Cuthy into the stratosphere because he was on the end of both tries, but that second belonged to Tips. He could easily have scored it, but his decision to pass sums up his entire personality. You couldn't hope to meet a humbler bloke; all the talent in the world, but without an ounce of arrogance to accompany it.

During that period, our first-choice back row was Lydiate, Warburton and Faletau, all of whom were incredible players, but Tips was in a class of his own. He and I were kindred spirits, in that neither of us were Gats's first pick and only got our chances through injury. Both of us spent a long time in the shadows before we could convince people of our true worth.

There was a misconception with Tips that he didn't do enough of the 'grunt work' and wasn't willing to stick his head where it hurt, which was total nonsense. His showreel moments might paint him as a Flash Harry, but I can tell you definitively that he was as strong and brave as anyone I've played with. I defy you to watch him for eighty minutes and not come to the same conclusion.

No one could believe what was happening when we went over for that second try. The crowd were chanting, 'Easy, easy' and we could all begin to enjoy a feeling that's all too rare in Test match rugby; the sensation of being able to relax knowing the job is done.

We could be spectators as well as participants in those final fifteen minutes. The mindset changed from 'we could win the Championship' to, 'Jeez, we've absolutely battered them.' You could tell they were cooked and had nothing left to give. We'd taken things up to a level that they simply couldn't live with, and trampled their Grand Slam dreams into the dust.

When that dust settled, it was a record Welsh victory over England, 30 points to 3, a scoreline that still makes you look twice. I've heard it referred to as the perfect performance, but if you watch it back it was far from perfect; we actually played pretty poorly when we were in their 22. We might have retained the ball well, but we didn't penetrate much. We were just disciplined and won enough penalties to keep the scoreboard ticking over. Cuthy's first try was a counterattack rather than a crafted score, and the drop goal was opportunistic rather than planned.

What it was was error-free rugby. We did nothing differently to what we'd done previously under Gats. We just executed our game plan ruthlessly and kept the error count low. That's winning rugby. It's not sexy, but done right it's bloody effective.

They dropped the lights for the trophy lift, which only added to the drama. Our names were called out one by one, and each was greeted by the deafening roar of 75,000 manic fans. Amid the fireworks, the champagne and the pumping music, we felt like rock stars.

I didn't enjoy the celebrations as much as I should have because I had this irrational fear that it was going to be taken away from us. I was even worried about where to stand during the trophy lift. It seems comical reflecting on it now; there I was, with a Six Nations winners' medal around my neck, and I was fretting about where to stand and how to act. But when Ryan and Gethin hoisted the trophy skyward, the fireworks exploded around us, and all those concerns melted away. It was such an incredible, life-affirming feeling. When people ask how we can bear to make such great sacrifices and miss out on so many things – children's sports days, weddings, stag dos, family gatherings – the answer is for moments such as those. Time stops, and it doesn't matter if you're a centurion earning a king's ransom, or a young kid on peanuts. Nothing separates you; you're a band of brothers, a team. And not just any team. A *Championship-winning* team.

Little moments remain vivid in my mind, not least the photo I had with Shaun Edwards and the trophy during a lap of honour. That was the moment I thought, *I've made it*. The fact that Shaun Edwards – the unsmiling, intimidating tyrant, who'd spent two months tearing strips off us – had his arm around me and was beaming from ear to ear meant the world. The English boys were wandering around looking crestfallen, ruminating on their broken dreams. It's difficult not to feel a little sympathy in those circumstances, but that day was all about us, the victors. They'd come to our home, believing their own hype, and had been vanquished.

Alex is a massive royalist, so when she discovered Prince William had been in the changing room to congratulate us all, she was beyond excited. Alex wanted to pore over every detail. She was far more interested in that than our record win. While I tried to play it cool, it was pretty special to think that something you'd achieved had brought the future king into the changing room.

Once we were all showered and changed, Rob called us into a huddle and thanked us sincerely for all our efforts. He'd been through the mill personally – mocked mercilessly online, derided in the press, and even questioned by some of his own charges – but, despite all that, he'd stood firm in the path of a raging storm, and finished up a Championship-winning coach.

As someone who appreciated his forensic approach, and understood how hard he worked behind the scenes, I was delighted for him. It was an emotional exchange and, as we were all about to disperse, Mike raised his hand and asked earnestly if he could say something.

Rob nodded and handed him the floor.

Mike cleared his throat, paused for dramatic effect, and said, 'It was me who ordered the fucking burgers.'

8

FROM DESPAIR TO WHERE

It's 30 April 2013, a glorious spring day. I'm in London to meet my agent and I have a few hours to kill. I've found a cool little coffee roastery and have settled down on a bench with a take-away flat white. Plugging in my earphones, I tap on the Sky Sports app – the British and Irish Lions squad for the tour to Australia is about to be announced.

In an age of endless emails, texts, DMs and WhatsApps, the Lions squad announcement remains resolutely old school. If you're in, you find out when everyone else does. In the next few minutes, I'll discover whether I've achieved a lifelong dream and been invited to join one of the most illustrious teams in world sport: a team comprising the very best rugby players from Wales, England, Ireland and Scotland.

I'm feeling reasonably calm. A few weeks earlier – just after our Six Nations win – I'd received a letter telling me I was in contention. 'Don't book any holidays yet' was the message that around eighty players had received. A week or so later, I'd bumped into Warren Gatland at a rugby dinner. His parting words to me were, 'Make sure you keep your phone on.' The letter, the record win over England, and the knowing wink from the head coach. I didn't want to get ahead of myself, but for once it seemed the stars were aligned for me.

As I stared at my phone screen now, the legendary Lions figure of Andy Irvine mounted the podium to announce the squad of thirty-seven. I took a warming gulp of coffee and turned up the volume.

The players were being named in position order, starting with full backs, and the first to be announced was Leigh Halfpenny. I felt an obvious surge of pride as I heard his name. More of my teammates followed: Cuthy, George, Foxy, Jamie. All in.

Irvine cleared his throat and, in his resonant Edinburgh brogue, announced: 'Outside halves. Owen Farrell, Saracens and England. Jonathan Sexton, Leinster and Ireland.'

There was a brief pause before I heard him say, 'Scrum halves', and that was when my stomach fell. I was devastated.

When the shock subsided, my overwhelming emotion was embarrassment.

I'd been a key figure in our run to the title, and had controlled things tactically in that glorious finale against England, but I was not considered good enough to go on the Lions tour. My opposite number that day, Owen Farrell, had been picked ahead of me.

It didn't register then, but it turned out that of the fifteen Welsh players who started in that historic 30–3 victory, I was the only one not to make the cut for the Lions tour.

It was difficult not to take it personally. Why had Gats given me false hope? Why had I allowed myself to believe? I'd thought my role in the Six Nations had elevated me from bit-part player to first choice, but clearly I was wrong.

I felt isolated and alone. I called Mum. She was angry on my behalf and protective of her son. She struck the perfect tone, telling me to cherish those memories of the Six Nations and reminding me that I wouldn't have had that chance were it not for Priest's injury. I kept telling her how embarrassed I felt, and no matter how many times she told me how nonsensical that was, I couldn't shift the feeling.

Warren later admitted that the Wales–England game had had a profound effect on his final selection. Names that had been firmly pencilled in were scrubbed out, while others in the 'maybe' column were upgraded to dead certs.

Tips definitely turned Gats's head that day, showing him what most of us at the Ospreys already knew. Hibs's kamikaze approach and heart for the battle had also got him on the tour, as had Ian 'Ianto' Evans's classy performance.

On the flip side, Chris Robshaw, who'd at one stage been bookies' favourite for the captaincy, slid completely out of contention. But I was the outlier in that I was the only one from the winning side who was overlooked. It resurrected all those insecurities I thought I'd buried. I was still the guy who could borrow the shirt until someone better came along.

Shaun Edwards had been the Lions defence coach in 2009, on that epic tour of South Africa, and like me, he'd been overlooked for this one. Warren had picked Rob Howley as his backs coach, but chosen Andy Farrell – Owen's father – as his defence guru. Shaun kept his counsel at the time, but revealed later that the snub almost drove him back to rugby league. When I arrived in the Wales camp ahead of that summer's tour to Japan, he made a point of pulling me aside and offering some moral support.

Looking me in the eye, he said, 'I don't know what anyone else has done to deserve that spot ahead of you, but I need you to use all that anger and experience to drive this young team forwards.'

Amid all the sympathy and support I'd received, Shaun's voice cut through the noise. Hearing that from him gave me a real boost after a miserable few weeks, during which I had battled to convince myself I wasn't a failure.

I let the disappointment drag on during the Japan tour. With most of our Six Nations players down under with the Lions, our Welsh team was young, green and inexperienced. There were eleven uncapped players in total, and we'd left the likes of Ryan 'Jughead' Jones, Hooky and Matthew Rees at home. Some of those picked had barely played regional rugby, and that just strengthened my feeling that I was in the wrong place. I was there thinking about what might have been, but I was surrounded by a bunch of boys who thought they'd won the lottery.

I hope that doesn't sound disrespectful, but it was a difficult place for me to inhabit mentally. I was expected to lead but found it impossible to put on a front. I was grumpy and unsmiling, and my attitude was poor.

Before leaving, we trained against the Lions at the Vale, and we were due to eat together afterwards. I just couldn't do it. The thought of laughing and joshing with all those boys in Lions kit was just too much to bear. Alan Phillips did his best to change my mind, but I was adamant. I'd like to think I'm an obliging bloke, and I'd usually do anything Thumper asked me to, but this was a line I couldn't cross. I'm not great at putting on a front, and my emotions were still way too raw for that.

We scraped a win in the first Test, before losing the second convincingly. It was the first time Japan had beaten a side in the world's top ten. They were undoubtedly a team on the rise, and within two years they'd be beating South Africa in the World Cup, so it wasn't a total disaster, but it was a low moment for me personally. I felt strangely disconnected from it all.

I tried to avoid following the Lions tour, but it was impossible to ignore it completely. What was hardest to swallow was seeing Stuart Hogg line up at 10 in one of the midweek games. He's not a number 10, is he? And when they played the Brumbies, Warren summoned a load of extra English players to essentially act as cannon fodder – guys like Billy Twelvetrees, Brad Barritt and Christian Wade, who weren't even first-choice picks for their country.

And then, at the age of thirty-six, and two years into his inter-national retirement, Shane Williams got the call. That was the point my embarrassment at not being picked curdled into anger.

I love Shane, obviously, but he was on a Gullivers trip at the time, swigging booze with a load of tourists. After everything I'd achieved that year, it felt downright insulting seeing those boys run out against the Brumbies with the Lions crest on their shirt.

A friend of mine was moving house in Neath and asked if

I could help. I deliberately arranged to borrow a van on the day of the deciding Lions Test, so I would have a concrete reason not to sit and watch the game. By the time we'd finished lugging furniture to the new place, we plugged in the TV to discover the Lions had won. And, as weird as it sounds, one of hardest bits to swallow was seeing the actor Daniel Craig in the changing room swigging champagne with the team. It underlined to me that I'd missed out on something unique and career-defining. Lions series are notoriously hard to win, and that was the first time it had been done for seventeen years. It was gut-wrenching.

I've always tried to keep my feet on the ground, but being an international sportsman gives you a sense of status that is inextricably tied to your self-esteem. Mine took a battering that summer. Missing out on the 2011 World Cup squad had lit a fire in me, driving me to higher standards. Missing out on the Lions tour in 2013 had the opposite effect. I just wanted to get off the treadmill and take a break. In fact, the end of the tour felt liberating, like a dark cloud had lifted and I could move on.

The 2014 Six Nations campaign was disappointing both for me, and for us a team. Whether it was Lions fatigue or a general drop in standards, we seemed unable to string a series of performances together, and it soon became apparent that the chances of winning a third successive tournament were slim. Rhys Priestland was fit again, and drafted straight back into the team, meaning I was again surplus to requirements. He started the first two games against Italy and Ireland, a limp victory followed by a humbling defeat.

Gats told me that Rhys Webb and I would be starting in round three against France, but when the team was announced, I was on the bench. I felt dejected, naturally, but didn't even question his flip-flop. I persuaded myself that being among the reserves was better than not being involved at all.

I had twenty minutes off the bench against England, who avenged the 30–3 defeat with a comfortable win at Twickenham, before finally getting the start I craved against Scotland.

Twenty minutes in, I found myself splayed out on the turf seeing stars. I'd launched a kick skywards and Stuart Hogg flew at me, shoulder-first, and caught me in the jaw. My head whipped back violently, and I hit the deck with a thump.

The referee, Jérôme Garcès, immediately brandished a yellow card, to the howling disapproval of the Welsh crowd. Moments later, having seen the sickening replays, he upgraded it to a red.

In today's more enlightened times, I'd have been taken off for a head injury assessment, but after a couple of minutes I was declared safe to continue. It didn't mean I'd forgotten the incident, and was still complaining loudly when Neil Jenkins came on shortly after with the kicking tee. Jenks, never the most sympathetic, told me to stop moaning and put the ball between the posts. I did, and we went on to record a ruthless 51–3 victory.

I was delighted with my performance. Patting me on the back on the way down the tunnel, Shaun Edwards said, 'That's *exactly* how an international number 10 plays.'

I'd done nothing flash, but felt I'd controlled things perfectly, playing with poise and precision. Short, sharp passes, delivering the ball early to my strike runners, and putting the team in the right positions through accurate kicking and calm decision-making. Shaun usually only spoke to me about defence, so for him to make an observation like that spoke volumes.

I was in the showers when one of the boys shouted someone was here to see me. I rushed out, dripping wet, and slipped on the tiles, careering into a mournful-looking Stuart Hogg. We grappled a bit as I tried to retain my balance, and one of the boys started shouting, 'Woah, woah . . . round two, is it?' It was pure slapstick.

Hoggy had come to apologize and was visibly upset. He knew

the challenge had been reckless and felt personally responsible for the defeat.

For a second, I considered ripping into him about taking my place on the Lions tour, but he looked like he'd had a rough enough day already. We shook hands, and I told him there were no hard feelings.

It was a wonderful way for me to finish the campaign, but overall, it felt like a regression in terms of my development. It was difficult going back to being a foot soldier after being a key general twelve months earlier. It was a stark reminder that I wasn't one of Gats's golden boys. I had to fight the devil on my shoulder telling me to confront him, but the brutal truth was that doing so would be more likely to deliver a fatal blow to my career than improve it.

It was another injury to Rhys Priestland that pushed me back to the forefront ahead of the 2014 summer tour to South Africa. To address the accusation that we were often undercooked going into international campaigns, Warren organized an old-school Probables v Possibles trial in Swansea. I was in the Probables' starting line-up, and we took the Possibles to the cleaners.

The Tests were being played in Durban and Nelspruit. The strength and conditioning staff had mentioned the potential effects of altitude in Nelspruit, which – at around 3,000 feet above sea level – isn't as high as Johannesburg, but would still put a bit of strain on the lungs. Arriving in Durban, we headed straight to the beach for a bit of stretching and recovery, confusing the fleece-clad locals as we strode into the ocean in our budgie smugglers.

The conversation turned back to the pressures of playing at altitude, with several of the boys who'd done so before offering advice. We'd got a connecting flight from Jo'burg, and Jamie – who'd toured with the Lions in 2009 – mentioned that we'd been nearly 6,000 feet above sea level at that point. Hooky – who'd also toured with the Lions but had a less enquiring mind – shook his head in disbelief. Then, after a brief pause, while literally standing up to his waist in the Indian Ocean, he asked, 'So what altitude are we at here, then boys?'

Playing at King's Park was amazing. It was the antithesis of a sleek, modern stadium, but those rickety old stands and musty changing rooms were dripping with history. It was a privilege to be there, but any pleasure derived from running out at one of the world's most iconic grounds was immediately wiped out by the onslaught we faced.

It was like nothing I'd ever experienced; a dark green tidal wave washed over us, churning us around and spitting us back out. There was no respite or relief from the constant pressure; make a tackle, get back up, make another, and another, and another. It was relentless. I knocked over two drop goals in the first half to keep us in touch, but it was finger-in-the-dam stuff, and it wasn't long before it burst.

Adam Jones, aka Bomb, was winning his one hundredth Test cap, but there was little room for sentiment. A message came on after twenty minutes saying if he didn't shape up, he was coming off. Sure enough, ten minutes later he was gone.

The failings of the team were being laid squarely on his shoulders, and he was forced to trudge diagonally off the pitch, prolonging the humiliation he must have felt. He wasn't accompanied by medical staff, so it was obvious to all that it wasn't an injury replacement. He was being publicly shamed. Five years earlier, he'd been lauded as the world's best tight head, after destroying Tendai 'Beast' Mtawarira with the Lions in South Africa. It was a horrible way for one of our greatest ever players to end his Test career.

The aftermath was brutal. Shaun and Gats tore into us with a level of rage they rarely showed.

There were ten Lions in our side, and we'd travelled with genuine hopes of a first ever victory on South African soil. After a 38–16 defeat, that ambition suddenly seemed risible.

'If you think you're on holiday next week,' Gats yelled, 'you've got another thing coming.'

There was no hiding place in training. The coaches ordered a full bone-on-bone contact session to replicate the intensity of a Test match. The likes of Alun Wyn loved that kind of old-school approach, but most of us backs hated it, and conspired to go easy on one another, falling into contact and taking the tackles rather than trying to bust through them. We weren't fooling Shaun. He stopped the session abruptly and yelled, 'Have all of you fuckers got a gentleman's agreement, or are you going to start actually fookin' tackling each other?' We quickly realized we'd better shape up or the afternoon was going to get a whole lot worse.

It must have worked because we were a team transformed in that second Test. It was one of the craziest, most topsy-turvy games I've been involved in. We came out all guns blazing and motored into a 17–0 lead courtesy of tries from Jamie and Cuthy, before we went into collective meltdown.

Luke Charteris was sent to the bin for collapsing a driving maul, and I followed shortly after for a similar offence. Faced with a bristling stampede of Springbok forwards thundering towards me, I'd had two options: jump out of the way or hurl myself into the fray. Unwisely, I chose the latter and got trampled unceremoniously into the turf like Wile E. Coyote from the Road Runner cartoons. When I peeled myself off the floor, several yards from where the try had inevitably been scored, I was confronted by the sight of Steve Walsh brandishing a yellow card in my face.

For the record, I have no idea how to actually collapse a maul.

We worked our way back into a 30–17 lead late in the second half before the Southern Hemisphere curse struck again. They scored twice in the last eight minutes and the last was an absolute sickener. They worked the ball wide to Cornal Hendricks on the right wing, who seemed destined to score before Liam Williams came from nowhere and clattered him into touch with a kami-kaze tackle reminiscent of his namesake, JPR Williams.

It was an apposite comparison; at that stage in his career, 'Sanj' Williams had long, flowing locks and a languid running style that recalled the seventies icon. He also possessed the same level of bravery, and an appetite for the tough stuff that belied his skinny frame. It looked to all the world like he'd pulled off a heroic, try-saving tackle, until the replays showed his elbow had caught Hendricks in the face.

He turned from hero to villain in the blink of an eye.

Steve Walsh promptly awarded a penalty try, and what would have been a difficult touchline conversion became a simple chip in front of the posts. The score was 31–30 with eighty minutes on the clock; it was the only time South Africa had been in the lead.

We were absolutely distraught when the whistle blew, none more so than poor old Sanj. Slumped in his cubicle with a towel over his head, he didn't move for around ten minutes. Every one of us went over in turn to console him, but he wouldn't respond to anyone. He was bereft. He didn't even look up when the South Africa coach, Heyneke Meyer, came in and told us how well he thought we'd played and how desperately unlucky we'd been. That could have come across as patronizing, but he sounded genuinely sincere, and we appreciated it.

Liam received a barrage of hate mail and abuse after the game. It was disgusting. He was an impulsive, committed young player who lived on the edge, and none of us blamed him for what hap-pened. We'd left it a good few hours after the final whistle before bringing up the fact it had cost us around £7,500 a man in win bonuses. We knew he was back in the room when he told us all roundly to 'fuck off'. Nearly a decade later, when he signed his big-money contract in Japan, I politely suggested it was time for me to call in that debt and got a similarly brusque response.

As much as we tried to cling onto the positives of the narrow defeat, our dismal record against the southern hemisphere's big three could not be denied. Since Warren Gatland had taken over, we'd played the big three a combined twenty-five times, winning just once. It was becoming a loaded question for Warren: how can you be one of Europe's consistently best sides, yet fail so predictably against the big beasts from the south? Unlike the dark days of the nineties, we were now as fit and well prepared as anyone, which meant it could only come down to that frustratingly nebulous reason: the psychological hurdle. Or was it, as some sections of the Welsh press delighted in suggesting, down to our limited game plan? When confronted by teams we couldn't pummel into submission, did we have the subtlety or imagination to plot a course to victory? Could we pick locks as well as batter down doors?

We had further opportunities in autumn 2014 when all three teams came to Cardiff. Australia were up first and notched a tenth straight win over us, despite being outscored by four tries to three. New Zealand followed, with a comfortable 34–16 victory, extending their winning sequence over Wales to a mind-melting sixty-one years. Consequently, our only chance of salvation came against South Africa, who we hadn't beaten since 1999.

What unfolded will never get a commercial DVD release, and I'd advise no one to waste eighty minutes of their lives watching it back, but it represented a paradigm shift.

It was an absolute pig of a game but after eighty tense, frenetic minutes, we emerged battered, bloodied . . . and victorious.

It was a huge result: revenge for the summer, vindication of all our hard work and two fingers up to the doubters. How we did it was irrelevant; the win was everything.

To top it all off, I was named Man of the Match. It was as close to perfection for me as any Test I'd played; a demonstration of what I am and what I want to be remembered for. I wasn't fizzing long passes out to the wings, ghosting through defenders, or sidestepping my way to the try line, because that's not me. I was nailing big tackles, battling for every last blade of grass, keeping a cool head, and making split-second decisions on when to kick, pass or run. And when I kicked, I used every tool in my box to keep them pegged back: long raking touch-finders, fiendish little grubbers, delicate chips, and booming up-and-unders. I was much more about blood, guts and determination than deception and delicacy, and I couldn't have felt any prouder. After all those lean years, and all that time on the outside looking in, I felt like the wheel was finally starting to turn in my favour.

Finally, I had been entrusted with the shirt, and I was able to show everyone what I could bring to the number 10 role for Wales.

It was also one of the rare occasions when Mum, Dad and Rachel all came to the game. It had been impossible for Dad to make it when he was living abroad, and even when he was in the country, he rarely made it to the stadium because his nerves would get the better of him. That day was the exception, and we have a lovely photo of the four of us together in the family room.

The 2015 Six Nations was a big leap forwards for me personally. Rhys Priestland was fully fit, but for the first time I was picked ahead of him. We were doing a kicking session at the stadium the week of the England game, and the highlights of the South Africa win were playing on the big screen.

'Jesus, Bigs,' Rhys grinned, 'you asked them to put this on a loop, did you?'

He'd been through a rough patch, suffering a dip in form after his return from injury, and had been booed by a section of Welsh fans when he'd come on for me a few weeks earlier in the Australia game. As much as Rhys and I were rivals for the jersey, he was someone for whom I had the utmost respect, and it was shameful to see so-called fans act that way towards him.

He was a private bloke and wasn't as emotionally volatile as me, so it was difficult to gauge how he was feeling. Our relationship wasn't particularly close, so he never spoke to me about much other than rugby, but I could relate to his experience as a Welsh number 10, knowing what it felt like to have your every action pored over, analysed and judged. I'm not saying we should be immune to criticism, but the incessant public commentary can be insidious and harmful, and I've seen the effects it has on people's mental health.

It was bitingly cold on the Friday night we played England at the start of the 2015 campaign. It was the first time they'd returned to Cardiff since the 30–3 game, and the Welsh Rugby Union went all out trying to recreate the hype, with thumping hip-hop, strobe lights and pyrotechnics, in stark contrast to the traditional build-up two years earlier. Some games just don't need the big sell, though, and this felt over the top.

In fact, the bit of theatre that really ramped up the rivalry was entirely unplanned. We were about to come out of the changing room, when a frantic floor manager ran up and told us to stop. We were in battle mode and didn't take kindly to having our momentum stalled. The longer the delay went on, the more agitated we became.

Thumper and this floor manager were arguing about it, and by this point, England were lined up further down the corridor. They'd refused to go out when called, claiming we were planning to leave them stranded on the pitch, at the mercy of the hostile crowd at the Millennium Stadium.

In truth we'd had no such plans, but it was clear now that this had become a stand-off, with neither side wanting to cede ground. Foxy, generally one of the most laid-back members of our squad, was getting increasingly uptight, and when the floor manager tried to explain what was happening, he shouted, 'Just fucking get them out there.'

Prop Paul James, one of the hardest blokes in our squad, was eyeballing England captain Chris Robshaw from across the corridor, while Robshaw was avoiding eye contact, trying to play it cool. The referee, Jérôme Garcès, eventually got involved, insisting we had to get moving, at which point Gethin 'Melon' Jenkins said, 'We're not rushing now just to accommodate them.'

It was in danger of turning into a farce, but I'm sure it was TV gold.

The stand-off appeared to work in our favour, as we raced into a ten–nil lead. All was going swimmingly until I clashed heads with Melon – the worst person on either side to bump heads with. His nickname comes from the shape of his head, but not from the texture, I can assure you. The blood started to gush immediately, pouring from a cut above my eye. I got patched up, and managed to knock over a drop goal that took us into a 16–8 half-time lead. We'd never surrendered a half-time lead to England in Cardiff, so the omens were good.

I could contribute nothing to the team talk, as I spent the entire fifteen minutes being stitched up. The medics used a local anaesthetic, so I could only really hear noise and chaos coming from the main changing room. It bothered me somewhat; as a leader and the main tactician, I would normally be involved in those discussions. The fact I wasn't led to a bit of a disconnect at the start of the second half. We were stodgy and sluggish, losing our way and failing to add a single point to our tally. England were allowed to steal victory.

It was a deflating experience, especially after 2013, which to some of us had felt like a generational shift, what could have been a catalyst for a sustained period of dominance over the old enemy. But England had had other ideas; they'd come back to the scene of their massacre and claimed revenge.

In fact, that turned out to be the only bad half of rugby we would play in that whole campaign, and it probably cost us a Grand Slam.

In the second round, and for the second year running, a Scotsman was ordered off the field after an illegal challenge on me. It was Finn Russell this time, who was given a yellow for tackling me in the air. We scraped an edgy win at Murrayfield to get our title challenge back on track.

It wasn't pretty, but Shaun Edwards reminded us that this is what we do; we respond to a setback by winning on the road. Part of his creed was never to over-celebrate one-off wins; he'd say we could celebrate when we'd got a medal round our neck or a trophy in our hands.

His parting message was to go to Paris and do the same, and we did. It was our fourth consecutive win over France, which felt significant, not least because I scored my first try for Wales. I found myself on the end of a neat little offload from Lyds after Webby had made one of his sniping breaks.

I couldn't have been more grateful to see the try line appear as I was running out of space and gas. I was so used to running up to people to celebrate their tries, it felt odd to have my teammates running to embrace me for once.

Ireland beat England that same weekend, keeping their Grand Slam dreams on course. We were playing them next in Cardiff, and still had a big say as to the destination of the title. Little did we know quite how dramatic the climax of the tournament would be.

The Ireland game in round four ranks among my favourite ever Test matches. You probably have a fair idea what makes me tick by now, so it won't come as a surprise when I tell you this game wasn't a scintillating, end-to-end exhibition of running rugby. It was a brutal, no-holds barred clash between two sides unwilling to give an inch. Ireland were defending champions and on course for a Grand Slam, but they came up against us at our obdurate best.

There are games when you feel you're chasing it, and others when you're gliding serenely above the fray. This was the latter. At one point, Rob Kearney launched a seventy-metre spiral kick from his 22 to ours, and I leapt skywards, plucking it from the air, and spinning it back infield in one fluid movement. Leigh then kicked it back into their half, won it back in the air, and within minutes we'd earned a penalty.

It's often things like this that stick in my memory, rather than some wonder try. When you feel like you're *on*, you play with a sense of freedom, and you try things. The inner voice that urges caution is silenced. It was a revealing insight into my state of mind; knowing the jersey was mine was a liberating experience.

During the second half, Ireland were relentless, spending an eternity in our 22 and at one point racking up thirty-three phases before ultimately being repelled. After about fifteen of those phases, I remember thinking, almost perversely: *this* is what I play the game for, making tackle after tackle, reloading, knocking people backwards, and refusing to yield. We had a virtually foolproof system under Shaun and trusted each other implicitly. We were rarely stressed without the ball as we might have been under other regimes. Shaun made us love the art of defence: 'Attack sells tickets, defence wins trophies.' And he'd won more than virtually any other coach in the business.

You might think it strange to hear a fly half opining about how much he loves defending, but I mean it. I made twenty-seven tackles that day, which is more than a blind-side flanker normally gets through. I get as much satisfaction from repelling an attack as I do in creating a try with a fizzing thirty-metre pass or a cross-field kick. Defence becomes a weapon; during that ten-year period, it was a brutal blunt instrument. We'd suck the life out of teams and take pleasure in watching their morale crumble before our eyes. It was a proper man test, and that day we came out on top.

The final weekend was a broadcaster's dream and an administrator's nightmare. There were three teams still in contention for the title, and none of them were playing each other. There's one official Six Nations trophy and a replica, so the decision was made to send the official trophy to London where England were hosting France, and the replica to Edinburgh, where Scotland were taking on Ireland. That meant there was nothing in Rome, where we kicked off proceedings against Italy.

There was a logic to this. England, Ireland and Wales were all on six points after three wins apiece, but those two had a superior points difference to us. England were on +37, Ireland were on +33 and we were on +12. On the balance of probability, the trophy would end up in England or Ireland's hands, and this was looking even more likely as we found ourselves 13–11 down approaching half-time.

Before the game, Gats had referenced a league game when he was at Waikato when they'd needed a certain winning margin to take the title. He said he'd focused minds by giving players individual targets, and he did something similar with us in Rome.

'Leigh – if you get eight shots at goal, I want you to get at least seven of them. Warby – we need three turnovers from you today; get stuck in and go after them. Scott Baldwin, you're allowed one lost lineout and no more.'

Then, looking around the room, he picked out George North and said, 'What's your target going to be?' George panicked and said, 'I'll get forty touches.'

Gats broke into a broad grin, replying, 'If you get forty touches, I'll pull my pants down in the middle of Stadio Olimpico.'

Setting those individual targets took the pressure off the team as a whole. If the aim had been to secure every single lineout and win the game by thirty points, it would have put a heavier, collective load on the team. It was a clever bit of man-management.

It wasn't quite working out on the field in the first forty minutes, though, where our mindset had changed from going all out for the title to just winning the game and perhaps finishing second. At half-time Gats acknowledged that things hadn't exactly gone to plan, but encouraged us to go back to those targets we'd set. How many of them could we achieve in the next forty?

The answer was pretty much all of them. George might not have managed forty touches, but he made a hell of an impression, scoring a hat-trick inside ten minutes. Webby was at his impish, elusive best, Sanjay was purring, Tips was everywhere, and I kept knocking over the conversions as the tries began to rain down. When George scored his second, pushing us through the

30-point barrier, we all locked eyes and instantly turned our minds once more to winning the championship.

Jeez, boys. *It's on.*

In the dying moments, we were back in their 22, 61–13 ahead and pressing for a ninth try when Gareth Davies dropped the ball, gifting them possession that led to a length-of-the-field score.

In any other circumstances it wouldn't have mattered a jot, but on a weekend where every point was precious, it was immensely frustrating. A fourteen-point swing.

Had we scored, the end result would have been 68–13, a winning margin of fifty-five, as opposed to the forty-one-point margin we ended up with.

It was a record victory over Italy, and one of the most complete attacking displays we'd put together under Gats, but we felt hollow at the final whistle.

As Luke Charteris and I were walking off to a standing ovation from the Welsh fans, I turned to him and said, 'I don't think it's enough, is it?'

He grimaced and shook his head.

We showered and changed and settled in for the Scotland–Ireland game, desperate for Scotland to pull off a shock, or at least to keep things tight.

Our scoreline meant Ireland knew exactly what they had to do – beat Scotland by twenty-one points or more and hope England didn't run riot against France.

We'd been told to stay sober, as the BBC had arranged a room in Rome's Presidential Palace to present us with our medals in case events took an unexpected turn. It soon became apparent that they weren't going to – Scotland pretty much rolled over and threw the towel in – and the Peroni began to flow like the Tiber.

England and France delivered a topsy-turvy twelve-try classic at Twickenham, but we were too far gone to remember much. The drunker we got, the more it numbed the pain.

It had actually been Gareth Davies's first Six Nations game, so we all toasted him, with Gats drily adding, 'Congratulations, and thanks for dropping the Six Nations.'

That was it for poor Gar, bless him; he was already morose with guilt and that tipped him over the edge. He clinked bottles with Gats, necked what was left of his and immediately popped the cap on another.

Suffice to say when the taxis arrived to take us to a nightclub, Gareth was nowhere to be seen. Priest eventually found him curled up in a corner, comatose and dribbling, and started berating him for being such a lightweight.

Gats – who's fond of a drink himself – gave Rhys a stern look and said, 'Leave him.'

And so it was that mere hours after making his Six Nations debut, young Gareth was being tenderly tucked into bed by Neil Jenkins.

Because we finished third, the 2015 Six Nations campaign hasn't gone into the annals of Welsh rugby folklore like those of 2012 and 2013, but we were arguably an even better side that year. Were it not for a bad half against England, we'd have won the Grand Slam. As clichéd as it sounds, the margins in international sport are perilously thin. A ball brushing the tips of someone's fingers rather than landing in their palm can be the difference between glory and despair.

9

THE AGONY AND
THE ECSTASY

Twickenham Stadium, 26 September 2015, 9.48 p.m.

My legs are trembling. Not with nerves, but exhaustion and adrenaline. There are six minutes left of what's been a titanic, bone-shuddering Test match between England and Wales.

It's the World Cup and England are the hosts.

The scores are tied at 25 apiece, and we've just been awarded a penalty. Seven times in this game, I've placed the ball on the kicking tee, seven times I've sent it sailing through the posts.

This one is different.

It's forty-nine metres away, at the very edge of my range, and my legs feel like they belong to someone else; they are leaden, and coursing with lactic acid.

Rugby is the ultimate team game, but there are moments when it becomes an entirely solitary pursuit. This is one of them.

I wanted this kick. I wanted the responsibility.

It was exactly what I'd been waiting for.

There are moments like this where your senses become heightened. Every noise becomes amplified, every twitch more keenly felt. Smells are stronger, colours are sharper and your heart thumps a little harder. Except this time, the opposite happened. Lining up the kick, I withdrew into a bubble. The faces of the 80,000 spectators became hazy and indistinct, the noise a distant blur. Neil Jenkins's words of advice went unheard. I was wrapped in a fog with only the posts visible through it all.

I tilted the ball at its usual 45-degree angle, pulled up a few blades of grass, and stood, placing my right foot next to the ball before beginning my routine.

My run-up in reverse. Five steps backwards, bend down, toss the grass in the air to check the wind, run my hand through my hair, bounce up and down at the hips, touch both shoulders, another hand through the hair, touch the right shoulder, wiggle both shoulders forwards and backwards, all while staring intently at the ball. Then a slow, deliberate look at the posts.

Then, stillness. Hands in front of me, legs apart.

This is it. The same kick I've practised thousands of times: on the lawn in Llangennith with the Atlantic breakers at my back, at Banwen RFC, the Rec in Penclawdd, at Gorseinon RFC, the Gnoll in Neath, and countless thousands of times in Llandarcy and Wales's training base at the Vale.

Except this time, it's in front of millions, it's at Twickenham, and it's for victory. A game of unimaginable tension between two of the biggest rivals in world rugby, and it's all come down to this.

I close my eyes, take one last deep breath, and begin my run-up.

Destiny had led us to this point. Almost three years earlier, in the unlikely surrounds of London's Tate Modern gallery, the draw for the 2015 World Cup had been made.

The timing couldn't have been worse from a Welsh perspective. We were seven defeats into an eight-match losing streak, and had tumbled down the rankings. Drop outside of the top eight, as we did, and you find yourself swimming in pretty choppy waters.

Once the draw was complete, we were only too aware of the scale of our task; if we were to progress to the knockout stages, we'd have to negotiate a group containing our old nemesis, Australia, and our bitterest rivals, England, who also happened to be hosting the tournament.

Little wonder then, that it was dubbed the 'pool of death'.

By this point Warren Gatland had abandoned the Polish experiment, and had decided on some new venues for our World Cup training camps. The first was a little village nestled in the Swiss Alps called Fiesch. It was the sort of place you'd associate with leisurely days on the slopes and sundowners on the balcony. Unfortunately, it's forever etched in my mind as the location of the most savage, unrelenting physical examination I've ever experienced.

The objective was obviously to improve our fitness, but also to separate the mentally strong from the weak. The camps were designed to test the more subtle gradations of mental toughness. You might be strong, hard and indomitable, but were you borderline masochistic? Were you able to delve into your deepest reserves, to find an extra 1 per cent when your vision was blurred, your legs felt like cement, and you were seconds away from vomiting up the contents of your stomach.

It was a Darwinian trial, survival of the fittest, with the losers missing out on a World Cup place.

One or two bad sessions, and that could be your time done. Gats doesn't care if you're not as fit as the next guy, but he cares if you're not trying to be.

Whereas Poland was all about the cryotherapy, the concept here was to live and train at altitude, where the air was thinner and the strain on the lungs more intense. 'Live high, train low' was the buzz phrase, but it should have been 'train high, live even higher', because everything was up in the more rarefied air of the Swiss Alps.

Our accommodation was around 2,200 metres above sea level, and we were training about 1,000 metres lower down. All journeys were made on the gondolas, and there was a certain grim irony to jumping into them and marvelling at the breathtaking views, knowing that once they shuddered to a halt, we'd be beasted to within an inch of our lives.

Gats loved the mind games, pitting us against one another,

fostering little rivalries between those battling for the same shirt. He'd put big forwards up against each other in tug o' war competitions, and place bets on the outcomes. Nothing would motivate Warby more than overhearing Gats say he thought Dan Lydiate was going to beat him.

That power-endurance stuff – tyre flips, tug o' war, bag slams, wrestling – was a proper man test, and one that we backs were far less keen on than the forwards, but Gats wanted us on the edge and would secretly enjoy it when things got a little feisty.

Every conversation you had with Gats was loaded. 'How was yesterday?' he'd ask. 'Bit tough? Need us to roll things back a bit?' Was he being genuine, or was he testing you? You'd think, 'All right, I've got a bit more in me to give.'

One of his favoured instruments of torture was the 'Heini Müller', a figure-of-eight sprint drill. Starting on the halfway line, you would sprint diagonally to the try line, jog across to the other corner, then sprint diagonally back to the halfway line. He'd always chuck them in when you were least expecting it, and usually at the end of a hideous, lung-busting session.

We'd refer to such days as 'def con' days, after the US military defence alert codes, when Gats would gleefully announce a few Heini Müllers to wrap things up after two long sessions. You'd go up against those fighting for the same shirt, and even if you were regarded as first-choice in that position, coming last against your colleagues would flood your mind with doubt. That was enough for most of us to find an extra gear.

As brutal as the Switzerland experience was, at least the torture took place in a spectacular setting and in relatively temperate climes. The same couldn't be said of our second camp in Qatar, where the scenery was as uninspiring as the heat was murderous. Our first session was at seven in the morning, and it felt like running around inside an oven. While the forwards were practising scrums, I looked up to see Gats leaning gingerly against a palm tree, looking woozy and delirious just watching.

It was an arid, dry heat that stuck to the back of your throat, making you feel permanently parched. I couldn't think of anything worse than scrummaging in those conditions, and it didn't take long for the session to descend into a medical emergency.

There was a commotion by the halfway line, and everyone started sprinting for the tunnel, voices raised in panic. Once we'd reached the sanctuary of the air-conditioned changing room, we were greeted by the sight of Tomas Francis splayed out like a crucifix, wearing a ventilation mask and looking like a pregnant mother about to give birth. He was swaddled in ice blankets and looked panicked and disoriented.

A rugby environment is the last place to come for sympathy, and once it became apparent that he wasn't going to die, the mood swiftly changed to one of rampant piss-taking and abuse. Everyone was scrabbling in their kitbags for their phones, callously snapping pictures of poor Franny as he lay prone and wheezing on the floor.

He'd arrived in camp as something of a wild-card pick; a tubby, overweight prop not long out of university, who'd been plying his trade in the lower leagues with Doncaster and London Scottish.

Gats had clearly seen something in him – a rough diamond in need of a polish. He'd become one of my closest friends in the squad and my long-term roommate, but back then it looked as if his Test career would be extremely short-lived.

That incident has passed into legend as the most vivid indicator of how gruelling that Qatar camp was, and it prompted a drastic change in the schedule. From that point on, we'd only train before sunrise and after sunset.

The sessions were still horrendous, and our results were posted in the team room for all to see. Those numbers would prevent you from relaxing; if I clocked that Priest or Gareth 'Chicken' Anscombe had racked up a better score than me, my mind began to whirr as to how much harder I'd have to work the next day.

There was one session that the boys still talk about, and you can taste the bile in the back of your throat just thinking about it. It was another one of those interminable sprint drills, where you're forced to run continuous shuttles to the point of exhaustion. The forwards had gone first, and when we arrived we were greeted by a scene of utter carnage. Most of them were splayed out on the floor, their chests rattling as they heaved dry desert air into their wheezing lungs. Their faces were an alarming shade of beetroot red. Others were bent over, retching violently and trembling from head to toe. It was a vivid, terrifying premonition of what lay in wait. Poor old Dan Lydiate looked as though he was ready to quit. Lyds is supremely fit and an absolute warrior, but he's also a hill farmer from Abbeycwmhir – a remote hamlet which is covered in a blanket of snow for three months of the year. Doha – with its oppressive humidity and blistering temperatures – was about as far from his comfort zone as you could get.

These moments of abject misery and despair are meant to equip you for similar experiences in a Test match; those moments when it feels like you're about to collapse, where every sinew is strained to breaking point, every breath seems snatched, and your limbs seem filled with lead. When a chorus of negative voices are screaming at you to give up, to keel over, but you don't. Because you've been to the well all those times and you know there's more left inside you. Mental strength is not about blocking out negative thoughts; it's about not giving into them.

The idea for this drill was to run for ten seconds and rest for ten, but that was only if you covered the required distance in the first ten. Jamie Roberts, never the most agile of backs, was struggling big time. He'd been playing for Racing Metro in Paris, and it was clear his fitness levels had dropped off a little. He was taking about eighteen seconds to cover the ground, leaving him just two to rest and, as a consequence, was running pretty much continuously.

As much as I was struggling myself, bent over with my hands on my knees between sets, the sight of Jamie lumbering around like a Shire horse was too funny to ignore. I started laughing, and the more I laughed, the more frustrated he became.

The scrum halves – Lloyd Williams and Gareth Davies – were

gliding around, barely breaking sweat, while Jamie hauled himself clumsily back and forth between the cones. The number 9s might not have it their way with the power-endurance stuff, but it's always the little guys with the fast-twitch muscles and stumpy legs that boss the sprint sessions.

During the last shuttle, I was out on my feet, fighting a constant urge to keel over and collapse, but I kept going, fuelled by all the sessions we'd banked in Switzerland. I eventually fell at the line, ignoring orders from the coaching staff to 'stay tall' and control my breathing. I was absolutely done, my battery drained, but a strange sensation overcame me nonetheless. I felt serene, as if I could handle whatever was thrown at me.

It was an epiphany of sorts; a realization that there was a point to all of this, and that you could reach a level where instead of feeling wrecked and defeated, you almost felt superhuman.

We faced Ireland home and away in our warm-up games for the 2015 World Cup, with Warren Gatland and Ireland's head coach Joe Schmidt coming to a gentleman's agreement around selection. They picked experimental line-ups for the first game in Cardiff – where Ireland won convincingly – and first-choice XVs for the second game in Dublin, which we won 16–10.

It was the first time Ireland had lost there for two years, but any positivity was shattered when we played Italy in the final warm-up, and lost Rhys Webb and Leigh Halfpenny to sickening injuries. You could tell in an instant that their World Cup dreams were over, and I was totally gutted for both. We'd already lost Jonathan 'Foxy' Davies, so that was three of our first-choice backs gone before the tournament had even begun. And as callous as it sounds, my next thought was that I'd now be Wales's front-line goal-kicker, with all the extra pressure that would entail.

When you think of World Cups, you think of travel and adventure, of journeying with your band of brothers to the ends of the earth and putting your body on the line for your country. To that end, popping over the border to England felt a little tame. Our first game – a routine victory over Uruguay on 20 September – was actually played in Cardiff, making it seem even less exotic.

With that victory in the bank, all attention turned to our game against England. After three years of fevered anticipation and hype, this quake-inducing fixture had finally arrived. This was the old rivalry on steroids. The loser would be on the back foot and scrambling – with the Wallabies lurking menacingly on the horizon – whereas the winner would have one foot in the quarters. The fact that England and Australia had already beaten Fiji meant the group had been reduced to a three-horse race. It felt like a knockout game before the knockouts.

England sprung a surprise with their team selection, picking the rugby league convert Sam Burgess at inside centre. Burgess was a mountain of a man and had switched codes the previous year amid a whirlwind of hype and expectation. There was no doubting his credentials. He'd guided the South Sydney Rabbitohs to their first NRL title in forty-three years with a Man-of-the-Match performance, and was a decorated Great Britain and England international in rugby league.

When Bath had secured his signature, it was just a matter of time before he was fast-tracked into the England squad, but there was a sense of confusion around his best position. Bath had picked him as a blind-side flanker, whereas England saw him as a 12, and that's where Stuart Lancaster picked him for the game at Twickenham. It added another layer of intrigue to a game that was already one of the most hotly anticipated in World Cup history. The fact that he was directly up against Jamie Roberts was a headline writer's dream, with every variation on the 'irresistible force versus the immovable object' trope appearing in the English press. He essentially became *the* story, and there were some who genuinely seemed to believe he could win the game on his own.

Rob Howley was secretly delighted at the selection, suggesting to us privately that it smacked of desperation. It was the biggest gamble of Lancaster's tenure, and a sure indication they were

It was the round ball that first captured my heart – and my Manchester United obsession continues to this day – but eventually rugby would turn my head.

Home is where the heart is

Left: Our home on
the Gower.
Below: Me with my big
sister, Rachel, and my
favourite book –
one I now read to my
boys at bedtime.

Visiting Dad
in Dubai during
the holidays.

With my
beloved Mamo
and Dado, who've
both had an enormous
influence on my life.

A rare moment
with Mum, Dad,
Rachel and me all
together, celebrating
my Man-of-the-Match
award against South
Africa in 2014.

My first start for the Ospreys, aged eighteen, in 2008.

My Wales debut against Canada, later that same year. I may have been in a yellow shirt, as opposed to the fabled red one, but it was still the realization of a dream.

European heartbreak in San Sebastian, 2010, as my last-minute drop-goal attempt sails wide.

Left: With Mike Phillips, celebrating our Magners League Grand Final victory over Leinster in 2010, two years after my debut . . .
Below: . . . and repeating the feat two years later, beating the back-to-back European Champions on their home turf.

My relationship with Warren Gatland has been a complicated one, but there's no doubting his coaching credentials.

My old buddy Leigh Halfpenny, whose career has followed the same path as mine, from the muddy fields of Gorseinon to some of the greatest stadiums in the world.

Always an honor to play against you. One of my idols, huge respect #DanBiggar @welshrugbyunion

Above left: I'm my own worst critic, but it means the world to me when those I admire pay me a compliment. Romain Ntamack is one of the finest 10s of this generation. *Above right:* History may not judge Wayne Pivac as kindly as he deserves, but he achieved some incredible highs, including a first ever win in South Africa. I liked him and was sad to see him go.

An invitation to the
Directors' Lounge at
Old Trafford turned into
a messy night in the company
of Usain Bolt. I was a little
worse for wear the next day!

Left: My confrontational
manner has got me into
trouble a few times, including
on this occasion when Owen
Farrell and I clashed during a
2023 World Cup warm-up.

Right: Huw Bennett, Owen
Watkin, Gareth Davies, Liam
Williams and me (left to right).
Downtime is important during
World Cups, but sailing a leaking
dinghy around Japan's Lake
Shidaka wasn't our best idea.

From my teenage years at the Gnoll to
sold-out stadiums across the globe,
Neil Jenkins has been my shadow,
constantly refining my technique.
I owe him an enormous amount.

Siya Kolisi and I were opposing captains in 2022, when Wales won for the first time ever on South African soil. We shared a huge amount of mutual respect.

My Man-of-the-Match display against South Africa in 2014 may not have earned points for style but, in terms of grit and obduracy, it was one of my very best.

History was made at the 2022 Six Nations, when Northampton provided both captains for the England v Wales match.

thinking more about us than themselves. Worried about Jamie's reputation as a bruising ball carrier, they'd bulked up their midfield with an equally monstrous presence, but rugby union is more strategic than league; the battle for the gain line is more nuanced. We were confident we could isolate and expose him.

Alan Phillips had used every contact in his little black book to persuade some of Wales's most feted celebrities to come and present our jerseys and, understanding the significance of the England game, Thumper knocked it out of the park.

Ask people across the globe to name a single Welsh person and this guy's name would probably be one of maybe three or four that immediately spring to mind. He's that famous. But clearly his fame hadn't spread as far as Warren Gatland's corner of New Zealand, as our head coach announced, in hushed tones, that our jerseys would be presented by the one and only . . . 'Tom James.'

Out trotted the unmistakeable figure of Tom Jones, all perma-tanned and looking like a mini Mount Rushmore statue. To his eternal credit, he didn't correct Warren, but we were all mortally embarrassed on his behalf.

Later on, Gats was quietly fined £500 for the faux pas.

The day of the game dawned, and with the kick-off scheduled for 8 p.m., a yawning chasm of time opened up before me. How on earth was I going to fill it? The WRU put a bus on from Cardiff for all our families to come and see us for an hour over lunch. It was a lovely gesture, but I wasn't in the right headspace for it. Mum and Alex were on the bus, and I had to go down to tell them I needed to be by myself. It felt insensitive and self-absorbed, but the pressure of the goal-kicking was getting to me. I knew that one shanked kick could be the difference between victory and defeat. While everyone else was relaxing over coffee and sandwiches with their families, I was under the duvet in my room, alone with my thoughts. Was I really capable of running the game *and* kicking the points?

En route to the stadium, our bus slowed to a crawling pace and my mind began to race, worried that we'd be late and our preparation would be compromised. As my panic continued to deepen, the England team bus went hurtling past. As hosts, they had to arrive first, and whether we'd left early or they late, we'd been ordered to slow down and let them pass. Surely there was a protocol for this? Instead of the zen-like calm I needed to be accessing, my mind was boiling over with anger and frustration.

It continued when we reached the stadium, when Warby – stalking the changing room like an angry tiger – started protesting loudly that the temperature was too high. I began to wonder if there was some kind of sabotage going on. Were England messing with our heads, delaying our arrival, cranking up the heat in our changing room? It was bordering on paranoia, and I knew I had to escape onto the pitch to start my kicking routine. And it was there, on the immaculate Twickenham turf, surrounded by 80,000 seats, that it all changed.

I looked up at the stands; at the fans beginning to trickle in, at the flags being draped over the sides, and I thought, 'This is *exactly* where I want to be.' The knots in my stomach loosened, and the nerves drained from my body, and I knew I was ready.

Something special was brewing.

The plan was to kick off short. I normally hate doing that at the beginning of a match because there's no margin for error, but now I felt uber-positive.

I was going to land this kick exactly where I wanted – not too long, not too short, but right on the money. That tells you where my confidence levels were at, and it summed up my attitude that day from the first whistle.

We had a penalty in the second minute. The kind of kick I'd comfortably convert nine times out of ten. As I was lining it up, I emptied my mind of the pressure and thought instead of Mum and Alex up in the stand, picturing them with their hands clasped, looking down at me, and in that moment I almost forgot about the occasion. I just wanted to do them proud.

The ball squeezed over, just shaving the right-hand upright, and I felt a surge of pride and relief. Taking over the goal-kicking from someone as talented as Leigh had been a big deal, and I'd passed the first test.

It was a frenetic, breathless and combustible opening quarter that eventually erupted after Dan Lydiate flung himself at Tom Wood's ankles, sending him crashing to the floor. It was a trademark Lyds move, and the English boys were incensed, flooding in and starting a mass brawl.

No punches were thrown; it was essentially a load of pushing, shoving and verbal sledging, but importantly we didn't back down an inch. England's volatile full back Mike Brown and Warby had to be separated as Jérôme Garcès repeatedly blasted his whistle in an attempt to restore order.

Often these scuffles are just performative, but this time the aggression was real. This might have been Twickenham, and England might have been the hosts, but we weren't standing on ceremony for anyone.

England were first to seize the initiative, with a clever strike play. Sam Burgess and Billy Vunipola ran cunning decoy lines to free up space on the blind side for Jonny May to go cantering over. It was a hammer blow, and gave England a ten-point lead with half-time beckoning. We had to strike back before the interval and, when we were given a lineout just inside our own half, we called a play we'd devised to test Burgess's defence. We knew he was a brilliant one-on-one defender, capable of dominant, bone-crunching tackles, but doubted whether he'd be able to read intricate plays on the fly.

Off the lineout, I threw what we called a 'tunnel ball'; Jamie ran one of his trademark decoy lines, while Hallam Amos ran an arc around the back, and I rifled the ball 'down the tunnel' between the two of them to Scott Williams. We knew Burgess would hesitate over whether to take Jamie or Hallam, and it worked like a dream. Scotty drifted, caught the ball at pace and turned on the after-burners, gobbling up the yards all the way to the 22. He was eventually brought down, but England were scrambling and gave away a penalty in front of the posts.

I knocked it over, narrowing their lead to 16–9.

It was a small moment, but a significant one. Before I'd lined up the penalty, the big screens were showing replays of Scott Williams leaving a lunging Burgess in his wake. Burgess had caused a stir earlier in the week, replying 'who's that?' to a question in a press conference about our centre Scott Williams. Scotty is a pretty undemonstrative bloke, but he's hard as nails and that comment would have stung. He might have conceded a few stones and several inches to Burgess, but he bows to no one, regardless of size or reputation.

During those replays on the screens, as the England players were trudging towards the posts, Bradley Davies was bellowing at them, 'He knows who he is *now*, doesn't he boys?!'

The second half became a tense kicking duel and, as the penalty count mounted, so did the opportunities to kick at goal. Neither Farrell nor I were in the mood to miss, and a pattern developed where he'd nudge England further ahead and I'd claw us back: 19–9, 19–12, 22–12, 22–15, 22–18.

It was around the hour mark that we got within four points and sensed a tangible shift in momentum. It felt like we'd been hanging on until then, but as we entered the final quarter, we started to play a bit more rugby, and found some holes where previously there'd been none.

Slowly but surely, we began to inch our way back into the game, but just as we'd established a firmer foothold, the rug was yanked from beneath us. In the space of five disorienting minutes, we lost three key members of our backline as the team began to disintegrate in front of my eyes.

Scotty Williams was the first to fall, stretchered off with a ruptured knee ligament, shortly before Hallam Amos dislocated his shoulder. Liam Williams followed soon after, a stray boot to the head leaving him concussed.

The sporting gods are often cruel, but this felt positively

sadistic, especially given we'd already lost Pence, Foxy and Webby before the tournament.

It forced us into a desperate reshuffle, with George moving into the centre and Lloyd Williams – our reserve scrum half – filling in on the wing. Rhys Priestland came on at fly half, with the message that I was to move to full back.

I remember thinking, 'This cannot be happening.'

The biggest game of our lives, and we now had three players playing out of position.

Rhys had played full back before, so would have been the more natural choice there, but the coaches were anticipating a barrage of kicks from England and wanted me to deal with the aerial threat.

The odds of us pulling off an unlikely victory lengthened out of sight at that point. The four-point deficit now felt more like twenty-four, and a team with less resolve would have slumped into self-pity. But if those gruelling pre-season camps were for anything, they were for moments like this.

Gethin Jenkins gave away a stupid offside penalty shortly after, coming in at the side of a ruck right beneath the sticks, and I lost my rag completely. 'What the fuck are you doing?' I yelled. 'Use your head. Three points could be the difference!' He gave me his trademark death stare and bellowed back, 'I'd rather give away three than fucking seven.'

Farrell knocked over the kick to take them 25–18 ahead, but still we refused to buckle. We'd been knocked to the canvas but were determined to go out swinging.

England fans were no doubt relaxing at this stage, but little did they know that Twickenham was about to witness a climax as dramatic as any Hollywood movie.

As devastating as those injuries were, the simple truth is that we wouldn't have won the game without them. What had seemed a wretched twist of fate would become a glorious act of serendipity.

England had brought George Ford on for Sam Burgess, and

when we were awarded a lineout in our half, we formed a huddle to discuss our options.

'What's the call?' Jamie asked, the competitive spirit still burning intently behind his eyes. Rhys pointed to George Ford – a teammate of his at Bath – and said, 'See that fucker over there? I'll give you the ball and I want you to run over him.'

Not the most sophisticated plan, but it was a start. We won the lineout and Jamie thundered towards Ford, winning the collision decisively, as we moved quickly into our shape.

As we were working the ball back to the right-hand side of the pitch, I came into the line from full back, giving us an extra option. With Priest at 10, we now had two ball players in the midfield. Alun Wyn dummied to carry, before passing out the back to Rhys, who found me on his outside shoulder.

Now, if I'd been a natural inside centre, I'd have straightened and looked for contact, but instead I scanned, noting that Brad Barritt was defending narrowly. Sensing he'd commit to an early tackle, I sent a floated pass above his head to Jamie.

Jamie had Antony Watson marking him, and his midfielder's instinct told him to cut back rather than take him on the outside. That forced Watson to bite in, leaving Lloyd unopposed on the left wing. All he needed was the pass, which Jamie duly provided. *Whooosh.* Lloyd was away and accelerating down the touchline.

We were all running behind him, anticipating the next phase, when suddenly he kicked it away.

What's he *done*?

I was cursing him for squandering such precious possession, when something quite astonishing began to unfold.

Scorching into my peripheral vision came a lightning-quick Gareth Davies, accelerating rapidly onto the ball, which was now bouncing towards the try line. The England defenders had turned on their heels and were scrambling back in blind panic, but Gareth was too sharp for any of them, pulling away as he'd routinely done during those sprint drills in Qatar, leaving all and sundry trailing in his wake.

All he needed was a kind bounce; for that fiendishly unreliable oval ball to bob into, not away from, his grasp.

And as the entire stadium held its breath, it happened. He somehow gathered the ball with the very tips of his fingers, and touched down for the try that shook Twickenham to its foundations.

Devastating as those injuries seemed at the time, that try would not have been scored if our original backline had remained intact. A natural winger would have backed himself to step in, to use his footwork, and fend, but Lloyd's instincts were different. As a scrum half, he was adept at kicking off both feet, and Gareth had been tutored by Rob Howley to always run that inside support line. As a fellow scrum half, Lloyd *knew* he'd be there. For Lloyd to be thrust into a turbo-charged Test match and deliver a moment like that was truly outstanding, and Gareth's finish was out of this world. He'd touched down right under the posts, too, making the conversion a formality.

As I ran back, glancing at the big screen, I was greeted by the incongruous image of Prince William, in his Welsh top, goading his brother Prince Harry with a celebratory fist pump. It was the injection of belief we'd so desperately needed, and a little of our swagger returned.

A kicking battle ensued between me and George Ford, with each of us taking turns to send aerial bombs skyward. I hoisted a high one, aiming for the left side of the field, but it drifted towards the centre and into the arms of a leaping Mike Brown. Before he had time to think, he was enveloped on the halfway line by a swarm of rampant Welsh defenders. Warby buried his head in the ruck and clamped his arms over the ball like a mollusc.

Penalty, Wales.

This was it. The halfway line, and a kick to win it.

That year, my normally staid pre-kicking routine had evolved into something increasingly elaborate; in fact, Jamie had even accused me of inventing it to get more attention. The truth is that it came about by accident. During kicking practice in Qatar, I'd had to contend not just with the sweltering heat, but also the constant presence of flies. Before every kick I'd be tugging my shirt and arching my back to stop it sticking, wiping the sweat from my forehead and swatting away the flies. All these involuntary actions unconsciously made their way into my routine. Gifs and memes had been proliferating on social media; the routine had been dubbed the 'Biggarena', and set to the music of the 'Macarena', complete with twitches, bouncing and swipes of the forehead.

For me it had become a bit of a crutch, I suppose, and I went through the full range again there at Twickenham before locking my gaze on the posts.

Meanwhile, 150 miles away in the Gwaelod y Garth pub just north of Cardiff, my dad was tucked in a corner, nursing a pint of ale, when one of the locals piped up; 'This is where we need Halfpenny. This is well out of Biggar's range.'

Without revealing his identity, Dad replied that if I got it, the doubting Thomas would have to buy the whole pub a round, and they shook on it.

Back at Twickenham, I was in the zone. Disconnected from the noise and the chaos, I narrowed my vision. This was the moment when I couldn't give in to doubt. *Don't snatch at it, don't rush.* I began my run-up and swung my leg, connecting as sweetly as I could have hoped, and sent the ball sailing majestically through the posts with a couple of metres to spare.

After a brief pause during which it sank in, the Welsh section of the crowd went absolutely ballistic, and the noise came flooding in.

For the first time in the game, we were in the lead.

I turned to see Gareth Davies looking heavenward, with both fists clenched in triumph, and Priest ran up and enveloped me in a hug.

For the next four minutes, from a purely selfish point of view, I wanted that kick to be the difference.

England were frantic, as they could sense the World Cup

slipping through their fingers; they rallied for one last frenzied surge towards our line. Warby was hovering with a predatory look in his eyes, waiting to pounce on any loose ball, and he seized his moment, clamping down on Mike Brown in a near-identical movement to the one that had secured the penalty.

I was screaming at him, 'Let it go, let it go!' but it was too late.

A shrill blast on Garcès's whistle indicated a penalty, this time in England's favour. Such are the vagaries of the breakdown. On another day, with another ref, that would have been our penalty.

We were all unconsciously heading for the posts, assuming Chris Robshaw would take the three points and the draw, when I saw him point towards the corner flag. It was a seriously bold call that would come to define his tenure as captain.

This was now the defining moment.

With minutes left, we had to repel one final siege. Ford knocked it into touch and, as the lineout was being formed, Warby was stalking up its length with a demonic look in his eyes, bellowing, 'We do *not* give an inch. Don't you *dare* let them fucking score.'

Luke Charteris, one of the world's best maul defenders, was staring ahead impassively, like a man possessed. This was what Shaun called an 'attack set' – a defensive rearguard action with an attacking mindset. Don't just look to soak it up; get up in their faces and smash them back. You can't call one every time, because they'll lose their significance, but this was when everyone was to give an extra 2 per cent.

Jenks came on with the water, and I was screaming at him, 'Where am I defending? Who am I taking? Do I stand in the middle of the posts or the far side?'

I'd never defended at full back before, and Lloyd – who'd never defended on the wing – was having a similar conversation with Jamie.

I stared across at their backline, looking for clues as to who might be about to get the ball. I could hear Shaun's words in my head. *Stay square, stay connected and bury anyone who comes down your channel.*

The ball went to Robshaw at the front; an odd choice, given the circumstances. This was their last roll of the dice, and we'd expected them to throw long and launch a strike play. If you're gambling with a kick to the corner, you might as well gamble with the lineout.

So as soon as Robshaw landed, our pack came together as one and slammed into England like a wrecking ball crashing through a derelict building. Their flimsy maul splintered as our forwards ploughed mercilessly through it, dumping them all over the touchline in a heap of crumpled bodies and tangled limbs. It was a serious display of power and ferocity.

They did their best to disrupt our final scrum, swarming over Toby when he scooped the ball up from the base, but we weren't going to let it slip now.

I dropped way back behind the try line, Gareth rifled the pass to me, and I kicked the ball so hard into the stand that I nearly injured myself.

My first thought when the whistle blew was, *Shit, I've pulled my hamstring*, but my second was, *Jesus, we've just beaten England at Twickenham.*

Lloyd Williams was the first to embrace me, followed closely by Priest, who told me what an incredible performance I'd delivered.

I saw Gethin next, whose first words were, 'I told you three was better than seven.' He then asked if he could have my boots.

Caught up in the euphoria I agreed, only discovering later that he'd made a small fortune auctioning my right boot and Lloyd's left during his testimonial dinner. 'The boots that sank England' were apparently the subject of a fevered bidding war. Suffice to say, neither of us were cut in on the deal.

Ian Evans was doing some corporate work at the side of pitch, and he was welling up with emotion. I'd never seen him like that; Ianto was normally the most laid-back bloke you could possibly meet, the polar opposite of his long-term second-row partner, Alun Wyn. While Al was all brooding intensity and scowling passion, Ianto was a languid space cadet with his head in the clouds.

He never really loved rugby, he just played it because it was his job, so to see him so animated was revealing. If you were going to be involved in just one game as a Welshman, you'd have wanted it to be that one.

Warren Gatland was visibly emotional during his post-match TV interview. I was standing right next to him, waiting to receive my Man-of-the-Match award, when he was asked, 'How heroic was that performance from Dan Biggar?'

'Yeah well, he kept us in the game, didn't he? Two excellent kicking games from both teams,' came his rather perfunctory reply, before he proceeded to talk about the match in more general terms.

I couldn't believe what I was hearing. Talk about bursting my balloon.

I didn't want to be showered with praise, but could he not have been a *little* more effusive after what was undoubtedly my career high point?

As with most things with Warren, it seemed calculated, but I was damned if I knew what his motive was. Was he just trying to keep my feet on the ground?

The mood was dampened further when I was selected for a random drug test after the game, and – instead of celebrating with the boys – was sent to a medics room to give a urine sample. I was so dehydrated, it was touch and go whether I'd be able to produce anything in time to catch the bus back to the Vale. I just about made it, but the journey wasn't quite as debauched as I'd imagined it would be.

We were facing Fiji in five days and were told to get plenty of water down us to rehydrate. The same rules didn't apply to the coaches, who were quietly getting hammered down the front.

Supporters' buses festooned with Welsh flags and filled with drunken fans regularly passed us by, slowing down to wave, honk their horns and toast the victory with foaming cans of beer. It seemed like the entire population of Wales was travelling back over the border on a huge wave of euphoria.

We reached the Severn Bridge at around 2 a.m. and the barrier remained steadfastly down. Confusion reigned for a few minutes, as no one was manning the toll booth, and it looked as if the victorious Wales team would be marooned on the bridge until dawn.

Eventually Paul 'Bobby' Stridgeon, our fitness coach, seized the initiative. Fuelled by several cans of lager, he leapt from the bus and – in a scene that recalled the young Superman lifting a car – proceeded to force the barrier up over his head, grunting and wheezing as he locked his arms out victoriously like an Olympic weightlifter. He returned to a raucous round of applause, bowing theatrically as the driver restarted the engine and headed for the border.

By the time the bus pulled into the Vale at around 3 a.m., the adrenaline had left our systems, and we were desperate for bed. As we wound our way down the narrow lane towards the hotel, Warren stood up and cleared his throat.

We wondered if he had one last stirring speech in him, but he just grinned wickedly and said, 'Straight to cryotherapy, boys.'

And so we found ourselves – mere hours after beating England in the World Cup – hunched over and freezing our tits off in the Vale's cryotherapy chambers.

My performance had provoked interest in me to a degree I had never before experienced. The following day, there was a flood of media requests to interview me, but our press officer told us all to keep our heads down and focus on the next game against Fiji, which suited me fine.

The England game had put me in the limelight, but my every instinct was to withdraw from its glare. Dad called to tell me a BBC reporter was coming to interview him that afternoon, and I told him to cancel it immediately. Mum turned down a similar request, so the journalists ended up at Gowerton Comp speaking to my old teachers instead. Suddenly I felt like public property.

All I wanted to do was to put my feet up and chill, but not

surprisingly everyone wanted to come over and celebrate with me. Several of my mates dropped by, as did Mum, who'd blown about £50 on Sunday papers at the corner shop in Seven Sisters. They were all keen to revel in the afterglow of that magnificent result, but I found it exhausting.

The following day I was back in camp, and on the phone to my agent by the hotel foyer. My performance against England had caught the attention of a couple of French clubs, and some big-money offers had materialized. I'd been stalling on an offer of a central contract from the WRU, keeping my options open, and Gats had been pressuring me to sign it. I'd left the team room to take the call, and was acting a little furtively, not wanting anyone to hear, when Gats came ambling past.

I panicked, affecting an interest in the potted plants and doing my best to project an air of insouciance. He nodded in greeting and strode past, before instantly turning on his heel and saying – while I was still on the phone – 'Just so you know, that WRU contract needs to be signed within the week or it's off the table.'

Classic Gats – lobs a little grenade and disappears before you've had a chance to reply. *Shit.* Had he been eavesdropping? It seemed too much of a coincidence.

Toulouse and Montpellier were the interested parties; two amazing clubs from France's rugby heartlands in the south-west. The offers were flattering and extremely tempting. But Gats's comment hadn't been an idle threat or a negotiating tactic – he meant it. My agent had been inflating my ego, filling my head with grandiose thoughts about living in the south of France, while Gats had trundled by and casually inserted a pin in the balloon.

After seven years of playing for Wales, I'd finally worked my way into a position of influence. I was playing well and in the van-guard of a team that was going places. Finally I was one of Gats's go-to men, after years of trying to gain his trust and respect. Could I throw that all away by moving to France? It seemed a monumentally risky move. This was before the much-maligned 'sixty-cap rule' was introduced, which precluded you from selection if you were playing your club rugby outside Wales and hadn't yet won sixty or more caps.

It was an effective move. I'd been genuinely torn but this, along with a phone call to Mum, sharpened my focus. Mum told me this was my time to shine and, as usual, she was right.

Gats used to get quite involved in the financial side of contract negotiations. He'd always said that if you left Wales it would have to be for at least a hundred grand a year more, to compensate for lost match fees and win bonuses. As I was mulling all this over, I was struck by a sudden thought: *that* was why he'd been so dismissive of my efforts against England. He knew I was out of contract and didn't want to over-inflate my value, making it harder to keep me in Wales.

Suddenly it made sense. I should have known; Gats always has an ulterior motive.

As it panned out, I signed the WRU contract within the week.

A few days later, I was practising my kicking when Gats walked past with the analysis boys.

Stopping to watch, he said, 'This one's to send us into the World Cup final.' I blasted it between the posts from forty yards, and turned smugly to face him, point proved.

No words were exchanged; he just walked away. Hindsight has taught me to appreciate these moments for what they are. He was continually poking the bear, keeping me on edge, pushing me to work harder, aim higher.

The Fiji game was – without exaggeration – one of the toughest I'd played in in my life. They had some absolutely monstrous athletes, many of whom were playing in France's Top 14, and they'd come to Cardiff sniffing an upset. Fijian teams of the past had always been outrageously skilful but were usually lacking in structure and discipline. This vintage was a more complete outfit, combining brute strength with agile footwork and a delicate offloading game.

We'd only had four days' rest after the England game and it showed, as we became increasingly sluggish as the match wore on. I limped off with cramp eight minutes from time, by which point we'd been run ragged and were out on our feet. The 23–13 victory wasn't as emphatic as we'd hoped for, and any celebrations were muted.

It was a timely reminder that the England victory would count for nothing if we didn't qualify for the quarter-finals.

By the time we'd returned to the Oatland Park Hotel in the early hours, someone had clambered up to the sign and replaced the O with a G, rechristening it the Gatland Park Hotel. No one has ever taken the credit, but Thumper's smirk suggested he might have been responsible.

Our win over Fiji meant England had to beat Australia to progress. Naturally, all my mates were supporting Australia, not just because they were playing England, but because a Wallabies victory would grant us passage to the quarters. I therefore found myself in the slightly surreal position of hosting a Wallabies-themed house party during the World Cup, watching on while my mates, bedecked in singlets, shorts and cork hats were necking cans of Foster's and cheering on the Wallabies.

I'm not some jingoistic Welshman who delights in seeing England suffer, but when they were sunk by Australia, it felt like a seismic moment. They were gone; dumped out of their own World Cup with a game to spare.

It meant we'd survived the pool of death and the only question remaining was whether we'd finish first or second. Our final match against Australia would determine that.

Finishing top was a significant prize; it would mean a quarter-final against Scotland as opposed to South Africa. Though we'd recently ended our long losing streak against the Springboks, we'd never lost to Scotland under Gatland. It was obvious which route we'd prefer.

Australia had ripped England apart, scoring three tries and racking up thirty-three points, which served us notice that we couldn't just expect to turn up and grind out a win. Our attack would need to be as sharp and incisive as theirs and we'd need to go in search of tries.

The first half unfolded in a tense, cagey manner but we felt in total control, hemming Australia into their own half and suffocating their much-vaunted attack. Statistically we enjoyed 82 per cent of territory in that opening forty, but their superior scrum helped them to a 12–6 lead. Early in the second half, their discipline momentarily deserted them, and Will Genia and Dean Mumm were sent to the sin bin in quick succession. This was our chance to break their resistance. Losing one man is a handicap, losing two is a nightmare, and for seven minutes, it would be fifteen against thirteen. It felt like a huge momentum shift that we simply had to exploit.

What followed was the most frustrating period we endured in the tournament. Australia rallied to deliver a defensive display of exceptional guts and discipline. Outnumbered and under the cosh, they repelled every one of our increasingly desperate advances, hurling bodies into contact, lunging desperately at our runners, and repeatedly dragging us down. We laid siege to their line, battering relentlessly against an obdurate and unrelenting Wallaby wall. Three times, we breached it, three times we were denied a try: Jamie was scythed down millimetres short, Liam was hauled to the floor, and George was held up despite dragging three Wallabies over the line.

As heroic as their defence was, we only had ourselves to blame. We were tactically naïve and utterly devoid of guile or invention. A two-man advantage will always result in overlaps; eventually a gap will appear that cannot be plugged, but we lapsed into tunnel vision. Australia were defending intelligently, staying on their feet, and resisting the urge to dive into rucks. There's no doubt that I should have done better as a fly half; I should have been bolder and more inventive. Collectively, we made a succession of bad decisions – trying to milk scrum penalties instead of launching strike plays, trying to batter through traffic instead of looking for space out wide. Had we done that, we'd have walked in unopposed. The one time we did look to go wide, Adam Ashley-Cooper made a phenomenal read, sprinting out of the line and killing the move. Our chance had gone, and so had the game.

Rob Howley was barely able to contain his rage, telling us we'd blown a golden opportunity to top the group. 'How can you spend that long in the opposition 22 and not fucking score?' he yelled, addressing all of us, not just those who'd carried fruitlessly into brick walls.

A melancholy silence took hold, as people stared listlessly at the floor looking utterly deflated. I felt compelled to say something.

'Everything you guys have said is on the money,' I conceded. 'We should have got over the line and topped the group, but let's not forget we're in the quarter-finals of the World Cup.'

With the gloom lifted slightly, there was a knock at the door, and the Australian back row forward David Pocock stuck his head around. He was hoping to swap jerseys with Justin Tipuric. Tips reluctantly agreed, knowing what was coming next.

Pocock peeled off his jersey to reveal surely the most ripped, sculpted torso in world rugby: chiselled abs, granite pecs, bulging veins, and biceps the size of bowling balls.

Tips, with the greatest of respect, has a body like a bag of custard. He tentatively pulled his off and stood there pale and topless, with his sloping shoulders and spaghetti arms dangling. He was dying of embarrassment while Priest, Gareth 'Cawdor' Davies and I sniggered at his obvious discomfort.

You couldn't have two more contrasting shapes in world rugby. It's nuts how someone who's gone through all that physical conditioning can enjoy none of the visual benefits. Though in fairness, anyone who stood next to Pocock with their top off would suffer by comparison.

The post-match review left no stone unturned, with Rob

replaying the entire miserable seven-minute sequence when we'd failed to score. No one felt more responsible than us players, especially as the press had reheated all the same accusations about 'Warrenball' being to blame. The insinuation was that we'd become a team of automatons, our senses dulled by years of following a restrictive, low-risk game plan. It was a load of bollocks and we resented it. As if Gatland would tell us to ignore a four-man overlap and continue to run direct balls just because that was our ingrained game plan. There are times when you reflect after a game and wonder if the coaching had been poor, the tactics misguided or the messaging unclear, but this wasn't one of them. We'd been encouraged to play, and we'd gone into our shells of our own volition.

We had no one to blame but ourselves.

South Africa had lost to Japan during the pool stages in a result dubbed 'The Brighton Miracle', easily the biggest upset in World Cup history. That, and the fact we'd beaten them the previous autumn meant we approached the quarter-final with less trepidation than we might have. Having said that, they'd recovered well from the Japan debacle, hammering Samoa, Scotland and America along the way. Unlike the Aussies or the Kiwis, who could bamboozle you with flair and invention, the Boks just wanted to steamroller you into submission. That's what we were preparing to face that week and training was stripped to the very basics. Shaun Edwards declared early, 'I'm not going to bore you with video clips or expect you to spend hours on the laptops. When you play against this team you have to nail three things: kicking, tackling and maul defence.' That's all we worked on from a defensive perspective: kicking endless balls in the air, defending driving mauls, and tackling our bollocks off.

Our injury crisis was deepening, forcing Gatland into yet another reshuffle, with Gareth Anscombe being picked out of position at full back and the twenty-year old rookie Tyler Morgan thrust into the outside centre berth.

Physically, we were falling apart, but psychologically we were in a good place.

Gats had instilled a winning, no-excuses culture, and once we'd parked the Australia game, it was all about optimism and self-belief. Whatever people might have said about the game plan, you could never question the iron will of our squad.

The quarter-final unfolded exactly as we'd expected, with South Africa looking to physically batter us, but we seized the early initiative, sending George North thundering into the heart of their defence and almost all the way to the line. They had a battalion of heavyweight ball carriers, all conditioned to run hard into contact, and we were forced to tackle low to stall their momentum. The likes of Damian de Allende, Eben Etzebeth, and Duane Vermeulen were all giants, and were marauding around with menacing intent. The penalty count rose steeply, and we found ourselves 9–3 down without having done much wrong.

Our response was immediate, and the try we scored was the result of our analysis. Willie le Roux was a brilliant attacker but was defensively suspect and weak in the air. We'd planned to target him when the opportunity arose, and when Anscombe passed to me in our half, he pointed to an isolated Le Roux in the backfield. I sent the ball skyward and hared off after it. As it was hanging in the air, I was thinking *no one's blocked me, I've got a free run through to Le Roux*. I leapt to claim it from his grasping hands and shovelled an ugly pass away to Gareth Davies, who accelerated over for the try.

Those aerial skills were something I'd worked hard on. Watch it back and you'll see my jump was strong and purposeful, whereas Le Roux's was half-hearted and speculative.

Technically speaking I wouldn't have scored too highly; I hardly leapt with the grace of a gymnast, but in that moment, there was no way I was losing the contest. It was all about strength of will and who wanted it more. I'd expected to claim that ball whereas he'd merely hoped to.

Right on the stroke of half-time, I hit a drop goal that nudged us ahead.

The belief was growing by the minute.

In the changing room, cuts and niggling injuries were being attended to, and instructions were being barked into pounding, swollen ears. Shaun was banging his clipboard saying, 'Three things. What are the three things we've worked on all week?' We all chimed in unison, 'Maul defence, kicking and tackling.' 'That's right,' he said. 'Keep focused on those three things and we're going to win.'

We started the second half well, but after a while the Boks began to strangle us and they retook the lead. The tension was difficult to bear, knowing that one lapse could decide the game.

As we entered the final quarter, South Africa conceded a penalty and just as Wayne Barnes blew his whistle, I had an attack of nerves. As well as I'd been kicking, I suddenly felt apprehensive. It was just outside the 22 and not especially difficult, but I was wishing it was on less of an angle when Gareth Anscombe appeared on my shoulder and said, 'This is your moment here, go and win the game.' Those words had a transformative effect and I struck it perfectly, taking us into a one-point lead that we clung on to desperately, making tackle after tackle as South Africa surged forwards in waves.

One of those tackles sent me stumbling backwards leaving me dazed and disoriented. Prav Mathema and Geoff Davies hauled me off for a Head Injury Assessment and I was furious, aiming my anger squarely at the medics, who were entirely right in their actions.

I didn't handle it well, first refusing to leave the field and then arguing with Geoff all the way off, before petulantly kicking a pile of stray water bottles.

I should have acted with more grace, especially given what we now know about head injuries, but in that moment all I cared about was the fact I was being subbed off in the most important game of my career when our fate was still dangling in the balance.

I'm a terrible spectator and felt utterly helpless when South Africa delivered the killer blow five minutes from time. They had a left-hand scrum in our 22, one of those that are horrible to defend. There's always a dilemma of whether to put an extra body on the short side or leave it open and back yourself to make a decision on the hoof. They tried to march us backwards, but we held firm, forcing them to play.

Vermeulen picked up from the base and I knew we were in trouble as soon as he darted round the short side. What followed still gives me nightmares. I saw it unfolding in slow motion.

No one epitomized South African brawn more than Vermeulen, a bristling, snarling slab of muscle whose first thought was to marmalize whatever was standing in his way. Only this time – with the delicacy of a ballerina – he chose to pivot, sending a deft offload into the hands of Fourie du Preez, who'd materialized wraith-like on the blind side. Lloyd Williams had been the first to try to stop Vermeulen, and Cuthy – assuming the burly number 8 would try to bulldoze his way over – came flying in to help, giving du Preez a free run to the try line. Cuthy had endured a torrid period at the hands of social media trolls, and this was another reason for the haters to pile into him, but anyone would have done the same. When you prep for the Boks, you prep for brute force. No one would have seen that coming.

It was a genius move, and du Preez – who'd been coaxed out of retirement to play in this World Cup – deserves enormous credit. South African rugby may be all about big lumps of meat, but he provided that essential drizzle of spicy sauce.

There might have been time left, but we were done. Weakened by our injuries, and tottering on our heels, we managed to throw a few final jabs, but all the force had gone out of them. It was galling to watch from the touchline. We paraded onto the pitch at the final whistle to thank the fans, but I just wanted to disappear into a hole in the ground. Charts dragged me under his arm. He'd been there before, losing in the semi-final four years earlier, and knew from experience that the sun would still come up in the morning.

I still struggle to talk about that du Preez score. It was only the third try we'd conceded in the tournament, and I agonize over what we could have done differently.

Personally, I'd tapped into my richest-ever vein of form during that tournament, and a losing quarter-final didn't seem a just reward. People point out that we emerged from the most competitive pool in World Cup history and came within a whisker of beating the Boks, despite being handicapped by a crippling injury list, but that's no consolation.

We returned to our hotel, where our friends and families had gathered, and I stayed in the corner with Mum, Alex and my sister Rachel. It was an evening I had to endure rather than enjoy. I didn't want to talk about the game, didn't want to hear about how brave we'd been, or how close we'd come. I don't know what other people were feeling inwardly, but it seemed to hit me harder than the rest of the team. The defeat weighed really heavily on me.

You can sometimes seek solace in the booze, drinking to numb the pain, but I didn't want to do that either. I wanted the pain to be raw. I wanted to remember how low I felt so I could use it as fuel for the next time. Once the family bus left, I disappeared to bed, lying awake for hours with those feelings of regret tumbling through my mind.

The following morning, there were a lot of sore heads as we gathered in the lobby to disperse. Some boys were going on holiday, others back to their clubs in England, with the majority jumping on the bus to head home to Wales. Phillsy had drunk through the night and was prowling round reception with a mischievous glint in his eye. Gats appeared, and a gaggle of fans who'd arrived to wave us off gave him a hearty round of applause. Phillsy looked perplexed, 'Oh bloody hell, well done Gats,' he shouted across the lobby. 'A standing ovation for losing in a quarter-final, is it?' It was a comment dripping with sarcasm and born of frustration. Mike had been in the squad throughout but hadn't played a single minute of rugby. For someone of his stature and influence, it had been hard to take, and he was letting off steam. He was still roaming around in reception when the bus driver fired up the ignition and Tips asked innocently, 'Are you coming back with us, Mike?' In a show of mock humility, Mike replied, 'Oh, am I allowed? That's really kind of you. I know I'm shit now, but thanks for not leaving me behind.'

I cracked a smile for the first time since the previous day.

We might have suffered a heartbreaking defeat to South Africa, but the sun had come up, the world had kept turning, and Mike Phillips was still being Mike Phillips.

10

THE LONELY PLACE

I'd always wanted to be Wales's goal-kicker. Leigh Halfpenny was my best mate in the squad and arguably the best place-kicker in the world, but if he wasn't doing it, I wanted it to be me. The World Cup in 2015 had given me the opportunity to step up, and I relished it, converting all but two of my attempts for an overall tally of fifty-six points. My 100 per cent record against England, culminating in the match-winner from the halfway line, was a source of immense pride. But here's the curious thing – success doesn't always breed confidence.

After the World Cup, I allowed some demons to creep into my mind, and my kicking began to suffer. It's easy to ceaselessly practise your technique, but endless hours on the training paddock count for nothing if you begin to believe you're going to miss.

For a while after the World Cup, I felt a horrendous pressure to nail every kick for Wales and the Ospreys. It was unbearable at times. I began to understand those golfers or darts players who talk about the 'yips', and wondered whether I needed to rework my technique.

When we played Ireland in Dublin in the opening match of the 2016 Six Nations, I had a penalty ten metres from touch on the right-hand side, and I felt almost physically compressed by the weight of expectation. The day before, I'd done my kicking sessions at the stadium and I'd ended up spooning kicks left, right and centre. I had made no changes to my technique between October and February, but I just could not seem to knock a ball over. Predictably, I missed this penalty too, and the swagger that had accompanied every kick during the World Cup seemed to drain away.

I think maybe it was the realization that I was now the established goal-kicker. There had been pressure at the World Cup, but I felt like I'd been given a free pass in Leigh's absence due to an injury. Now, it was my job.

That one in Dublin drifted to the right, which was a sure sign of me being tense and tight. My heart doesn't necessarily beat faster when I'm lining up a kick, but any nerves manifest themselves in the tightness of my limbs. When I make contact with the ball, I'll be snappy and quick as opposed to fluid and relaxed. A lot of the kicks I missed during this period were because I'd 'pulled' the ball, a sure indication that I'd deviated from my technique. And it was all in my head.

In Neil Jenkins, I had the best coach and confidant around, but I was so proud I didn't want to reveal any weakness, preferring to confront my demons in private. It was a Catch-22; I needed more pressure kicks to help navigate this wobble, but more pressure kicks equalled more opportunities to fail.

We finished second in that Six Nations behind England, who recovered from their World Cup debacle to win the Grand Slam. By the end of the campaign, I'd recovered my mojo, kicking seven out of eight as we powered to a 67–14 victory against Italy.

I took a perverse sense of pleasure from the fact I'd 'cured' myself without any outside assistance. I am very stubborn and, rightly or wrongly, I see seeking help as an admission of weakness. Whenever I've suffered a period of hardship or bad form, I've dug myself out of it on my own. It's what I pride myself on, and stems from my belief that my achievements have come more from hard work and mental fortitude than natural talent. Ultimately, I'd rather be mentally tough than be blessed with Quade Cooper-esque skills but likely to crumble in the face of adversity. In normal circumstances, I've got this almost pathological ability to separate real life from the eighty minutes between the white lines.

We had a psychologist called Andy McCann attached to the squad, and a lot of the boys swore by him. Despite his numerous successes, Leigh Halfpenny has a tendency to internalize his emotions and can get overwhelmed with anxiety. He'll often spend days agonizing over a missed kick or tackle. So people like Warby and Pence considered Andy absolutely vital, and would regularly work through their mental demons with him. It's just not for me.

In broader terms, I didn't really think about what would happen when Leigh was back from injury. If I'm honest, he's the better kicker. He's that bit more accurate and strikes the ball more cleanly. If I miss, it's usually because I've not hit the ball well, whereas his kicks will always be sweetly struck and sail majestically through the air; they'll just sometimes drift left or right. His technique is different. He glides through his run-up, building momentum before the strike, whereas mine is more staccato.

That said, I can claim to be the better kicker out of hand. I just shade him on punting and drop-outs, and one of the best weapons in my armoury is the old-fashioned spiral bomb, which I'm delighted to see is back in vogue. There's nothing more satisfying for a kicker than launching a perfect one into the ether, and nothing more horrifying for the poor backfield player tasked with catching it. Rugby balls are fiendishly unpredictable things, but it's anyone's guess what direction it'll travel in when it's spinning on its axis and bobbing about in the thermals.

Leigh and I used to take the mick out of Neil Jenkins, telling him he was lucky we'd both come along because we're so diligent he barely has to do anything. The reality is, without him, we wouldn't be half the kickers we are.

We've worked with Jenks from a young age and his influence has been immeasurable. With his dodgy knees and wobbly gait, you'd never guess he was once an elite athlete, but his brain is like a supercomputer. He approaches kicking with the academic reverence of a university professor.

It seems like a lifetime ago that I used to meet him at the Gnoll in Neath as an impressionable teenager in the Ospreys Academy.

There must have been some nights that were mild, but in my memory, it was always freezing cold and pitch black. Jenks would go via the newsagent's to pick up a bottle of Coke and bar of Dairy Milk before settling in for a one-to-one session.

It's difficult to explain how privileged it felt having these sessions with a legend like Jenks. We were starstruck. He's easy company, but that didn't stop us feeling incredibly nervous lining up goal-kicks when he was standing behind us, forensically analysing our form.

Over the years, he's built up a mental dossier on our techniques, our habits and our foibles and, if something goes wrong, he'll have spotted what it is before the ball's landed.

Now it's all about tweaking minor things to maintain high standards, but back then, the advice was more broad. He'd spent a lot of time studying the best place to hit the ball. If you're kicking into the breeze, you've got to go a bit higher on the ball to drive it through the wind. A brisker wind needs a lower trajectory, whereas calmer conditions require a more lofted kick.

To kick higher, you strike lower, and vice versa. You can't kick a ball forty-five metres by punching it that way, but you'll get it to cut cleanly through the wind during its flight. I'd arrived like a nerd for my first session with a list of questions, but Jenks has such a deceptive way of simplifying things, I'd binned most of them within ten minutes.

He's a big advocate of stockpiling all the knowledge, but only tapping into the bits you need. He'd mastered the art of making something look easier than it really is, but he was a hard taskmaster who had no truck with laziness.

Don't get me wrong, it can get tedious. When you're knackered after a session and the boys are already in the tent getting their boots off, you can resent having to stick around for another half an hour kicking balls over and over again. Sometimes you wonder if it's genuinely worth it.

I'm sure there are people who'd think once you reach a certain level, you don't need that endless repetition, but it's like a muscle that needs constant flexing to stay supple. There have been periods when I've had tight hamstrings and not kicked for a fortnight, and I'll feel a noticeable loss of rhythm when I return.

As obsessive as I can be, I have to draw the line somewhere. Not for me the kind of mental torture Jonny Wilkinson would put himself through. Jonny would set himself ever more difficult challenges and castigate himself for failing to achieve them. He went through a phase where he'd insist on hitting the crossbar ten times in a row before finishing a session. If he got to nine, but missed the tenth, he'd start again, and would often still be out there at midnight. That would drive me insane. Jenks was always good at mixing things up, so you're not doing the same session over and over again. It's not like we're NFL players who only kick; we've also got to do weights, recovery, team sessions and units, and you physically can't just keep going on and on.

The closest we'd get to a Jonny-style routine was the seven-kick session that Jenks devised. Seven kicks from forty metres out. Starting on the left, five metres from the touchline, and gradually creeping across the field until you're five metres from the opposite touchline. You have to nail all seven to finish, but they have to be consecutive so if you miss the sixth, you go back to the start. The session could be done and dusted in seven kicks – a great incentive – but you could still be out there hacking away fifty or sixty kicks later. It's human nature that the more you fail, the more frustrated you become, and the harder it gets. It teaches you a valuable lesson in staying calm and focused.

The older I've got, the less obsessive I've become. I no longer feel the need to practise kicking on my day off. Having one day off a week helps you freshen up and prevents you compounding bad habits if you're not having a good day. It was Jenks who encouraged me to do less as I got older, to give myself a mental break, and enjoy twenty-four hours away from rugby. You need that release to stop yourself feeling overwhelmed. As much as it contradicts the philosophy of my early years, sometimes less *is* more.

When Jenks was in his pomp, he won games for Wales almost single-handedly with his metronomic goal-kicking. Games that should have been dead and buried were so often pulled from the fire by Jenks and those clutch kicks of his. His secret, he always maintained, was imagining he was in Cae Fardre in the Rhondda, knocking balls back and forth to his grandfather. It was a mental trick he'd play to escape the often unbearable tension. He was no longer in a packed Twickenham or Loftus Versfeld, surrounded on all sides by hostile fans willing him to miss; he was in his happy place, doing it for fun. Whether it's a failure of imagination or not, I've never developed a similar crutch. I simply cannot persuade my brain I'm anywhere other than where I am – usually in a sold-out stadium with something big on the line.

My method, in so far as I have one, is to focus everything on the mechanics of the kick, and hope this will empty my brain of all other distractions. It's not foolproof but it helps. Jenks taught me to look beyond the point you want the ball to land, so I'm not thinking about it going through the posts, I'm looking at a particular fan in the stand or, for example, a yellow jumper, or a piece of text on the hoardings. If it says, for example, 'N13', can I land it on the 1? If I miss the 1 by a fraction, it's still likely to go through. If I hit the ball cleanly, nine times out of ten everything takes care of itself. I'd love to be able to tell you about my zen ability to transplant myself to another dimension, devoid of doubting voices and fluttering nerves, but I can't, because it doesn't happen. My mindset when I'm standing over the ball is to take all emotion out of it as far as possible and focus on being technically precise. Whether it's a kick to win it in the last minute, or the eighth conversion you've struck during a one-sided romp, I try to approach it in the same dead-eyed way. If it's technically good, it'll go over.

I understand that sounds simplistic, and it's clearly delusional to simply say 'block out all the noise'; you'd have to be a sociopath not to be affected by the pressure that comes with taking a kick in an international match. The idea that some people simply have ice in their veins is a nonsense. Everybody who's ever taken a kick in those circumstances will know how it feels to have that seed of doubt in your mind when you're standing over the ball. When you're tense and tight, the tendency is to hit the ball hard, but unless you're hitting it from fifty-plus metres, you're never having to belt the ball. With a golfer, the slower and smoother the swing, the better it travels. And it took me a while to realize this, but missing kicks is part of the process.

I keep an old quote on my phone from Michael Jordan that I still refer to now: 'I've missed more than nine thousand shots in my career. I've lost almost three hundred games. Twenty-six times, I've been trusted to take the game-winning shot and missed. I've failed over and over and over again in my life. And that is why I succeed.'

No two kicks are ever the same. You could have one in the first minute when you're fresh and focused or one in the eightieth when you're knackered and your legs are like jelly. In theory the latter should be the hardest. Doing anything when fatigued is trickier, whether you're wiring a plug or mowing the lawn, but in my experience it's the earlier ones I find most challenging, when you haven't had time to settle in and establish a rhythm. They're tone-setters, those early ones. If you miss, it makes the second attempt that bit harder, and if you miss *that*, the posts will seem less than a metre wide for the third. That's why it's always nice to have a sitter early on. It's like golf; you want to make a solid par on the first hole, a good first tee shot followed by a routine putt, and you're on your way to a good round.

By the seventy-fifth minute of a game you're in the zone. Admittedly, if it's been an exhausting passage of play lasting several minutes, it can be tough physically, and it takes a little more effort to control your breathing and bring your heart rate down. Those might be the only kicks where the physical outweighs the mental. Otherwise, I'd say kicking is 90 per cent in the mind.

Prior to the 2015 World Cup, before Leigh's injury, we'd discussed me deputizing at certain points during a game. The analysts had discovered that a lot of Leigh's misses were after long, exhausting passages during which he might have covered a few widths of the pitch, sweeping back and forth. As 10s generally do less work in terms of defensive covering, I was going to be on standby to take over kicking duties in such scenarios. In hindsight it might have been impractical actually to bring that in as a policy – would Leigh have willingly handed over the tee? – but, as it transpired, it was never put to the test.

That kick to beat England in 2015 was considered one of my finest moments, but I was far more nervous for my first kick than that one. It was so important to get a good start and I hadn't hit the first one well. It was an edgy, snatched attempt that thankfully had enough to squeeze over, but it got me into the groove. And while we're exploding myths, the idea that kickers enjoy absolute silence is nonsense. It amuses me when messages appear on big screens imploring fans to 'respect the kicker'. I much prefer to take my kicks against a backdrop of booing and other ambient sounds. Lining up a kick somewhere like Thomond Park, where you can usually hear a pin drop, is far more unnerving than being sledged or abused. It's a reminder that every single person in the crowd is watching you. Hearing people laughing, drinking and talking bollocks is enough to persuade you that if you miss, maybe you'll get away with it. No one's paying attention anyway. Silence denies you such comforts.

Back in 2009, when we toured the US, we spent half a day watching the Chicago Bears train. There are more than fifty players on an NFL roster, and they were all on the field together, rehearsing countless offensive drives and complex strike plays. All except the place-kicker, Robbie Gould, who was on a separate pitch, endlessly practising field goals with his kicking coach. He came on at the end and just practised two field goals with the rest of the team, coordinating his run-up with the snap. It seemed like a dream gig to me, and I told him so. Everyone else was out there getting battered from pillar to post, and having to memorize reams of complex information, while all he had to do was come on and kick every once in a while. I explained that I had to do all the other stuff, *and* do the kicking. He looked at me through narrowed eyes, no doubt wondering who this Welsh upstart was, and replied, 'Sure, but if you miss a couple, you might get a bit of grief but that's all. If I miss a couple, I'm out the door. And I'm not talking one or two in a game, I'm talking one or two in a *season*.'

Perhaps he had a point.

11

THE LIMITS OF THE HORIZON

When Warren Gatland took the Wales job, he was asked by Roger Lewis, the CEO of the Welsh Rugby Union, what his priorities were. 'Playing the southern hemisphere big three on a regular basis' was his swift reply.

Gats believed that pitting yourself against the best was the quickest route to improvement so, in 2016, less than a year after New Zealand had been crowned world champions for the second time in a row, we were heading to the land of the long white cloud.

Gats had been canny in his choice of tours during his tenure, timing them to precede Lions trips to the same places. In 2008, the year before the Lions took on the Springboks, Wales travelled to South Africa. The 2012 Wales tour to Australia was the summer before the Lions faced the Wallabies. And this tour was a year before the Lions headed to New Zealand. As Gats had been appointed as Lions head coach again, these games served as auditions as well as full-blooded Test matches.

Our preparation was disastrous as we were battered at Twickenham by an under-strength England in a pre-tour friendly. Within days, an article appeared in the Welsh press listing six Welsh players who were out of form and 'playing for their places'.

I was among them, as was Gethin Jenkins.

It felt personal and entirely unjustified. The previous autumn, I'd been lauded for my performances in the World Cup, and in early 2016 Wales had come second in the Six Nations, losing just one game – narrowly – to the Grand Slam champions, England.

As much as I'd got used to batting away negative press, this article really pissed me off. I don't expect the Welsh press to be cheerleaders, necessarily, but this felt like they'd pre-loaded the gun, and couldn't wait for one bad performance to start firing bullets. Our press officer, whose job it is to keep those often-fraught relationships cordial, was trying to play it all down, but Gats was in full agreement with me and the other affected players, and in the end we got our way, making it clear we'd no longer be speaking to that particular publication. We didn't want to see their journalists in our press conferences, and we certainly didn't want to see them in our team hotel.

Every one of us knew we'd performed dreadfully in our friendly against England, and I had no issue with people critiquing my performance, but to call for my head off the back of one game, after all the credit I'd accrued, was insulting.

As you've probably come to realize, I like a fight, and this actually worked in terms of awakening a bit of revolutionary spirit among the boys.

Training felt like a punishment that week. Gats had put three double days in the diary, which was more than we'd ever normally cram into a single week. After getting flogged on Monday and Tuesday, we asked Warby to appeal for Thursday's session to be reduced to a single. Warby didn't want to rock the boat, so Melon and I approached Gats, framing it as a group decision.

Before I'd got to the end of my first sentence, he cut me off with, 'I don't give a shit what the boys think, we're doing another double on Thursday and they can fucking well get on with it.'

Rob Howley sat me down later that day and asked if everything was OK with me off the field. Rob didn't usually pull me aside like that, and I was tetchy and defensive in response. Yes, I'd been getting lots of attention after the World Cup, I was getting married that summer, and my agent had been fielding calls from several interested clubs, but none of this was affecting my form or my outlook. I began to suspect the critical article might have influenced his thinking, and I was left wondering whether my place was again under threat.

By the time I left for New Zealand, I was feeling riled and angry, as though there was a ton of pressure on me before a ball had even been kicked.

The first Test was in the intimidating surroundings of Eden Park, a near-impenetrable fortress, where the All Blacks hadn't lost since 1994. Wales – as we had constantly been reminded – hadn't beaten them *anywhere* for sixty-three years, but memories of that abject performance against England were soon banished as we ripped into the world champions.

First-half tries from Toby Faletau and Rhys Webb saw us take a narrow lead into half-time, and we clung onto it until the final quarter, when New Zealand raised the tempo to warp speed and left us clutching at shadows. They scored three tries in the last twenty minutes, giving the final scoreline of 39–21 a lopsided look that we scarcely deserved.

Ultimately, it was the same depressing outcome. A brave stand that eventually crumbled in the face of a merciless black tide.

Three days later, we were in Hamilton to take on Warren Gatland's hometown team, the Chiefs. They were missing most of their internationals, but any illusions we might have had about it being a midweek romp were dispelled when Brad Weber sliced through for a try in the opening minutes. Local hero Stephen 'Beaver' Donald – he who'd been summoned from a fishing trip to play in the 2011 World Cup final – was absolutely sensational. He might have been getting on in years, and carrying a few extra pounds, but he made our international players look like amateurs. When he was subbed off, the whole stadium rose to give him a standing ovation.

I was in the stand with four or five of my non-playing teammates, and it would have been churlish not to stand up and join in, so there I was, watching Wales lose 40–7 to a provincial side, and clapping off the bloke who'd orchestrated the victory.

The second Test followed a similar pattern to the first, but with our resistance crumbling a little earlier this time, due largely to the presence of Beauden Barrett. He'd come on for Aaron Cruden just before half-time, and wrested control of the game, taunting us at every turn as he jinked, danced and weaved his way through our defence at will. He'd done something similar at the national stadium in Cardiff a few years earlier and we've long joked that we should all be cut into his lucrative endorsement deals, as it was those two games against Wales that launched him into the stratosphere.

With the series already gone, the third Test was a game too far, and we got thumped 46–6 down in Dunedin. If our glass had been half-full after the first two Tests, it had been well and truly drained by the third. We were outgunned, outmuscled and out-thought. The only upside was that the Welsh football team were in the middle of a dream run to the semi-finals of the Euros, so the glare of the media's lens was mercifully pointing elsewhere.

The aftermath was excessively boozy. Dunedin is a student town, and most of us were trawling the bars until the early hours before heading to a vineyard the next day on virtually zero hours' sleep. By the time we arrived at the airport, we were well oiled, and headed straight for the bar once we'd boarded the plane. We were having a whale of a time until a scuffle broke out in the corner.

Tom James, our fiery winger, and Shaun Edwards were squaring up to one another, shouting in one another's faces. Things escalated quickly, and it might well have come to blows if Luke Charteris hadn't lunged from his seat and got between them.

At six feet ten inches tall and nineteen stone, Charts is a natural peacemaker; he was always the level-headed one who kept his cool in a crisis. TJ, however, was incapable of keeping his feelings in check. He was annoyed about how little he'd played on tour, while Shaun had been quietly fuming about the amount of tries we'd conceded. Those frustrations, fuelled by booze and lack of sleep, had resulted in an explosion of anger. There were some well-dressed passengers not far away, sipping cocktails and looking aghast at what was unfolding. I remember thinking that if I'd paid five grand for a business-class flight from Auckland to Dubai, I'd probably be a little peeved if a bar brawl broke out at 12,000 feet.

Once Charts had managed to cool their tempers, our team manager Thumper took over, coaxing TJ back to his seat and offering him a glass of champagne. What TJ didn't know was that he'd dropped a sleeping tablet into it, and within ten minutes he was dead to the world, snoring like a congested rhino.

We didn't hear another peep out of him until we landed.

Within a month of the tour ending, I was a married man.

I'd decided to make an honest woman out of Alex a few years earlier after nearly ten years together. I'd proposed in the middle of a Six Nations campaign, having commissioned the local jeweller to make a ring based on a Tiffany design she'd seen in New York. Asking her father for his permission had been the most nerve-wracking element of the entire process. Paul's a retired GP who doesn't suffer fools, and I'd put so much energy into approaching that right, that I'd forgotten to plan what to actually say during the proposal. So when Alex returned home and found the ring on the windowsill surrounded by candles, the first words out of my mouth were, 'I don't know what I'm meant to do now.'

Seizing the initiative, she replied, 'I *think* you're meant to go down on one knee and ask me to marry you.'

Thankfully, our wedding was planned a little more thoroughly. We got married at St Gwynour Church in Penclawdd, the same place her parents had tied the knot decades earlier. It goes without saying that Alex looked incredible, and even I scrubbed up reasonably well.

Ben Whitehouse and my mate Gwilym were my best men, and

began their speech with an elaborately rehearsed parody of my kicking routine to the tune of 'Macarena'. It was an amazing day with my friends and family, and kick-started a much needed eight-week break from rugby, during which I switched off completely.

It was during the autumn of 2016 that Northampton first showed an interest in me. The WRU had been discussing bringing in a sixty-cap rule to discourage players from leaving Wales. It was a sensible enough policy in principle, but a little impractical in the real world. The concern was that the Welsh domestic game was suffering because rich French, English and Japanese clubs were dangling big-money contracts in front of our top players and luring them away.

The solution they devised would put the onus on the player: move if you like, but unless you've won sixty caps, you can forget about playing for Wales again. It was a risky move. If players chose to look after their futures over playing for their country, the national side could easily slide into the doldrums.

I was on forty-seven caps when the offer came through from Northampton. Martyn Phillips, now CEO of the Welsh Rugby Union, was in the training barn one evening, and I asked if I could have a word with him and Gats. The gist of my argument was that this offer was too good to pass up, and if I didn't accept it now, it might not come around again.

Gats was reluctant to give any ground, saying there were stacks of highly paid players knocking around in the Premiership and there would be other opportunities over the horizon.

It was difficult to mount an argument when you didn't know what case you were trying to make. The cap rule hadn't yet been brought in, and the 'wild card' policy was a fudge open to interpretation and manipulation. Gatland had a quota of 'wild card' players he was allowed to pick from outside Wales, but the number seemed to fluctuate from season to season. There wasn't any rhyme or reason to it, and it wasn't much of a deterrent to those considering a move abroad because most of them still expected to be picked anyway.

Gats wasn't willing to make any exceptions for me; he's more inclined to brinksmanship than diplomacy, telling me, 'If you move away, you'll have to rely on a wild card.'

Then, wearing that deadpan expression of his, he listed those players already in that category: Jamie Roberts, Jon 'Fox' Davies, Luke Charteris, Leigh Halfpenny and Taulupe Faletau.

Toby Faletau was one of Gatland's favourites, so he was a guaranteed pick, meaning if he only had two wild cards, I'd be battling it out with all the others for that one remaining spot. Essentially Gats was never going to give me the answer I wanted, which was, 'If you go, I'll still pick you.'

Further complicating matters was the fact I was on a dual contract with the Ospreys and Wales, and I'd had similar short shrift from head coach at the Ospreys, Steve Tandy. Steve had explained gruffly that letting me go would set a dangerous precedent.

I felt really deflated. The dilemma occupied my mind for months, and after a disappointing Six Nations campaign in 2017, in which we finished fifth, Alex and I took ourselves off for a break in the Celtic Manor Hotel near Newport. It was while we were enjoying lunch overlooking the Ryder Cup golf course that the phone rang.

It was Northampton again, with another offer.

What if I was to sign on the line now, but not start until the 2018–19 season? That way they'd avoid buying me out of my existing contract, and I'd technically have enough time to amass sixty caps before moving.

I hung up the phone and, over a bottle of velvety Malbec, Alex and I mapped out our future. The money on offer was significant, and by 2018 I would have been at the Ospreys for ten years. It seemed an appropriate time to move on. Between then and the start of the 2018–19 season, there were nine Wales matches in the diary: four in the autumn and five in the 2018 Six Nations.

By now, I'd reached fifty-six caps. Barring a catastrophic loss of form or a long-term injury, I had to back myself to pick up four more in that period, but the stark truth was that if I ruptured an ACL and was sidelined for twelve months, I'd be walking away from my Wales career.

Despite the degree of jeopardy involved, we decided it was too good an opportunity to pass up, and the longer we talked, the more convinced I became that we *had* to roll the dice.

I told my agent to get things moving; my decade-long association with the Ospreys was coming to an end. Other than a year up in Dundee with Dad's work, I'd lived my whole life on the Gower Peninsula. Northampton wasn't the most exotic of destinations, but it was time to spread my wings.

Within the week, Martyn Phillips had called me to confirm that the sixty-cap rule was being signed off by the board and would come into effect in October 2017. His message was, 'Keep your head down, keep playing, and you should be fine.' I prayed he was right.

One of the reasons I was keen to leave was to escape the increasingly claustrophobic goldfish bowl of Welsh rugby. I was sick of my every move being scrutinized, and my character being constantly put under the microscope. During that miserable Six Nations campaign in 2017, I reached a genuine low ebb after we'd lost to Scotland for the first time in ten years. We'd been beaten comfortably, but much of the focus post-match was on an incident that occurred in the fifty-first minute.

We were trailing 16–13 and were awarded a kickable penalty that would have tied the scores. Alun Wyn was captain and had pointed to the sticks, but there was a bit of confusion as to whether Leigh would go for goal or kick to the corner. A conversation took place between Al, Leigh and me, and I ended up kicking to the corner. So far, so innocuous. We lost the lineout and Scotland snuffed out the danger, going on to win the match 29–13.

After the match, the media spun this ludicrous story about me deliberately undermining Al and kicking to the corner against his wishes. Part of our conversation had been picked up on the ref's mic, and it was pored over by a salivating media pack as though it was one of the Watergate tapes. Newspaper columns and TV debates followed about whether I was some kind of malign, disruptive influence. It was all utter fabrication, and the truth was a lot more prosaic.

Al had told the ref we were going for the posts, assuming that Leigh would step up. Uncharacteristically, though, Leigh didn't fancy the kick. I then asked if we were going to the corner. A simple conversation, but people chose to infer from my tone that I was barging in and seizing control.

It was all bollocks.

I don't mind admitting that it really affected me. I'd become so used to batting away negative press that I thought I'd become impervious to criticism, but this one sneaked right through my defences.

For several days my nerves were on edge and – for the only time in my career – I genuinely considered jacking it all in. I sat in the kitchen one night venting to Alex for several hours, threatening to call time on my Wales career. Without sounding like a martyr, it felt like every time I went out there and put my body on the line for Wales, I'd end up being slagged off and belittled.

Alex could see how much it had got to me and said, 'Look if you genuinely want to walk away from Wales, we'll talk about it and work something out, but don't act on raw emotion. Sleep on it and see how you feel after the tournament.'

That's rare from Alex, who'd normally respond to my moaning with a curt, 'Come on, we've got holidays to pay for', but there was a difference in the mood this time and she recognized that. She's been my beacon of sanity during a tumultuous and emotionally draining career, and there's no way I could have had the success I've had without her by my side.

Once I'd calmed down and got things out of my system, Alex quietly mentioned that she had something to say. It occurred to me that I'd been speaking non-stop for the best part of an hour, and she'd barely got a word in.

'Um, I'm pregnant,' she announced, with a tentative smile. It was the best possible news, and those two words swiftly put everything else into perspective.

On the Monday, Howlers called Leigh, Jenks, Al and me into a meeting to discuss the incident, and told us we'd taken the wrong option, that we should have kicked for goal.

Leigh admitted that he'd turned it down and I hadn't wanted to undermine him by stepping in, so the obvious thing to do had been to kick to the corner. Al was saying he hadn't been sure what the on-field consensus was, and I was sitting there thinking, What am I *doing* in this meeting? Why were we even *having* a meeting? It felt as if the media had created an entirely false narrative and we were giving it credence by discussing it.

I desperately wanted to go on tour with the Lions that summer, and eighteen months earlier had felt as though I was in the box seat. Lions tours are all about teamwork and working together for the greater good, and here I was being portrayed as some power-hungry narcissist. My form had also dipped and there'd been a real clamour for Sam Davies to replace me in the Welsh team. Not for the first time, I genuinely worried that the negative press might scupper my chances.

12

LIVING WITH LIONS

I've spent many a long hour in my own company, endlessly kicking balls through rugby posts, and that's where I found myself on the afternoon of 19 April 2017, just over the road from the Ospreys training base in Llandarcy. Apart from the whine of traffic from the M4, it was an unremarkable day. Low clouds were scudding through leaden skies, and there was a threat of rain in the air. Time seemed to have slowed, and I was gripped by an uneasy feeling. At two o'clock, the Lions squad for New Zealand was being announced. After the crushing disappointment of four years ago, I was worried I was about to go through it all again.

My international form had dropped off during the 2017 Six Nations. An Owen Farrell-inspired England had won the tournament, and his club Saracens would go on to win the Heineken Cup that year. Ireland had come second, and Leinster too were on fire domestically and in Europe.

Just like four years earlier, Sexton and Farrell were the front-runners for the Lions tour, and I was very much in their slipstream. I had to be absolutely bossing games to be challenging for a place alongside those two, and I wasn't.

It's difficult to describe what loss of form looks like; often it's just an intangible feeling. Things just don't *feel* right. Movements that are usually fluid and natural become stilted and awkward. Decisions normally taken instinctively and in a split-second take longer. And then the mistakes happen. Those are the tangibles: dropped passes, shanked kicks, missed tackles. With every one of those came an imagined black mark next to my name in Gatland's Lions notebook. The loss to Scotland and its fallout felt like a killer blow, and the prolonged scrutiny only deepened the sense of gloom.

Would that cost me Lions selection? Had it irreparably tarnished my reputation?

All these dark thoughts explained why I'd taken myself off on my own when the squad was due to be announced. Several of the Ospreys boys were in the running and they'd hung around the clubhouse to watch it as a group. I couldn't think of anything worse.

I started to pack the balls back into my net just as the clouds darkened, and I wondered if that wasn't a portent of some kind. Taking a deep breath, I pulled out my phone and checked the messages. There were around fifty on there, which could mean one of two things.

My thumb hovered tentatively over the first, from Alex, and I tapped the screen.

'You've done it!' she'd written. 'Love you loads!'

A beaming smile spread rapidly across my face, and I mouthed a silent 'yes'.

I crossed back over the road towards Ospreys HQ, and the Sky Sports cameras were already there. I literally could not stop smiling. Alun Wyn, Tips and Rhys Webb had been selected as well, so there was a really good vibe around the place.

Other people have spoken of the elation they've felt being selected for the Lions. I felt differently, and not because I didn't crave it desperately, but because by then I'd been playing international rugby for nearly ten years, and I'd begun to wonder whether I'd end up one of those players who starred for their country, but never made it as a Lion. It would have left a glaring hole in my CV.

The 2013 snub had scarred me badly; in some ways, it also took the gloss off my 2017 selection. I'd felt so much pressure to get picked, and had agonized so much about my loss of form, that my reaction was more a sigh of relief than a jump for joy.

My parents did the jumping for joy on my behalf. Dad was waiting with a bottle of champagne when I got home, and Mum had already called to offer her hearty congratulations. She was over the moon, and outwardly far more excited than me.

The press was already accusing Warren of Welsh bias, and I was wondering aloud whether I'd made it because of familiarity over form, when Mum told me to stop questioning it and enjoy it for what it was. 'You're a bloody Lion!' she exclaimed excitedly, and I tried to park those negative feelings.

For those not steeped in rugby history, the Lions is a baffling concept. Every four years, you gather the best players from four different countries – who've been conditioned to dislike and mistrust one another – and meld them into a single team in a matter of weeks. You then travel to the other side of the globe and take on the toughest sides in world rugby. It shouldn't even come close to working, and yet it does. And the presence of around thirty thousand travelling fans is testament to how much it captures the imagination.

Our first squad get-together was at the elegant Syon Park Hotel near London. Al offered to drive myself and Tips up and my nerves started to jangle when we hit traffic on the M4. I was twitchy as hell, and couldn't believe it when they suggested stopping for a coffee at Reading services. The two of them were so relaxed, having done it all before, whereas I was like a tightly coiled spring, shuffling nervously in the back seat and worrying that we'd be late.

When we eventually arrived, the atmosphere was relaxed and informal. It felt really odd to be wandering around among men you'd normally be eyeballing in the tunnel, or sledging on the field, and realizing they were now your teammates.

England had the biggest representation with sixteen players in the squad, and Wales weren't far behind with twelve. The only Scots in the room were Stuart Hogg and Tommy Seymour, a cause for consternation among Scottish fans, who felt they'd deserved more.

I'd heard people talk of national stereotypes – the Welsh meek and withdrawn, the Irish garrulous and outgoing, the English posh and superior, and the Scots just happy to be there – but those proved to be nonsense, of course, and as soon as we gathered in the cavernous surrounds of Syon Park, any barriers melted away.

The English lads might have had a bit more swagger, but they'd just won the championship so that was probably justified. I fell into conversation with Stuart Hogg. I hadn't known how to take him before. On the field, he'd always seemed a little brash and cocky, pretentious even, and we'd had our fair share of run-ins. But now I saw him stripped of all that bravado, smiling and cracking gags, and I realized that the image I'd formed in my mind was a caricature based on his worst on-field qualities.

We were ushered into a massive kit room, where piles of gear had been neatly stacked for collection. That was the moment it sank in, as I picked up my Lions-branded kitbag with my initials embossed on it, turning what had felt nebulous into something real and tangible. There hadn't been a misprint; this wasn't a hoax: I was going on a Lions tour. And in addition to the symbolism of it all, the stash itself was on another level – brand new shiny Beats headphones with Lions logos on the sides, personalized Bluetooth speakers and all manner of other gizmos and treats. It was better than any Christmas stocking.

The Lions tour of 1997 is the one that arguably re-energized the concept. Not only was it a victorious tour, but the whole enterprise was captured on camera for the seminal *Living with Lions* film. Its warts-and-all approach, which captured the grit as well as the glamour, and was essential viewing for my generation. My first real Lions memories are of the 2001 tour to Australia, though – where Brian O'Driscoll carved his way into our consciousness, and Justin Harrison had the last laugh, stealing the crucial lineout that snuffed out the Lions' chances in the deciding Test.

I had to remind myself that I was now a part of that historic team, and had a chance to weave a few of my own threads into that century-old tapestry. I was under no illusions about the task ahead, though, having recently seen up close how formidable the All Blacks were on home soil. After beating Wales 3–0, they'd smashed their way through the southern hemisphere's Rugby Championship, winning all six matches, including two emasculating defeats of the Springboks. It was going to be a Herculean undertaking.

We were greeted by a traditional Māori welcome in Waitangi, where three hundred Māori warriors gathered to salute our arrival. It was an awesome spectacle, with the warriors in traditional dress performing a fearsome haka under cobalt blue skies, and the Bay of Islands glistening in the background. It was like nothing I'd ever experienced, and underlined the significance of what was to come.

Warren Gatland had hammered home the importance of respecting their culture, and ensuring we had something to offer in return. We'd formed a choir, led by Ken Owens, and in response we sang our tour songs: 'Calon Lân', 'My Highland Home', 'Fields of Athenry' and 'Jerusalem'. There'd been cynicism from some quarters about the choir, and a reluctance among some Welsh boys to sing 'Jerusalem', but at that moment we realized the significance of it all. It wouldn't have looked good if we'd just shuffled our feet and mumbled a few words of thanks in response. A hearty chorus of 'Calon Lân' wasn't as visually arresting as 300 Māori warriors wielding spears and performing a spine-tingling haka, but it certainly sounded pretty good.

The whole experience was a welcome tonic from the previous day, when we'd limped to victory against the New Zealand Provincial Barbarians up in Whangarei. We'd arrived in the country three days before and imagined the opener – against a largely amateur side that had a fruit picker and a sheep farmer in its ranks – would be a gentle loosener. It wasn't, and for a while there was a real fear we'd slip up. Warren's son Bryn was playing at fly half for the Barbarians, and he very nearly engineered the most disastrous of starts for his dad. Without taking anything away from Bryn and company, jet lag had been an obvious factor in our lacklustre performance, so while it was discouraging, it was easy enough to put it in perspective. After the game, we got an insight into just how tribal the New Zealand press can be. 'The Lions reached unimaginable levels of mediocrity' screamed one headline, and much of the criticism was directed at Warren. Most Lions are desperate to start the first game on tour but, given the way things panned out, I was glad to have missed that one.

My opportunity was to come against the Auckland Blues – then the lowest-ranked of the Super Rugby sides – as Gats made fifteen changes, but I lasted less than half the match after going off with a head knock. We were 10–5 up at that point, and I had to watch from the bench as the Blues conjured a last-minute victory. Johnny Sexton had replaced me at fly half, having started the first game, and if Gats was going to honour his pledge to give everyone a chance in the opening three matches, Owen Farrell would be starting the next against the Crusaders. The only thing I could cling to was the fact that Johnny seemed to be playing within himself. He'd looked a little lost against the Barbarians, and couldn't impose his usual authority on the Blues game. It was an interesting dynamic between the three of us. Ostensibly, we were very similar players – tactically astute, kicking fly halves who shared an indomitable competitive instinct. We got on fine superficially, but there was definitely a keen rivalry developing as we jockeyed for position during the tour.

As intense as I am, I'm able to push rugby to the side once I'm off the paddock, but I got the impression Owen couldn't. He was obsessive on a much greater scale, and I found it quite difficult to socialize with him. Johnny was equally driven, but better able to switch off.

My burgeoning friendship with Johnny got me access to the Irish inner sanctum, which happened to be the kit-man Rala's hotel room. Rala O'Reilly was a living legend in Irish circles; an absolute gentleman with a gift for putting people at ease. Rala always had the best room in the hotel, having persuaded the management he needed a luxury suite with a kitchen to chuck all the kit in. All the Irish boys would congregate there, drinking Rala's tea, stealing his biscuits and generally abusing his hospitality. They'd repay his generosity by 'affectionately' trashing his room the night before every game. I witnessed one such incident, instigated by the normally earnest Peter O'Mahony, who encouraged us to lob spare kit all over the floor, empty the cutlery drawers, and squirt shower gel over every available surface. Rala had the patience of a saint and would accept such behaviour as a 'good bit of craic', while stoically cleaning it all up the next day.

The Crusaders had a strong claim to be the best club side in the world. They were the dominant team in Super Rugby, and were accustomed to burying opposition sides under an avalanche of points. The match was likely to be the toughest on tour behind the Tests, and Gats had picked his strongest side to try to salvage some pride.

As predicted, Faz started at 10, with Johnny on the bench. What followed was a serious statement of intent that completely altered New Zealand's perception of the Lions. Against a Crusaders side littered with All Blacks, we delivered a performance of controlled fury, completely shutting out a side that was so used to running riot. The final score of 12–3 was a testament to our parsimonious defence. They'd been scoring at an average of thirty-seven points a game prior to that. Our defence coach, Andy Farrell, was beyond delighted, claiming afterwards that, 'They couldn't fucking breathe, boys. They got absolutely schooled on how to play at this level.'

We later learned that three points was the lowest score they'd ever registered in their history. Perhaps we weren't such a hapless rabble after all.

If that win was a massive stride forwards, we suffered another misstep against the Highlanders, surrendering a 22–13 lead to succumb 23–22. I'd been picked for that one, and a narrative had started to develop that the midweek team was being exposed, while the Saturday team was crystallizing into the Test side.

It was immensely frustrating, as I wasn't able to make a compelling case for selection. My anger boiled over during the fraught final quarter, when I unleashed a tirade of abuse in the direction of my roommate, Justin Tipuric.

We'd conceded a penalty and, seeing Tips's distinctive blue scrum cap nearby, I screamed blue murder at him. His expression darkened as he yelled back, 'It wasn't me, you prick.'

'Bollocks,' I replied, 'sort it out!'

God knows what the opposition were thinking as he advanced towards me, jabbing his finger in my chest and saying, comically, 'I'll see you back in the room tonight.'

I felt that I'd played really well in that game, but the stark reality was that we'd lost the two games I'd been involved in.

The schedule had been really punishing both emotionally and physically. We'd been made to fulfil all kinds of sponsors' commitments – visiting schools in remote areas, driving for hundreds of miles cooped up in the backs of Land Rovers – and had barely had any time to switch off. I feared that this once-in-a-lifetime opportunity was disappearing before my eyes.

Owen strained his thigh in training before the 'unofficial fourth Test' against the Māori All Blacks, which saw me elevated to the bench. You never wish ill on your teammates, but this was a chance to do something as part of the Saturday squad.

I got on for a fifteen-minute cameo, but only once the game was safely won, and Johnny Sexton had completely recovered his mojo. If Johnny had delivered another under-par performance, it could have been the sliding doors moment I'd been waiting for, but he was excellent that night. With his Irish half-back partner Conor Murray inside him, he'd stamped his authority on the game and guided the Lions to an emphatic 32–10 victory. Everything that had been absent from his game to that point had returned in spades.

We might not have been matching the Kiwi sides for guile

and ingenuity, but we'd found a way to suffocate them. This was the template we'd need to follow if we were to prevail in the Test series.

We'd just finished a particularly rousing rendition of 'Jerusalem' after the game, when I looked at my phone to see I'd missed fifteen calls from Alex. Panicking, I called her straight away. We were having a hot tub delivered, and they'd been unable to fit it around the side of the house, so they'd been trying to persuade Alex to hire a crane at great expense to lift it over the garage. I was 12,000 miles from home, in my muddy kit, on top of the world after my first Lions win, and there I was in the corner of the changing room trying to haggle with an impatient builder over the price of a crane. That pretty much wiped out my match fee there and then. First world problems.

Speaking of problems, there was an almighty one brewing in camp. In a bid to preserve his front-line players, Gats had parachuted in six reinforcements in an unfortunate echo of what he'd done in Australia four years earlier. The move went down like a turd in the punch bowl in certain quarters. Cory Hill, Gareth Davies, Kristian Dacey and Tomas Francis were already in New Zealand for a Welsh tour match against Tonga, and Alan Dell and Finn Russell were just across the Tasman in Australia. With the exception of Franny and Gareth 'Cawdor' Davies, these players weren't the next cabs off the rank, so to speak. They'd essentially been picked as cannon fodder because they were closer geographically than the Irish or English players who were touring South Africa and Argentina respectively.

It developed into a full-blown PR disaster, with the All Blacks coach Steve Hansen and the England coach Eddie Jones weighing in, piling more pressure on an already beleaguered Warren Gatland. Eddie objected to the fact that more worthy candidates – like Joe Launchbury and Dylan Hartley – had been overlooked simply because they were further away. The 'Geography Six' debacle became another brickbat for the Kiwis to hurl at Gats, who doubled down angrily, claiming he was here to win a Test series and nothing else mattered.

I did my best to welcome the new players into the fold, but they got a pretty frosty reception elsewhere. The England props Joe Marler and Dan Cole – both of whom I had a lot of time for – were the most aggrieved. It was a combination of sympathy for their overlooked English colleagues in Argentina, and anger because they'd not made it into the Test reckoning themselves. They clearly thought the arrival of the Geography Six had cheapened the whole experience.

Until then I'd got on well with Joe; his eccentricity and wacky sense of humour made him a great tourist, and he was constantly dropping amusing videos into the WhatsApp group. He'd rinse the security guards he claimed were 'stealing a living', surreptitiously filming them when they were at their most idle – sucking lollies, staring into space, or casually doing weights in the gym.

The Six did their best to make light of the situation when they were forced to stand up in front of the squad and introduce themselves. Gareth's dad owns a car dealership with branches all over West Wales – Cawdor Cars, hence his nickname – and he used his intro as a mock sales pitch, handing out business cards and promising cut-price deals. Franny's was based on his chubby period playing for London Scottish, and consisted mainly of slides of him eating cake. Cory absolutely nailed his, putting up a fake Gullivers Sports Travel poster advertising supporters' tours for the Lions trip to South Africa.

'I've just told Gats I've booked onto this one,' he said, 'so I'll be looking to do this again in four years' time.'

He won over most of the doubters with that, though there were still a few stony faces at the back.

There were two more midweek games left against the Chiefs and the Hurricanes, two of the best provincial sides in New Zealand. A bit of chat started going around the so-called 'Midweek Veg' that they were going to refuse to be subbed off during those games. They'd rather twice play the full eighty than see a member of the Geography Six run on.

Ironically, it was a Joe Marler yellow card that gave Alan Dell his chance against the Chiefs, and he embraced it, driving them backwards convincingly during his first scrum. Other than that, the Geography Six remained rooted to the bench all night, with Alun Wyn coming on at one stage ahead of Cory Hill – so much for preserving our Test players.

Marler had virtually cracked his head open once he returned to the field, and had to be heavily bandaged, but he refused point-blank to leave the fray. It was obvious that the coaches had been stung by the backlash and were leaving the new guys out of it, making them feel even more redundant. Had there not been such an outcry, I'm sure they'd have unloaded the bench on sixty minutes, because by then we were coasting to victory.

From a personal perspective, we'd finally won a game I'd started in, and I'd played seriously well in the process. Gats had claimed it was a final audition for the first Test, but I'm not sure how many people truly believed him. I'd had a bout of suspected shingles during the build-up and had slept through most of the previous day, but still managed to summon the energy to perform, nailing all my kicks in a 34–6 victory.

Despite the tension surrounding the Six, we played with a real sense of togetherness, and were clapped back in enthusiastically by the Saturday side. Gats congratulated us all on a job well done and reminded us that they hadn't picked the Test team yet.

It went quiet for a moment as his words sank in, before James Haskell cleared his throat and yelled, 'So you're saying there's a chance?!'

I didn't think there was a chance for me. Playing on a Tuesday and backing it up on a Saturday is tough, but Gats was true to his word and picked Elliot Daly and Liam Williams in the Test side, both of whom had played against the Chiefs. Sanj had played the full eighty, and would normally do the bare minimum when it came to looking after himself, but in those five days, he did every form of recovery imaginable: ice baths, saunas, compression socks, deep-tissue massage, the lot.

While those selections raised eyebrows, the one that generated all the headlines was Warby's omission from the starting XV. Peter O'Mahony had been given the captaincy, relegating Sam to the bench. While it filled reams of newspaper pages, it wasn't a huge surprise to us. Pete had led really well in the Māori All Blacks game, and had been a commanding presence on tour, whereas Warby had largely been a peripheral figure. He wasn't fully fit or producing the types of performances we were accustomed to, and he was humble enough to admit that. As for me, my instincts were right: Faz was picked to start, with Johnny on the bench.

The match followed a depressingly familiar pattern; we were competitive for sixty minutes, before the All Blacks accelerated away in the final quarter. Watching from the stand, I noted that New Zealand had subtly altered their tactics, eschewing the dinks and chips Beauden Barrett had become renowned for, and choosing instead to batter around the fringes. They kept things suffocatingly tight and strangled the life out of us. The fact we scored one of the greatest tries in Lions history – a length-of-the-field effort started by Sanj and finished by Seán O'Brien – was of scant consolation.

The final score of 30–15 might have flattered the All Blacks, but it was a sobering reminder of the scale of the challenge. New Zealand had now gone forty-seven Test matches unbeaten on home soil.

The local press was gleeful in the aftermath, mocking Gatland openly and claiming he'd blown it. The *New Zealand Herald* ran a front-page cartoon, depicting him as a red-nosed clown. There was a real nastiness to it, and it stuck in his craw big time, as did the coverage surrounding the Provincial Barbarians game his son had played in. He'd mentioned beforehand that he'd warned Bryn he'd have to make a few tackles, and the headline in the following day's *New Zealand Herald* had been, 'Gatland to target

Barbarians' weakest link – his son.' I'm sure that deep down Gats would have been craving some kind of approval from his own people. This was provocative and unnecessary.

The last midweek game of the tour was against the Hurricanes, five days before the second Test. Sadly, the furore surrounding the Geography Six reared its head again and cost us victory. I'd converted two tries and knocked over four penalties as we built what seemed an unassailable 31–17 lead, but once again, players were refusing to be subbed off.

At one point Joe Marler was arguing loudly with our forwards coach, Graham Rowntree, while he was still on the pitch. He'd had his ankle strapped by then, and Dan Cole was clearly blowing out of his backside, but neither would budge. The only reason Finn Russell got on was because I'd had to leave the field for a Head Injury Assessment. It was farcical. We'd clearly lost a bit of energy and momentum in the final quarter, but our refusal to use the bench allowed the Hurricanes to roar back and salvage a draw.

In the final reckoning, four of the Six – Franny, Gareth Davies, Cory Hill and Kristian Dacey – didn't get a single minute of game time. Russell and Dell only got on for medical reasons, and Gats admitted that his decision to keep them sidelined had been influenced by the backlash the whole saga had generated. I felt desperately sorry for the Welsh boys, who left after ten days having experienced nothing but misery and opprobrium through no fault of their own. They didn't consider themselves Lions and would rather not have bothered.

The team for the second Test was named two days later, with Gats making three changes. Feeling that we'd lacked a creative spark in the first Test, he brought Johnny Sexton in at 10, and shifted Faz to 12. Having two 10s in the starting line-up wiped out any slim hopes I'd had for a bench spot.

The other changes saw Warby return to captain the side, and Maro Itoje slotting into the second row. The guys they replaced – Peter O'Mahony and George Kruis – were dropped from the twenty-three altogether. It was a huge fall from grace for them, and they were drafted straight into the Midweek Veg, who'd planned a massive bender that night.

Kruiser's socially awkward manner had already marked him out as an oddball on tour, and his brutal axing was greeted not with sympathy but hilarity by the Veg, who ripped the piss out of him relentlessly.

At the start of the tour when we'd first assembled on the bus, we were unsure whether everyone was on board, and Kruiser had stood up and earnestly suggested we all shout out our name and Lions numbers. Such an eminently sensible suggestion was greeted by a chorus of mocking jeers. It set the tone for his treatment on tour.

James Haskell, it won't surprise you to learn, was the unofficial leader of the Midweek Veg. If the melding of four nations is all about confronting prejudice and confounding expectations, Hask probably summed up the Lions' spirit more than anyone else.

I'd been with Tips watching Sky Sports News when we heard of his call-up and we'd both rolled our eyes in despair. I genuinely thought I'd hate him. He'd always projected this image as a loud-mouthed English posh boy who loved the sound of his own voice. The rest of the Celts shared our concerns, despite the English boys insisting we were going to love him.

As it turned out, they were absolutely right. He *is* a loud-mouthed English posh boy who loves the sound of his own voice, but he's also a relentlessly upbeat ball of energy who gets on with everyone. On long tours, guys like that are worth their weight in gold. Never have my initial perceptions of someone turned out to be so spectacularly wrong.

Hask had arranged for us to go to a 'gourmet Italian restaurant' to kick off our night out, so we were a bit perturbed to discover it was essentially a shed in some guy's back garden. Haskell and Rory Best were leading the charge. I've never seen a man drink like Best. You'd take one sip from your beer, and he'd already be ordering the next round. He could comfortably put away twenty bottles in a session.

Haskell introduced a drinking game where you all had to stand up and perform an action; the Paul Pogba 'dab' dance, the Usain Bolt 'lightning bolt' – or whatever took your fancy. The next person had to copy that and add one of their own, and so on until you were trying to memorize around ten moves and perform them in sequence. If you got it wrong, you had to finish your bottle in one glug. Things got predictably messy. At one point I had six on the go trying to keep up.

Eventually the bill arrived, and it was getting on for two grand for around ten of us. Rory whipped the receipt from the tray and announced authoritatively, albeit with a slight slur, that it would be decided by 'credit card roulette'. In other words, everyone puts their credit card in a bowl, and they're withdrawn one by one, until there's only one left, and that unfortunate soul has to pay for everyone.

After ten interminable minutes, it came down to the last two: George Kruis and Joe Marler.

Marler turned to Kruiser and said, 'Mate, you've had a shit week. You've gone from being a rock star and starting in the first Test, to drinking in someone's shed with us muppets. I'm happy to split it with you.'

It was a generous enough offer, but Kruis declined, saying he was backing himself. Inevitably, he lost, and the worst week in his professional career came to a costly end.

We of the Midweek Veg might have known we were out of contention for the second Test, but we still had a role to play, and ripped into the Test team in training that week. Our brief was to play like the All Blacks, to execute plays we thought they'd run and do our best to break down the first XV. That was the week the real Sexton re-emerged. His swagger had returned, and several of the boys were on the receiving end of his famous expletive-ridden tirades.

Rhys Webb was a target during one session, having several strips torn off him when he mis-read the play. Faz was equally vocal, reacting furiously to every dropped ball. At the opposite end of the scale stood Courtney Lawes, who'd watch Farrell's tantrums with a bemused smile, muttering, 'Chill out, Faz', before melting someone with one of his trademark bulldozer tackles.

The second Test was played out in horrendous conditions, with squally wind and rain sweeping around Wellington's 'Cake Tin' Stadium. The defining moment came in the twenty-fourth minute, when their talisman, Sonny Bill Williams, was sent off for leading with his shoulder in a sickening collision with Anthony Watson. It was the first time an All Black had seen red on New Zealand soil and was clearly a crushing blow, but they dug in and built an 18–9 lead regardless.

Then the magic happened. Refusing to buckle amid the deluge, we fought back and scored twice through Taulupe Faletau and Conor Murray, levelling things up at 21–21. With four minutes left, Faz showed balls of steel to bang over the winning penalty, consigning New Zealand to their first home defeat in forty-seven Tests and whipping off their cloak of invincibility in the process. The red card was a huge factor, but like we'd done against the Crusaders, we'd neutered a side renowned for shredding opposition defences. It had been three long years since New Zealand had been held try-less.

Gats was on combative form in the post-match presser, repeatedly referencing the negative press, insisting it had been a galvanizing force and declaring wryly that he was a 'happy clown' that night.

Four years earlier, during the Lions tour to Australia, Warren had received a barrage of criticism for taking his squad to the beachside resort of Noosa the week before the final Test. It had worked though, because a refreshed Lions side had battered the Wallabies in the decider. Looking to repeat the formula, we had a few days in Queenstown, a magical otherworldly place on the South Island, nestled in spectacular Alpine scenery. It's the self-styled adventure sports capital of the world, and the perfect place to open the release valve and relax.

A number of players had gone 'off tour' by this point, knowing they had no meaningful involvement left and were determined to have a good blowout before returning home. Several of the boys did a bungee jump, and Kruiser's reputation took a further nose-dive when he stood suspended 100 metres above the Kawarau River, gripped by fear and refusing to move. The poor bloke was eventually pushed off after fifteen minutes, and was rinsed about it for the rest of the trip. I took what I thought was the tamer option of a jet boat ride, until someone told me afterwards that a tourist had been decapitated years earlier while poking their head out for a better view.

Watching that third Test was really hard. As much as I was yearning for the boys to claim a historic victory, I also desperately wanted to be out on the field. I'd enjoyed the tour, and played well, but I felt a little cut off, like I had the ticket, but not the VIP wristband. At the final, critical moment, when everything was on the line, I was sitting in the stands wearing a suit.

Rory Best was in a similar position, but Gats asked him to deliver a team talk to the squad about the so-called Black-lash that was coming. The previous year, Ireland had beaten the All Blacks in Chicago for the first time in their history. A week later, back in Dublin, they were smashed by the same team who tore into them with a vengeful rage. Besty warned the Lions to brace themselves for a similar experience, and it duly arrived.

You could almost hear the bones crack and see the blood spill from up in the stands as the wounded All Blacks came out in full berserker mode. Both try lines remained intact, but the All Blacks built up a 12–6 half-time lead. It was a brutal Test match, and at one point it looked like a war zone down there. Seán O'Brien's arm was dangling limply from its socket, Johnny Sexton's heavily strapped ankle looked bulbous and deformed, and Alun Wyn's swollen forehead was bleeding profusely.

Both sides were taking chunks out of each other, pausing hostilities only when penalties were awarded. An absolute howitzer from Elliot Daly brought us level at 12–12, and it was down to Faz to tie the scores again at 15–15 with three minutes to go. This was sporting theatre at its very best – intense, nerve-shredding drama that dared you to look away.

But that's what we all wanted to do seconds after the restart when a shrill blast of the whistle signalled a penalty to New Zealand. Liam Williams had reached for the ball and knocked it into Ken Owens who'd strayed offside. Ken instinctively caught the ball, before panicking and dropping it, raising his arms in the air and pleading clemency. But the look on his face said it all. According to the laws, it was a penalty, and he knew it.

It surely couldn't end like this. Warby, who'd always been unfailingly polite with referees, cut through the mayhem, and asked Romain Poite to check the replay. He later admitted that he didn't even know what he was asking him to check, but it worked like a Jedi mind trick. After reviewing the footage, Poite – realizing this one decision would decide the outcome of the series – downgraded the penalty to a scrum.

I'm not a rugby scholar and I don't know the laws inside out, but it *looked* like a penalty, and the New Zealand captain, Kieran Read, was furious.

I'm obviously biased, but ultimately I thought it was the right decision for the integrity of the series. To lose on a technical offence would have been horrendous, and Romain realized that Ken's faux pas was accidental rather than deliberate.

It was the strangest end to a Test series imaginable. Confusion reigned for several minutes among the fans and the watching millions as to whether there'd be extra time, but ultimately that was it. It was all over.

In a thunderous, epic three-match series, during which we'd led for just three minutes across three games, we'd ended with a share of the spoils. The celebratory photos were utterly unique, as Warby and Read hoisted the trophy together, while the players all mixed in as one; a battered and exhausted troop of warriors clad in red and black.

Warren had the last laugh, arriving for the press conference wearing a red nose. A drawn series wasn't a victory, but it was vindication for a proud Kiwi who'd been unfairly pilloried during the seven weeks he'd spent in his home country.

Personally though, I felt like it was unfinished business. I'd been part of the expedition, but I hadn't planted my flag at the top of the mountain. Until I played in a Test match, I couldn't consider myself a proper Lion.

Gats and Andy Farrell both told me they'd been impressed with my attitude, praising me publicly for remaining 100 per cent committed even when it was obvious I was out of the reckoning for the Tests.

My own professional pride ensured that was the case, but it's also true that Gats was my national coach, and I couldn't afford to drop my standards. Those from the other nations who'd been consigned to the Midweek Veg, like Joe Marler, were more inclined to go 'off tour' because their relationship with Gats wouldn't endure beyond the trip. That's not a criticism, as I felt for them, but it's hard to maintain that laser focus when you're receding from the picture and unable to change the coaches' minds.

While I'd been away, Alex had been house-hunting in Northamptonshire, and had bought a place without me even seeing it. So, the day I arrived home – at 7 a.m. and jet-lagged up to my eyeballs – Mum and I drove up for me to have a first look, and to find out what I'd spent my wages on.

After seven weeks away, it was lovely to spend six hours in Mum's company, though we did talk incessantly about rugby. Mum has always been my biggest supporter; she implicitly understood how that tour was simultaneously an amazing honour and a massive disappointment.

My Lions business was very much unfinished.

13

SAINTS, PARENTHOOD AND PASTURES NEW

The autumn internationals in 2017 were loaded with jeopardy. With my Northampton contract signed and sealed, I had to play in all of them to reach the magic total of sixty caps. Any notion that the policy was toothless was dismissed when Rhys Webb became its first high-profile victim. He'd signed a contract with Toulon and was told that by doing so, he'd sacrificed his Wales career. He'd only won twenty-eight caps, but couldn't resist the big money on offer in the south of France. There was a murky backdrop to it all – a suggestion he'd been privately assured he'd be OK – but if such a promise was indeed made, it turned out to be a hollow one. It was clear that I could take nothing for granted.

The first game was against Australia on 11 November. Alex was due to give birth to our first child on 29 October. A week after the due date, he'd yet to make an appearance and I was already in the Wales camp. Nothing was more important to me than the birth, but there was a situation unfolding in which I might have to choose between being with Alex or playing against Australia. My international career might depend on it.

It seemed surreal that it had come to this. Thankfully, Alex went into labour on the Monday, six days before the match. I drove her to Singleton Hospital with her mother, Mandy, at seven in the morning. With an overwhelming sense of guilt, I told her I had to head to training, thinking that missing even one session could preclude me from selection. She was amazing and told me to go.

You can imagine how I felt during that journey, driving away from my pregnant wife to essentially kick a ball around for an hour or two. It seemed so trivial, but that session had become so significant in my mind. I couldn't give Gats *any* reason to not pick me.

I might have been physically present, but my mind was back at the hospital, and I broke the speed limit to get back there the minute the session was over. Alex had had an epidural and was surprisingly relaxed.

James arrived just before midnight and, like any parent will tell you, it was the most wondrous and life-changing experience you can possibly imagine. In that moment, nothing else mattered, and the three of us stayed in hospital overnight, revelling in that bliss that accompanies the arrival of a new life.

Alex's mum Mandy arrived at the crack of dawn, enraptured by the sight of her first grandchild, and she and Alex ordered me out to make that day's training session – my first as a father.

It felt unreal. I was exhausted, emotional and sleep-deprived, but simultaneously floating on air. I'd been up all night, staring at this beautiful, fragile little thing, terrified I was going to break him.

By the time I arrived back on the Tuesday, my mum and sister were there, and Mum was holding James in her arms, declaring tearily that she didn't think she'd ever experience love in that way again.

Alex stayed in hospital for a week, so I was shuttling back and forth to the Vale, showering in the health club, and functioning on pure adrenaline.

We lost again to Australia – our thirteenth defeat in a row to them – but however bad it sounds, I didn't really care. My motivations that autumn were selfish, and reaching sixty caps was my main priority. Knowing I had a son back home made a loss to the Wallabies seem far less important.

It was a way of thinking that felt entirely alien to me, and it came with a big dollop of guilt. I didn't want to be that person who's not bothered about winning or losing. Rugby's a team sport, and you don't want to let your comrades down. Had I been a tennis player or a golfer, I'd have just taken the tournament off, but you don't have that luxury as a rugby player.

By the end of the autumn, I'd played in all four Tests, which culminated in another victory over South Africa. I ended that match with a concussion, but also consumed by a huge sense of relief that I had finally reached the magic figure of sixty caps.

It was a good job I had, because I suffered a bad shoulder tear in the lead-up to the Six Nations in early 2018, and ended up playing in only two of the five games. The first was against Ireland, where my temperament was once again called into question. I was tackled in the air while taking a high ball, and complained to the ref while the tackle was still being made. He didn't blow his whistle, the ball went loose, and they shifted it wide and scored. We lost by ten points, so it wasn't a defining score, but a disproportionate amount of attention was paid to my conduct during the fevered post-match analysis. Martyn Williams told the BBC's *Scrum V* programme that I needed to stop moaning to referees, and reckoned my teammates needed to start grabbing me by the scruff of the neck and pulling me aside.

During my one-on-one kicking review with Jenks, he paused on that incident and said, 'Look, it's one hundred per cent a penalty, but you've just got to get on with it, you can't react like that.' I knew he was right, but I do get pissed off with referees because I don't feel they are held to account in the same way players are.

All the talk afterwards was about my reaction rather than Glen Jackson having missed the offence. It was another easy headline for the tabloids; more clickbait, more grist to the mill.

I called Mum on my way home to vent, and she said, 'Forget it; you've got a son waiting here who absolutely adores you, so come home and give him a big hug.' It was a timely reminder of what was important in my life. The knowledge that I'm building a future for my family is what motivates me now, and I make no apology for that. When I retire, I'll miss the matchday experience, and the camaraderie, but not the rugby itself, or the constant character assassinations. The number 10 shirt made me fall in love with the sport, but it's also made me resentful of it. At the end of the day, the sport doesn't love you back.

When I cross the white line, I'm performing. Not in a contrived way, but I'm channelling a different part of myself. It's fanciful to suggest – as many have – that I'm switching from Dr Jekyll to Mr Hyde. It's still me – just a distilled, ferociously competitive and confrontational version of myself. I never watch a match back and feel like I don't recognize that guy on the field; it's just an extension of who I am. Ask those who know me well what I'm like and they'll hopefully tell you I'm polite, thoughtful and considerate. Ask a bunch of rugby fans the same question, and they'll probably say I'm arrogant, gobby and impulsive. They're only seeing the rugby player, not the person.

Mum once told me I was incapable of hiding my feelings, and it's true I'm an open book. In the real world, though, I'm able to contain those frustrations, whereas in the emotionally charged arena of Test rugby I allow them to spill out. I *need* to be at a certain emotional level to play well.

People have told me to chill out before games, to channel my inner calm, but it doesn't work for me; I have to invest everything – mentally, emotionally and physically – into it. I can't flick in and out like some can. The desire to win trumps everything. I'm not like Justin Tipuric, who spends those pre-game hours soaking in a deep bath, or Taulupe Faletau, who can turn up his emotional dial as and when required. Level one is zen mystic, level ten is Test-match animal. Because I'm less talented than them, I have to rely on emotional anger to carry me through. I can only deliver Test-quality performances when I'm on full blast.

I'm also a perfectionist, which is difficult in a team sport when so many things are beyond your control: the weather, the referee, the performance of your teammates. I may nail every kick, fizz every pass, and even score a try, but if I miss a tackle or drop a ball, it colours everything else. I've got better at accepting these things over the years, but I still strive for perfection every time I take to the pitch.

Most coaches I've worked with have recognized that my innate competitive streak is an essential part of who I am, and to dilute it would be to dilute my effectiveness as a player.

Wales toured Argentina in the summer of 2018, and I was among a number of players rested. I didn't want to be – the neurotic in me worried that a winning team might replace the established order – but Rob Howley assured me that it was part of a concerted plan to build more depth. After the New Zealand tour and our injury-ravaged experience in the World Cup, Martyn Phillips of the WRU and Warren Gatland had identified the need for a deeper talent pool.

Eleven new caps had been awarded on the South Seas tour the previous summer, and they all kicked on during the South American trip. Argentina is a fiendishly difficult place to go and play, especially since they've joined the Rugby Championship competition, so to go into the unknown with a group of inexperienced players and come away with a 2–0 series win was seriously impressive.

We all owed them a debt of gratitude, because there was a clause in our contracts that increased our match fees if we got to fourth or above in the world rankings. Those wins in San Juan and Santa Fe achieved that so, come the autumn, we were all earning £10,000 a game, instead of the usual £8,000.

Martyn Phillips deserves a lot of credit for that. Unlike some CEOs, who act like glorified accountants, he had a wider vision, realizing you had to speculate to accumulate. He understood the power of incentives and did everything he could to look after the players. That's not to say he was a walkover; everything he did came from a shrewd business perspective, but he was always transparent and understood that the success we provided on the field helped the business to flourish.

The men's international team is the biggest source of revenue – from multimillion-pound TV deals, to sold-out stadiums – and he understood that a winning side meant more money for the entire game. It's no coincidence that his stewardship coincided with some of our best years.

My enforced rest over the summer meant I was fully refreshed at the start of the new season, and ready to grasp the nettle at my new club. I hadn't really wanted to move to Northampton when they first expressed an interest, but once I'd made the commitment, I realized it was absolutely the right thing to do.

There was one minor hitch to address, though. When I'd signed for them, Jim Mallinder had been the director of rugby. By the time I'd arrived, he'd been sacked and replaced by Chris Boyd. I was nervous, concerned that he wasn't the guy who had wanted me, but those fears were allayed during our first meeting, where we spent more than two hours chatting in the Director's Lounge at Franklin's Gardens. I liked Chris immediately. He had an easy-going charm, coupled with a thoughtful, considered intelligence. And having recently coached the Hurricanes to the Super Rugby title, he had an impressive pedigree.

His fly half there had been Beauden Barrett, and I spent much of those two hours picking his brains about Beauden's routine and attitude, his strengths and weaknesses. Part of me was worried that Boyd would have preferred a Beauden-type player, but what he said put me completely at ease.

He explained that 'Beaudie' was only as good as his inside centre, because he relied on his 'second five-eighth' – as they call them in New Zealand – feeding him information. He'd perform at a much higher level with someone like Ryan Crotty outside him because Crotty acted as his eyes and ears.

Fly halves have to be ruck-focused, because that's where the ball is, but while you're looking at the ruck, the picture can quickly change out wide or in the backfield. That's where a communicator at 12 can make all the difference. They have those extra few seconds to scan and assess things, and if they keep you abreast, you're in a position to take advantage when the ball emerges.

Chris explained that he wanted to create that axis at the Saints, and pair me with a ball-playing centre like Rory Hutchinson. It was music to my ears. There is nothing worse for a fly half than a centre who doesn't talk. As Chris rightly prophesized, that partnership with Rory would become a key part of our success at Northampton. Rory would talk constantly. If we were in our own half and needed to kick for territory, he'd tell me what my options were before I even looked up. Those visual cues buy you vital seconds and can be the difference between cutting the line or being swallowed up.

There might be less than two hundred miles between Swansea and Northampton, but culturally it was an entirely different experience. The English boys were a different breed. However experienced I might have been, I was still the new kid having to feel his way in, and tune in to a different wavelength.

The first thing I noticed was that they *loved* the gym. Weights sessions would be long, sweaty affairs, and some of the plates attached to groaning barbells would have seriously big numbers on them.

Welsh players often get unfairly branded as gym monkeys, more comfortable chucking tin than honing skills but, believe me, the English boys are gym *gorillas*. I hate the tedious monotony of the gym, and had reached a point at the Ospreys where I'd coast through sessions at around 80 per cent, seeing them as a necessary evil rather than a vital part of my prep. There was no such luxury at Northampton, where every session was monitored and scored.

It took a bit of adjustment on my part.

The changing room was referred to as the Monopoly board, with the bigger, more capacious lockers labelled as 'Mayfair' and 'Park Lane', whereas the rusty, shoe-box-sized ones were 'Old Kent Road' and 'Whitechapel Road'.

The stars like Luther Burrell, Dylan Hartley and Courtney Lawes claimed the former, while the latter were reserved for the academy boys.

I'd been petrified driving into training that first day, worried about how I'd be received. I thought I might have been labelled a highly paid mercenary and given the cold shoulder.

As I was getting out of the car, Dylan Hartley wandered by carrying a portable safe, and I fell into step alongside him. It was an absolute gift to the rest of the boys, who immediately started laying into me: 'Here he is, Europe's highest-paid player, and he needs a safe to carry his wages around with him!'

It was the perfect ice-breaker.

Luther Burrell and Harry Mallinder took me under their wing and gave me the tour, introducing me to everyone. I was so keen to make an impression and stopped to chat to everyone.

After about fifteen minutes, Luther turned to me and said, 'Mate, will you stop saying, "Hi, I'm Dan." Everyone *knows* who you are!'

As time went on, I got really friendly with some of the younger lads, and they later told me that there'd been a big split in the camp between them and the senior players. I'd inadvertently bridged that divide, not through my skills as a diplomat, but because I was so desperate to make friends!

My arrival coincided with the inaugural Blakiston Challenge, named after Freddie Blakiston, the legendary Northampton and England player who fought in the First World War. It's a horrendous fitness drill that has since become a vital part of Northampton's pre-season regimen – something the players dread.

It was a boiling hot day, and it remains one of the most gruelling tests I've ever done. Starting with a 2.5-kilometre run, it morphed into a series of shuttles while carrying 20-kilogram sandbags. The final stretch was another 2.5-kilometre run, this time up the steep track to Castle Ashby. It had nothing to do with rugby, and everything to do with physical and mental endurance.

Given how eager I was to impress, I resolved to win the whole thing.

Dylan Hartley sprang out of the blocks, setting off at an explosive pace. The academy boys and some of the more supple youngsters followed in his slipstream, kicking up dust on the trail and pounding the parched ground.

I smelt a rat and hung back, determined not to blow a gasket on the first leg. As I suspected, Hartley soon slowed to a leaden-footed trundle and several of his fellow pacemakers faded badly.

It was at this point that I kicked like a middle-distance runner and started overtaking people. By the time we reached the final straight, I found myself in the lead, and dug into whatever reserves I had left to cross the line in first place.

I couldn't have been more delighted. Doing that in front of my new coaches and teammates felt significant. It sent a message to anyone who thought I was only interested in the status and the pay cheque. I was as willing to dig in and graft as anyone.

At the entrance to the gym, there's now a Blakiston honours board, listing all the past winners going back five years. It's an enormous source of pride that my name is at the top.

It took me a while to tune into the English banter, which was significantly less savage to what I was used to. While the Welsh boys will seize on any blunder and gleefully rip the piss, the English lads seemed far more earnest and polite. I remember once coming into the changing room after missing a couple of kicks for Wales, and Liam Williams piped up, 'Wearing your fucking wellies today, were you Bigs?' During my Northampton debut against Gloucester, I put two restarts out on the full, failed to reach the 10-yard line with another, and missed a couple of kicks at goal. Those were the things I was meant to be good at, and I was privately devastated.

After the third fluffed restart, I was in the middle of the pitch wishing the ground would swallow me up, when a chant of 'what a waste of money' began to reverberate from 'the Shed', the notoriously hostile stand at Kingsholm. I managed a wry smile, but

I'm sure a few of the travelling Saints fans were silently thinking the same.

I felt the need to apologize in training the following week, and assured my new teammates it wouldn't happen again. To a man, everyone was supportive and told me they were right behind me. Had I done that in Wales, the response would have been along the lines of, 'Ice up that shin and practise a bit harder, you prick.'

Mostly I was blown away by how geared the environment was to self-improvement. They already had a richly talented squad, but every one of them was eager to learn and get better.

Our attack guru, Sam Vesty, was a massive rugby geek, and his attention to detail was mind-boggling. Some of the more insecure players would complain about his overtly critical approach, and I'd tell them I wish he'd been my coach when I was a youngster.

I felt like I was starting over and learning the game differently, like a painter switching from watercolours to oils. My mind was opened up to new ways of seeing things. We weren't a team who could do what Wales had done for ten years, in terms of suffocating the life out of teams; we had to manipulate defences through guile rather than smashing them with brute force.

I was also able to explode the myth that I was a one-dimensional kicking number 10. Once I'd settled into that team, we broke the Premiership record for the number of tries in a single season. That's not to say I'd been stymied in the Welsh environment, just that my toolbox had always contained more elegant attacking weapons – scalpels and rapiers as well as chisels and hammers. Now I was just getting the chance to use the full range, and it felt refreshing.

The athletes we had at Northampton were blessed with more finesse and speed. We wanted as much ball as possible, whereas Wales were often happier without it. With Wales, we had one of the world's best crash-ball centres in Jamie, whereas in Rory Hutchinson we had one of best footballing 12s in the league. Jamie and Foxy are world-class centres, but neither are naturally gifted ball players like Hutchinson and Piers Francis. At

Northampton, we were encouraged to express ourselves, and I loved it.

Going back and forth between Wales and Northampton made me twice the player, and I was able to bring elements of both camps to bear. I could help Northampton with aspects of their structure and game management, and Wales with a sprinkling of attacking flair. It's things like this that are overlooked when arguments rage about keeping players in Wales. I understand the need to protect your own domestic league, and to attract new fans by keeping hold of your best players, but denying them the opportunity to play in another country is denying them the chance to progress and improve, both as players and human beings.

Northampton is an out-and-out rugby town. The supporters live and breathe it, and rare is the home game that isn't a sell-out. It's so different to playing for the Ospreys, where we shared the Liberty Stadium with Swansea City Football Club and rarely played to a full house. The Liberty Stadium is out of town and difficult to reach, and has the sterile, impersonal feel of a lot of modern stadiums, whereas Franklin's Gardens is an authentic old-fashioned rugby ground, with history oozing from every pore. Every home game felt significant; the fan zone was always bustling, the concourse was festooned with pop-up food trucks, and there'd always be a live band pumping out the tunes to get people in the mood.

The crowds were passionate too and, given my temperament, it was often a combustible mix. I was sent off against Gloucester for a high tackle on Chris Harris and, as I was approaching the dugout, a Gloucester fan, who'd clearly had his fair share of scrumpy shouted, 'You're a fucking disgrace.' I was already angry with myself, and he pushed me over the edge.

Eyeballing him, I replied, 'Do me a favour mate, why don't you just fuck off?' He looked genuinely shocked, claiming, 'You can't speak to me like that.'

I told him, 'Don't have a go at me and then start crying about it when I come back at you.'

It was beginning to get awkward when the stewards stepped in and began to escort him out.

'Don't do that,' I shouted. 'I've got no problem with him having a pop; just don't expect me to stand here and take it.'

It simmered down a little, but he was still mumbling 'we pay your wages' as I took my seat in the dugout. I honestly don't have a problem with fans mouthing off from the stands. They pay their money and they're entitled to their say, as long as it doesn't cross the line into abuse. Just understand that if you have a go at me, you'll get it back with both barrels.

I've actually stopped going out after games, because I worry – given my short fuse – that I could run into a bit of trouble. Cardiff is a small city, and on international weekends it's impossible to blend in. Back when I used to venture into town, the night would rapidly descend into a succession of selfie requests and boorish accounts of the game from people whose wits had been dulled by litres of booze. I'm not precious, but neither am I inclined to take advice from a portly stranger who might once have played for Cwmtwrch Thirds. I'm not able to bite my tongue in those circumstances, so I've decided it's not worth the hassle.

I don't resent the attention, but I don't enjoy it either. There are those in the Welsh squad who are downright rude when being asked for photos, and those who can't get enough of it. I always try to be as obliging as possible, but there are times when it feels intrusive. For someone who values their privacy, it can be difficult. I was once asked to sign an autograph at my grandfather's funeral; on another occasion, when I was visiting a friend in hospital, all the nurses asked for a group shot. Both requests just felt inappropriate.

Even after all these years, there's a voice inside me asking, 'Why do they want a photo with me?' I still feel like a normal bloke from Llangennith who kicks a ball around for a living. I do understand it in some ways; on the occasions I've been in the Director's Lounge at Man United, and I've seen David Beckham or Petr Cech, I've been desperate to get my photo with them and spend a bit of time in their company, but I still find it really difficult to understand why anyone would feel the same way about me. Those guys are global icons, and I still feel like someone who's gate-crashed the party and is hoping no one will find out.

On that note, I had one of the best nights of my life when Man United played Villarreal in the Champions League. I'd forged a few connections at Old Trafford, and was invited to bring a few friends up for the game. I took James Grayson and Rory Hutchinson from Northampton, and my old mate Ben Whitehouse, now a rugby referee like his dad Nigel, who never needs a second invitation.

On arrival, we were told, 'You've got a good guest on your table tonight', and I speculated that it might be someone from the Treble-winning side, maybe, like Phil Neville or Nicky Butt perhaps. At that moment the door to the President's Lounge swung open, and this tall, statuesque figure with a shimmering aura loped in, immediately rendering the room silent.

It was only bloody Usain Bolt!

From that point on, any notion we'd had about staying sober ahead of our game at the weekend went out of the window, and we all started caning the champagne.

Despite our obvious starry-eyed reverence, Usain was the most laid-back, easy company, and we had an amazing night swapping stories and talking about our mutual loathing of the gym.

United won with a couple of late goals and Alex Ferguson celebrated by ordering bottles of his favourite wine for all the tables in the President's Lounge. I remember looking around at one point to take it all in – Usain necking shots of Sambuca, Fergie and Beckham chatting animatedly in the corner, and singer Alexandra Burke and *Strictly* star Gorka Márquez dancing around tables, all framed against the floodlit field of dreams that was Old Trafford – and thinking, if Carlsberg did nights out . . .

Anyway, I digress. Part of what kept me grounded was the company I kept, especially at Northampton. I didn't feel like an eighty-cap international. I was surrounded by up-and-coming young kids, like George Furbank, James Grayson, Tommy Freeman and Fraser Dingwall. They were coming through and having to prove themselves, and their youthful exuberance rubbed off on me. I felt as though I was learning from them as much as the other way round.

As that season progressed, I continued to marvel at Sam Vesty's inexhaustible work ethic and at the amount of pride he took in improving players under his watch.

After every session, I felt like I'd improved. It was specific, individually tailored stuff. He'd watch you like a hawk, identifying little foibles or idiosyncrasies and recommending tweaks and fixes. Rather than just say, 'Practise your passing', he'd talk to me about rotating my hands to give it more control and accuracy – 'pushing the pass through' was a big thing with Sam.

He'd coach you on the breakdown too, encouraging you to always fall forwards so you wouldn't be presenting the ball like a gift to the opposition jackallers. He'd pose philosophical questions about defence: who's attacking who? When we have the ball, are *we* attacking the defence by running straight and staying square, or is the defence attacking *us* because we're lateral and not challenging the line?

You might think someone like me, with ten years' international experience, might not need that level of granular detail, but I relished it. I'd got stale at the Ospreys, and sometimes a different voice can guide you to new creative territory. Critically we were not only told what to do, but *why* we were doing it. It's a small but crucial distinction, and encourages players to engage their brains rather than become robots trained to follow orders.

My imaginary playbook turned from a thin pamphlet into a weighty tome, crammed with ideas and variations. I began to see the rugby field like a chessboard, in which you could consciously manoeuvre the pieces into the right positions before striking the killer blow.

I might have only made small improvements skills-wise, but the level of my game understanding soared. It was like emerging from a narrow tunnel into a golden vista of expanding horizons. That's not a slight on my previous coaches; just an acknowledgement that – at that stage of my career – I needed to be pushed to the next level.

14

GRAND SLAM GLORY

'We're going to give Gareth a go.'

It was with those words, delivered casually by Rob Howley, that I learned I'd lost my Wales shirt.

Gareth Anscombe had played at number 10 two days earlier in an international against Scotland in November 2018. It had been a strange choice of fixture, being against a home nation rather than one of the southern hemisphere giants, and it sat outside World Rugby's Test window, meaning I was ineligible for selection.

Martyn Phillips had advocated for it, arguing that it would give us a better chance of getting our autumn campaign off to a winning start.

As Wales's first-choice fly half for more than three straight years, I was fully expecting to be restored to the starting line-up for the next match against Australia. The game had added significance, as we'd been drawn in the same World Cup pool again, and this was our last chance before then to bring a miserable thirteen-game losing streak against the Wallabies to an end.

That's why I was totally blindsided when Rob told me Gareth Anscombe had kept his place. I like Chicken a lot, and while we shared a keen professional rivalry, our friendship trumped that. I felt more sanguine losing my place to him than I might have to another rival, but I never liked surrendering the jersey to anyone.

When a losing streak is as long and psychologically damaging as ours was, you don't care how it ends, which was lucky because the match was dreadful. I ended up replacing Leigh after he was injured in a nasty collision with Samu Kerevi. It meant when the defining penalty was awarded four minutes from time, with the game tied at 6–6, I was the one tasked with kicking it. Mercifully, it sailed over, and, with one swipe of my right boot, our ten-year hoodoo against Australia was finally laid to rest. Perhaps more significantly, it was our seventh win in a row, which saw us climb to a heady third in the world rankings.

Warren tested his squad depth by making fourteen changes for the next game against Tonga, which included my restoration at fly half. After a sticky start, we romped to a 74–24 victory, and I moved up to fifth place on the list of all-time scorers for Wales, winning Man of the Match in the process.

During my post-match interview, I said, 'These are the games I've got to play in these days.' It was a joke for the players' benefit, who'd been mocking me about my supposed 'demotion', but also a cheeky reminder to the coaches that I wasn't ready to be put out to pasture yet.

Deep down I knew a Man-of-the-Match performance against Tonga wouldn't be enough to dislodge Chicken, and I was again named on the bench for South Africa.

It was a blow to my ego, but not a crushing one. I felt I was still playing an important role in the squad. England's coach, Eddie Jones, would later face derision from some quarters when he rebranded his substitutes as 'finishers', but he had a point. It's not like the old days when subs could get splinters on their backside from spending so long on the bench. In the modern game, deployed tactically, they can have a profound impact on the outcome.

We'd stumbled on this combination and I thought it could really develop into something.

Chicken and I had a solid relationship and wanted to help one another. You might find this difficult to believe, coming from someone whose competitive instinct borders on maniacal, but part of me enjoyed it. It was almost like a sabbatical, in that I wasn't having to lead meetings or press conferences, and the spotlight wasn't shining on me with such burning intensity. All I want is to be successful and to win, and we were doing that. That said, I certainly wasn't about to roll over, particularly with a World Cup on the horizon. I wanted the jersey back but, in the meantime, I thought this could be a good thing for my body and my mind.

We appeared to be coasting to a comfortable victory over South Africa after establishing a 14–3 half-time lead courtesy of tries from Tomas Francis and Liam Williams. Franny's was a genuine collector's item; the first ever scored by a Welsh prop against one of the southern hemisphere 'big three'. It's just a shame that whenever it's replayed, he'll have to relive the shame of having the worst mullet the game's ever seen.

As the match entered the final quarter, the Boks had clawed themselves back to 14–11 and the old demons began to creep in. That's when I entered the fray with the instruction to stick the ball in the air and 'get back into their territory'.

Tactically it worked a treat, and we wrested back control. Two penalties from my right boot helped us to a 20–11 victory: our fourth in a row over the Springboks.

The fifteen-year losing streak we'd suffered against them was fast becoming a sepia-tinged memory, and it was our ninth consecutive win overall, consolidating our third-place world ranking and underlining our status as genuine World Cup contenders.

Gats had always loved to stay under the radar in the run-up to big tournaments, but our performances were garnering the kind of attention we usually shied away from.

It was a game in which Ellis Jenkins experienced both ends of the emotional scale – stepping in at short notice to replace Dan Lydiate, he delivered an epic Man-of-the-Match performance against a much-vaunted Springbok back row, only to be stretchered off with a devastating knee injury that would ultimately keep him sidelined for two years. It was especially cruel, because Sam Warburton had retired after the Lions tour, and Ellis was being touted as his long-term successor.

Gats changed tack in the build-up to the 2019 Six Nations, declaring on the eve of the tournament that if we beat France in Paris, we'd win the Grand Slam. Gone was the false modesty of previous years, and gone was the desire to stay below the radar. This was fighting talk, and we felt as if we could back it up.

I arrived in camp with a knee injury and was forced to train on my own during the first week. Given the niggling injury and the fact the autumn had gone so well with Chicken in the hot seat, I doubted whether I'd be back in the frame.

Any confidence we'd built up was shredded in the rain-lashed opening forty minutes in Paris. We were as abysmal as France were impressive, and were it not for Morgan Parra's misfiring boot, we'd have been dead and buried long before I had the chance to bring my experience to bear. The swagger we'd displayed in the autumn had been replaced by a nervous, faltering anxiety, and we were 16–0 down at half-time. We didn't know it then, but if we were to win, we'd have to pull off the biggest comeback in Six Nations history.

It was an understandably muted changing room. Even Shaun Edwards was quiet, and it fell to Huw Bennett to seize the moment. Benny's an emotional bloke whose wholehearted commitment had dug Wales out of many a deep trench in the past. He raised his voice purposefully. 'Boys, we've got forty minutes to turn this around. If we go out there feeling sorry for ourselves, the Grand Slam dream, the winning run, and *everything* we've worked for will be gone.'

It shocked everyone out of their torpor, and Sanjay stepped in. 'Instead of going out and trying to win the game,' he said, 'let's go out and make a mess of it. Get up in their faces, harry them, hassle them, force them into mistakes, then hoover up the crumbs.'

It was a bit of Saracens terminology Liam had brought in, meaning if you can't win with elegance and elan, do so by smashing things to bits. Liam has a pronounced stammer, and rarely does press for that reason, but he doesn't suffer those same insecurities in the team environment. He's a confident leader, and his intervention decidedly changed the mood.

We had to score first, and did so through Tomos Williams. Moments later, Yoann Huget committed the mother of all howlers to gift us our second. The referee was playing advantage, and I could see from the bench we were running one of our set moves. Jon Fox had his hands up to receive the ball, when Hadleigh Parkes went rogue and grubbered through. It was an ugly kick, coming off his shin and bouncing harmlessly over the French line, too far for any of our chasers to reach it. But Huget made a monumental hash of covering back, allowing the ball to squirt out of his hands like a bar of soap. George North pounced on it and scored a second try.

We knew France had the capacity to implode, and it was happening in front of our eyes. They were suddenly screaming at one another, and the crowd – joyous and upbeat in the first half – had become restless and agitated.

The call came down to get me on. There were twenty-five minutes to go, and we were two points adrift. As the game entered its final quarter, I nudged over a penalty to take us ahead for the first time.

Then came the ultimate act of self-destruction by France: Sébastien Vahaamahina, the towering lock, launched a wild, speculative pass, which missed its target by some distance, and landed in the grateful arms of George North. George had to juggle it a little, but once he'd pinned his ears back, no one was catching him.

That's the moment the fans remember when they recall the victory – George haring down the pitch and gobbling up the yards – but Owen Watkin is worthy of a special mention too. In those dying moments, France threw everything at us, running into contact with blind fury, unable to believe they'd thrown the match away so carelessly. Owen was freakishly good at stripping the ball in contact, and he killed their final attack dead with one of his trademark rips. Shaun reserved special praise for Owen's contribution, because that's arguably what won us the game.

Gats cut a relieved figure afterwards, saying we'd dodged a bullet, but it was our tenth win in a row, and it was as if we'd genuinely forgotten how to lose. Adam Beard didn't even know what it *felt* like to lose. His Wales record at that stage read played fourteen, won fourteen.

We had Italy in Rome next and, rather than fly home, we headed south to the French Riviera. It was part of a plan to replicate the feel of a World Cup, and the boys didn't need much persuading.

We watched the Ireland–England game in a bar on the seafront, and I remember being seriously impressed. It was a stark reminder that we'd have to raise our game significantly to compete with those two. There were a fair few English and Irish fans in the pub, and at some point someone twigged that the entire Welsh squad was there tucking into the Guinness. There was plenty of banter flying around after that, with the more confident English fans declaring loudly that they were going to win the Six Nations.

We all got a bit carried away, and nearly forgot about the midnight curfew that had been imposed by Thumper. With visions of him angrily standing in the lobby with a register, we all sprinted home down the Promenade des Anglais, clutching half-eaten burgers we'd picked up along the way.

Franny and I collapsed into bed, bloated after all the Guinness and junk food. At some point in the early hours, I was startled awake by a strange guttural sound, a little like a choking pig. There, bathed in silhouette next to my bed, was the prone figure of Franny, crouched on all fours, vomiting voluminously onto the carpet. Lurching backwards in disgust, I buried my head under the covers. It wasn't until morning – when I awoke to an acrid stench – that I discovered it was my designer jeans that had borne the brunt of Franny's – how to say this tastefully – projectile disgorgement.

It remains the only time he's apologized to me about anything.

Over breakfast, he reminded me that we'd made several drunken calls to his boss, Rob Baxter, leaving a series of increasingly inarticulate messages asking when he was planning to sign me for Exeter. We vowed not to get so over-excited next time we were allowed out.

On our day off we took a trip to Monaco, which was an eye-opener. None of us had ever seen opulence on that scale – yachts worth £250 million, grand old hotels with vast ballrooms and crystal chandeliers, Ferraris and Lamborghinis gliding down the boulevard. If that didn't make a group of Welsh boys feel out of place, the drinks bill at the Monte Carlo Casino certainly did; it was ten quid for a glass of Coke!

For some reason, management had booked us into a really posh hotel in Rome as opposed to the usual Marriott. We knew we were in a more exclusive environment when Dolph Lundgren sauntered past during check-in, reducing a bunch of international rugby players to a rabble of over-excited kids as we queued to get our picture taken with him.

We came through against Italy, but our victory was far from convincing. For the first time in my career, I felt the need to apologize to my coach. Gats had emphasized the need for squad unity and was refusing to distinguish between his first- and second-choice line-ups, but the ten changes he made for Italy undoubtedly weakened the side. Subconsciously, I must have felt the need to perform to push my case for playing in the England game a fortnight later, and nothing I did went right. I put three or four kicks out on the full, and felt edgy and clumsy throughout.

Stepping onto the bus afterwards, I said sorry to Gats, admitting I was nowhere near my best. His reply was philosophical. 'No problem, Dan. That's the way it goes sometimes.'

He'd admitted to the press that making so many changes had been a mistake and had stalled our momentum. But, dodgy performance aside, we'd extended our winning run to eleven, equalling a record that had stood for more than a century.

Everyone wanted to play in the England game, and training was absolutely savage. Without any prior warning, Gats insisted on a brutal series of fitness sessions that recalled the dark days of Qatar. They were horrendous, but after the World Cup camps, we knew we'd reap the rewards come game time. There was loads of hardcore running, followed by 'game blocks' to test our ability to perform under extreme fatigue. They'd go on for five minutes non-stop to replicate such scenarios in a match, and as the sessions continued, tempers began to flare, especially among the forwards. A furious Ross Moriarty and Samson Lee had to be dragged apart amid a flurry of flying fists.

England came to Cardiff at the peak of their powers, having won their last five Six Nations games in a row. They'd scored four tries against Ireland, and six against France, obliterating both in the process.

As is always the case when England come to town, the hype machine went into overdrive. The press conferences were stuffed to the gills with dozens of Fleet Street journalists, and even the quieter players were piping up in training. The narrative was similar to 2013; they were crossing the Severn, brimming with confidence, to face a Welsh side yet to fully hit its straps.

Gats preferred it that way. He was publicly embracing the underdog tag while privately telling us there was no way we were going to lose.

I remember being amazed at how slick we were in the captain's run, our last training session before the game. The energy levels were right up there, and there was an intensity and focus that hadn't been evident at the start of the campaign. Alun Wyn worried it had been too good, that we might have jinxed it by playing the game a day early, and he might have had a point when we found ourselves 10–3 down early on. I started on the bench but, despite us going behind, my sense from there was that we were the stronger team. What pleased me the most was the full-blooded commitment of our forwards. Spurred on by a vociferous home crowd, they were hurling themselves into collisions with a total disregard for their welfare. It was an impressive display of guts and tenacity, and I could sense England starting to tire even before half-time.

In the second half, we started winning all the 50-50s, and blasting holes with our pick-and-go strategy. Their line speed had improved considerably under John Mitchell, but because we kept our carries tight to the rucks, they weren't able to blitz the way they wanted to, and it upset their rhythm. Their discipline started to creak, and some of their more volatile players were getting prickly.

Gats had told us to target Kyle Sinckler, seeing him as a ticking time bomb, and in Rob Evans we had the perfect guy to get under his skin. Rob's the ultimate wind-up merchant, who hasn't got an off switch, and at every scrum he was needling him, goading him, telling him Gats thought he was shit.

It worked. The more frustrated he got, the more of a liability he became. He was penalized for a late shoulder charge on Chicken, and again shortly after for a choke hold on Alun Wyn. Eddie Jones hauled him off before he was sent off, by which time we'd reduced the lead to 10–9.

The difference in attitude was probably summed up in that incident. Sinckler was the very definition of a boggle-eyed maniac, fired up and ready to erupt, while Al was the picture of calm, laughing derisively as Sinckler completely lost his cool.

Manu Tuilagi was the next to blow a gasket, grabbing Liam around the throat and spoiling for a fight. Two or three years earlier, Liam would have swung for him, but this was a different, more serene Sanjay, who'd learned from bitter experience.

It was quite telling watching this all from the sidelines, seeing how controlled we were and how wound-up England were getting.

I was brought on for the final quarter. Though people have

since told me it was the perfect twenty minutes, it actually started badly.

My first job was to engineer an exit from our 22. We had a scrum fifteen metres in on the right-hand side, and I made the wrong call. Toby should have gone blind and passed it to Gareth Davies for him to box-kick long down the tramlines. Instead, I called a play that saw Toby run to the open side and pass to Hadleigh Parkes. England flooded the breakdown and won a penalty bang in front of the posts.

Once I'd recovered from that, though, I started to feel invincible, like a show-stealer in the final act of a dramatic play. In sharp contrast to England's kick-heavy approach, we decided to keep hold of the ball, chipping away at their crumbling defence and driving remorselessly upfield. For phase after punishing phase, we recycled the ball with a swiftness of purpose that kept England rocking on their heels. Ten phases, fifteen, twenty. Onwards we marched.

That sequence is what playing 10 at Test level is all about. You're conducting the orchestra, scanning, assessing options, and making snap decisions on the fly. I was allowing the forwards to play off the scrum half, stepping up when I needed to, keeping my passes simple and precise. Twenty-five phases, thirty. I felt in total control, never a moment when I was doubting my options. I just *knew* what to do.

We had them exactly where we wanted. For those few minutes I was in a zen state, seeing bodies colliding in a blur of jumbled limbs, but floating above it all like a jazz musician; adding little lyrical flourishes while the rhythm section kept things moving propulsively forwards.

Eventually, I pulled the trigger, releasing George on the right-hand side, where he drew the attention of three tacklers, dragging them all to within inches of the line. I played scrum half at the next ruck, passing to Cory Hill who'd run a brilliant angle to smash his way over. The thirty-five phases that led to the try lasted five minutes – the exact length of time Gats had made us practise our aerobic games.

Gats always loved to peddle the theory that we were fitter than everyone else, and on the evidence of this, perhaps he was right.

The touchline conversion put us 16–13 up.

Shortly afterwards, Gareth Davies was charged down in our 22, and amid the ensuing panic, I scooped the ball up and launched a torpedo kick sixty yard upfield. Usually, as a fly half, I'd have been the one chasing Cawdor's kicks, but I'd had a sixth sense to hold back. Courtney Lawes and Joe Launchbury had been close to a charge-down on a couple of occasions, and I could smell the danger. We ended up with a lineout deep in England's territory.

This is it, I was thinking. *Let's finish them.*

It was one of those rare moments when I felt utterly invincible.

With three minutes to go, our pack delivered the coup de grâce, reducing England's scrum to rubble inside their 22. The penalty was coming but we wanted more. I'd clocked Josh Adams hugging the touchline and, receiving the pass one-handed, I launched a high, hanging kick up towards him. Elliot Daly has a few inches on Josh, but Jaddsy timed his jump to perfection, snaffling the ball in mid-air, and juggling it on the way down before burrowing over the line.

It sent the stadium into raptures; seventy-five thousand voices combining in a deafening roar as hundreds of pint glasses were thrown skyward in gleeful abandon.

It had been tough to lose my starting spot, but those twenty minutes meant I was still making huge contributions to a winning team. It was entirely different to being dropped or usurped, as I was still coming on and delivering big moments. We'd been losing against both France and England when I came on, so I could argue with conviction that I'd shifted the balance in our favour.

The belief soared to another level after that win. England had been red-hot favourites, and we'd made them look ordinary. It brought our five-game Six Nations losing streak against them to an end and set a new record for consecutive Welsh victories.

We'd now won twelve in a row, and that was the moment we knew the Grand Slam was on. It would be tough up in Murray-field, but if we overcame the Scots, we'd be back in Cardiff for a Championship decider against Ireland.

Somebody referred to what happened in the build-up to the Scotland game as an 'absolute clusterfuck' and they weren't far wrong. On the Monday, the entire squad was summoned to an emergency meeting, where Martyn Phillips and Julie Paterson from the WRU announced that the Ospreys and the Scarlets – two of rugby's bitterest rivals – were to merge, and the contracts making it official were to be signed that afternoon.

Here we were, preparing for leg four of a potential Grand Slam, and the WRU decide to plant a dirty great bomb beneath it all. Those two teams supplied the bulk of players to the Welsh squad, and now they were all wondering whether they'd have a job beyond the Six Nations.

Martyn calmly explained that a new development region would be formed in North Wales, and that a number of players would be sent up there to play. There was also talk of a new pay-banding system that would lead to significant pay cuts. For thirty seconds the room was stunned into silence.

We literally couldn't believe what we were hearing.

Once we'd recovered our senses, we asked for all the coaches and execs to leave so we could process what we'd heard. It was only then that the room exploded into life, and all the anger bubbled to the surface.

As a nation we're not great at standing up to authority, but we resolved to fight our corner this time. When Julie and Martyn returned, they faced a fusillade of angry questions, led by a particularly animated Gareth Anscombe. The answers coming back felt like a piss-take, like a scene from *The Office*. Those who asked if they would be ineligible for Wales if they were forced to take work elsewhere were effectively told yes.

If there'd been nothing on the Scotland game, things might have got more militant. Chicken floated the idea of strike action, but we didn't want the bureaucrats to skewer our Grand Slam dream. So for the time being we just told Martyn and Julie that we were vehemently opposed to the proposals and intended to fight them tooth and nail.

Unsurprisingly, it was desperately hard to concentrate on the rugby over the next few days. Rumours were spreading like wildfire, and angry WhatsApp exchanges were being leaked to the media, which didn't help with squad unity. We were finding out the latest developments in the papers or on Twitter rather than through official channels. As much as I had enormous sympathy for all my colleagues in Wales, I couldn't help but feel an almighty sense of relief that I was locked into a contract in Northampton, far away from all this madness.

By Thursday, we'd resolved to park it and concentrate as well as we could on the Scotland game. Gareth Anscombe and Alun Wyn talked about the siege mentality we'd need to adopt; how we'd need to channel this anger into our performance.

Flying to Edinburgh felt like an escape.

Scotland had been playing some great attacking rugby under Gregor Townsend, and we weren't about to underestimate them. I worried that our minds might be elsewhere during the game, but those concerns proved unfounded in the first half, where the off-field turmoil had a galvanizing effect, and we produced some of our best attacking rugby of the campaign. I was watching on contentedly, again from the bench, anticipating a relaxed second-half cameo with the game comfortably won. It proved to be far from that.

Liam Williams went off with a stinger injury, and I was summoned on early in the second half. God knows what had been said in the Scotland changing room, but they came back out possessed. They were already back in it before Hamish Watson appeared from the bench like a snarling rhino for one of the most astonishing cameos of the professional age. It was like watching a computer game on cheat mode as he rampaged around, pumping his knees, and bouncing off tacklers like a human cannonball. The crowd could sense a turning of the tide and Murrayfield became a boiling cauldron of Caledonian fervour. I'd never seen one man make such a forceful impact.

The entire second half was played in our territory and all we did was tackle – making an energy-sapping 160 in total. It was a total implosion, but despite the overwhelming pressure, we had an inner belief – hardened by that run of twelve consecutive wins – that we'd somehow prevail.

We finally got out of our half and won a penalty in their 22. Knowing we had the advantage, Jonathan Davies swung wildly at the ball, with the worst drop-goal attempt since Arthur Emyr's in the 1991 World Cup. Thankfully when Chicken took the shot on goal moments later it sailed over, and we'd got out of jail.

The atmosphere in the changing room was flat. We'd spent the entire second half on the edge of our nerves and weren't in the mood to celebrate. Gats looked as relieved as anyone. 'Whenever you win a Grand Slam,' he said, 'there's always one half you look back on and think, "we got away with one there".'

Liam was hidden from view by a pillar, and he piped up, 'Fuck me, we've had one of those in every game so far.' There was a nervous pause as everyone waited for Warren to react. Thankfully he cracked a smile, and the whole changing room erupted into laughter.

Shortly after, Martyn Phillips arrived to tell us the merger was off and to apologize for all the unrest it had caused. It was a difficult moment for him, but he'd built up a lot of credit with the players and we respected the fact that they'd listened to our objections. Who knows what had gone on in the boardroom over the previous few days, but it seemed odd that an apparent 'done deal' was suddenly dead in the water. We were essentially told to forget it had ever happened.

We entered the final week as the only team able to win the Grand Slam.

Standing in our way were the defending champions, Ireland – a side that had beaten the All Blacks in the autumn and were officially the second-best team in the world. After losing to England in the opening round, they'd gradually recovered their rhythm and were coming to Cardiff with the Championship in their sights.

That final week of a tournament, when titles are on the line, is usually when the tension is ratcheted up to its highest level, but this time, we felt uncharacteristically serene. Our other tournament victories under Gats had largely been against the odds, but there was a sense of destiny attached to this one.

The night before the final round, as we tucked into a feast of chicken goujons drizzled in mayonnaise and ketchup, we felt supremely confident. Before lights out, Franny and I had a conversation about how good it felt to be part of this team. There were no cliques or rivalries; it felt like being in an Under-14s club side with your mates. There was no way we were going to lose.

That conviction was only strengthened during Al's team talk, when he implored us to go and 'do it for someone you love, someone who means the world to you.' He'd lost his father the previous year, and we all knew how much he'd have cherished his dad being there when he led his country out for a Grand Slam decider.

The game couldn't have started more perfectly. Chicken put a delicate chip over their onrushing defence, which landed sweetly in Parkesey's grateful arms, putting us 7–0 up after two minutes. Dreamland. It was the sign of a team in perfect harmony. After the opening game against France where we'd looked clumsy and disjointed, we were now a well-oiled machine, capable of reading each other's thoughts.

Parkesey's cult hero status didn't need burnishing, but what he did next pushed him into the annals of Welsh folklore. Ireland were given a penalty deep in their own half, and Johnny Sexton bamboozled our defence – feinting to kick long before sending a cross-field kick into the expectant arms of Jacob Stockdale.

That kind of trickery was something we'd prepped for, but I could see from the bench on the far side that George was down, leaving us a man short defensively. Stockdale caught it in full stride, handing off Gareth Davies before accelerating away.

The green-shirted hordes were already up on their feet, celebrating a sure try, but they hadn't reckoned on Hadleigh Parkes. Astonishingly for a man whose pace is usually on a par with a milk float, Parkesey turned on the after-burners and chased down Stockdale like the Terminator, wrapping him up in the tackle and hauling him into touch.

All the GPS stats in the world couldn't explain how he managed it. It was pure heart and desire. Momentum in games is such a strange, nebulous thing. Single incidents can have a huge influence, and that was undoubtedly one of them. Had they scored and levelled the game at 7–7, things could have turned out very differently.

George had been down for a reason – he'd broken his hand. With less than ten minutes gone, I was on at fly half, with Liam moving to the wing and Chicken to full back. It was only when I ran on that I realized how relentless the rain was. I was soaked to the skin before I lined up behind the first scrum.

We won a penalty from that scrum, and it set the tone for the victory.

Our forwards were magnificent all day, and Rob Evans was at his effervescent best – relentlessly taunting Tadhg Furlong at every engagement. He and Gar Davies were like a tag team. At one point Tadhg dropped to his knee, panting heavily, and Gar, looking perplexed, asked, 'What's he doing, Rob?'

'His belly's so big he can't support his own weight, can he?' came Rob's reply.

With the rain continuing to fall, the enforced changes worked in our favour. With both Chicken and me on the field, we had two kicking options and were able to put a stranglehold on the game.

It's ironic that a Grand Slam decider turned out to be one of my easiest games for Wales. We had not won any plaudits during the tournament for our pragmatic approach, but we didn't give a shit about garnering good reviews. We just wanted to win.

We kicked the leather off the ball, chased hard in defence, piled into breakdowns and won a succession of penalties that Chicken knocked over with metronomic accuracy.

I had no issues with him taking the kicks; he'd started the game and earned the right. I was happy to step in if needed, but Gareth nailed everything that came his way, and I had nothing but admiration for him.

We were 16–0 up at half-time which, coincidentally, was the exact same scoreline we had been losing by in round one, and the conditions were almost identical.

Ireland's cynical decision to keep the roof open had backfired on them. Coming back from three scores down in decent conditions when you can throw the ball around is one thing; doing it beneath relentless sheets of rain, where handling is hazardous, is quite another.

Ireland's discipline – generally such a hallmark for them under Joe Schmidt – deserted them in the second half, and every kick of ours that sailed between the posts chipped away at their morale. Their generals, Sexton and Conor Murray – usually the barometer for their poise and control – became ever more flustered, and we knew their challenge was fading. In the space of a few minutes, Sexton – who was the reigning World Player of the Year – kicked a restart out on the full, and passed the ball directly into touch.

Those signs were as indicative of Ireland's collapse as the 22–0 scoreline. He'd completely lost his grip. Gats had built up a dossier of players' strengths and weakness from his time as Lions head coach, and he knew Sexton's psyche as intimately as anyone's. He'd told us to target him unremittingly, and it had worked.

If one thing summed up the relentless nature of that Welsh side, it was Alun Wyn's fury when we conceded a try two minutes into injury time. It was but a mere consolation for them, but Al was fuming that we'd let our guard slip. Most of us were already thinking ahead to the celebrations, but he ordered us to line up and charge at the conversion attempt with as much desperation as we would have done in the first minute.

That's why he was our captain; he was always on a ceaseless quest for perfection. He'd been outstanding in that campaign; probably the best he'd ever been, and worthy winner of Player of the Tournament. From the first minute in Paris to the last in Cardiff, he'd been an absolute machine.

The victory parade was glorious despite the rain, which continued to fall long after we'd lifted the trophy. Alex and my son James came on to the pitch to celebrate, and despite Alex's concerns about her perfectly coiffured hair getting wet, we got a brilliant photo of the three of us which remains on the mantelpiece to this day.

Forty-five minutes after the final whistle was blown, we were all still out there in the teeming rain. Gats's suit was sopping wet, but he was oblivious, waving to the enraptured crowd on what he thought was his final appearance in the Six Nations.

Three Grand Slams in eleven years told its own story, wrapped up with a record win against the very team that had sacked him from his first job in international rugby.

We didn't play extravagant attacking rugby or score many tries, but we had an unshakeable self-belief, a dogged refusal to roll over, and an obdurate defence. If titles were awarded on style alone, England would have romped home. They scored more than twice as many tries as us and broke the 30-point barrier in four of their five games.

But when it really mattered, they didn't have our spirit. Our game against them in round three had been the real Grand Slam decider. We might not have been the most gifted team in the tournament, nor the most pleasing to watch, but we were unarguably the best.

15

STRANGLED INTO SUBMISSION

I learned pretty early that scaling one mountain may reward you with a magnificent view, but there are always other, more challenging-looking peaks looming on the horizon. The Grand Slam had been amazing, but we now had our sights set on the World Cup. It was the one competition Warren had never won, and after the heartbreak of the last two campaigns, we were determined to go deeper than ever before.

By the August of 2019, I'd reclaimed my place in the team, after Gareth Anscombe suffered a bad knee injury during a warm-up match against England. If, going into that game, we were a team that had forgotten how to lose, we were given a stern reminder that day. The 33–19 defeat brought our record-breaking winning run to an end and robbed us of one of our best players.

It also prompted J. J. Williams, the celebrated former Wales winger, to declare, 'Wales would never win the World Cup with Dan Biggar in the team.'

It seemed every time I was back in the spotlight, the same old criticisms reared their head. I wasn't creative enough, I wasn't a running threat, or a good enough footballer; all guts and no guile.

I started in the return fixture against England and won Man of the Match in a victory that saw us climb to the top of the world rankings, nudging New Zealand off the spot they'd held for a decade.

During my post-match interview, I couldn't help myself, thanking J. J. for his comments and sarcastically reflecting on how 'really motivating and supporting for the team' they had been. I said it with a wry smile, but it was motivated by anger. It felt good to get that off my chest.

Our pre-World Cup training camps had a similar feel to 2015 – a return to Switzerland for more 'live high, train low' punishment. Switzerland was simultaneously as beautiful and brutal as we remembered it.

The gondolas between the accommodation and the training grounds came every forty minutes and missing one would leave you at the mercy of the increasingly pernicious fines committee.

Imagine our delight then, when on the final day Bobby and Benny, the two senior strength and conditioning coaches, were nowhere to be seen. Members of the fines committee were rubbing their hands gleefully, dreaming up a vengeful punishment to get them back for all the misery they'd put us through, when our eardrums were assaulted by a deafening blast from the PA speakers.

The *Mission Impossible* theme was being pumped out at maximum volume, and in the distance, we spotted two paragliders floating down the mountain. As they got closer, we could see that it was Bobby and Benny, grinning inanely.

They landed in an ungainly fashion right in the centre circle and rose to their feet looking inordinately pleased with themselves. We were all gutted, having convinced ourselves the session would be cancelled, and no one was more gutted than the members of the fines committee.

Next we headed off to Turkey for a warm-weather training camp. My abiding memory of the trip was the notorious incident of the 'Turkey Six'. For reasons only Gats will know, he decided to give everyone over the age of thirty the afternoon off.

I had a hip injury and couldn't train anyway, which turned out to be a blessing in disguise. The anointed Six were given a bit of rope and abused it like an excitable Jack Russell on an extender lead. While the rest of the squad were being beasted, the Six – Parkesey, Tips, George, Ken, Al and Foxy – headed to the all-inclusive beach bar and hammered the cocktails, working their way through the menu at a rapid pace. They then retired to the main bar to start on the beers, and were about four or five deep when the rest of the squad returned drenched in sweat and aching from limb to limb.

Foxy cracked a gag about the state of them all, and it went down about as well as a fart in a lift. Foxy's brother James – also known as 'Cubby' – was in the squad, and he took umbrage on behalf of the rest, getting up in Foxy's face and telling him he was 'bang out of order.'

Foxy staggered unconvincingly to his feet and shoved Cubby in the chest, asking, 'Who are *you* to tell me I'm out of order?' It was a comical re-enactment of a scene that had surely played out innumerable times during their childhood in Bancyfelin, but the other hotel guests looked a tad perturbed to see two burly blokes squaring up to one another in the middle of the day.

I genuinely don't know what Gats's rationale was, but it drove a bit of a wedge between the squad for a day or two. The rest wouldn't have minded if the Six had just had a few drinks, but they'd taken the piss – and admitted as much afterwards.

One of the Russian guests approached me when things had simmered down and asked which one of us was the stag. We had to explain that we were international rugby players preparing for the World Cup. She looked at me quizzically, wondering if I'd just used the world's least convincing chat-up line.

The excitement levels were high when we met at 5 a.m. on 11 September for the bus journey to Heathrow. There was a real spirit of adventure that had been absent four years earlier when the World Cup had taken place on our shores.

Japan, unlike England, was an exotic, mysterious and distant land.

Twenty minutes in, Adam Beard started complaining about his stomach, moaning softly and struggling to get comfortable. Naturally, we were all taking the piss, telling him to get over it and to stop dampening the mood.

Our team doctor Geoff Davies gave him a couple of paracetamols and told him to chill out. It wasn't until we were all in the departure lounge that we noticed Beardy had disappeared. Someone piped up that he'd gone home, so we all started phoning him, leaving wholly unsympathetic messages, accusing him of being a lightweight and a hypochondriac.

Alan Phillips had apparently come off the bus at Heathrow, and said to Geoff, 'I know I'm not a doctor, but I think he's going to be all right.' Not the most scientific diagnosis and, as it turned out, wildly inaccurate, as a couple of hours later poor old Beardy was in a Cardiff operating theatre undergoing emergency surgery to have his appendix removed.

We later heard that if he'd got on the plane, we would have had to make an emergency landing, and he'd probably have ended up in some Russian hospital in the middle of nowhere.

We'd been told that our first training session in Kitakyushu was to be open to the public, but we didn't think the locals would be particularly keen. They'd seemed pretty reserved until then, and while Japan was the host nation, rugby remained something of a curiosity to the population at large.

Leaving our units session, I noticed that barriers were being erected on the road to the stadium, and idly wondered what might be going on. Further on, a lengthy queue was beginning to form, and I assumed some big star was coming to town. A few hours later, as we walked to the ground, we saw the queue had quadrupled in size, and it slowly dawned that it was *us* they'd come to see.

Though they'd been queuing for hours, there wasn't a scrap of litter anywhere or any sign of disorder. They were the most impeccably behaved fans we'd ever seen, and once we were inside, twenty thousand of them – *twenty thousand* – rose to their feet and started singing.

I thought we were about to be treated to some Japanese folk song by means of a welcome, but it was soon apparent that they were singing the Welsh National Anthem. Not some mangled, third-rate version, but a flawless rendition with every syllable perfectly enunciated, and sung with the same level of gusto you'd expect at the national stadium in Cardiff.

Then, as if to prove a point, Gats flogged us to the point of exhaustion. He has a reputation as a hard taskmaster, and clearly wanted to show the Japanese public – who have a strong work ethic – just how much effort we put in.

That evening, we had our cap presentation in the City Hall, and en route we were made further aware of how much the locals had taken us to heart. Several vehicles we passed were emblazoned with Welsh flags, local buses were plastered with images of dragons, the train station was festooned with huge posters of our players and Kokura Castle was illuminated in shimmering red.

We'd planned to sing 'Calon Lân', but the Japanese beat us to the punch with their own superior version, embarrassing us into singing 'Ar Lan y Môr' instead because we knew we couldn't compete. It was genuinely humbling.

My phone buzzed on the bus back. There was a message in the senior players' WhatsApp group from Warren. Foxy, Alun Wyn, Ken, Tips and I were summoned to meet him as soon as we got back to the hotel.

I knew instinctively that it had something to do with Rob Howley. A few people had noticed that Rob hadn't been on the bus, but assumed he'd be heading to City Hall separately. When he didn't turn up, the whispers began, but the consensus was that he'd probably had some dodgy sushi and was resting up at the hotel.

When we convened in one of the conference rooms, an ashen-faced Gats explained that Rob was being sent home. World Rugby had received a tip-off that he'd been making hundreds of bets on matches, including games that Wales had been involved in. This amounted to corruption under World Rugby's guidelines, and there was no option but to suspend him.

A later investigation would reveal no evidence of match fixing, and that he'd lost rather than made money. Despite the outrage the revelations generated, it was just a simple tale of human fallibility. Rob had been reeling from the death of his sister and had turned to gambling as a source of comfort. We were all devastated for him and found it difficult to process.

Howley and Gats had been joined at the hip for decades, and after twelve years in charge during what had undeniably been our third golden era, this was supposed to be their swansong. As a double act they'd amassed a boatload of trophies with both Wasps and Wales, but the one that had eluded them was the World Cup. You could argue that their entire twelve-year tenure had been leading to this, and suddenly the ground had opened up and swallowed Howlers whole. As disastrous as the whole scenario was, it also felt uniquely, depressingly Welsh.

We knew this could derail our campaign and, with that in mind, Warren's man-management was vital. He said that if we allowed any negativity to swell it could quickly permeate the entire squad, and stressed the importance of appearing decisive and focused. He gave us a series of options. Should we empower the players to lead the attack? Should we call Alex King, who'd helped out in 2017 when Gats was with the Lions? Or should we summon Stephen Jones, who'd be taking over in a few months anyway, when Gatland handed the reins to the new regime? That seemed like the obvious solution, and our agreement was swift and unanimous.

The news had leaked out, so the questions came thick and fast when we returned to the team room. The mood was one of bewilderment. We knew Howlers enjoyed an occasional bet, but none of us had any idea he'd sunk into a hole that deep.

We delivered the facts as dispassionately as we could before Gats arrived and explained what would happen next; Stephen would be arriving within the next forty-eight hours. As callous as it sounded, we had to draw a line under it quickly, and move on.

Rob had never been truly appreciated in Wales. He was – despite the prevailing narrative – an innovative and pioneering coach. But beyond that, he'd been a great mentor and friend to me. He'd been among my staunchest defenders. A pillar for me to lean on when times got tough. As a former Wales captain, he knew only too well how debilitating the constant carping and criticism could be and he always ensured I didn't fight that battle alone. I felt truly sorry for him, knowing that this time he'd been the one privately battling demons.

Once the practicalities had been dealt with, my immediate concern was for Rob's welfare, and I turned to Gats and asked, 'Where is he?'

Gats told me he'd packed his bags and was waiting in the lobby for his lift to the airport. He looked pale and glassy-eyed when I found him slumped in a chair like a deflated balloon. It was as if all the life and vitality had drained from his system.

He stood to shake my hand, and I swatted it away, enveloping him in a bear hug and telling him sincerely that this didn't affect my opinion of him in any way. I told him how much I appreciated everything he'd done, and that whatever we achieved in this World Cup would be down to his hard work.

His voice was shaky and hesitant, and he kept apologizing, insisting that he'd let everyone down. I assured him that that wasn't the case, but it was clearly weighing heavily on him. He was contending not just with the sense of shame, but with the guilt that came with it.

Emotions are heightened anyway during a World Cup, when you're far from home, and that only served to intensify things. I'd witnessed close-up the passion and dedication he'd brought to the job, and losing him at such a critical point was painful.

I woke up at 4 a.m. after a fitful night's sleep and looked at my phone. Everyone was leading on the story, and any fantasies I'd had about it being a jet-lag fuelled nightmare were quickly dispelled. Some of the others – who weren't as close to Rob as I had been – might have thought it was merely an inconvenience, but I couldn't help but worry about how his absence might affect us.

Despite the upheaval, we switched quickly into work mode. We'd developed an almost robotic ability to shut out the noise and focus on the task in hand, and the collective experience of that squad played a decisive role.

The mood was a little strange for twenty-four hours while the news continued to percolate, but Al led the group well, holding on tight to those leadership reins and guiding us through the chaos.

I felt a huge amount of admiration towards Rob for the way he handled the aftermath. He could easily have come out defending himself against some of the more aggressive takes in the press, but he kept his counsel, knowing the longer the story dominated the headlines, the more damaging it would be to our campaign. It wasn't until months later that he sat down with a journalist to give his side of the story.

Steve Jones, to his credit, didn't try to change anything. He just asked what we'd been working on and suggested a few tweaks here and there.

He and I hunched over the laptop for a few hours after he arrived, going through clips and helping familiarize him with some of the patterns we'd devised. We were going to be one of the last teams to actually play, so against the backdrop of all this drama, we'd had to wait and watch every other team strut their stuff. We were so relieved to have finally got into the rhythm of a Test week and were champing at the bit to get out there.

We were in Pool D along with Australia, Fiji, Georgia and Uruguay and were slated to play Georgia first. Though nominally a tier-two nation, they'd long been the best of the rest in Europe, and there'd been a concerted lobby for them to replace Italy in the Six Nations.

During our last encounter with them, we'd just held on amid allegations of cheating as the match descended into a series of tense, creaking scrums near our try line. It had served as a clear warning that you take Georgia lightly at your peril.

Howlers had analysed their defence and devised a series of strike plays to exploit their soft edges and positional naivety. The plan was to strike hard and early to sap their spirit.

The first thing I noticed when jogging out for the warm-up was how many fans had already packed the stands, and the second was how muggy and humid it was. Fatigue was going to be a factor, and the slippery ball would make handling a challenge, so a fast start was important. The other main message was to kick the ball whenever we were in our own half. We didn't want to gift them any set pieces in our territory.

Howler's imprint was all over that game, and the first three tries we scored were down to his forensic eye for detail. Two minutes in, we called our play 'Crusaders', which worked like a dream, with Foxy cruising straight under the sticks. My first kick of the World Cup was an absolute sitter; the kind I could have back-heeled with my eyes closed. I missed it. Running on to collect the tee, Jenks looked utterly bewildered. 'Fucking hell, Biggsy', was all he could muster.

To add insult to injury, or rather injury to insult, I'd taken a smack in the face from Liam Williams while celebrating the try. There's nothing better than seeing something you've practised so assiduously come to fruition on the pitch, and Sanj and I – understandably excited – mistimed our embrace.

We were clinical – two more strike plays were deployed with ruthless precision, and we were 22–0 up before the game was twenty minutes old. The second half wasn't as slick and we lost some of our rhythm, but we were already looking ahead to the next game against Australia. That was the one likely to shape our destiny.

Unbelievably, Adam Beard reappeared the following week. He arrived just as we were setting off for Thursday's training session. In place of the powerful, broad-shouldered colossus we'd left behind was a lanky, undernourished beanpole. But if he was expecting sympathy after his ordeal, he'd come to the wrong place.

As he unfolded his six-feet-nine-inch frame from the taxi, he stood there grinning like an idiot. We immediately slapped him with a fine for poor timekeeping, and another one for wearing the wrong kit. When he protested, we added another for the weight loss. He claimed to have lost about half a stone, but I reckon it was closer to two. His stomach had shrunk after the op, and he was struggling to put the weight back on, claiming to the press that he was eating extra eggs and porridge at breakfast. In reality, the conditioners were frog-marching him to McDonald's after dinner every night to force-feed him Big Macs and fries. For four or five days, he had licence to eat whatever the hell he wanted.

On the one hand he was loving it, but on the other he knew that his chances of getting back to a decent fighting weight to play a part in the World Cup were slim, if you'll pardon the pun.

We lucked out in Tokyo. We'd pulled accommodation out of a hat, and found ourselves at the New Otani, which is by some distance the best hotel I've ever stayed in. The top floor was essentially our team room, and the window framed a broad panoramic sweep of the Tokyo skyline, with the Olympic Stadium surrounded by glittering skyscrapers, and the dramatic outline of Mount Fuji looming in the distance.

It was like gazing into an oil painting. There were thirty-seven restaurants in the hotel, catering to every taste imaginable, and a 400-year-old Japanese garden within the grounds, featuring ornamental bridges, carp ponds, a profusion of colourful flowers and a tumbling waterfall. There was even a Bentley dealership, should one of the guests fancy an impulse purchase. The only drawback was that it was eye-wateringly expensive, as I discovered when I sank into one of the sumptuous leather armchairs in the Satsuki bar and ordered a club sandwich and Coke, only to be charged £46.

Gats had developed a sixth sense in terms of reading the mood and, once we'd settled in, he gave us two days off and told us to soak up the atmosphere. It was the first time most of the boys had been to Japan and, as much as we were there to work, it would have been a real shame not to embrace the culture, and sample Tokyo's unique, exotic ambience. Most of us wanted to disappear into the city for a while, to wander its streets, meets its people, sample the cuisine, and let it all wash over us. Alex had flown out, along with several other of the players' wives, so we got to spend some precious family time together. Accompanying her was our friend, Vicky, who'd recently got married and chosen to come to Japan *instead* of going on honeymoon with her husband, Damian. That's commitment for you.

On the first night, keen to make a good impression, I treated them to a lavish gastronomic dinner at an incredibly posh restaurant, seriously denting my bank account in the process. The following night we dined at a dingy kerbside café, where the entire bill came to around a tenner and – gallingly – the food was much tastier.

A lot of the boys disappeared to Disneyland for the day, but Adam Beard came back all depressed because at six feet nine he couldn't fit into any of the rides.

On 29 September, the day of the Australia game, we walked from the hotel to a local park and ran through some starter plays under the maple trees. As we were heading back, Shaun Edwards put his arm around me and said, 'I fancy a drop goal could be quite important today.'

It was classic Shaun; just a whisper in the ear and a knowing look. But I took it on board. If he thought a drop goal could be crucial, it probably would be. During the bus journey to the ground, I was thinking constantly about drop goals, picturing them soaring through the Tokyo night sky.

Out on the pitch, I spent ten minutes knocking over drop goals amid all the clamour and the noise. I was striking the ball crisply and felt like my radar was locked in. This match was so important: win, and we were in pole position; lose, and our World Cup dreams would hinge on the next game against a fired-up Fiji.

We made the perfect start, smashing into Michael Hooper from the kick-off and turning the ball over at the ruck. Two phases later, after Wyn Jones and Jake Ball had punched big holes in the Aussie defence, I dropped into the pocket with Shaun's words ringing in my ears. Cawdor rifled a pass to me, and I aimed for the posts. As soon as I hit it, I knew it was over. Thirty seconds gone, and we were 3–0 up against one of the best teams in the world.

Given our history against the Wallabies and the significance of the game, it felt enormous. Striking the first blow puts you on the front foot and your opponent on their heels.

We had a different mindset for this game and were willing to shift the ball from our own half and take some risks. Within ten minutes, we'd scored the first try from a cross-field kick.

I'd been surprised to see Hadleigh Parkes underneath it rather than George, and my initial thought had been, *What the hell's he doing there?* Parkesey can barely get off the ground in training, but like he'd done with his heroic tackle on Stockdale, he managed to transcend his natural ability and soar above Marika Koroibete. He made no mistake with the grounding.

I knocked over the touchline conversion and remember feeling troubled by the sensation that it all felt too easy. I should have known not to think that way – the moment you switch off against a top team, you're made to pay.

Their frustrations were boiling over, and their captain Michael Hooper was penalized for a later shoulder charge on me. Refereeing inconsistencies had been the subject of feverish debate during the tournament, and we'd seen yellow cards given for such challenges, but Hooper avoided a sanction despite howls of outrage from the Welsh supporters.

The Wallabies hit back through Adam Ashley-Cooper, with a try not dissimilar to our own. Shortly afterwards, I was forced from the field. Australia were on the rampage, and I found myself as the last defender with the bullocking Samu Kerevi thundering down the wing.

I somehow managed to bundle him into touch, but got myself concussed in the process. My tackle technique was awful, and my head ended up on the wrong side. It didn't feel like a particularly heavy blow, but something felt amiss. I got to my feet gingerly, feeling a little trippy and disoriented.

Tips was alongside me, shouting 'well done', but his voice was muffled and distant. My vision wasn't exactly blurry, but it felt like things were happening around me in slow motion. The medics were alongside me in a flash, telling me I'd have to come off.

I desperately wanted to stay on. I knew I was experiencing the classic symptoms of concussion, and fully understood the perils of playing through it, but the gladiatorial instinct had kicked in. As a number 10 it's easy to persuade yourself you're indispensable. You're the general, directing things on the pitch, and it felt as though the Wallabies were getting right back into it. I *needed* to be there.

Geoff Davies was shaking his head, dismissing my nonsensical claims that I'd 'be fine'. It wasn't until ten minutes later – when I'd comprehensively failed the HIA – that I came to my senses, realizing there was no way I could have carried on. Regardless of the personal risks, knowing what we now do about brain injuries, I'd have been a liability. My reaction times would have been slower, my ability to read the game would have been impaired. I thought I was letting the team down by leaving the field, but the reality is I'd have been letting them down by staying on.

Rhys Patchell looked assured when he came on. His first penalty attempt was during my ten-minute HIA period, when HIA replacements apparently aren't allowed to kick at goal. Liam pointed this out to him while he was preparing to take the kick – presumably fancying a pop at it himself – and Patch told him pointedly to mind his own business. He nailed it, which helped him to settle.

His second penalty followed another controversial incident, where Kerevi was deemed to have struck him in the neck when carrying into contact. Despite Hooper's audible protestations that Patch's 'terrible tackle technique' had been to blame, Roman Poite awarded us the penalty, and Patch duly slotted it over from forty-five metres out.

From the restart we landed the killer punch. Australia were in possession, but Genia's pass was laboured, and Gareth Davies flew out of the line to intercept it before scorching up the field like a Lamborghini gliding through its gears.

Cawdor is so good at that; it's his signature move but, even when sides prep for it, it's virtually impossible to stop. He's given the freedom to lead our defensive line and genuinely spooks opposition half backs with his lightning-quick acceleration. Once he'd picked off the ball, the despairing cover defence didn't stand a chance. It's his speed of thought as much as his athletic ability. His brain is constantly whirring, making these micro-calculations about when to go for it. He's a shy bloke off the field, but on it he transforms into this strutting, swaggering rock star, with an uncanny knack of producing those big moments on the biggest stages.

With that try, we completely seized the initiative, and the tempers – which had been gently bubbling – boiled over during the walk down the tunnel. Their scrum half, Nic White, was complaining loudly about something or other, and despite my inner voice urging calm, I told him, a little impertinently, to 'Shut the fuck up and get inside.' It led to a bit of a scuffle, which underlined just how rattled they were.

The start of the second half was a mirror of the first, with Patch knocking over a drop goal during our first attack. It wasn't as cleanly struck as mine, mind, but it bobbled over and bagged us another three points. At 26–8, I thought the game was dead and buried. But I was forgetting that critical component of the Australian psyche; they *never* know when they're beaten.

What followed was something of a waking nightmare, as they ripped into us, playing with a desperate, almost kamikaze fury. Watching that second half – during which we barely touched the ball – must have aged me ten years.

They scored twice through Dane Haylett-Petty and Michael Hooper, and a penalty brought them to 25–26 with thirteen minutes to play. It was excruciating. My heart was thumping every time the ref blew his whistle, and I was willing the clock to tick faster, desperate for those eighty minutes to be up. It's immeasurably worse living out those moments helplessly from the sidelines. It was difficult to believe that our seemingly unassailable lead had been whittled down to a mere point. Even when Patch nudged us further ahead at 29–25, it did little to relieve the tension.

I've never felt relief like it when the final whistle blew. It was sheer force of will that got us over the line; the knowledge that we'd gone on that winning run and clung on against overwhelming odds in places like Paris and Edinburgh. Our fitness had been a huge factor. All that misery we'd put ourselves through in Switzerland and Turkey had been for moments like this.

We had a few quiet beers after the game, but deliberately didn't go overboard. We'd come to Japan with the express aim of winning the World Cup and weren't getting ahead of ourselves.

When the dust had settled, we realized that we'd beaten one of the southern hemisphere big three for the first time in the pool stages of a World Cup.

After those thirteen agonizing defeats, we'd now beaten Australia twice in a row, including this one, when it really mattered. And in a tight game, in which we were outscored by three tries to two, what had proved the difference? Those two drop goals at the start of each half.

I told you Shaun Edwards was always right.

After the high drama of the opening week, we had a chance to decompress, with a ten-day turnaround before Fiji. Relocating to a beach resort down on the coast in Beppu was meant to be a chance to recharge our batteries, but after the sensory overload of Tokyo, it felt strangely drab and uninspiring.

To alleviate the boredom, Sanj, Cawdor, Owen Watkin, Huw

Bennett and I decided to go jet-skiing on Shidaka Lake, but were told on arrival that it was off the cards because of the choppy conditions. We were, however, welcome to sit in a dinghy and be towed around by a speedboat.

It didn't sound particularly appealing, and as it turned out, it wasn't. The dinghy had a hole in it and started sinking minutes after we'd left the shore. The water – which we spent most of our time partly submerged in – was perishingly cold.

The intentions had been good, decamping to the coast for a bit of R and R and the chance to unwind, but the reality didn't live up to our expectations.

Management also tried to force us to swap roommates while we were there, sparking a rare note of discord among the group. Some of the boys felt we were being bossed around, and Franny organized a revolt, encouraging us all to swap back when they weren't looking. It was a good idea in principle – trying to stop cliques developing – but it seemed unnecessary when the group was already harmonious. It might sound trivial, but we were stuck in this remote little outpost where nobody spoke a word of English, and we just wanted to cling to what was familiar. Franny and I had been roomies for four years. We might seem an unlikely coupling, but we'd got on brilliantly since the day we met.

During the 2015 World Cup we'd had a cards group, consisting of me, Franny, Luke Charteris, Gethin Jenkins, Scott Baldwin and Matthew Rees. Foxy joined in once, but he proved a shameless hustler, fleecing everyone of their cash, and was swiftly barred.

Not long after, Charts, Melon and Balders all got the chop, leaving Franny and me as the sole survivors, so we remade the group in our image, declaring ourselves leaders and vetting any new recruits that wanted to join. That was the moment we became joined at the hip.

If our relationship began around the cards table, it developed around our mutual love of sweets, crisps and chocolate. If you're ever in need of a Haribo fix, you're guaranteed to find a healthy stash in our room, where we'll happily munch our way through our bodyweight in confectionery.

Woe betide anyone who leaves any stray wrappers on the floor, though. I'm no slob, but Franny's a clean freak with more than a touch of OCD. The minute we check in, he'll rearrange the furniture according to some inner feng shui that only he understands. It usually involves moving everything to the outer edges of the room to maximize the floor space. His kit will always be ready the night before, neatly folded, ironed and separated into little piles, whereas mine is randomly lobbed into a pile in the corner, which I have to comb through to find whatever creased or worn garment I need. He won't admit it, but it definitely bothers him.

As an illustration of how close we'd become as a squad, we lobbied to change how the money was shared out at the 2019 World Cup, arguing that every member of the squad deserved equal pay. Previously everyone would get an overall 'squad fee' for the tournament, but only the matchday twenty-three would get match fees and win bonuses on top.

Being away for so long, we felt it right that we should split everything between the thirty-one players on tour. For senior players like me, Al, Foxy and Ken, who were likely to feature in every game, it amounted to a pay cut, but we strongly believed it was the best way to maintain unity.

There's an argument that it's an even harder slog for those who don't make the matchday squad because they've had to work just as hard in training, but don't get the reward of actually running out onto the field.

Those who were set to benefit were the likes of Aaron Shingler and James Davies, who weren't likely to be front-line players, and they were among the most vocal advocates of the more 'socialist' system being proposed. But given Beardy's situation, and Cory Hill's injury struggles, Shings soon realized he might end up playing a whole lot more, at which point his enthusiasm for the deal waned considerably!

When we presented it to the WRU CEO Martyn Phillips, and

gathered in the team room to sign it off, Shings and Cubby – tight West Walians that they were – piped up from the back saying, 'I think we've changed our minds.'

We moved from Beppu to Oita, where the Fiji game was being played, and it was there that we discovered the *'onsens'*, or natural hot spring baths. Oita was the *onsen* capital of Japan and they were *everywhere*: steam baths, mud baths, sand baths; every kind of bath you could imagine.

Oita was considerably livelier than Beppu, and these baths were wonderful little sanctuaries from the bustle and craziness of urban Japan. I thought that perhaps I was going a little too often, but my fondness for the healing waters was nothing compared to Cory Hill's fully fledged addiction.

Any time of night or day I wandered into one, Cory would already be there, floating meditatively, his flushed complexion and shrivelled skin suggesting he'd been soaking for some time. He was days away from being flown home after failing to recover from a stress fracture in his leg and might have been hoping for a miracle cure.

Every time we play Fiji, the plan is the same: keep it tight, drive the lineouts, drain their energy during scrums, milk penalties, and kick the ball off the field at every opportunity. And every time we play them, we veer violently off script, doing virtually none of those things. So often in the past, we'd been sucked into their chaotic way of playing – chucking miracle balls, running from deep, and engaging in long, breathless passages of play.

We had to remind ourselves constantly that week: don't let it happen again.

Lining up in the tunnel, I don't mind admitting I felt a bit intimidated. I was craning my neck to look up at every one of them. They were huge men – broad-shouldered, barrel-chested slabs of bristling muscle – and were it not for the numbers on their shirts, it would have been impossible to distinguish between backs and forwards. As I walked out, Cubby turned to me and said, 'Christ, it feels like *Space Jam*, butt.'

He was referencing the kids' film where Michael Jordan and Bugs Bunny have to take on an invading horde of muscle-bound aliens. He wasn't far wrong.

The conditions were bone-dry, the roof was closed, and the pitch was rock-hard. Basically, the worst conditions imaginable to be playing Fiji, and for the first fifteen minutes we played worse than we ever had under Gats. For quarter of an hour, we were sucked into a frightening Fijian vortex. They ran hard and fast, thundering into contact and bouncing off tacklers with alarming ease.

All week we'd spoken about the importance of starting well, and after a quite astonishing opening salvo from the Pacific Islanders, we found ourselves 10–0 down after ten minutes. To make matters worse, we had a man in the bin after Ken had seen yellow for WWE-style tip tackle.

We were under the sticks looking utterly shell-shocked and I remember saying, with comic understatement, 'It's not ideal this, is it?'

I glanced at the big screen where the TV cameras had picked out Gats in the crowd, and he looked completely bewildered, like he genuinely couldn't comprehend what was going on. It was one of the few times in my career when we simply had no answers. It felt as if we were playing a different sport against a different species.

We spent a bit more time in their half, and gradually started winning things – one or two aerial battles, one or two loose balls on the floor – and the momentum shifted a bit. Josh Adams scored in the corner off a cross-field kick, which helped restore his pride after he'd been bulldozed by both Tuisova and Murimurivalu when they'd powered their way to the try line.

We had another penalty, and there was a long discussion about whether to go for goal, kick to the corner, or take a scrum. We could get back to 10-all but there was a feeling that slowly, imperceptibly, we were turning the tide, and we spurned the three points to go for seven.

Our ambition paid off, and we put Josh in again at the corner. With the conversion, we were four points ahead.

They cut to Gats again on the big screen, and the difference in his demeanour was stark. His ghostly pallor and haunted expression had disappeared, to be replaced by a flush of relief and the merest hint of a smile.

Fifteen minutes into the second half, Fiji put a kick up and Sanj and I hared towards it from opposite directions. As we leapt to claim it, Sanj elbowed me in my head, knocking me off balance, and sending me tumbling downwards where I smacked my head on the turf.

I was already out cold before he collapsed on top of me, his bony hip landing another blow for good measure. Three knocks to the head in less than three seconds.

I can only tell you this having watched it back, because I have no memory of it happening. Unlike the glancing blow I took against Australia, this was a serious impact and I was completely sparked out.

Several seconds passed before I gingerly I opened my eyes, vaguely aware of physio Mark 'Carcass' Davies clutching my head and asking if I could hear him. For a split second I was completely disoriented. Where was I, what was I doing? But here's the strange thing; once I'd come to my senses, I felt absolutely fine. In contrast to the aftermath of my previous head knock, where I'd felt dizzy and lethargic, I felt energized and alert. There was absolutely no way I was able to play on, but I felt as though I could have.

By this point, the buggy had trundled onto the field and was waiting to take me to the tunnel, but I waved it away dismissively, preferring to jog off.

The Head Injury Assessment was carried out, beginning with a balance test which amounted to walking along a straight line without veering off course. I passed that comfortably, and was then given several cognitive tests, like reciting the months of the calendar backwards, and repeating back a sequence of random words like *lemon, sugar, paper* and *baby*. They score you against a baseline set at the start of the season so, for example, if you remembered eight out of ten when you'd done it before, any less than that would be considered a fail.

I'll be honest; it's a really difficult thing to do. I struggle to do it when I'm sitting down at home with no other distractions, but when you're in that headspace where the adrenaline is pumping, and your brain's already a bit scrambled, it's far tougher.

Regardless of the result, I knew I wasn't going back on, but had the decision been mine alone, I wouldn't have hesitated. That's why it's so important that such decisions are taken entirely out of the players' hands, because – as idiotic as it sounds – most of us would fight to get back out there. Even in these enlightened times, when there is little doubt about the damage that can be done, we're still ruled by an animalistic desire to re-enter the fray, consequences be damned.

The tension eased when Josh scored his third try after a bit of midfield genius from Foxy.

At the final whistle, everyone was utterly spent. We'd won and secured our passage into the quarters, but the mood was far from celebratory.

The changing room looked like a field hospital, with each of us sporting an array of cuts, welts, bumps and bruises. We were all in agony.

I was closing in on a hundred caps and can say without hesitation that that match, and the one we'd played against the same opposition four years earlier, were the most physical games I've ever played in.

Most teams will contain one or two players who combine size and power with guile and speed, and you can target them accordingly. Against Fiji, you're up against fifteen of them.

A few of the Fijian boys came in to swap shirts, and it looked a bit like when you raided your dad's wardrobe as a kid. Their shirts were hanging off us like tents, and ours looked like crop tops on them.

No one felt like going out, least of all me, as my head injury had ultimately left me feeling groggy and tired. Once the adrenaline had left my system, I realized I wasn't right after all. My limbs felt heavy, my movements were slow, and my head was all fuzzy. My continuing participation in the World Cup was out of my hands.

After a good night's sleep, I felt entirely back to myself, but I'd need to be given the all-clear before returning to play. The fact I'd had two head knocks in two games put me in a different category. Secondary concussions that occur before your brain has properly healed are potentially more harmful than the original injury.

The media was following the story with rabid interest, because it was about far more than one man's health; it was a test case for how seriously rugby was taking brain injuries, and any misstep could be extremely damaging for the game's image.

What bothered me was that certain people thought we were trying to cheat the system and do whatever was necessary to get me back for the quarter-finals. I've heard plenty of stories about coaches putting pressure on medics to pass players fit when they're not, but in my experience with Wales I never witnessed anything but the utmost professionalism. That's why I was pissed off on Geoff and Prav's behalf when the keyboard warriors rushed to judgement, some inferring that Wales would exploit any loopholes necessary to get me back on the field. It's immensely frustrating when you pick up a paper or see things online which are so far removed from the truth.

We relocated to Kumamoto where the Uruguay game would be, and Foxy and I were taken to the local clinic for scans; him on an injured knee and me on my brain. It took longer than usual to receive the diagnosis, as it came through three people – the Japanese doctor told our liaison officer in earnest, grave-sounding tones what was on the scan, our liaison officer then translated it to Geoff, who then explained it to me in layman's terms.

Thankfully, my news was positive, which came as an enormous relief. Foxy's wasn't so good, and his chances of being fit for the quarter-final were slim. Phase two of my assessment was a Zoom consultation with an independent Australian doctor called Michael Makdissi, who'd worked extensively in the AFL and with the Australian Olympic team. Assuming I passed all the return-to-play protocols, the decision on whether I'd be allowed to carry on rested with him.

He was thorough and methodical, asking what I remembered about the incident, how I'd felt in the immediate aftermath and since, and what side-effects I'd been suffering. He knew his stuff and, even if I'd wanted to, there was no way I could pull the wool over his eyes. The longer the consultation went on, the more nervous I became. I was aware that this doctor could extinguish my World Cup dream with one swipe of his pen.

Thankfully, after he'd reviewed the footage and interrogated me on my symptoms, he was happy for me to play in the quarter-final.

Our final pool game against Uruguay coincided with the arrival of the most powerful typhoon to hit Japan in more than sixty years. For weeks, forecasters had been monitoring the progress of Typhoon Hagibis, and there was a real fear that if it struck the mainland, it could wreak untold devastation. Buildings could easily crumple in its path, and thousands of lives were at risk.

The fate of the World Cup hung in the balance. Scotland's game against Japan in Yokohama was under threat, and its cancellation would have seen them dumped prematurely out of the competition. In the end, only two key matches had to be cancelled on the Saturday: the New Zealand game against Italy and England against France.

Meanwhile, tucked away in the coastal backwater of Kumamoto, we were 700 miles away, well out of the typhoon's path, and it felt surreal watching the apocalyptic news footage of buildings being washed away amid devastating landslides, and Tokyo sky-scrapers wobbling in the face of raging biblical storms. We didn't miss a single training session but, after the Rob Howley and Adam Beard episodes, we felt we'd had our share of drama and were relieved to be able to go quietly about our business.

We beat Uruguay in a scrappy encounter which earned us a quarter-final against France. Their final pool game against England had been cancelled because of the typhoon, meaning – depending on your opinion – they'd either be well-rested or undercooked coming into the last eight.

On reflection, we were over-confident going into that game. There was an unspoken feeling that we expected to win, and we collectively took our foot off the gas in training. The coaches still ran a really tight ship, but some of the players – myself included – dialled down the intensity somewhat. We'd won seven of our last eight against the French and allowed a bit of complacency to creep in.

Foxy was named in the team and trained all week, but it was obvious he wasn't right. He'd been in outstanding form, but his knee wasn't healing quickly enough, and we knew it would be a miracle if he pulled through.

Owen Watkin had been sketchy all week, wondering whether he was going to start in the game of his life, and he eventually found out on the morning of the match when a pithy message from Prav landed in the players' WhatsApp group saying simply, 'Foxy's out, Owen's in.'

Not the most orthodox way of finding out you're playing in a World Cup quarter-final, but Ows was pretty damn excited, nonetheless.

France's winger Yoann Huget stoked the fires in the build-up, claiming Wales played 'boring rugby', which was a bit rich con-sidering we'd scored twice as many tries as them en route to the quarter-finals.

It turns out France were refreshed rather than rusty from their week off, and looked sharper and hungrier than us from the first whistle. Before we'd had a chance to find our rhythm, they'd surged into a two-try lead. They were slick and precise in everything they did, whereas we were clumsy and stuttering. We needed a decisive moment, and Jake Ball provided it.

He'd slipped off a tackle for France's first try and had been looking for someone to take his frustrations out on. Guilhem Guirado was his unfortunate victim, as Jake virtually broke him in half with a bone-crushing tackle.

Waino pounced on the loose ball and disappeared into the distance like a high-stepping gazelle. No one got near him as he cantered over for a try. It was the least he deserved after a brilliant tournament.

He'd been one of Gats's left-field picks. He'd been a footballer through most of his youth, who'd only picked up a rugby ball at the age of seventeen when Cardiff City's academy let him go, and here he was, five years later, scoring a try in a World Cup quarter-final.

The reprieve was brief, though, and we were lucky to only be 19–10 down at half-time. Gats was angry in the changing room, his right hand chopping out the rhythm of his sentences like a furious conductor in charge of a symphony. His last words were barked angrily: 'Get out there and show us the team we know you can be.'

Seven minutes into the second half, a French maul was advancing ominously towards our line, when I heard a howl of outrage from within. Sébastien Vahaamahina had elbowed Waino in the face. Not in the claustrophobic confines of a scrum or a ruck, but in full view of the crowd, and it looked worse with every slow-motion replay.

A red card was the only option.

It was a big turning point, and we assumed – naively – that the game would now fall in our favour, but we continued to play poorly. With fifteen minutes left, and the score 19–13 to France, I remember thinking, 'We'll be on a flight home tomorrow morning.' It felt like a lost cause.

With seven minutes left, France had a defensive scrum five metres from their line. Our reserve props Dillon Lewis and Rhys Carré had been suffering a bit of criticism for their supposed weak scrummaging. They took all that criticism and used it as fuel for that one scrum, piling into the French and rocking them backwards.

Charles Ollivon picked up the loose ball, but Tomos Williams was on him like a limpet, digging his fingers in and ripping it from his grasp. Time stood still as the ball flew into the air, resulting in a mad scramble to retrieve it. Tips reacted first, scooping it up and surging for the line. He was held short, but Ross Moriarty plunged over in his wake. Mayhem ensued, with the French insisting the ball had gone forwards while we leapt around, pumping our fists with glee.

After watching the replay, an unflappable Jaco Peyper decided there was no clear evidence the ball had gone forwards and told the despairing French that the try would stand.

The conversion – just to the right of the posts and ten metres out – would have been a gimme if it was a golf putt, but I suddenly felt overwhelmed with nerves.

As much as I try to empty my mind of extraneous thoughts, there are times when they flood in anyway, and this was one of them. It was all on this.

I was probably the only person in the stadium that thought I could miss. The relief that surged through me when it went over was immense, and it ultimately proved the last score.

For the remaining six minutes we reverted to our old selves, rolling up our sleeves and choking the life out of them. Who knows how things might have panned out had Vahaamahina not had his moment of madness.

As Gats said to the press afterwards, the best team lost. No one could argue with that, but in many ways that performance typified what we'd become: a gritty, stubborn, awkward side that could dig in and find a way to win.

The excitement levels in the changing room were more fevered than usual because of the emotional rollercoaster we'd been on. To have snatched victory from the jaws of defeat in such a breathless manner was exhilarating.

The room was all beaming smiles, high-fives and back slaps when Gats approached me and said pointedly, 'You weren't at your best today.'

It caught me off guard and I bristled, snapping back, 'You didn't take me off though, did you?'

I was angry. Gats rarely got his timing wrong, but he did then. Had he spoken to me after the Monday review, I'd have accepted it, but to do it then amid a backdrop of such elation and relief felt heartless. For an hour or so afterwards, the anger lingered, and I was pursuing the argument with him in my mind, dreaming up pithier, more cutting responses, and wishing I'd had a better defence. I felt deflated. It wasn't until later when I checked my phone that my spirits rose. There was a video of Alex and James dancing in the kitchen chanting, 'We're going to Tokyo, we're going to Tokyo.' It was the tonic I needed.

The coaches didn't do much wrong during their tenure, but I thought the tone of the week leading into the semi-final against South Africa was a bit negative. After a game like the France one, where we'd got out of jail, you're better off acknowledging that and focusing on the positives, but the review seemed draped in negativity. Yes, we'd ridden our luck, but we were in the semi-final of a World Cup, and that fact seemed to have got lost amid the recriminations.

The analysis boys pieced together a sequence of our defensive lapses, several of which focused on me being out of position or being slow to react. It was a tough meeting, and I remember breathing a welcome sigh of relief when it was over.

Gats approached me after the meeting and said he wasn't naming the team until later in the week, so I'd have to wait to see if I was playing. Normally by the Tuesday session, the team will have been named, and you train according to your status within it: shirts for the first XV, bibs for the reserves.

For this session – five days out from a World Cup semi-final – Gats was telling us to swap in and out because selection was still up in the air.

Warren clearly had his reasons, and I'm assuming he thought it would drive up everyone's standards, but it felt contrived and unnecessary to me. A World Cup semi-final week should be exciting and enjoyable, but this felt tense and psychologically draining. It wasn't the time for mind games. It was a week where we needed absolute clarity and, frankly, a little bit more positivity around the place.

Once the team was named on Wednesday, everything settled down a little bit. It was essentially the same team that had faced France, expect that Foxy had battled his way back to reclaim the number 13 shirt.

Thursday was declared a bone-on-bone contact session, designed to replicate the ferocious battle we'd face against South Africa. A sound idea in principle, but one loaded with risk. With minutes to go, Liam was tackled from behind and collapsed clutching his ankle in obvious distress.

As he lay there writhing in agony, the mood darkened instantly. I was gutted for him because he'd become such a key player, and his absence would be keenly felt. Losing him was an absolute sucker punch.

The captain's run went poorly too. The stadium was an hour's drive away in Yokohama, and we got stuck in traffic en route, arriving late to find the pitch waterlogged after heavy rain. It was impossible to train meaningfully or to practise kicking, and that added to the growing sense of tension.

The silver lining was the presence of Alex and James – who I hadn't seen for six weeks – at the hotel when I got back. My son's running hug from twenty metres away in the hotel lobby was an amazing boost after a difficult week.

Alex's mum and dad had come out too, and we all went out for dinner and watched England demolish New Zealand to reach the final. It was a strange result to process. Besides the fact that England had beaten the tournament favourites, it meant that if we won our match, it would be a Wales–England World Cup final.

Heading back up to my room, I felt a twinge in my lower back and doubled over in pain. I managed to shuffle into the room, and collapse into my bed as Franny looked on, bemused.

'What's up?' he asked. 'My back's seized up,' I groaned in reply. 'Mate, we've got a World Cup semi tomorrow,' he said jauntily, stating the bloody obvious. 'Why don't you give Geoff a ring?' Moments later, the team doctor was handing me a couple of industrial-strength muscle relaxants and telling me to get them into my system.

I did so, before clambering into bed to watch the football on my iPad. The next thing I knew, I was waking drowsily with my headphones still clamped to my ears. The iPad was still emitting a blueish glow, but the football had long since finished. I'd barely seen a ball kicked before I'd passed out.

I drifted back to sleep feeling completely spaced out, and when I next awoke, the painkillers had worn off and my back had seized up again.

It occurred to me that I might actually have to pull out of the game, but Prav proved that morning why he's the best in the business. I rolled onto his physio bench feeling stiff and tight, and within half an hour I rolled off it again, now feeling supple and sinuous. I wanted to hug him with gratitude, but he warned me there was an inflammation there that could yet be aggravated. 'Dose up on painkillers,' he advised, 'and keep your fingers crossed.'

I didn't dare sit down on the bus to the stadium, pacing nervously up and down the aisle, pausing every now and then to lunge gently, and praying nothing would happen. It dominated my thoughts to such an extent that I barely noticed the electric atmosphere in the ground during the warm-up.

Our fitness coach Bobby Stridgeon saw how stiff I was when

placing the ball on the tee so he raced on with another couple of paracetamol. As I was bending over like an arthritic pensioner, I remember looking to the other side and seeing the monstrous figure of François Steyn, all rippling thighs and powerful quads, booming the ball over with ease from fifty metres.

He was a much bigger man than I'd realized, and I couldn't help but feel vulnerable. Had this been a regular season club match, there's no doubt I'd have withdrawn, but when the stakes are this high, your attitude changes. At a time when I should have been contemplating the game, thinking about the opening few phases, memorizing the calls, I was wrestling with this emotional dilemma. Should I pull out for the good of the team?

With the fanfare building around me, and the Taiko drummers pounding their rhythms from the sidelines, I decided I had to give it a go.

The game unfolded exactly as we expected it to, as an unapologetic kick-fest. It was physical, attritional, and definitely not easy on the eye. Memories of our last quarter-final were at the back of our minds, and while it wasn't a revenge mission per se, there was a feeling of unfinished business. We were refusing to budge in the scrums and were competing for every scrap in the air. At times it was like looking into the mirror as their tactics were virtually identical to ours. Both teams were happier without the ball, sending kicks skyward and inviting the opposition to try their luck against virtually impenetrable defences. Passing became a luxury neither team was willing to indulge in.

The injury curse struck again before half-time, and we lost Franny and George North in quick succession. South Africa's scrum had been chewing up the opposition en route to the semis, so losing our most destructive scrummager was far from ideal.

Shaun Edwards reassured us at half-time that things were on track. We just needed an opportunity to pounce.

His last words were, 'You're forty minutes away from a World Cup final.'

Hearing it said out loud really rammed it home, and we

The two women in my life. Mum was always an inspiration to me, and Alex has been by my side every step of the way. I wouldn't have had the career I've had without them.

Whether we're on the Gower or the Med, we'll always
feel at home with James and Ollie by our side.

Above left: It was a revelation moving to Northampton, where my knowledge and understanding of the game deepened considerably. *Above right:* I miss Mum every day and remain eternally grateful for everything she did for me. It's a real source of comfort that she spent three wonderful years as James's grandmother before she passed away. *Below:* The 2019 Grand Slam ultimately saw us reach number one in the world, and it was great to have Alex and James on the pitch to celebrate.

Left: The 2017 Lions tour of New Zealand was a sensory overload, epitomized by this spectacular Maori welcome in the Bay of Islands.

Right: Conflicting emotions after another defeat to Australia. James had been born earlier in the week, and I needed to reach the magic figure of sixty caps to continue playing for Wales. My head was elsewhere, but pulling out wasn't an option.

Above and right: By way of contrast, the Lions tour in 2021 was bittersweet. I was finally considered the best fly half in Britain and Ireland, but the lack of crowds made for an underwhelming experience.

The South African fans were incensed by my confrontation with their golden boy, Cheslin Kolbe. Little did we know that we would meet again as teammates at Toulon by the end of the year.

Above and left:
Arguably my finest moment in a Wales jersey: nailing the winning kick from the halfway line to beat England at Twickenham in the 2015 World Cup.

It sometimes seems surreal mixing with royalty, but Prince William's role as patron of the Welsh Rugby Union meant he was a regular presence.

Above left and middle right: What a difference eighty minutes makes! The pride I felt running out for my 100th cap in 2022 soon turned to rage after a hapless defeat to Italy.
Bottom right: I was exasperated by the media coverage of my on-field argument with George North during the Fiji match at the 2023 World Cup. Not for the first time, I was painted as the villain, but I make no apology for my fiery temperament.

I've suffered some devastating lows in the red jersey, but few were as gut-wrenching as the semi-final loss to South Africa at the 2019 World Cup. There wasn't a single bloke in our squad who doubted that we could beat England in the final.

My last ever game for Wales, at the quarter-finals of the 2023 World Cup in Marseille. It wasn't the fairy-tale ending I'd hoped for, but I was glad I got to bow out on my own terms.

returned to the field with renewed vigour, levelling the scores with an early penalty.

It remained locked at 9–9 for nearly twenty minutes, before the moment that still haunts my dreams.

Faf de Klerk dummied to go right from a ruck before passing left. We had the numbers to cover, but when their bruising centre Damian de Allende ran at me, I lunged too high, and he swatted me aside. I scrambled desperately to make amends, but you rarely get a second chance in Test rugby.

Once he'd broken my tackle, he'd as good as scored. I was immediately gripped by that sinking feeling. It was a horrible, exposing moment, and I had nowhere to hide.

In a game where neither side had managed to find much space, it felt pivotal. Missing a tackle is a much bigger dent to your pride than throwing a poor pass or slicing a kick. It was technique that had failed me, pure and simple, but I knew my courage would be questioned and I hated that. I couldn't shake that feeling for a good few minutes afterwards. It was futile and damaging, but I couldn't help myself. I knew it could have been the turning point. At a time when I needed to be forceful and decisive, I became hesitant and unsure. For those few intense minutes, it felt like I was the only bloke on the field and every set of eyes was boring into me.

Gats's sixth sense kicked in and he made the call to replace me for the last twenty minutes.

That hurt. You want to be on until the bitter end, to be the guy who makes the difference; instead I was on the sidelines, powerless to influence the end result.

Rhys Patchell came on and immediately sent a brilliant touchfinder deep into South African territory. After a series of raids, we were awarded a penalty five metres out, and Al opted for the scrum.

The Boks love that kind of man test, and as soon as the ball was in, they marched forwards, looking to splinter our scrum. We started to buckle but Ross Moriarty managed to dig the ball out and palm it on to Tomos. Two crisp passes later, Jaddsy was strolling over the try line.

It had been a bold call to take the scrum, and a gutsy move to attack the short side. Leigh's nerveless conversion made it 16–16, and swung the momentum firmly back in our favour.

Cawdor and I were now on the bench together, daring to believe, urging the boys to keep South Africa on the hook, to keep stressing them, testing their discipline and luring them into giving away a penalty. But that's a hazardous game to play because you risk giving one away yourself, and that's exactly what we did.

Al carried into contact, and Francois Louw shot in and snaffled the ball. Shit. Our relentless pressure had amounted to nothing, and they were able to clear their lines.

The relieving kick put them back in our half, and we all knew what was coming.

They claimed the lineout, clustered into a phalanx of beefy Boks, and motored forwards with an irresistible momentum. With that many bodies moving in the same direction, the inevitable happened and the whole thing collapsed in a heap of tangled limbs.

Jérôme Garcès blew his whistle and thrust his arm out decisively.

Penalty, South Africa.

My heart sank. Handré Pollard was one of the most accurate marksmen in world rugby, and when he pointed towards the posts, I knew there could be only one outcome.

A hushed silence fell as he swung his leg languidly towards the ball, sending it end-over-end into the Yokohama night sky and through the posts. It was a horrible, soul-destroying moment. There were four minutes left, and only three points in it, but it felt like the killer blow.

The last painful moments were spent desperately trying to free ourselves from their grip, but it was futile. They'd done what we'd done to so many of our victims over the years. They had us in their jaws now and weren't letting go.

The official reason for the final penalty was that Rhys Carré had lost his footing, and Dillon Lewis came in from the side, but having spoken to some of our forwards, the boys reckon Duane Vermeulen dragged it down from the inside and conned the referee.

If so, it was a cute move by an experienced campaigner, but to lose a game of that magnitude on such an arcane technicality felt difficult to stomach.

I've never felt lower after a match than that. Everyone was slumped in their cubicles, shrunken and glassy-eyed, trapped in their own silent reveries. If we could have jumped on a plane and flown home that evening, we would have done. No one wanted to spend another minute in Japan, let alone play in a meaningless third-place play-off.

The bus back to Tokyo was deathly silent, as everyone continued to ponder what might have been. Thinking about the work we'd put into the campaign – the horrendous lung-busting training camps, the sacrifices we'd made, the time away from our families, the fourteen-game winning streak, the glorious against-the-odds victories, the dizzying rise to the top of the world rankings.

Had it all been for nothing?

Every time we'd been backed into a corner, we'd come out swinging, digging deep into our reserves to find a way to win. But when it really mattered, we couldn't.

You often find solace in the company of your teammates, but that night I wanted to be as far away from them as possible, and I knew that salvation wouldn't be found in the bottom of a beer glass.

I went out for dinner with Alex and her parents, but I was barely present, lost in my own thoughts. I was equally antisocial during the team get-together on the Monday. Being around the squad served as a reminder of what had happened, and I couldn't just breezily push it to one side. This one felt different to 2015, when our injury-ravaged squad had limped through to the knockout stages. We'd been genuine contenders this time; we'd built the depth, conquered our southern hemisphere demons, and arrived at the tournament as Europe's best side.

On top of that, there was the lingering feeling that it had been the last chance for this set of players, and possibly for me as well. Would I still be around in four years' time? It felt like not so much the end of the tournament, as the end of a golden era.

I was also consumed by the feeling of having let people down. My family and friends, and the thousands who'd spent their savings flying halfway around the world to watch us. I found myself apologizing to people, as though it was all my fault. There was nothing anyone could have said to soothe the pain.

South Africa blew England away in the final, which led to the inevitable hypothesizing: if we'd made it, would we have done the same? I still carry that disappointment around with me, and while it recedes with every passing day, it never disappears entirely.

16

PIVAC AND THE PANDEMIC

As a lifelong Man United fan, I know what it's like to follow in the wake of a successful dynasty. Under Alex Ferguson, United won thirteen Premier League titles, five FA Cups, two League Cups, and were twice crowned kings of Europe. Whoever followed in his footsteps was doomed to fail.

By 2020, the World Cup aside, Warren Gatland had won every competition he'd entered, including the Heineken Cup (twice), three Premierships, four Six Nations titles (including three Grand Slams), and a Lions series.

He was, to put it mildly, a tough act to follow.

The man chosen to succeed him was another Kiwi, Wayne Pivac. They might have hailed from the same island, in the same part of the world, but they were polar opposites.

Gats was cagey, earnest and difficult to read, whereas Wayne was open, avuncular and quick to smile. As someone who'd been a beat cop in a rough part of Auckland, regularly dealing with the aftermath of murders and violent robberies, you might have thought he'd be a strict disciplinarian but, on the contrary, he was refreshingly laid-back.

Their differences also extended to their rugby philosophies. Wayne had transformed the Scarlets from mid-table toilers to a swashbuckling, Championship-winning side in just a few seasons. They played some spellbinding rugby during their surge to the Pro 12 title in 2017, their all-out attacking philosophy a stark contrast to Gats's more conservative approach.

The burning question on everyone's lips was, could that work in the more rarefied atmosphere of Test match rugby?

Wayne had a sly sense of humour, as I was to discover on my first day back in camp. He called me aside the week before we were due to play the 2020 Six Nations opener against Italy to explain that they wanted to build some depth at fly half and were leaving me out of the squad.

What the fuck?

I was quietly fuming, and it must have shown, because he immediately cracked a smile and said, 'You looked like you believed me there for a second.'

My expression softened considerably, as he continued, 'Just joking, you're starting, and I want you to lead the backline.'

He might have strung it out longer had I not looked so furious.

Later that day, we had a full meeting with all the heads of department. Prav delivered his usual opening address, reminding us at the end that we had a trophy to retain, but when Wayne stood up, he corrected him, saying this was a new group, and we had a trophy to *win*.

It was a subtle break with the past.

We opened our campaign with a 42–0 romp against Italy, and it appeared that the transition might be smoother than we'd imagined. Unfortunately, that was the last time we'd taste victory in the tournament.

We were well beaten in Dublin, before losing narrowly to both France and England. Ironically the more adventurous style of rugby we'd played in those two games was what the Welsh public had been longing for, but we'd just ended up on the wrong side of the ledger.

It wasn't easy to adjust after more than a decade of following an embedded game plan, and when you're under pressure, it's natural to revert to what you know best.

Everyone in that squad, bar Alun Wyn, had only ever played

under Gatland, so to a degree we were institutionalized. We'd become conditioned to wanting territory rather than possession, and would instinctively kick the ball away, inviting teams to run into the maw of our defence. That involved playing "off nine" a lot more, with lots of box-kicking and short passes to marauding pods of forwards.

Conversely, Wayne preferred playing off the fly half, which has its benefits but can invite teams to smash you behind the gain line if you don't get your timing right. His concept made sense in theory, and I enjoyed having the ball in my hands more, but it was difficult to implement in the Test arena.

Gats's game plan involved winning collisions, punching holes, and getting over the gain line, whereas Wayne's was based on guile and evasion; getting the ball along the backline and exploiting gaps out wide. Looking for space rather than heavy traffic.

If you're playing off 10 on the touchline, for example, you accept that you'll lose ground on the first contact, but you'll then be in the middle of the pitch with two sides to play to. Wayne would speak about 'chopping their chain', which loosely translates to shortening their defensive line. The idea was that within a few phases, they'd have fewer defenders on their feet, enabling you to isolate them with tip passes and lots of ball movement.

What Wayne hadn't reckoned for was the claustrophobic nature of international rugby, where opposition defences are all over you like a rash. What worked for the Scarlets was often killed at source with Wales, and it meant that when we did kick the ball, it was out of panic rather than part of a plan. I'd find myself kicking aimlessly to get rid of the ball, as opposed to accurately so I could regather it. If we kept hold of possession, we often found ourselves going backwards. But we were never going to flick a switch and transform ourselves overnight.

Six Nations camps are all-consuming affairs, and it's easy for events in the real world to pass us by. But there was a news story that developed during the 2020 campaign that got stranger and more alarming as the weeks passed.

A mystery virus from China, supposedly originating in a bat or a pangolin, had begun to spread across national borders and was infecting and killing humans. What had initially seemed an abstruse and distant concern suddenly became very real when the disease arrived in Europe. The news footage from Italy, where the death toll was mounting, was distressing in the extreme, and it soon became apparent that the virus would be coming to the UK before too long.

Covid-19 was declared a global pandemic, and the world was about to change beyond all recognition. Live sporting occasions, where tens of thousands of people clustered together in close proximity, were suddenly seen as dangerous 'spreader' events, and it wasn't long before the sight of fans in stadiums felt like a memory from a bygone era.

After much deliberation, our final match of the Six Nations – against Scotland – was cancelled within twenty-four hours of kick-off, with tens of thousands of Scots already crowding the capital city. Within weeks, Cardiff – along with every other urban centre in Britain – would become a ghost town.

The day after, I was in a meeting at Northampton, being briefed on what might happen next, when the chief executive burst in and told us to grab our bags and go home. The league had been suspended indefinitely. No one knew whether this meant days, weeks, months, or potentially even longer.

Alex and I decided to head back to Wales and hunker down on the Gower where we had more space. I need to be careful how this comes across, because I'm aware of how wretched and depressing this period was for so many, especially those who lost loved ones in such desperate circumstances, but I have really fond memories of lockdown. We were incredibly fortunate in that no one we knew got seriously ill, we were financially secure, and we were able to enjoy a period of uninterrupted family time during what turned out to be a gloriously sunny spring. For the first time since I was a teenager, I had no schedule, no demands on my time, and nowhere I had to be. As much as the majority of the population felt imprisoned and claustrophobic, I felt strangely liberated.

The only communication we had with the club was a weekly Zoom call, during which everybody would be lounging in their gardens, tending barbecues, sipping beers and soaking up the sunshine.

I stayed fit and healthy, improvising exercise routines with a small pile of weights and fitness bands the WRU had given me, but other than that I gave my body a well-deserved rest. Over time every little niggle, ache or strain I'd been managing over the years slowly disappeared, and I felt in the best shape of my life.

We'd been having conversations with Northampton about the need to take pay cuts of 25 per cent as the club tried to steer itself away from the financial cliff edge. While some of the boys were opposed, I took a more philosophical stance, reasoning that if I felt this healed and physically refreshed after a few weeks off the hamster wheel, I might end up extending my career by a couple of seasons.

The final round of the Six Nations was eventually played during the last weekend in October 2020 and was followed by a completely contrived tournament called the Autumn Nations Cup, devised purely to keep the cash-strapped unions afloat.

The country was still in the grip of the pandemic, though, and the Principality Stadium – formerly the Millennium Stadium – was being used as a field hospital, so our home games took place in an empty, windblown Parc y Scarlets in Llanelli. We lost dismally to Scotland, condemning us to fifth place in the Six Nations, just eighteen months after we'd won it in such emphatic fashion. It already felt like an eternity ago.

There was no sign of our defence coach, Byron Hayward, the Monday after the defeat, and everyone assumed he must have tested positive for Covid and was self-isolating. We soon learned that he'd been sacked.

Warby – who'd been part of the coaching staff as a breakdown specialist – had also disappeared three weeks earlier, and the press began speculating wildly about mutinies and internal unrest. Admittedly, the optics didn't look great; we'd suffered our worst Six Nations finish since 2007, endured a first home defeat to Scotland in eighteen years, and now it seemed we were haemorrhaging coaches. It had the look of rats leaving a sinking ship, and that was the narrative that took hold, but the truth was more prosaic.

Warby had been a left-field appointment in the first place, and soon realized he wasn't cut out for the job. It had been more like a hobby for him, and we needed someone who was fully invested. He's a big family man, and decided he'd prefer to be with his wife and kids than holed up in a Covid-secure bubble at the Vale.

As for Byron, that was a really difficult call for Wayne. He'd been one of his key lieutenants at the Scarlets, and they were really close. If anything, Byron had had an even tougher job than Wayne in terms of stepping into someone else's shoes. Shaun Edwards was probably the best defence coach the game had ever seen, and we'd all been his devoted disciples. Anyone following in his footsteps would have been fighting an uphill battle.

Byron was a hard-as-nails former boxer who spoke well, and knew his stuff, but he came from an environment where he'd been nurturing and developing club players. It was an entirely different dynamic when the guys sitting in front of you were gnarly, experienced internationals.

Gethin Jenkins was swiftly summoned to replace him, and tasked with instilling again that no-holds-barred defensive intensity that had served us so well under Shaun.

The Autumn Nations Cup was a drab and uninspiring affair compared to the usual autumn internationals. The teams involved in the Six Nations were joined by Georgia and Fiji (Japan had to withdraw due to travel restrictions). For Wales, defeats to England and Ireland were offset by unconvincing wins over Georgia and Italy. It was beyond strange to play in empty stadiums. While the shock of the early days of the pandemic had given way to a grim acceptance of the new normal, the idea of playing an international match in front of vacant, silent stands was surreal. Without that sensory rush of crowd noise that accompanies a burst from a winger, the collective intake of breath that follows a big tackle, or the visceral roar that greets a try, the whole endeavour soon loses its lustre. It all felt hollow and unreal.

On the plus side, World Rugby had decided to freeze the world rankings during the pandemic, which eased the pressure in terms of results. We knew that, regardless of what happened, we'd be seeded fourth in the next World Cup, and with that in mind, victories weren't Wayne's biggest priority.

He made it clear that his aim was to blood new players, test different combinations and continue the transition to his style of play. A lot of new guys got their first taste of international rugby during that campaign, including Kieran Hardy, Callum Sheedy, James Botham, and an emerging star by the name of Louis Rees-Zammit.

During the review of the Ireland defeat, Gethin Jenkins showed a few clips of what he considered defensive lapses. He paused one, pointing at the screen, and saying, 'Look at this. I've got my 10 here with his back turned, talking to the referee, my 12 not looking remotely interested, and my 13 looking at the posts.' I could feel my temperature rising. What had happened was that Ireland had kicked for touch, and I was asking the ref a legitimate question about their forwards being slow to set at the lineout. The clip was entirely misleading.

Melon carried on, accusing us of lacking focus.

'This is ridiculous,' I snapped. 'We've got enough things on our plate without you piling negatives on negatives.'

Melon, eager to assert his authority, snapped back, and things quickly got heated between us, with Wayne eventually having to intervene.

The adrenaline was still coursing through my veins as I made my way to training. A grinning Elliot Dee sidled up to me and said, 'Congratulations, Bigs.' I was on edge and barked back,

'What do you mean?' He raised an eyebrow and said, 'I think you just announced your international retirement back there.' As I was warming up, Wayne approached and asked if I was all right. 'I'm fine,' I snapped, 'but don't expect me to take that kind of shit and just roll over.' He smiled breezily and said, 'I liked it. That kind of confrontation can be a good thing.'

Steve and Jenks sought me out after for a chat. They'd noticed a change in my demeanour and were worried the pressure was getting to me. They knew exactly what I was going through in terms of my workload: goal-kicking, running the team, making the calls, doing my extras and analysis. They could practically see the weight of responsibility bearing down on me and talked about the need to delegate. They'd noticed me sermonizing about defensive structures earlier and told me to give it up. 'That's not your job, leave it to someone else, clear your plate of unnecessary distractions.' It wasn't the most revelatory observation, but it was a lightbulb moment nevertheless. I resolved not to stress over the team as much and trust my teammates to do their jobs.

The fact that it came from those two had more impact too. Between us we were the three most capped fly halves in Welsh rugby history, and only they understood the unique demands and pressures that come with that jersey. Each of us had been scarred by that shirt in some way, and we'd spent our careers constantly having to prove ourselves.

The fact they'd approached me was also key. Even though I had their wealth of knowledge at my disposal, I'd never sought their counsel because I'd always wanted to do it my way. I never wanted to be a cut-and-paste version of someone else.

For Wayne to emerge from Warren's shadow was difficult. To persuade the squad to embrace a whole new vision was challenging. To do both during a global pandemic was nigh on impossible.

Whether this influenced the vibe he sought to create, I'm not sure, but it was definitely looser and more relaxed than it had been under Gats.

Practically speaking, the progress we'd made during the Six Nations had completely unwound, and we had to start from scratch ahead of the 2021 edition.

We were being governed by strict medical orders and told to stay in the Vale all week. Any journeys to and from home would risk infection. Covid was still raging, despite the punitive lockdown measures, and were it to infiltrate our bubble, games could be cancelled, nudging the WRU and the sport itself closer to financial oblivion. It was that serious.

Sold-out home matches are worth up to £10 million to the WRU, so the longer we played to empty stadiums, the further the coffers depleted. Television money was the only thing keeping us all from going under.

We began to suffer from cabin fever, with the Vale of Glamorgan increasingly feeling like the Jail of Glamorgan. It was an emotionally draining time, and we'd heard stories about other teams being banished to their rooms once training had finished and not being allowed out until morning. Wayne recognized how debilitating that would have been and instead helped us make the best of a bad situation, creating a glorified youth club with dart boards, pool tables and Scalextric tracks.

The experimentation of the autumn was over, and a line drawn in the sand. It was time for Wayne to prove he was the right man for the job. Public levels of scepticism were soaring, and there were plenty of critics who considered Wayne out of his depth. Results had been undeniably poor, but things were slowly bearing fruit behind the scenes and, as time went on, some of the cynicism among the players began to melt away.

To his credit, Wayne hadn't come in and completely swept away the old regime. It was very much a case of evolution, not revolution. His experience of quelling an early mutiny when he took over at the Scarlets had prepared him well for what could have been a difficult period, and he struck a good balance between being authoritative but also open to feedback.

In the weeks leading up to the Six Nations, Jenks and Melon acted as a pragmatic counterweight to Wayne and Steve's more adventurous leanings. As coaches schooled in the Gatland way, they talked a lot about the importance of structure and organization. In other words, we didn't have to run *everything*.

On the Wednesday before the opener against Ireland, the senior players were summoned to an emergency meeting. A picture had emerged on social media of Josh Adams at a baby shower for his expectant fiancée. Nothing was a starker sign of the times than this. The strict social-distancing rules introduced by the government meant no one was allowed to socialize with anyone outside of their immediate family. What would normally have been a delightful and innocent photo was – in these dark times – evidence of law-breaking, and management knew they'd have to act.

Being able to play sport while most of the population was confined to their homes was a privilege, and one we couldn't abuse. Their instinct was to slap a fine on Josh and ban him for the opening two matches, but we argued that was too much. Eventually we talked them down to just the ban, though obviously it amounted to a financial penalty too, as he'd be missing out on match fees and potential bonuses, as well as those two caps. It remains the most expensive baby shower in British history!

Suspending Josh was a big call as we'd already lost Liam to a ban following a red card he'd picked up playing for the Scarlets. That meant two of our first-choice back three were out of the opening game in a tournament in which Wayne was already under a huge amount of pressure.

Training that week was highly charged and erupted spectacularly during a forwards session when Jake Ball and Alun Wyn started swinging wildly at one another following a collapsed maul. Tomos Williams – the only back in the session – had a ringside seat, and subsequently declared it a score-draw after they both managed to land a few blows, though Al definitely looked the worse for wear, sporting an angry-looking shiner all the way up to match day.

Internationals at the Principality Stadium normally take place in a swirling cacophony of noise, in which you can barely hear yourself think, let alone speak. During that game against Ireland, you could hear *everything*: the subs chatting on the sidelines, the messages coming on, even the opposition's team talks in their huddles. It was surreal and unnerving, and we had to keep reminding ourselves it was an actual Test match in the Six Nations.

After having beaten us in the autumn, Ireland were understandably confident, and no one was giving us a prayer. Fourteen minutes in, Peter O'Mahony came flying into a ruck, nearly taking Franny's head off. It was a sickening collision, but the ref, Wayne Barnes, thought otherwise, initially waving play on. Nigel Owens had come in to give us a referee's briefing before the tournament, and told us that English refs were less inclined to punish head-on-head collisions, advising us to draw attention to any that occurred, and to protest any lenient decisions.

With that in mind, Franny hounded Barnes, insisting that he checked the replay. When he eventually did, the evidence was damning and O'Mahony was sent off.

Ironically that's when the game swung in *their* favour. The red card galvanized them, and Conor Murray and Johnny Sexton reverted to their belligerent best, orchestrating things brilliantly and keeping the ball well out of our grasp.

It was classic low-risk, one-pass rugby and, in our exasperation, we started giving away penalties, allowing them to take a 13–6 lead into the break.

Wayne spoke at half-time about the Leinster–Scarlets semi-final in 2017, when the Scarlets lost Steff Evans to an early red card, but still managed to grind out a win. He was watching that unfold in reverse, and urged us to move the ball around more, to get away from the set piece and find those holes where the missing man would normally have been.

Eight minutes into the second half, we finally made our advantage count. Turning the ball over on their 22, we snapped into attack mode, recycling with merciless efficiency, before Josh Navidi put George North into a hole for the try. It was a reassuring glimpse of the George of old – strong, fast and ruthless. Ten minutes later, Louis Rees-Zammit added another, burning down the touchline before leaping acrobatically to dab down in the corner. It was a sensational finish and took us into a 21–16 lead which we held until the final few seconds of normal time.

We just had to run down the clock and belt the ball into the stands, but for reasons I still can't fathom, Cawdor decided to pluck it from the scrum and grubber it directly to Ireland's full back Hugo Keenan. Cue pandemonium as the game descended into a breathless, frantic finale, in which Ireland expended every last ounce of energy trying to conjure a winning score.

You could see the panic in Cawdor's eyes as he flung himself around like a berserker, flying out of the line and doing everything he could to kill Ireland's attack.

They smelt blood and won a penalty, and we were out on our feet as Billy Burns prepared to kick to the corner.

All he needed to do was knock it into touch, and give them a chance to set up one of their trademark driving mauls.

I winced in anticipation as he swung his leg towards the ball . . . and kicked it dead.

As much as I was elated at the win, I felt a huge amount of sympathy towards Billy, and made a beeline to console him. It's always a risky kick, as you want to get as close to the line as possible, but I told him to forget about it, that it wasn't the reason they'd lost. I knew, though, as someone who has carried similar burdens, that it would torture him for some time to come.

There was only a six-day turnaround for the Scotland game, and our squad was riven with injury. We'd lost both our number 6s against Ireland: Lyds to an ACL and Navs to a neck injury, but midfield was the biggest concern, with George and Johnny Williams both joining Foxy on the casualty list.

I've never liked playing at Murrayfield, and that day was right up there as one of my worst-ever experiences. Snow began to fall during the warm-up, it was bitterly cold, and the cavernous stadium felt desolate and inhospitable. The injuries and the travel had contributed to a collective sense of ennui, and we just couldn't get things going.

It's comfortably one of the worst games I've played for my country.

As a team, we were heavy-legged and lethargic and struggled to find any kind of rhythm. Scotland exploited that, harnessing the flamboyant stylings of their head coach Gregor Townsend and scoring some scintillating tries. At 17–3 behind, for the first and only time in my career, I considered subbing myself off. Someone needed to light a spark and it wasn't me. Were it not for Louis's try on the stroke of half-time, we'd have been dead and buried.

I missed the conversion and jogged in feeling empty inside. I needed to be put out of my misery.

Wayne clearly shared my sentiments and, ten minutes into the second half, he replaced Gareth and me with Callum Sheedy and Kieran Hardy. It paid immediate dividends as their added zip and vigour helped put Sanjay away for a try.

We looked much slicker with them at the helm, and they began to manoeuvre us around the field with a precise exhibition of tactical kicking. Callum might have been green at this level, but he'd had a hell of an apprenticeship at Bristol, playing with world-class athletes like Charles Piutau and Semi Radradra. He wouldn't have felt too intimidated stepping up.

Unbelievably, for the second week running, we found ourselves with a one-man advantage after Zander Fagerson clattered into Wyn Jones at a ruck in what amounted to a flying headbutt. It wasn't as clear cut as the O'Mahony one a week earlier, but it was illegal, and he was given his marching orders.

Then came the moment that turned Louis Rees-Zammit from a rising star into a global sensation. Willis Halaholo goosestepped his way into space, making a strong outside break before rifling the ball to Zammo on the wing.

Zammo was surrounded by defenders and had virtually no space, but without breaking stride he chipped the ball over the top and gave chase. As the Scots turned to scramble, he glided past them all, leaving them trailing hopelessly in his wake. The ball bounced kindly into his arms, and he dived for the line.

It was an extraordinary bit of skill, yet he made it look entirely effortless, and with that one inspired intervention he took us into the lead. He claimed afterwards that he'd accrued an extra 50,000 Instagram followers within an hour of the final whistle.

In a game of heart-stopping drama, that wasn't the final act. We were defending a slender one-point lead with the clock in the red when Scotland launched one last desperate attack, splintering our defence and putting Duhan van der Merwe into space. Summoning every last ounce of energy, Owen Watkin launched himself at Duhan and swiped at his ankle. There are few defensive plays more satisfying than the ankle tap; the softest of contacts that can instantly transform a charging rhino into a clumsy giraffe.

Duhan collapsed in a heap, and with him so did Scotland's challenge. Owen might not be a glamour boy like Zammo, but that tap was every bit as important as the try.

During the post-match huddle, I thanked the boys for their never-say-die spirit and asked for a round of applause to acknowledge 'Willis's first cap and my last.'

I'd had an absolute shocker and wanted to get the gag in early before the boys declared open season. Sometimes you just have to buckle up and take the flak.

Zammo had already developed a glowing reputation in the Premiership, but he proved that day that he could do it at Test level too. As a Cardiff boy, he couldn't be further removed from the Welsh stereotype – with his slicked hair, perma-tan and confident swagger, he's everything most young Welshmen are not.

Wayne had worked him hard in camp, instilling a strong work ethic to go with his outrageous natural talent. There'd been a few fitness concerns when he'd first arrived and Wayne had gone public about that, conscious that the Welsh fans were already salivating over the emergence of a generational talent and wanting to keep his feet on the ground.

He was able to produce these incredible 'YouTube' moments but didn't have the same endurance that the rest of us did. He had come last among the backs in fitness testing the previous year, and knew he'd have to address that before he'd be considered as a Test starter. Not that it stopped him pushing his case.

He once ambushed Stephen Jones in a coaches' meeting, asking in full earshot of everyone why he wasn't being picked. Steve politely explained that he was competing against Lions and fifty-cappers and would have to bide his time.

It was an audacious move, but I think they quietly admired his confidence. Later, after training had finished, he was wandering to his car when Jenks accosted him, asking where he was going.

'To the showers,' he replied, bemusedly.

Jenks pointed over his shoulder, 'You know all those other boys who you think you're better than – what are they doing right now?'

Zammo turned around to see the likes of Leigh, Josh and Sanj doing their extras, diligently practising their kicking and aerial skills.

With a bashful grin, he turned on his heel and joined them.

By the time of the 2021 tournament, he'd addressed his failings, and we were all indebted to him for his contributions in those opening two games. He was on a red-hot streak.

We had a casino night after the Scotland match, and I'd gone on decent run on the roulette table. Towards the end of the night, he and I were the last men standing, with a sizeable pile of chips at stake. I suggested we go red or black for the final winnings rather than split it fifty-fifty. I don't know what I was thinking. Of course the golden boy of Welsh rugby was going to win; he was untouchable right then. Sure enough, he cleaned up and I walked away with nothing.

After the Scotland game, a narrative developed in the press that we'd been lucky; that we'd only scraped two wins because our opponents had been shown red cards. What the press failed to consider in their rush to discredit us was the fact that *we* hadn't been carded. Our discipline had been on-point and that was no coincidence.

We knew how much head contact was being policed, so we had spent a lot of time practising tackle technique and ruck entries. It was a big point of focus for Wayne, who'd drilled it into us that cards can decide outcomes. The upshot was that *we* didn't put any high shots in, *we* didn't lead with our heads or our elbows, so – guess what? We didn't get any cards.

The constant griping felt like sour grapes, particularly from the Scots, who never live up to their perennial hype. Given the number of times we'd beaten them, I thought it was more than a little churlish of them to question *our* credentials.

But actually I didn't really care about what was being said. We were two from two, and that was all that mattered.

Our next fixture was against England in Cardiff two weeks later. I was genuinely worried that I'd be dropped for that game, and part of me wondered if I'd reached the end of my road. Sheeds had come on and seized control against Scotland, and I couldn't have complained if Wayne had stuck with him.

The usual arguments were being reheated in the press about my supposed lack of creativity, and questions were being asked about whether it was time to hand the reins to a new generation. So I was very relieved when Wayne gave me another chance, but Cawdor wasn't so lucky, missing out to Kieran Hardy.

Wales–England games are rarely without incident, but this one was absolutely *littered* with controversy. If the Scots had been fuming about their red card, the English were apoplectic about what unfolded during the first half in Cardiff.

We were given a penalty in England's 22 after repeated infringements, and the referee – Pascal Gaüzère – told Owen Farrell to speak to his players about their discipline. As Owen gathered them on the try line, I asked Pascal to tell me when time was back on. I could see Josh Adams creeping towards the left touchline, and knew what he was thinking.

Faz finished speaking to his players, but they were still bunched up near the posts and I thought sod it, I'll chance my arm. Swivelling to the left, I sent a punt over towards Josh. I knew it was an audacious move, but at worst Pascal would have just blown the whistle, and we'd have had a shot on goal.

Nothing ventured, nothing gained.

Josh is the ultimate poacher, and had already anticipated the kick, keeping him one step ahead of George Ford who realized too late what was happening. He leapt in vain to try to snaffle the ball, but Josh was already airborne and scooped it from under his nose. Try, Wales.

Farrell was absolutely seething, yelling at Gaüzère that he hadn't given them time to set, but Gaüzère was unrepentant, replying simply, 'When I call time on, it's play on.'

I wasn't without sympathy for Faz – I'd probably have reacted the same way had the shoe been on the other foot, but you play to the whistle, don't you?

If that try upset the English, the next sent them spiralling into a rage. We worked the ball across the backline before Josh dinked a grubber through for Zammo. It bounced awkwardly and Zammo knocked it on, but before it touched the ground, it hit his leg and bounced backwards. He yelled in frustration, thinking a golden opportunity had gone, but Sanj kept playing, sweeping up the loose ball and crashing over the line.

Any celebrations were muted, because pretty much everyone thought it had been knocked on. Everyone, that is, but the TMO.

My French was pretty limited, but while the referee was

consulting with the TMO, I heard the word *'Essai'* repeated several times with conviction.

I turned to Foxy and asked, 'Doesn't that mean "try"?' He raised his eyebrows and nodded in mock disbelief. 'He's going to give it.'

Zammo's reaction when he did was priceless. His stunned expression – magnified on the big screen – summed up what everyone was thinking; we'd massively got away with one there.

Our third try was another example of quick thinking. England conceded a penalty in their 22 and, assuming we'd go for the posts, they let their guard down. Kieran Hardy had other ideas though, tapping quickly and scorching through a dozing England defence.

I'd come off by that stage, having tweaked my hip flexor, so was again in the position of watching helplessly from the sidelines as England mounted a nail-biting comeback.

It was 24–24 going into the final quarter, but I still felt we were the better, fitter side.

You could sense our belief growing; we'd toughed it out against Ireland and got lucky in Scotland, but this felt like a far more controlled performance. The Pivac imprint was beginning to take effect. We were playing more instinctively, but winning more collisions and developing a relentless rhythm.

Callum really stepped up in those last twenty minutes. He'd missed a few kicks at Murrayfield and suffered a ton of abuse from keyboard warriors. Privately it had knocked his confidence, but when England's discipline began to falter, he punished them decisively. In the space of five feverish minutes, they gave away three penalties and Sheeds nailed them all. His third took us two scores clear and snuffed out any lingering hopes of a comeback. Then Cory Hill's last-minute try gave us a precious bonus point and ensured we won the Triple Crown with a flourish.

It had been an astonishing transformation.

The lacklustre performances in the autumn had been banished, and we'd found a fresh focus. Not many would have believed we'd be celebrating a Triple Crown months after limping to victory over Georgia – if having a solitary beer before driving home qualified as 'celebrating', that is.

Covid robbed us of the chance to properly indulge, but it also meant we were able to linger longer in the changing room without being dragged away for the usual corporate and media commitments.

Zammo wanted a photo with me as a companion piece to one he'd taken three years earlier. He flicked through his phone before alighting on a blurry image of the two of us in a dingy Cardiff nightclub. I vaguely remembered that confident teenager approaching me for a selfie in Tiger Tiger, and here we were, three years later, clutching the Triple Crown as international teammates.

Predictably, there were those who believed we were still riding a wave of outrageous luck and good fortune, and being gifted questionable tries. It was a baseless argument because we'd beaten England by sixteen points. There was no doubt we'd been the superior side, and we'd proved it in those final twenty minutes by grabbing the game by the scruff of its neck.

England had been strong favourites and were defending champions, but there weren't many willing to give us credit for knocking them off their perch.

I spoke to a few of the England players after and they told me they'd been feeling increasingly claustrophobic in camp. Our situation wasn't ideal, but we'd done everything we could to keep spirits high.

If you noticed any dodgy barnets during that campaign, it's because Prav had taken a crash course in hairdressing, and had set up a 'salon' in the hotel so he could use the boys as guinea pigs. We'd also established a 'Covid Caff' from the start, which was going from strength to strength. George North was excelling as head barista, Foxy was head waiter, and Josh had been saddled with washing-up duties as an extra punishment for his Covid breach. Meanwhile I'd been told to continue with the laundry duties I'd been tasked with since my earliest days in camp. Come to think of it, it was pretty much all of us senior players grafting on our days off while the new breed – Zammo, Sheeds, Kieran 'Kizza' Hardy et al – sat around eating croissants and ordering endless coffees.

Something had clearly gone wrong with the power balance.

Wayne made a statement with his selection for the round four Italy game in Rome on 13 March 2021, resisting the urge to make sweeping changes and telling us to put them to the sword. We went for the jugular, scoring four tries in the first half-hour. The 48–7 victory was a fizzing statement of intent, a message to France that we were coming for the Grand Slam.

France's third-round match against Scotland had been post-poned following a Covid outbreak in their camp, supposedly caused by a bunch of their players breaching lockdown rules to go and eat waffles in Rome. 'Wafflegate' had nearly derailed the entire competition, but after a bit of scrambling behind the scenes, a decision was made to reschedule the game for the week after our final fixture against the French.

It was only a minor distraction for us as we knew our destiny was in our own hands; beat France in Paris and the Slam was ours, regardless of what happened the following week.

The match was frenetic and breathless from the very first whistle. Four tries had been scored within the first twenty minutes, including a rare one from myself. If there had been a crowd in the Stade de France, they'd already have had their money's worth.

But if the first half had been characterized by Gallic flair and Celtic grit, the second could be summed up by one word: carnage.

What happened still infuriates me to this day. Following a

lineout on the French 22, our forwards formed a powerful rolling maul that began to accelerate irresistibly towards the line.

A try appeared inevitable when their prop, Mohamed Haouas, dragged the maul to the floor. The ref, Luke Pearce, called advantage and declared loudly, 'He's going lads', meaning Haouas would be heading to the sin bin.

Knowing we had an advantage, we spun the ball swiftly to the right, where Zammo leapt acrobatically and touched down with an outstretched arm.

It was another sensational finish and we leapt for joy, thinking it was game, set and match. There was, however, a smidgeon of doubt about the grounding, and after an interminable series of replays, the TMO decided the ball had been touched against the base of the flag. It was a blow, but I was actually quite relieved as I was convinced a penalty try was forthcoming, which would mean a guaranteed seven points and no need for me to attempt a touchline conversion.

To our collective amazement, Pearce despatched Haouas to the bin but denied us the penalty try, saying he wasn't convinced it would have been scored. I was astonished. From my standpoint, it was a cast-iron penalty try. The only reason Haouas had collapsed the maul was because he knew we were about to score. It would have put us 34–20 up, and there was no way they would have come back from that.

Unable to control my anger, I unleashed a fusillade of abuse in Pearce's direction. Tips glared at me indignantly, telling me to calm down.

'Tell him to do his job then', I yelled, pointing at Pearce, 'and maybe I *will* calm down.'

I was in danger of getting carded myself when Cory Hill piped up, 'Biggsy, come here *now!*'

'*What?*' I snapped angrily, spoiling for a fight with my own teammate.

'Listen. I know he's a cunt and you think he's a cunt. But if you want to call somebody a cunt, call me a cunt, because I *am* a cunt!'

The carnage continued down the other end when Brice Dulin hit back for France, only to have it chalked off when an act of blatant foul play came to light during the replay. In the previous ruck, Paul Willemse appeared to have gouged Wyn Jones and, after another lengthy TMO referral, the decision went from a penalty, to a yellow, to a red card in the space of five minutes. For the third time in five matches, a member of the opposition had been sent off.

My last contribution was to slice the relieving penalty kick to touch. I knew as soon as it left my boot that I'd miscued, and what should have been a lineout on the halfway line, ended up being just outside our 22.

Wayne then made a raft of changes, taking me, Foxy, Ken and Franny off in one fell swoop.

It was a big mistake. Between us we had more than three hundred caps' worth of experience.

We were ten points up with thirteen to play, but Foxy and I had been around long enough to sense there'd been a virtually imperceptible momentum shift. France weren't dominating necessarily, but the tide was turning slowly in their favour, and we'd responded by taking our wiliest campaigners off the field.

We won the lineout, and Sheedy hoofed it upfield, but Willis Halaholo strayed offside chasing the kick. It was an innocent mistake, but one Foxy wouldn't have made. That's no slight on Willis, but he'd arrived cold into the game and hadn't yet gauged its rhythm. They moved back into our 22, and were only denied a try by a heroic Sanjay tackle. Toby had been caught offside in the build-up and was sent to the bin, nullifying the advantage gained from Willemse's red.

There was a creeping sense of dread about those last ten minutes. They got within inches again before dropping the ball, and any relief we felt soon evaporated when Sanj was binned for diving off his feet at the next ruck. It was another massive call, and another that was completely unjust. A penalty, perhaps, but not a yellow card.

With him and Toby now alongside me, Foxy, Ken and Franny in the dugout, there was an unspoken realization that all our serial winners were off the pitch when cool heads and experience were what we needed most.

It was with a sense of inevitability that Charles Ollivon eventually bagged the try they'd been threatening to score, reducing our lead to three points with minutes to play.

We clung onto possession for two of them before conceding yet another penalty. What followed was *the* most heart-stopping, nerve-jangling sequence of play I've witnessed, as France – to their credit – threw everything at us.

Not for them the safety-first approach; they were flinging wild passes from one touchline to another, and I watched with an increasing sense of desperation as eventually, inevitably, they found a gap.

As our defence got narrower, France pulled the trigger, floating a pass to the unmarked Brice Dulin, who cantered gleefully over the line. It was the last play in the last second of one of the most pulsating matches I've ever been involved in.

Foxy and I swapped agonized glances, utterly crestfallen, tears welling in our eyes.

How on earth could that have happened?

The devastation quickly turned to anger and, emotions raging, I made a beeline for Luke Pearce and gave him a piece of my mind. 'You're an absolute disgrace,' I told him as he hurried to get off the field. 'That was a penalty try all day long!'

He stood his ground, saying I had no right to speak to him that way.

I snapped back, 'You've just lost us the Grand Slam, I'll speak to you however the hell I want.'

I then had an argument with our media manager, who was trying to feed me a load of meaningless platitudes to spout to the press. He wanted me to be magnanimous and congratulate

France on their victory, but I was in no mood to toe the party line. I told him to stick me in front of a microphone so I could tell people what I really thought; that we'd been robbed.

I lost the plot in the changing room, ranting and raving at no one in particular. I was pissed off at being taken off, pissed off at the refereeing decisions, and pissed off at the decision to gag us.

I was looking to pick a fight with anyone.

Elliot Dee had to step in and physically drag me away. He reminded me I was on ninety-two caps, adding, 'Make sure you get to a hundred. Don't do anything to jeopardize that.'

With that he frogmarched me to the hot tub on the other side of the changing room, where we got stuck into the Heinekens with Franny, Tomos Williams and Cory Hill. None of us had eaten a morsel of food or drunk any water, so it didn't take long for the beer to take effect. Within minutes we were loudly putting the world to rights, getting increasingly drunk and lairy. We continued to drown our sorrows at the hotel bar, where the gallows humour kicked in.

Tomos and Sheedy started a drinking game, saying, 'Hands up if you came on when we were thirteen points up and ended up losing?' Whoever put their hand up had to finish their drink, and so it continued.

'Hands up if you just lost the Grand Slam; hands up if you've played your last game for Wales; hands up if you lost us all thirty grand?' and on and on.

Looking back, it was probably a little insensitive, as there were guys in that squad who'd have been feeling genuinely tormented by the mistakes they'd made.

Franny dialled up Stuart Hogg on FaceTime and we were all bellowing down the phone at him, telling him we'd hold him personally responsible if Scotland didn't beat France the following weekend.

By then we'd done the maths and knew France had to win with a bonus point *and* by a margin of twenty-one points to knock us off the top of the table. The Grand Slam dream might have evaporated but, once the mist had cleared, we were still favourites to win the title.

When the sun came up, Sheeds, Toby and I were still slouched in our seats at the bar, beers in hand, eyes all bleary and bloodshot, as the rest of the boys started trickling down for breakfast.

All-nighters were fairly commonplace for Toby, but it had been the first one I'd pulled in a while. I slept like the dead the following night, dreaming of blown chances and yellow cards.

I was in Northampton on my own that week, and continued to comb over the details of the match, torturing myself and dragging everyone around me down too. My parents and Alex actually told me to stop calling until I could do so without ranting.

I was consumed by nerves on the day of the France–Scotland game. It was an odd feeling in that everything hung on the outcome, but there was nothing I could do to influence it. I felt helpless and impotent while it was on, constantly fidgeting and changing channels. In its way, it was as compelling and nervewracking as our game had been the previous week, and was similarly decided at the death. There was no need to get the calculators out though, as Scotland won for the first time in Paris since 1999.

So, when I officially became a Six Nations champion for the third time, I was in the house on my own. I couldn't even crack open a beer as I was playing for Northampton the following day. It couldn't have been a more shuddering anti-climax. We should have had a proper celebration with the trophy in the Stade de France, yet here I was in my slippers and tracksuit bottoms, feeling entirely alone and underwhelmed

I was playing against Worcester the following day when my Wales teammates had a trophy presentation in the training barn at the Vale. It was a far cry from lifting the cup in Paris amid an explosion of fireworks and adrenaline, but it was something, and they did it together.

I drove back to Swansea from Sixways under gloomy skies and called in at the Vale on the way. The hotel was deserted but for a lone receptionist, who knelt beneath the desk to retrieve a padded brown envelope with my name scrawled on it in biro.

Inside was a Six Nations winner's medal.

17

THE MORE THINGS CHANGE,
THE MORNÉ STEYN THE SAME

May 2021 was the month my life turned upside down and would never be the same again.

On 6 May, I was selected in the Lions squad to tour South Africa. Eleven days later, my beloved Mum died.

Never had joy turned so rapidly to grief and despair.

Six weeks earlier, on the morning of 2 April, I'd slung my kitbag in the boot of the car, nosed out of the driveway and had begun my journey to Franklin's Gardens.

As always, my phone connected to the Bluetooth, and I called Mum. I spoke to her every day without exception, and the morning call was a daily ritual. There was no answer.

Unusual, I thought, but not alarming.

I finished training and tried again. Still no answer.

I drove back and loaded my new dining table into a van I'd borrowed, and began the long journey to our other home in Three Crosses on the Gower Peninsula, where I'd planned to drop the table off and spend the night.

It was my sister Rachel's birthday, so I called to wish her a happy one and asked if she'd heard from Mum. She hadn't either.

Mum not picking up the phone was unusual; not calling Rachel on her birthday was unheard of. After a flurry of panicked calls to her friends and neighbours, we discovered she'd been rushed to Morriston Hospital in Swansea.

It was a day we'd been dreading. Mum had been diagnosed with ovarian cancer a few days after her fiftieth birthday in 2004.

She'd lived with it for seventeen years, but had been so brave and stoic, you'd barely have noticed.

We'd hoped that an operation she'd had in 2005 would have given her the all-clear, but it returned soon afterwards. She had a slow-growing tumour that had been kept under control by periodic bouts of radiotherapy, but she'd always remained resolutely upbeat, playing down her symptoms, and watching her sprint around the tennis courts in Llandarcy, or walking her dogs for hours on end at the Gnoll, you would never have suspected she was living with cancer.

That's why the end was so difficult to process.

From the moment we received the news she'd been admitted to Morriston, she deteriorated alarmingly, almost disappearing before our eyes.

At the end of April, Rachel and I were called in for a meeting with Mum and the consultant, where we were told that Mum had days to live. There was an option for surgery which, if successful, would give her a bit more time, but we were told to prepare for the worst.

I'm not the first person to have lost a parent, but I can't begin to describe that crushing sense of despair we felt in that moment. As they prepared Mum for theatre, we had to say what might have been our last goodbye.

Mercifully she pulled through, but I was shocked by how desperately ill she looked during my next visit. She was a withered, shrunken version of herself, drained of her vitality.

In all the years she'd had cancer, she had never *looked* ill, and it was disorienting to see her that way. I offered her my iPad and BT Sport login and she turned it down. She couldn't even summon the energy to watch a bit of rugby. I knew then that it was the beginning of the end.

I drove up to Leicester to play in the East Midlands derby, agonizing over whether it appeared callous for me to carry on as though everything was normal. I was named Man of the Match in a rare win at Welford Road, and though Mum's voice was shaky and weak when I called, I could hear the joy in it.

When I walked onto the ward on the day of the Lions squad announcement, her first words to me were, 'Don't you even think about not going.'

She'd read my mind. As much as it had been an enormous honour to have been selected, I'd already decided I couldn't go with Mum like this. I'd never have forgiven myself if I'd been 8,000 miles away in South Africa when she passed away.

Things moved disturbingly quickly after that, and within days Mum had been moved into her own room. We knew it was serious when the hospital lifted Covid restrictions for us, telling us to stay as long as we liked.

For the next week, Rachel and I kept a bedside vigil, watching heartbroken as her breathing became increasingly laboured. By then, she'd stopped responding to our chatter, but the lovely nurse told us that hearing was the most acute sense at this stage and asked if we wanted to play some music.

Mum had always loved Jon Bon Jovi, so we put one of his albums on and held her hand. By the fourth song, she'd gone.

I divide my life into before her death and after.

If grief can be defined as learning to live in the world without someone you love, I'm still learning. I miss her every day, and every time I drive to training, I have that impulse to call her, to tell her what I've been up to, to ask for advice.

I had lots of lovely thoughtful messages in the wake of Mum's death, but I'll always remember the phone call I received from Alun Wyn.

My relationship with him has been a complex one, and we're not necessarily the closest, but it took a lot of courage for him to actually call and speak to me rather than send a text. He'd recently lost his father and knew how I'd be feeling.

Everything that happened from that point on was coloured by Mum's death.

As proud as I was to be selected for the Lions, it paled com-pared to the grief I was experiencing.

I had never experienced that rush of elation you'd assume would greet selection for the Lions. In 2013 I had suffered the crushing disappointment of not being included. Four years later, I'd been plagued with anxiety in the run-up to the announcement of the squad, so relief was the overwhelming feeling when my name appeared.

This time, without sounding arrogant, I expected it.

I was Wales's first-choice number 10 and a Six Nations winner. Ironically, I think my stock had risen as a result of being taken off for the last fifteen minutes of the France game. I had the strong feeling we would have won had Foxy, Ken and I stayed on the field, and absence can sometimes be as powerful as presence.

We flew to Jersey for a training camp and enjoyed a bit of team bonding – paddle boarding in St Brelade's Bay, boat trips around the lighthouse at La Corbière – as we got to know each other. It soon became apparent that the Ireland centre, Bundee Aki, would be the squad enforcer.

During one contact drill, the Scottish prop Rory Sutherland was putting himself about a bit, clattering into contact and bumping people off, and he built up a head of steam as he approached Bundee. What followed caused us all to gasp as Bundee planted his feet and absolutely *melted* him. Sutherland went down like a collapsed deckchair, his ego presumably as bruised as his sternum.

As with 2017, there was a good deal of feeling our way around one another. There was no love lost between Finn Russell and me. We were polar opposites, and had had our fair share of bust-ups. Nothing major, but we'd usually get stuck into one another during matches, sledging and lobbing verbal digs at each other whenever we were within earshot. He was definitely not the person I would have gravitated to in normal circumstances, but

I found myself at a table with him and Owen Farrell in Jersey and realized, after several hours in his company, that he wasn't such a bad bloke after all.

I never wanted to second-guess Gats, but I sensed a slight shift in the power dynamic between Faz and me. This time, rather than hanging around in his slipstream, I felt I was there as his equal, and had a hunch I'd be in pole position to start come the Tests.

I started the warm-up match against Japan in Murrayfield, which we won comfortably, but at a considerable cost. Alun Wyn and Tips both went off with shoulder injuries. At a stroke, we'd lost our captain and one of our most experienced campaigners. Adam Beard and Josh Navidi were swiftly summoned ahead of that night's flight to Johannesburg.

In an echo of the O'Driscoll fallout of 2013, the Irish press was frothing at the mouth over Beardy's selection at the expense of James Ryan, and the old tropes about Gats's Welsh bias started to resurface.

There was no great conspiracy, though. I just think Gats wanted the biggest men he could call on, and they don't come much bigger than Beardy.

I was chuffed to have started the game as it felt like an early vote of confidence, and winning Man of the Match didn't harm my cause.

It also marked a stepping stone on the road back to normality as twenty thousand fans were allowed in; the first time we'd played in front of a crowd for well over a year.

Although we were playing for the Lions, the experience was nothing like a 'Lions tour' would normally be. Nothing will diminish the sense of pride I felt in putting on the shirt, but every other emotion was dialled right down. With its large rural population, lack of access to medical care, and the unsanitary conditions in its townships, Covid had inflicted a terrible toll on South Africa. It was a miracle the tour took place at all, and certainly none of the usual immersion in the country's culture and landscape was possible.

On arrival at an eerily deserted Johannesburg Airport, all our luggage had to be tested and sprayed before we could board the bus to our quarantine hotel. We were tested every day before breakfast, and couldn't move about freely until a negative result had been confirmed.

We were based in Montecasino, a huge leisure and casino complex in Johannesburg. Normally buzzing with activity, it now looked like the set from one of those post-apocalyptic movies, where everything was caged off and abandoned and all signs of life appeared long since extinguished. As much as we had to remind ourselves how privileged we were, staying there was a thoroughly depressing experience.

We cruised to victory in the opening match against the Sigma Lions. It was in the build-up to the second game, against the Sharks, that the spectre of Covid raised its head for the first time.

Cawdor, Sanj, Wyn Jones and I had invited Anthony Watson into our card crew as an honorary Welshman. That, and the fact he was rubbish, so represented easy pickings.

On the morning of the Sharks game, Anthony failed his Covid test, which meant all five of us in the card crew had to withdraw from the team. The rest of us had tested negative, but anyone deemed a 'close contact' of a positive case had to go into quarantine too. Bobby and Benny were measuring the circumference of the table to prove it was longer than two metres – the distance within which 'close contact' was deemed to have occurred – but their efforts were in vain.

We were despatched to our rooms like pariahs. Any kind of outbreak could put the whole tour in jeopardy, and the South African Rugby Union was already on the verge of bankruptcy, so no risks could be taken.

The more immediate concern for the coaches was to cobble

together a team to fulfil the fixture. The boys from the card crew had all been picked to play, so at a stroke Gats had lost a third of his run-on team. As we were cursing our luck, word spread that the entire Springbok squad had been quarantined after a larger outbreak in their camp. Things were getting twitchy. From a personal perspective, I was really annoyed. Finn had laid down a strong marker in the first game, and I'd been hungry to assert my credentials.

From what we were later told, the journey to the ground felt more like a summer tour trip for Aberbargoed Thirds than the British and Irish Lions. In scenes bordering on farce, Prav was at the front shouting, 'Who's played full back before? Anyone fancy a go on the wing?' Gats had to make eight changes in all, essentially sending out a scratch side, with only one back among the reserves.

Owen Farrell took a scrum cap with him just in case he was forced into emergency back-row duty. The jerseys had to be reallocated as well, with Zammo wearing my number 10 shirt, as it was a little too snug on Faz. He'd clearly been spending more time on the pec deck than me.

Back at the hotel, the five of us in quarantine watched the game on our iPads, carrying on a running commentary as the boys romped to a 54–7 victory.

Confined to my room for two further days straight, I managed to pretty much complete Netflix. By the time I was allowed out, I'd resorted to watching niche documentaries on YouTube about people who'd been lost at sea. The only thing keeping me sane was a bundle of surprise packages Alex had hidden in my case for me. There were ten in all, each designed to lift my mood. The labels said things like, 'open when you're feeling lonely', or 'open when you're feeling homesick'. One said, 'open when you want a cosy night in' and, as I was having a cosy two days in, I tore it open to reveal a big bar of chocolate.

Nutrition be damned, it was gone in one sitting.

The box for when I was lonely had a teddy bear inside, with a recording of James telling me he loved me. I'm normally quite stable emotionally, but hearing that while locked in my room more than eight thousand miles away absolutely slayed me.

A Covid outbreak in the Bulls camp put paid to the fourth game of the tour, leading to a hastily arranged rematch against the Sharks in Pretoria. It was the first time I'd been to the iconic Loftus Versfeld and, despite it being empty, I was only too aware of the history emanating from those creaking stands. That stadium had borne witness to some of the most memorable Test matches ever played, not least between the Lions and the Springboks. It was there, twelve years earlier, that Morné Steyn had landed the monster penalty that claimed the series for South Africa. Jenks and I had a wander around the pitch prior to kick-off, trying to locate the exact spot from which he'd struck that fateful penalty.

It was a relief to finally get a start on South African soil. After showing a bit of first-half resistance, the Sharks ultimately proved toothless, crumbling to a 71–31 defeat. It was our third romp on tour and, however satisfying that was, it still left us feeling worried about how undercooked we were likely to be going into the first Test, which was now just a fortnight away.

Before the series rolled around, though, real life intervened again as South Africa erupted into a frenzy of chaos and violence. The flashpoint was the imprisonment of the former president Jacob Zuma for contempt of court, which plunged the whole of Gauteng province – where we were staying – into a violent wave of civil unrest. Buildings were being destroyed and set on fire, looters and rioters were laying waste to the streets, and hospitals were struggling to cope. Not only were people dying in their hundreds, but the sudden profusion of protestors on the streets inevitably sent Covid cases surging again.

Against this grim backdrop, the lunacy of us proceeding with the whole expedition was laid bare. A rugby tour suddenly seemed utterly inconsequential.

Meanwhile the Springboks themselves were almost at the point of no return. Their internal Covid outbreak led to the cancellation of their second warm-up match against Georgia, meaning they would enter the series having played just one Test match in the 600 days since their 2019 World Cup triumph.

In a desperate bid to save the series, the entire operation was moved to Cape Town, away from the increasingly volatile Gauteng Province.

The next match on the schedule was against South Africa 'A', but this was actually a Springboks side in all but name, containing no fewer than 522 caps and seven World Cup winners.

I was picked to start again, but had to withdraw when I injured my ankle during training. I was gutted and could sense my chances of starting in the Tests slipping through my fingers. Gats shrugged when I told him I'd have to pull out, saying he'd pick me for the Stormers game in four days' time – the last provincial match before the first Test.

I prayed my ankle would have recovered by then.

South Africa A gave us a bruising reminder of the scale of our task, delivering a thunderous performance of precision and brutality, as we fell to our first defeat of the tour. That same side, burnished with a few extra Springboks, would be what we would face in ten days' time.

I spent the whole week wondering whether I'd be playing that Test, trying to get the inside track off Prav in between tedious sessions of soaking my foot in an ice bucket and performing the same repetitive mobility routine every hour, on the hour. By the Friday, I confessed to Prav that I didn't think I'd be right for the Stormers match. Covid protocols and the sprained ankle would now have kept me out of three games, and it felt as though my influence was slowly ebbing away.

The young England fly half, Marcus Smith, had been flown out as cover for Finn, who'd been struggling with an Achilles strain, and Prav told me the coaches had already decided to start him against the Stormers.

My heart sank a little when I heard that, as I could feel history repeating itself. I couldn't help but imagine Marcus playing a blinder and forcing his way into Test contention.

Prav sensed the drop in my mood and put a reassuring hand on my shoulder. 'Bigs, it's a good thing,' he said. 'If he's keeping you and Faz out of the firing line, it means you're both going to be involved in the Test.'

He was right. I needed to start viewing my glass as half full, not half empty.

If Marcus Smith's summons had raised a few eyebrows, it was the appearance on the bench of another recently arrived player that dominated the headlines. Eighteen days after dislocating his shoulder against Japan, Alun Wyn Jones had undergone a Lazarus-like recovery and rejoined the party.

If anyone was going to confound medical science like that, it was Al, but even by his standards this was nothing short of miraculous. He landed on the Thursday and was selected on the bench for Saturday. His last-quarter cameo proved he was back up and running, and he was immediately restored to the captaincy. Poor old Conor Murray – who'd been made skipper in his absence – must have wondered what he'd done wrong.

When we gathered on the Monday to hear Gats read out the Test team, I was consumed with anxiety.

Rather than his usual method of reading names off a crumpled piece of paper, Gats announced the team in the form of a slide show, starting with the front row and working his way through to the back three.

So it was around halfway through that I saw and heard my name. *Dan Biggar, Lions fly half.*

I closed my eyes and thought of Mum. Of how proud and emotional she'd have been, and how bittersweet it felt that I'd achieved my ultimate dream, and she was no longer here to share it with me.

After eight years of Lions disappointment, I felt I had earned this. It would have left a glaring hole in my CV if I hadn't played in at least one Lions Test. The trip so far might have felt like the antithesis of a 'real' Lions tour, but in that moment, it felt as special as it ever could have done.

I messaged Alex straight away, simply saying, 'I'm in.'

It occurred to me then that I had no idea who'd be playing alongside me. Usually when a team is read out, I'm privately assessing the choices – *that's a big call* or, *I'm not sure he's the best centre we've got* – but this time they'd all gone over my head. It wasn't until later I realized Jaddsy – who'd scored an avalanche of tries on tour – hadn't been picked. It was a crushing disappointment for him, particularly given that he'd missed the birth of his first child by coming out.

Stuart Hogg – who'd spent two weeks in Covid isolation in Johannesburg – was preferred to Sanjay at full back, and Taulupe Faletau didn't even make the twenty-three.

My half-back partner would be the Scottish scrum half, Ali Price. Conor Murray, stripped of the captaincy in the week, had now also been denied a starting spot.

Even by Gatland's standards, it was a bold, eyebrow-raising selection.

As we were leaving for training my phone buzzed. It was a message from James Haskell. 'Test starter! fucking hell, Bigs. You've come a long way since you were slumming it with me in the Midweek Veg.'

The session that followed was fiery. There were a lot of emotions swirling around, and a lot of disappointed players with points to prove. The normally mild-mannered Mako Vunipola was particularly aggrieved at being left out and was eager to vent his anger. It was meant to start as a 'grab' session, which is somewhere between a walk-through and full contact. The defending team are meant to grab jerseys as opposed to whack people, but Mako made it clear from the start that he'd be engaging in no-holds-barred full contact. I stooped to tackle him a few minutes in, and he bounced me several yards backwards. That set the tone, and a few minutes later, there were bone-crushing tackles flying in from all angles. We were lucky to come through it without any injuries.

Gregor Townsend delivered a memorable presentation based on the infamous 'Rumble in The Jungle', when Muhammad Ali beat George Foreman. Foreman was a monstrous brute who liked to physically dominate his opponents, whereas Ali was leaner and lighter on his feet. Ali was a massive underdog but won using his celebrated 'rope-a-dope' tactics – absorbing Foreman's punches, and tiring him out before going in for the kill.

This was to be our template against South Africa; we had to box clever and sap their energy. 'Make them miss and make them pay' became our mantra in the build-up.

We gathered in the team room that evening, unaware that the analysis boys had prepared a video of all our families sending us messages from the other side of the world.

Alex later told me that it took around twenty takes for James to nail his 'good luck Daddy' message, but it definitely melted a few hearts in Cape Town.

The reaction to Courtney's message was less affectionate when one of the English boys, on seeing his kitchen in the background, blurted, 'Fucking hell Courts, how much are they paying you at Saints?'

During South Africa's anthem, I stared into the vast emptiness of the Cape Town Stadium, up at the desolate-looking stands, and wished desperately that things were different. I wished they'd been packed to the rafters with passionate fans from both sides, and I wished beyond anything that Mum could have been there among them.

I'm not the religious sort, but I gazed skywards and silently asked Mum if she was looking down and, if so, could she lend us a helping hand.

The first half was an absolute onslaught, and our ill-discipline was the only thing that separated the two sides. Most teams aim to keep the penalty count down to ten or fewer, and we'd conceded nine by half-time.

The Springboks chiselled their way to a 12–3 lead, but we felt good in ourselves.

It had been eighty-three years since the Lions had recovered from a half-time deficit that big, but Gats was completely unflustered, telling us simply, 'Keep your discipline and we'll win the game.'

We turned down two penalties at the start of the second half and kicked to the corner instead. It was a ballsy move against a side that hadn't conceded a try from a driving lineout for three years, but we had to try something different. It worked the second time as we out-Bokked the Boks with a powerful surge to the line.

Courts claimed the ball from the middle and, once he landed, the rest of the pack latched together and ploughed through them like a pneumatic drill through wet cement.

It was a bristling statement of intent against the self-styled hardest team in world rugby.

The conversion was an ugly one – just crawling over after my foot slipped on the turf – but it got us right back in the game.

The Boks struck back hard, scoring through Faf de Klerk after an earlier effort had been ruled out for the most fractional of offsides. It was obvious this was going to go to the wire.

With the words from Gats ringing in our ears, our discipline held as theirs started to crumble. We had three penalties in range, and I nailed them all. The last was one of the most sweetly struck of my entire career and put us in front for the first time. I ran back, flushed with adrenaline at the thought that that kick could have won a Test for the Lions.

With ten minutes to go I caught a glancing blow to the head from Siya Kolisi's shin and was forced to leave the field. It was during those last few minutes that we almost blew it, losing our composure and shovelling on bad ball needlessly, until it was fly-hacked through by Damian de Allende who gathered to score.

Had it not been for a knock-on in the build-up, we'd have been in deep trouble.

That was our get-out-of-jail moment, and with two minutes remaining, Faz made it safe with a final penalty.

It was a monumental victory given the circumstances, and I can only imagine what kind of decibel-shattering noise the travelling fans would have made when Hoggy blasted the ball into the stands at the final whistle.

The fallout was immediate and intense.

South Africa's director of rugby, Rassie Erasmus, began retweeting posts from a Twitter user named 'Jaco Johan' which were heavily critical of the referee's performance. The extremely knowledgeable Johan had clearly analysed every decision in painstaking detail. Curiously, he only had three followers and his account had only just been created. It didn't take a sleuth to figure out that 'Jaco Johan' was someone from inside the Springbok set-up, and most likely Erasmus himself.

He vehemently denied such an accusation, but this was just a prelude to a far more damaging episode.

Within days an hour-long video had appeared online in which Rassie dissected around thirty individual incidents from the game, accusing the referee Nic Berry of bias and suggesting he treated Siya Kolisi with a lack of respect.

Rassie claimed the video had been meant for Joel Jutge, the head of referees at World Rugby, and it had been leaked by nefarious means. Most observers believed he had leaked it himself. Either way, it unleashed a whirlwind of controversy, with most journalists and pundits from this side of the equator lining up to condemn him.

As unedifying as it seemed, I actually had no issues with it. It might have piled unnecessary heat on the referees, but I thought those who leapt on their high horse over it were the same people who are usually desperate for drama and controversy to fill their newspaper columns. I actually think he's a genius, as well versed in the art of distraction as the likes of José Mourinho or Jürgen Klopp. The hour-long rant was his 'dead cat' strategy. It's all anyone was talking about, meaning no one was focusing on the Springboks' underwhelming performance or the way they'd surrendered their lead.

The bunker mentality continued that week, with Covid dictating everything. The entertainments committee had arranged a whale-watching trip for our day off, but even that – our one bit of escapism from the drudgery – was cancelled, when two of the crew tested positive.

If there was one man who kept us all sane amid the gloom it was Kyle Sinckler. He fell firmly into the James Haskell category of tourist: loud, brash and hyperactive but ultimately loveable. He'd hold court in the bar, getting on the microphone and rinsing everyone with his quick wit and dry humour. The only other thing that passed for entertainment in camp that week were the amateurish DJ sets by Tadhg Furlong and Tom Curry, whose double act – Scrum 'n' Bass – struggled to lure many onto the dance floor.

The second Test was a crushing disappointment. In a reversal of the way things had unfolded the previous week, the Springboks looked fitter, hungrier and more powerful. They dominated the aerial battle, squeezed us up front, and crunched through the gears with the arrival of their 'Bomb Squad' from the bench. Their lack of preparation coming into the first Test had left them significantly undercooked, but they were nicely broiled by the second and we were well beaten.

There was plenty of conjecture afterwards about whether the referee, Ben O'Keeffe had been subconsciously influenced by Rassie's rant and acted too leniently towards the Boks, but I think that was largely mischief-making.

The review was brutal and the coaches didn't pull their punches, accusing us of being bullied, contact-shy and lazy. It was a direct appeal to our animal instincts, for us to go out there and rip into them in the decider.

In the final Test in early August, the dark clouds over Cape Town could have been a portent for what was to come. Only ten minutes into the match, and my game, series and Lions career was over following a whack to my shin. It actually felt as if I'd broken it, but I hoped it would be something I could run off. As soon as I'd hauled myself to my feet, though, I realized my tour was over.

There was no TV in the medical room, and I was happy to disconnect from it all. The wound required stitches, but I asked if I could be left alone for two minutes. I sat in silence, looking down at the gash on my shin, and allowed my jumbled thoughts to percolate. I'd achieved my dream and had started all three Tests on a Lions tour. I forced myself to acknowledge that fact, rather than agonize about this one being cut short.

I knew, though, that the legendary Lions, the ones people still talk about decades later, are the ones who won. Whether I was involved or not, that was still within our grasp. I was back in the dugout in time to see Ken Owens bundle over for the game's opening try after another ballsy decision to turn down three and kick for the corner. We held on to that lead until the fifty-fifth minute when Cheslin Kolbe produced a moment of magic, ghosting through our defence to score. But within five minutes, Finn had kicked a penalty to level things up at 13–13.

It was at that point that thirty-seven-year old Morné Steyn entered the fray.

British and Irish players who are fortunate enough to have a long career can play for the Lions as often as they're chosen. For those who play *against* the Lions, though, it's meant to be a once-in-a-lifetime thing. But this was that same Morné Steyn who'd kicked the Springboks to glory *twelve* years earlier in the febrile cauldron of Loftus Versfeld.

Rassie had picked him for a reason, and his appearance felt like a very dark omen.

With two minutes to go, the score was locked at 16 apiece. South Africa were awarded a penalty inside our half, and Herschel Jantjies impulsively ran it before being swallowed up by our defence. It was a terrible call, but he got away with it; the referee ruled that he hadn't taken the tap from the right mark and gave them another chance.

In a finale that even Hollywood would have rejected for being utterly implausible, Morné Steyn grabbed the ball and pointed towards the posts.

I half expected the sky to darken and a crack of thunder to envelop the stadium.

The outcome was as predictable as it was gut-wrenching. There was no way someone of his ability and experience was ever going to miss. After all that sacrifice, all those weeks stuck in the hotel, all that time away from our loved ones, the tour was over, the faint flicker of victory snuffed out by one confident swing of the boot.

Like so much of the series, it felt a little dreamlike at the end. In the same way a crowd amplifies emotions, the absence of one sucks out much of the drama.

In the immediate aftermath, I just felt empty, though nowhere near as emotionally wrung out as I would in the days that followed.

The series will be remembered for a number of reasons, but the quality of rugby won't be one of them. That doesn't bother me, but I did feel a little down that much of the coverage of the final Test focused on Finn Russell's swashbuckling performance, as it seemed like a particularly depressing episode of déjà vu. Ultimately for me, though, winning trumps style every time, which is why I have such a grudging respect for the Springboks.

Because we were flying from a red-listed country, we knew we would have to quarantine in an airport hotel for two weeks if we landed back at Heathrow. A better alternative was to fly to Jersey where – as long as we tested negative each day – we'd be allowed to roam free.

We landed there at midday, and I was still cooped up in my room awaiting my test result when there was a knock on the door. Expecting it to be the medic, I opened it grumpily, only to be enveloped by my son James, who leapt into my arms and gave me one of the best hugs I'd ever had.

Back home after the tour, Rachel and I honoured our promise to our Mum to 'chuck her off the end of the worm'.

She'd never been one to stand on ceremony, and used to say this to us when she'd had a few glasses of her favourite New Zealand Sauvignon Blanc. 'I don't want any fuss when I'm gone; just chuck me off the end of the worm.' She meant Worm's Head, the iconic Gower headland that had been a constant landmark throughout the shifting tides of our childhood.

On what would have been her birthday, Rachel, Alex and I met Alex's mum and dad, and Mum's best friends Jenny and Spike at the Worm's Head Hotel for coffee and cake before the three of us set off on the hike to the end of the peninsula.

What we feared would be a grave, sombre trip soon turned into a happy occasion, full of laughter and comedy moments. Both Rachel and Alex stumbled comically during the rocky ascent. Rachel broke her fall with the bouquet of flowers we'd brought, crushing them in the process, and Alex stuck her foot in a rockpool, with the splashback giving her an unfortunate wet patch that made it look as if she'd had a different kind of accident.

It was blustery and overcast by the time we reached the top, and we thought we had the place to ourselves until Rachel spotted a random woman perched on a ledge eating an avocado with a spoon. We were paranoid the ashes would catch in the wind and end up inadvertently seasoning her picnic.

Mum would have loved the sheer absurdity of it all.

Five weeks after she died, her beloved dog Millie had followed her, so we scattered both sets of ashes over the edge of Worm's Head and said our final goodbyes.

Rachel and I had emptied Mum's house the previous day, so it had been an emotionally intense forty-eight hours. Among her possessions, we found a letter she'd written before her first operation back in 2005. She'd been preparing for the worst even then and had signed off with 'the sadness won't last forever, the happiness will return.'

It was a comforting thought as we watched the sun dip towards the horizon, bathing Worm's Head in a crimson glow.

18

FEAST TO FAMINE

It's 3 a.m. and I'm blind drunk, swaying unsteadily, and holding court in Neil Jenkins's kitchen. Seeing headlamps appear in the driveway, I run outside as Jenks's teenage daughter Georgia climbs out of a taxi, and rugby tackle her onto the lawn.

As we're rolling around in the dewy grass laughing maniacally, Jenks appears and says, 'Bigs, I think it's time you went to bed.'

Hauling me to my feet and brushing some stray blades of grass off my knees, he ushers me towards the idling taxi. Earlier that day, I'd won my one hundredth cap for Wales.

This wasn't how the day was supposed to end.

I was filling my car up on the M40 between Northampton and Redditch when Wayne Pivac called to casually ask, 'How would you like to be captain for the Six Nations?'

I knew Alun Wyn had been ruled out with a shoulder injury, but I didn't see this coming.

While I'd long been part of the leadership group, I'd always thought I was too feisty, and too temperamental, to ever be captain.

Wayne clocked my hesitation and asked what was holding me back. I laid my cards on the table and said I'd only take it if I didn't have to change.

I wasn't willing to become a yes-man, or a diluted version of myself.

Wayne chuckled down the phone. 'Dan, that's exactly the reason I want you as my captain. We need a bit of fire in our bellies.'

That weekend, Alex and I treated ourselves to a weekend away in Bath, and while we were in our hotel, she insisted I call Mamo and Dado – my dad's parents – and tell them. You could feel Mamo's smile through the phone as she said, 'We've been waiting all our lives for this moment.' She was overflowing with pride.

What I forgot to tell her was to keep it under wraps, as the news wasn't being officially released until Monday. Naturally, she put down the phone and called everyone in Onllwyn and beyond, to tell them her grandson was the new Wales captain. My phone soon lit up with dozens of congratulatory messages from her neighbours, and various distant family members. My first job had been to keep it a secret until the official announcement, and now the entire Dulais Valley had found out before the press.

Sanjay was the first to greet me in camp; not with a hearty congratulations as you might imagine, but a laugh of utter incredulity. 'You cannot be serious,' he grinned. 'You expect me to be captained by *you*.'

Clearly, I'd have to work on the 'respect' thing.

I'd made a vow to myself to be honest and transparent, having grown bored of watching other captains trotting out tired platitudes to the press. That wasn't my style. Welsh rugby fans are a knowledgeable bunch, and they deserve better than that. As players, we'd always been encouraged to keep our heads down and say nothing, which had always stuck in my craw. I was determined to do it my way.

In the end, my debut as captain in February 2022 was memorable for all the wrong reasons. We were ravaged by injuries and got hammered in Dublin by a revved-up Ireland, who absolutely smashed us off the park. Add that to the defeats we'd suffered against New Zealand and South Africa in the autumn, and the shine from last season's triumph was rapidly coming off.

The game against Scotland was a chance to reassert our status as defending champions. This one was at home, and would mark my one hundredth international appearance (ninety-seven for Wales, and three for the Lions). It was also the first time I'd led my country out at the Principality Stadium.

Covid restrictions had been entirely lifted and, after eighteen months of playing in barren, empty arenas, the Principality was once again awash with red, and reverberating with hymns and arias.

Waiting in the tunnel amid that cacophony felt special. That was *my* team behind me. After fourteen years in the jersey, I'd joined the select band of individuals who had captained Wales.

The weather was atrocious, but that suited us just fine. Scotland arrived full of verve and swagger, having beaten England, but we dragged them into a street fight we knew we had the wiles to win. I knocked over the decisive drop goal in the last ten minutes, which just about got us over the line.

I described the victory as one of the best in my Wales career and I meant it. After the rude awakening in Ireland, we'd shown real spirit and resilience to turn things around.

A bit of Northampton history was made at Twickenham, when Courtney Lawes and I were opposing captains at the end of February. Nothing illustrated our polar-opposite personalities more than the coin toss. I was five minutes early, twitchy, agitated, and desperate to get out there, whereas Courts loped up the corridor three minutes late, before giving me a big hug and asking how I was doing, like we were meeting for a mid-morning coffee at Franklin's Gardens.

We lost the match after another ponderous start, allowing them to stretch into a 17–0 lead before we eventually clicked into gear. It was disappointing, but there were enough positives to take, not least the re-emergence of Alex Cuthbert, who'd rolled back the years with a superb display of attacking rugby.

Against France I enjoyed one of my best individual performances for Wales. It was one of those rare games where I felt entirely in the groove, nailing a 50:22, hitting a perfect seventy-metre spiral bomb, and slotting three penalties as we went toe-to-toe with the tournament favourites. The decisive moment came on sixty-two minutes, when we were trailing 13–9. We broke down the short side, and Faletau passed inside to the onrushing Jon Davies. If Foxy had held onto the ball, we'd have scored and gone on to close the game out, I'm convinced of it. They held on to claim victory, but it could so easily have gone our way.

With our long-time defensive guru Shaun Edwards having swapped his red tracksuit for a blue one, France had added a layer of defensive steel to their natural attacking elan and were the form side in Europe. Losing to them was no disgrace.

Three defeats from four was way below where we wanted to be, but no one was talking of implosions or a looming catastrophe. We could easily have beaten France and England. No one was remotely prepared for what was to come.

We had Monday and Tuesday off, which isn't unusual in the final week of a campaign when everyone's up to speed and the fitness work is in the bank. But that only really works if the team remains the same and disruption is kept to a minimum.

Instead, Wayne tinkered heavily with the line-up, making seven changes, which – with hindsight – showed a lack of respect to Italy.

Alun Wyn had recovered ahead of schedule, and was thrust back into the starting line-up for what would be his 150th cap. As much as Al is one of the best players ever to have pulled on the jersey, it was the wrong call. He displaced Will Rowlands, who'd been our outstanding performer and deserved more than anyone to keep his place.

It was also my one hundredth cap, which had long been a target of mine, but those two milestones lent the week a bit of a carnival vibe; as though we were preparing for a testimonial rather than a full-blooded Test match. The individual milestones were being given more prominence than the actual game plan, and I got a bit too wrapped up in it as well.

Plans were being made for an elaborate celebration for the two of us. Alex had made an enormous cake with '100' written on it in icing, and the kit-man had prepared a special jersey with a quote from my mum – 'Thinking of you today, forever and always' – embroidered in gold on the breast. The game was increasingly becoming a sideshow.

Italy were on a thirty-six-match losing streak in the tournament and had conceded an avalanche of points against Ireland the week before. Plenty were questioning their presence among Europe's elite, and pondering how long it would be before they were replaced by Georgia or South Africa.

When we did speak about the game, the chat was all about going after a bonus point and a third-place finish. That hubris translated into our performance where we tried to run before we could walk. We tapped penalties we should have kicked, played too much in our own half, and spurned easy points to kick to the corners. It was a turgid, disjointed display, and we were fortunate to only be 12–7 down at half-time.

Despite our efforts to inject some pace into the game, we lacked any kind of spark. It felt like trying to light a damp matchstick. We eventually managed to grind our way into the lead, but the longer the game went on, the more twitchy we became.

It still pains me to recall this, but as we were nursing a slender 21–15 lead, Ange Capuozzo – their diminutive full back – received the ball in his own half and set off on a mazy, spellbinding run that screamed danger from the minute he hitch-kicked his way through the first tackle. He shimmied and swerved past everyone in his path, leaving a trail of flailing arms and lunging tacklers in his wake. When Edoardo Padovani appeared on his shoulder unmarked, our worst fears were realized.

There were tears flowing down Paolo Garbisi's cheeks when he nailed the winning conversion.

I was incandescent with rage and hurled my boots forcefully at the floor. It took Sanjay to bring me to my senses, quietly pointing out that Alex and James were behind me in the crowd. I was forced to compose myself, so James didn't see Daddy lose his shit so publicly. But it was hard to keep those emotions in check when, from a rugby perspective, it felt like the world had ended.

Caroline Morgan, the WRU's 'fixer' had arranged a hospitality box for my friends and family to enjoy my one hundredth appearance. Instead, they'd witnessed a historic humiliation – Wales's first ever home loss to Italy.

James jumped into my arms and remained there – incongruously – while I addressed the team in the huddle. His presence might have diluted my anger, but I didn't mince my words.

I told the players we were all in the last-chance saloon, and another abject display like that would likely signal the end of our careers. My words later got twisted by the press, where it was claimed I'd said some of them would never play for Wales again. I never said that, but I did say we'd plumbed new depths with that defeat. How we react to this, I said, would define what kind of team we really were.

Any celebrations that had been planned for Al and me were canned, and we had a muted presentation in the changing room that we neither wanted nor deserved.

Gerald Davies presented me with a commemorative '100th' cap and a gold watch, and the team was spared my rendition of Billy Ocean's 'Love Really Hurts without You' that I'd been practising diligently for weeks.

The plan had been to meet friends and family for some gourmet cuisine in Cardiff's Le Monde restaurant, but all I wanted to do was drink. The seafood platter looked magnificent but barely a morsel passed my lips as I downed bottle after bottle of beer before moving on to the wine. By the time the trays of Sambucas arrived and we were singing along drunkenly to the Backstreet Boys, the events of earlier had disappeared into an alcohol-soaked haze.

It was back at the Vale in the early hours that I decided to call Neil Jenkins. 'Oi Jenks, where are you mate?' I slurred. 'In the house,' he replied, through a fug of sleep.

'I'll be over now,' I replied, hearing his wife say, 'Is he having a laugh?' just before I hung up.

His house backs onto the golf course at the Vale, and I was there in minutes, dragging a load of my bewildered schoolfriends along for the ride.

And so it transpired that I spent the fag end of the night drinking bottles of Heineken with Jenks until the sun came up, with a brief foray into his front garden to rugby tackle his daughter for no apparent reason.

It ended up being an extended therapy session, with me venting all my pent-up frustrations, while Jenks nodded sagely, and my schoolmates shuffled uncomfortably wondering what the hell was going on.

I emerged from my bed at around lunchtime the following day with nothing to show for my efforts but a stinking hangover and a head full of regrets.

I was still consumed by anger and torment on the Monday when I was driving back to Northampton. Chris Boyd called and asked whether I needed anything from him. Bear in mind I was one of his marquee signings and I'd already been absent for the best part of six weeks, yet here he was asking if *I* needed anything.

We had two important Premiership games coming up against London Irish and Bristol, but I said I'd love to have a day with my family in Wales just to decompress and get my head straight.

'Do it,' he said, ordering me to turn the car around. 'We'll see you tomorrow.'

I thanked him profusely, and just before hanging up, he added, 'Bigs – don't worry about Saturday. It's not going to define you, mate.'

He just got me in every way.

I called Wayne the next day and told him that what had happened proved we *had* to play our best team every week and to start building momentum ahead of the World Cup.

It was a tough conversation because he was a proud man and was hurting as much as anyone. As the first Welsh coach to lose to Italy at home, Wayne was feeling the heat, and considered himself personally responsible. We picked over the game, discussing at length the disallowed Wyn Jones try that should have taken us out of sight, but it was a pointless raking over of the coals.

The truth is, we'd got what we deserved.

He agreed we'd not taken the game as seriously as we should have, but he refused to sink into a trough of despair, insisting we channel this anger and disappointment into something positive. This was one of Wayne's best qualities: his glass-half-full optimism. He never got too down, and was able to rationalize things without allowing emotions to cloud the bigger picture.

We were headed next to South Africa, to the home of the world champions, who were still sitting pretty at the top of the rankings after their series victory over the Lions. If the combined might of the home nations hadn't been able to dethrone them, what hope was there for a disorganized rabble already dismissed by most as a busted flush?

We were languishing at our lowest ebb, and I was now captain of the team. I couldn't have asked for a more daunting test of my credentials.

When we gathered for our June training camp, I laid out my vision for the tour. If we travelled into the belly of the Springbok beast with the same attitude we'd shown against Italy, we'd be steamrollered. We needed to make it ultra-confrontational; get in their faces, make life horrible for them. Perhaps we'd become a bit too 'nice' to play against. I wanted us to be their worst *nightmare*.

In the modern game, where there's such an emphasis on discipline, you're often encouraged to back away from confrontation. I wanted us to go looking for it. That had essentially been my blueprint throughout my career, and now I wanted to mould this team in my image.

We also addressed the environment. When Wayne took over,

he pretty much kept to Gats's weekly schedule, which felt familiar and comfortable; in truth we had probably slackened off a bit, become a bit complacent. One or two of us had started skipping recovery sessions, rushing through our video analysis, or cutting corners in the gym.

In elite sport, even a 1 per cent drop in intensity can make a huge difference. We had to change.

From now on, if the coaches told us we were doing four sessions a day, we were doing four sessions. If the conditioners arranged an early recovery session before breakfast, we'd all be there without fail. If the nutritionists banned the tuck shop, there was to be no argument. I'm not saying we'd been getting away with murder under Wayne, just that over a period of time – almost imperceptibly – we'd allowed our levels to drop.

A persistent criticism of the Pivac era was that we looked like a team caught in two minds. Unlike in the Six Nations, where you're coming up against different teams with different styles every week, a three-Test series against the same team could really focus the mind. We knew what was coming and what we had to do to stop it. The coaches had done a detailed review since the Six Nations. There hadn't exactly been a split before, but there had been a definite divergence in philosophy between Wayne and Steve on the one hand, and Melon and Jenks on the other. Now, they all seemed to be on the same page, and the strategy was clear.

There was to be a lot of kicking infield, and we'd be looking to make the Springboks' lives difficult with an energetic kick-chase and an aggressive defence. To the trained eye, it didn't look too dissimilar to a Gatland game plan.

Psychologically it also helped to get out of Wales, into another environment entirely where we felt under far less pressure. The weather in South Africa was superb, the hotels were luxurious, and life post-Covid was back to normal. From the minute we touched down, we felt fresh and focused, and the coaches were ruthless in their quest for perfection.

*

The opening Test was in Pretoria, and marked the first time the Boks had played in front of a crowd since the World Cup final nearly three years earlier. As such, there was a febrile, combustible atmosphere during the build-up, like a tinder box ready to explode.

In stark contrast to the empty, desolate boulevards we'd driven down a year earlier, the road was rammed with parked cars and thrumming with humanity. Hundreds of green-and-gold-clad Afrikaners lined the streets, tending their smoking braais, tossing enormous hunks of raw meat onto the flames, clinking stubbies and generally having a whale of a time.

After the misery and despair of the lockdowns, it was amazing to see so many smiling South African faces, even if they were hoping their team was about to pulverize us. After the soulless experience of Loftus Versfeld the year before, this was epic.

There's something animalistic about the crowd in Pretoria, and while I was practising my kicking, I was overwhelmed by the dizzying riot of colour, movement and commotion in the stands. After the disappointment of the Six Nations, we wanted to have our mettle tested to its limit, and there was no bigger challenge than this.

We had the dream start, working the ball wide to Zammo, who showed the watching South Africans what we already knew – that he's the fastest man in world rugby. He'd bagged a second try after half an hour, and we were flying.

There had been plenty of niggle during the opening forty minutes, with the referee, Nika Amashukeli, calling Siya Kolisi and me in at one point and ordering us to calm things down. 'Do you just want us to roll out the red carpet for them?' I said, sarcastically.

As far as I was concerned, my team were doing exactly what I'd asked of them, and I wasn't willing to back down one iota. We weren't coming just to 'play our part'.

The one flashpoint that got the crowd particularly animated was my stand-off with Cheslin Kolbe. Kolbe is the darling of

South African rugby, and they didn't take kindly to him being roughed up. He tried to wrestle the ball off me after it had rolled dead, and I gave him a fairly harmless shove.

Enraged, he swivelled round and cocked his fist.

'What are you going to do?' I asked. 'Punch me?'

He lunged forwards, hoping I'd flinch and said, almost comically, 'Do you want some?'

It was more of a schoolyard scuffle than an actual fight, but just another example of our refusal to back down.

There were plenty saying afterwards that as captain I should have led by example and dampened the flames, but I wanted to keep them burning. It was clear we'd got under their skin, and they didn't like it one bit.

After the Kolbe incident, I became a pantomime villain in the eyes of the crowd, and they relished it when I got yellow-carded before half-time. I'd prevented a try with a despairing tackle on Faf de Klerk, when the ref despatched me to the bin for not rolling away.

I couldn't have been further from the dugout when I was ordered off, giving the 52,000 rabid fans ample opportunity to boo me aggressively as I trudged off, shaking my head theatrically at the injustice of it all.

After eighteen months of silence on the terraces this was visceral and real, and the anger they felt was because – at 18–3 ahead – we had them flailing on the ropes.

Unfortunately, a rash of yellow cards and ill-discipline saw it all unravel spectacularly in the second half, as the referee completely lost control of the game, and with five minutes left we found ourselves behind for the first time, with only twelve men on the field. We'd all read this script before.

We weren't done yet, though, summoning all our fighting spirit to hit back through Dewi Lake, who took advantage of our own powerful driving maul. My conversion would have nudged us back in front, but it slid to the right of the posts: 29–29. A draw would have felt like a defeat given the lead we'd had.

We desperately wanted to close it out but in those critical clos-ing stages we had a mini-meltdown.

Tomos kicked a bit long from a lineout, and we didn't have anyone chasing on the blind side. I scrambled across to fill the space, leaving us short on the open side. The Boks clocked it, finding an outside edge and making serious yards into our half.

We'd worked all week at flying up in defence and getting in their passing lane to stop them getting the ball to their wings. I did just that as they launched their next wave of attack and was penalized for a deliberate knock-on.

Sometimes the best-laid plans go awry. Willie le Roux, whose pass I'd blocked, started celebrating wildly in my face.

I protested half-heartedly to the ref, arguing that I was going for the interception, but it was futile.

Damian Willemse's penalty was the last play of the game. Having been three scores up, we eventually succumbed 32–29.

It was a golden opportunity missed. For seventy-eight minutes, we'd had the better of the world champions in their own back yard. We'd executed our game plan to perfection, exorcizing the demons of the Italy game in the process. But still, we'd lost.

It was hard to accept. I was asked about the prickly nature of the match in the press conference, and doubled down on our rhetoric; we hadn't come here to pander to anyone. We were going to go out there and scrap for every last blade of grass and make life as difficult for our opponents as we could.

I held the gaze of all the South African journalists in the room and told them they could expect more of the same next week.

Some seemed taken aback by my honesty, but I made no apol-ogy for it. Rugby does a terrible job of promoting itself, and part of the reason is because players are muzzled by paranoid press officers.

It was nice to have reached a point where I could say whatever the hell I wanted, consequences be damned.

*

Nothing sums up the South African psyche better than what they did next. Having sneaked the victory with a last-minute kick, most teams would pick their first-choice side for the rematch and tell them to go out and finish the job. Instead, Jacques Nienaber made fourteen changes, a move even the great Gareth Edwards decried as disrespectful.

I didn't see it that way.

Nienaber flipped it and said those he'd selected would be offended to be referred to as a 'B' team.

Their starting side still contained the likes of Pieter-Steph du Toit, Handré Pollard and Eben Etzebeth, and a lot of those involved had been in better form than their more decorated colleagues. André Esterhuizen, for example, was the English Premiership Player's Player of the Year, and I knew from experience just how good he was.

After the previous week's can't-take-your-eyes-off-it nerve-jangler, the rematch was a turgid slugfest; the 3–3 half-time scoreline tells its own story. But the nature of the game and the chat about it being a weakened Springboks won't be what's recorded in the history books. When people look up what happened in Bloemfontein on 9 July 2022, they'll discover that Wales beat South Africa *in* South Africa for the first time ever.

It was a monumental team effort, but two people deserve special mention: Gareth Anscombe for his utterly nerveless touchline conversion that transformed a narrow loss into a historic win, and debutant Sam Wainwright for facing down the world's most fearsome pack and locking out the final scrum.

Chicken had replaced me in the second half after I'd injured my shoulder and missed a couple of my shots on goal. He missed another on seventy minutes, and it felt as though the game would be defined by wayward kicks. But with three minutes left and hope fading, we conjured the game's only try. A looping floated pass from Chicken to Jaddsy was enough to create some precious space, and Josh made no mistake with the finish. The conversion was sensational.

The feeling of elation was impossible to describe.

In the late nineties, Wales had been humiliated in South Africa, losing 96–13 with only a dropped ball over the line preventing the Boks from racking up a century.

For fifty-eight years, we'd been searching for that elusive win on South African soil, and now, under the Bloemfontein floodlights, we'd finally pulled it off.

I told the boys to stick together that night, to enjoy each other's company and cherish every moment, because these things don't come around too often. We'd deserved victory in the first Test, and this felt like justice.

Tommy Reffell was awarded Man of the Match and given a cheque for 12,000 rand, which was immediately appropriated by the entertainments committee and thrown into the kitty.

He and Lyds had been unbelievable over those two games, with Lyds rolling back the years, and Tommy looking every inch the Warby for a new decade. There had been rumours of internal unrest in our squad, of mutinous machinations following the Six Nations, but I can tell you unequivocally that we were all united and got on brilliantly.

Alun Wyn had been a little distant on tour so far, as he'd struggled to adjust to his new role as a substitute. For so long he'd been the beating heart of the team; the talismanic leader everyone looked up to. It was entirely understandable that he'd felt a little disoriented by his loss of status. Now he'd been shown yellow for the second game running, and those personal frustrations, combined with the historic win, saw him go hard on the piss. It was actually great to see him lower his guard for the first time in a while.

After the backwoods feel of Pretoria and Bloemfontein, Cape Town was like a gleaming mirage in the desert. We'd appointed 'tour guides' for each location and in the 'Mother City' the responsibility fell to Gareth Anscombe.

As the bus trundled in from the airport, Chicken was up on the mic, educating us all with nuggets he'd been busy researching: Cape Town's population, its colonial history, its flora and fauna, and various other titbits about Table Mountain and the Western Cape.

As we rounded a bend, he pointed out another famous Cape Town landmark: Mavericks Strip Club. 'That's one of Cape Town's most famous institutions,' he declared, 'with exotic dancers able to satisfy your every whim.'

Cue schoolboy giggles from the back of the bus.

'If you want something quick and simple, ask for the Louis Rees-Zammit,' he continued.

'If something slower and more languorous is your style, you can go for the Adam Beard.'

He paused to allow the titters to die down before adding, with a slight wobble in his voice, 'And if you show a yellow card on the door, you get the Alun Wyn Jones special.'

I wouldn't have been surprised if an actual piece of tumbleweed had blown down the aisle. No one dared look round to check Al's reaction, but I can tell you he was *not* amused. He stared impassively out of the window, refusing to even acknowledge the joke while Chicken tiptoed apologetically back to his seat. Catching my eye as he walked past, he mouthed 'too soon?'

I nodded firmly.

Cape Town isn't necessarily safer than other South African cities, but it's undeniably prettier. It's the kind of place you could spend a month exploring and still feel as though you'd only scratched the surface. There is probably no city anywhere else on earth with as arresting a backdrop. Wherever you wandered, the view was framed by the magnificent Table Mountain. Moody and mist-shrouded one minute, bright and sun-dappled the next. It was impossible not to be taken in by its sheer majesty. That final week on tour was everything the Lions tour wasn't. We got to hang out on the waterfront, gorge on sushi, wander through the shiny shopping malls, and generally absorb the vibes of a city the *New York Times* once declared the best place to live on earth.

We lost Chicken and Toby during the warm-up before the third Test. Losing one of them would have been challenging, two was a disaster. Taine Basham – who'd been swigging gin and tonics until the early hours, thinking his tour was done – was thrust onto the bench. Ultimately the hosts were too strong for our depleted side, running out 30–14 winners in a game in which Handré Pollard scored 20 points.

We had endured a long, tumultuous season, whereas the Boks were just getting into their stride. So although it felt like a game too far for us, there could not have been a greater contrast in terms of where we'd started and where we finished. We had definitively banished the memories of the Italy game, and significantly raised the bar, silencing many who had thought we didn't stand a chance against the Boks.

At the end of the game, I emphasized to all the boys that these were the standards we needed to maintain now. Siya sought me out to congratulate me on an epic series and, as we embraced, Cheslin and I made eye contact, and he came over to bury the hatchet.

As much as we were gutted, there was a tremendous vibe in the post-match function. We presented Eben Etzebeth with a bottle of Penderyn Welsh whisky to commemorate his one hundredth cap, and Jesse Kriel spent the evening trying to avoid the Welsh boys, who'd been told by Cory Hill that he had a contact for cheap Rolexes.

The conviviality continued at a downtown bar where the fans – starved of contact with their heroes for so long – were queueing up to lavish praise on the Boks.

It was getting rowdy; I could sense a bit of tension in the air and my sixth sense told me it would be wise to disappear. I enlisted the help of Adam Beard to hustle me out of there. With his considerable bulk, and six-feet-nine-inch frame, he cut a swathe through the drunker revellers with ease, and it occurred to me that when he knocks the rugby on the head, he has a decent career as a bouncer ahead of him.

The following day was among the most debauched I've ever experienced in rugby. Everyone met by the pool after breakfast, and what began as a quiet 'hair-of-the-dog' session soon degenerated into something far more raucous and disorderly.

Wayne appeared around midday with a flat white in his hand, doing the social rounds. As he weaved among the tables making small talk, Tobes, Tomos and I were discussing the etiquette of forcing him to neck a bottle of beer. Was it acceptable on the last day of a tour?

I parked any reservations and shouted across the pool, 'Oi, Wayne! Sod the coffee. See this off,' and held up a bottle of lager.

Without hesitation, he strode over, snatched it from my grasp and poured it down his gullet in just a few gulps. Exhaling with a satisfied smack of the lips, he asked, 'Boys, can I do another?'

I'm not sure how drinking games work in New Zealand, but in our world you rarely *volunteer* to drink more. He bolted about eight bottles in fifteen minutes, with each going down as easily as the last.

The boys were all exchanging bemused glances, thinking 'this guy's a legend.' We had not witnessed this side to Wayne, and it was genuinely nice to see him enjoying himself after such a torrid period in charge.

He placed his empty bottle on the table and announced he'd be back later, imploring us to 'neck every drink', before sauntering off without even a hint of a wobble. I gave him a wave and turned round just in time to see Al scoop Chicken off his sun lounger and lob him, fully clothed, into the pool. He'd been quietly nursing a grudge since the 'yellow card' gag and had spied his opportunity for revenge. Like a puppy wanting to join in the fun, Rhys Carré picked up Josh Navidi's hair clippers and lobbed them in after Chicken.

Josh – one of the most even-tempered blokes in the squad – calmy wandered over to Rhys, wrestled his phone from his grasp, and chucked that in too, watching it shatter as it bounced off the tiles and sank to the bottom. The other guests – who'd presumably been hoping for a peaceful morning by the pool – began to slink quietly away.

If the Pivac era was a rollercoaster, that tour was probably the part where we'd ratcheted our way up to the highest point and were deservedly enjoying the view. And we were mercifully unaware, as we relaxed by the pool on that sun-drenched morning, that we were about to embark on a gravity-defying plunge to the bottom.

In August 2022, I was enjoying a bit of downtime after the South Africa tour, when Phil Dowson, the head coach at Saints, messaged me for a chat. When he offered to drive to Swansea so we could chat in person, I knew that he was wanting more than just an idle catch-up, and I called him back and asked what was up.

After a few minutes of small talk, he cut to the chase. Like in Wales, English clubs were struggling to make ends meet post-Covid and were having to slash their outgoings. The salary cap was coming down, and the number of marquee players per club was being reduced from two to one. Courtney and I were Northampton's marquee players and our salaries had been exempted from the cap. The upshot was that they could no longer afford me.

I suggested we talk about a pay cut, but Phil said that any offer they'd be able to put on the table would be insulting. They were looking to groom the talented Fin Smith in my place. The forthcoming season at Northampton would be my last.

By now, Alex was pregnant with our second child, and we'd grown tired of the yo-yoing between South Wales and Northamptonshire. I had already begun idly wondering about moving on, and this conversation crystallized my thoughts. In the days that followed, Alex and I pondered our options. Japan? France? Elsewhere in England? I spoke to Wayne, who floated the idea of going 'home' to the Ospreys, but that felt like a backwards step and was swiftly quashed.

Japan was appealing, but there were complications. It's only a six-month commitment each year, and I started fantasizing about travelling for the other six; backpacking around China or island-hopping in Thailand, before Alex reminded me that we'd have a newborn and a five-year-old by that point. It was a fair point.

Things were still up in the air when our second boy, Oliver, was born. He was two days old and snoring on my shoulder, and I was settling down to watch Man United play Arsenal, when the phone rang. It was my agent, Tim, who'd have known the football was about to start.

What could he possibly want at this time?

Toulon were keen. 'They want you to sign now, for *this* season.'

They'd been expecting Louis Carbonel – their hometown boy – to re-sign, but he'd wrongfooted them by accepting a big-money move to Montpellier, and they were now in desperate need of a fly half.

Alex and I had planned to assess our options with a view to moving the following June. I looked down at Ollie snoozing in my arms, and thought, *We can't possibly disappear to France days after welcoming a new baby.*

I told Tim there was no way I could do this before the autumn, because I was rehabbing a knee injury and couldn't just pack a bag and abandon my family.

'Sleep on it,' he insisted. 'It's worth considering, and they won't wait for ever.'

The following day I had a Zoom call with the club president, Bernard Lemaître, the director of rugby, Laurent Emmanuelli, and the two coaches Franck Azema and Pierre Mignoni. They were charming and persuasive, explaining their desire to sign me for the rest of the season and two seasons beyond that.

I was intrigued to learn of their vision for the club, as there was no doubt it had undergone a significant transformation from the swashbuckling band of Galácticos that had dominated Europe for three years at the turn of the previous decade. They wanted to recapture that success, but without the drama and upheaval that accompanied the reign of the previous owner, Mourad Boudjel-lal. Boudjellal had made his fortune in comics, and developed a reputation as an eccentric oddball who'd essentially used his wealth and influence to assemble his own fantasy rugby team. He was the one who'd brought Tana Umaga, Jonny Wilkinson, Sonny Bill Williams, Matt Giteau, and a host of other global stars to the club. But he'd also upset a lot of people with his impetuosity, angry outbursts and tendency to publicly criticize his players. He was also accused of signing players purely for their star power, and not necessarily for their suitability.

The new culture at the club was one of hard work and honesty.

Pierre and Franck are big fans of good people; you could be a world-class player, but if you're not a good person you won't be on their radar.

I spoke to Leigh about his time there, and he said it sounded as if things had changed significantly. Leigh's recollections were of a looser, more laissez-faire approach, in which the English-speaking imports – many of them maverick by nature – took ownership of the team's direction, favouring flair over pragma-tism, and dragging the sleeping giant of the Med to the very pinnacle of European rugby. It worked then, but more by acci-dent than design. They'd fallen into something of a trough since, and this rebuild sounded more sustainable in the long term.

I picked Leigh's brains about places to live, and Alex grilled him about the availability of Ready Brek, Heinz baked beans and Robinsons squash. What sold it to me was Leigh recalling meet-ing his wife, Jess, at the beach in the evenings, where he would go for a bit of sea recovery before having dinner on the beach. I thought I could handle that, and I was impressed by the overtures from the club. They'd undoubtedly seen the bleak financial landscape of English rugby and spied an opportunity to plunder some prime assets.

The more I thought about it, the more I thought I'd be a fool to turn it down and, after a few weeks mulling it over, we decided to go for it. There was the small matter of me being under contract to Northampton for the remainder of the season but, luckily, Toulon agreed to pay a transfer fee.

For all my excitement about my new plans, it was with a heavy heart that I left Northampton. The four and a half years there had been the best of my career; I felt so at home there and the club had been so good to me. We'd narrowly missed out on the Premiership final after falling to Leicester in the semis that year, and it remains a huge regret that I couldn't help them lift that trophy. But now it was time to move on.

I was denied the chance to lead Wales again by a knee injury that kept me out of the 2022 autumn internationals. Justin Tipuric took my place, and any optimism we might have had going into the New Zealand game evaporated swiftly in the wake of a 55–23 drubbing; the most points we'd ever conceded at home. The match was shown exclusively on Amazon Prime, who'd wheeled out their latest big-name pundit – a certain Warren Gatland – to offer his professional appraisal.

He appeared less than impressed.

We restored some pride with a doughty win over an Argentinian side that had beaten England the week before, and New Zealand earlier in the year. At full time, Wayne and Warren appeared alongside one another on the TV coverage discussing the merits of the performance. It felt a little weird seeing Wayne being quizzed by his predecessor on live television. The image of the two of them shaking hands would prove oddly prophetic in the weeks to come.

The victory steadied the ship temporarily, but no one was prepared for what would happen next. On the day we played

Georgia, I was dressed as a Frenchman at a France-themed party my dad was hosting ahead of my move to Toulon. We were listening to French music, partaking in a French quiz and feasting on platters of cured meats and cheese.

During a lull in proceedings, I checked my phone and blinked hard at the headline, 'Georgia stun Wales with historic victory'.

I couldn't believe my eyes and ran to turn on the TV. It was true.

I immediately started texting the boys to find out what the hell had happened.

Chicken was the first to reply. 'Mate,' he said, 'the changing room is like a morgue.'

I came into camp on the Monday to show a bit of solidarity. Although I was no longer captain, I knew there were young players who'd be frightened to speak up and might have needed a sympathetic ear.

After a full squad meeting in the barn, I asked the coaches to leave us to it for ten minutes, before I asked the boys for an honest appraisal of what was going on.

Amid the mumbled replies, I gathered there had been a bit of disruption during the week about contracts, and some murmurings of strike action. That was unfortunate, but not an excuse for the Georgia defeat.

I said, 'Boys, if we need things to change, it's up to us to seize the initiative. If the structure of the week needs to change, if our style of play needs to change, those things need to be out in the open now.'

The room fell silent, and a depressing air of defeatism hung in the air, but eventually, after a bit of cajoling, someone admitted that the messaging from the coaches was inconsistent. Wayne and Steve were still intent on a more attack-minded approach, whereas Gethin and Jenks were more wedded to the defensive game plan we'd followed in South Africa. Three years since his departure, the shadow of Gatland still loomed large over the squad. Some also said that things had got a little stale and that maybe the schedule needed to be tweaked.

I was happy to act as a liaison between the players and the coaches, and resolved to sit down with Wayne at the end of the campaign. The World Cup was only ten months away, and we needed a good honest chat about the way forwards. As things panned out, we never got the chance.

The final game of the campaign was against Australia, and for fifty-five minutes, Wales were sensational. It was like a switch had been flicked, and Wayne and Steve had got their way.

We raced into a 34–13 lead, playing with verve, swagger and authority; we were rampaging and powerful up front, slinky and elusive behind. It might have been a patched-up Australia side playing their fifth Test of an arduous tour, but we were absolutely *dominating* them.

I was in Northampton that day for a bit of a send-off, and I turned it off after an hour, content that we'd wrapped up the victory.

When the Northampton boys arrived, they were shaking their heads in disbelief and asking how Wales had blown it again.

I was confused. Blown what?

One of them showed me his phone: 'Stunning defeat leaves Wayne Pivac on the brink.'

I was gobsmacked and – to this day, having watched it back – I still can't fathom how things unravelled so spectacularly.

Wayne was teetering on a cliff edge.

Regardless of my personal feelings about Wayne, if you lose at home to Georgia and Italy in the same year, you're going to be up against it. The chief executive of the WRU, Steve Phillips, called a Zoom meeting with me, Tips, Ken, George, Chicken and Al to explain that they were conducting a thorough review of the autumn series and wanted our input.

We weren't naïve; rumours had already begun to swirl about

Warren Gatland – the word on the street was that both England and Wales were now vying for his services.

Steve was waffling, so I interrupted and asked if changes had already been set in motion. He said that yes, there would be changes, and I said – if that was the case – what was the point of this conversation? It felt to me like he just wanted extra ammunition to load the gun he was already holding to Wayne's head, and I did not want any part of it. The truth was, I wanted Wayne to stay. He'd been good to me and I was still convinced we could do well in the World Cup. We would have the time to put a successful campaign together if we started now. But a few days after that Zoom call, Wayne was sacked, and Warren was parachuted back in on a lucrative four-year deal.

History has judged Wayne badly and wrongly. He was a much better coach than he's been given credit for. Among the criticisms he faced was that he'd come to rely on an ageing old guard and hadn't blooded enough youngsters. He actually capped more than twenty new players during his tenure, so that doesn't hold much water, but perhaps there were too many older guys past their prime, together with too many youngsters who lacked the coal-face experience. You always need a blend.

If I was to offer an explanation about what went wrong, it's probably the muddled thinking I mentioned earlier. Other than in South Africa, we weren't quite all on the same page as a coaching and playing group. Everyone was concerned about getting their own department right, as opposed to what was good for the team as a whole.

People might view the Pivac era through a prism of failure, but we experienced some incredible highs under him: a first ever win in South Africa, a Six Nations title that should have been a Grand Slam, a record points haul against England. Those things don't happen by accident.

I made a point of calling Wayne to thank him for everything. He and I had a good mutual understanding. He'd promised me the captaincy for the World Cup, and I'd been his first-choice 10 for his entire tenure. It had felt good to have the unequivocal backing of my coach, and I wanted to express my gratitude. Behind the salacious headlines, here was a decent bloke whose pride was hurting badly. The WRU had handled the affair in a shabby and insensitive manner. It was all a bit cloak-and-dagger, not to mention financially ruinous. At a time when the regions were struggling for money, and players were being told they'd have to take big pay cuts, the WRU was able to magically conjure £1.5 million to pay off Wayne, Steve and Gethin Jenkins, not to mention fund the bumper salary they'd be paying Warren.

There's an old adage that you should never go back, and that was my initial reaction to Gatland's reappointment. It all felt a bit retrograde, and I'm pretty sure Steve Phillips hadn't cast his net to include a wider pool of potential candidates. Gats just happened to be in the country, working for Amazon Prime. It felt like a coronation, another tawdry episode in the ongoing soap opera of Welsh rugby. It wasn't anything personal against Warren; I just disliked the Machiavellian machinations that brought about his reappointment.

Alex asked me how I felt about it, and I simply replied, 'He's not coming back with Shaun, is he?' Together, they'd had the Midas touch, and I wasn't sure the same magic could be summoned without that element. The WRU then vetoed Warren's request to bring Rob Howley back, who'd been cast into the rugby wilderness in Canada. Howley had served his penance, so it seemed spiteful to block his return, not to mention counterproductive. So on the one hand, the WRU had sacked most of the leadership team and opened the cheque book to lure back the main man. On the other, they were denying him the team he wanted to be successful. If we were talking about any environment other than Welsh rugby, it might have been surprising. But a lifetime of baffling episodes at the heart of our national sport had left me inured to the chaos of it all.

Self-inflicted wounds were the WRU's speciality.

19

RIVIERA DREAMING

I trundle down to the harbour in Carqueiranne, as the watery sunrise casts its golden glow over the glassy surface of the Mediterranean. Pleasure boats are bobbing gently on the tide as I wander into the boulangerie to inhale the rich aroma of freshly baked pastries. I exchange pleasantries with the girl behind the counter, who's seen my French develop from faltering to competent within a few months, and order my usual combo of two pains au chocolat – still warm from the oven – and a café au lait. Suitably fortified, I make my way to the gleaming compound that is Toulon's new training complex.

Leigh Halfpenny raised his eyebrows when I showed him pictures of the new place, recalling his days of changing in a Portacabin and attending meetings in a tent. Now, there is a shiny new set-up, complete with an airy modern gym, an academy HQ, and a gourmet brasserie where local businesspeople can host meetings framed by the glorious Mount Faron while the first XV trains below.

The 3G pitch is open to the elements at the sides, but sheltered under a closed roof, installed to offer sanctuary from the blazing Mediterranean sun. It's a place for us to practise our walk-throughs without fear of melting. The indoor barn in Wales serves a similar purpose, in that it protects us from the elements, but in Wales those are driving wind and rain as opposed to searing sunshine. It's barely an hour's flight away from Cardiff, but they're worlds apart.

Culturally, we're poles apart as well. There's a conviviality here that is uniquely French. Arriving at training at eight o'clock, I'll have shaken hands with dozens of people between the car park and the canteen. That's the custom here: a smile, a handshake, and a hug. They're open-hearted people, the French. I love it, though it took others a while to get used to. James Coughlan, our defence coach is a no-nonsense Munsterman, who was a little disoriented when he first arrived ten years earlier. After a few days of relentless hugs and hand-shaking, he called his mentor, the late Anthony Foley, for advice. Foley told him in his gruff Limerick brogue, 'I wouldn't be standing for all that bollocks. Tell them that where you come from, you shake hands with a man twice: once when you meet him, and once on his wedding day.' It took Coughlan a while to loosen the shackles, but he's one of the biggest huggers of the lot now.

There's a feeling right now that French rugby is *the* place to be. The clubs are all bigger, richer, and well insulated from the icy financial draught that's blowing through rugby in England and Wales at the moment. In France the Top 14 is thriving; every week the stands vibrate with vocal, passionate support, and clubs are frequently moving fixtures to bigger football stadiums to exploit the feel-good factor that's spread through the country in the wake of France's 2022 Grand Slam.

It came as a shock to me that the Sunday 9 p.m. kick-off slot is the most coveted, as it's a guaranteed sell-out, attracting enormous TV viewing figures.

Back in Wales, we're constantly engaged in wearying discussions about kick-off times and how convenient or otherwise they are. In France, fans' support is unconditional. Whenever and wherever you play, they'll turn up to watch.

Every Tuesday, Toulon allows the fans into the complex during training, and a hardcore of fifty or so dutifully trot in and watch transfixed as we run our plays in the shadow of the mountains. Afterwards they'll form an orderly queue, and politely ask for autographs and photos. There's a deep connection between them and the players and the coaches are keen to foster that.

I'd had to keep my move secret while contracts were being exchanged. I was rehabbing my knee in the Wales camp during the autumn of 2022, and the only people I'd told were Franny and Prav.

Once terms had been agreed, I had to take a medical before I could officially sign. I looked at flight options – there were a couple of easyJet flights to Nice, but with my knee in a brace I didn't really fancy a long drive on arrival.

I mentioned it to my agent, and within minutes he came back with, 'No worries, they're arranging a private jet.'

I was pretty excited until Alex brought up the recent Emilio Sala tragedy and said pointedly, 'I'm not getting on any private plane if it looks remotely dodgy.' We persuaded her it would be fine, and it was booked to collect us from Cardiff Airport at 7 a.m. the following morning.

There's a private hangar, separate from the main airport, which confused the hell out of our satnav, sending us on a seemingly endless detour. I'm a stickler for punctuality and started panicking, thinking word would get back that I was late for the jet they'd laid on especially.

Any concerns proved redundant as – when we eventually arrived – we were treated like royalty. There was no need for such tedious red tape as passport control or security. Our car was driven away by a valet, and we were offered a selection of drinks as we settled into a pair of leather armchairs. The likes of Gareth Bale and Aaron Ramsey are used to this level of service as they regularly shuttle back and forth from Madrid and Juventus, but it was an ultra-rare treat for me. That little glimpse into their lives showed me how far down the food chain I actually was.

The views from the plane as we approached the French Riviera were spectacular, and we took dozens of photos of the verdant hills rising above twinkling turquoise lagoons, not knowing that nestled amid them, on a slope overlooking the Giens Peninsula, was the house we'd end up living in.

There were three cars waiting for us at Toulon Airport. I was to be conveyed straight to the club for my medical, while Alex was taken house-hunting. I'm not sure she realized that within minutes of landing, she'd be whisked away in a car full of strangers, all speaking a foreign language. I removed my knee brace, not wanting their first glimpse of their 'star signing' to be me hobbling in like an invalid. It was a foolish move, but it felt like the right one.

I had blood tests, an ECG and an appointment with the cardiologist before I was able to eat anything. Alex and my agent Tim Lopez had been enjoying coffee and croissants on the flight, whereas I hadn't even been allowed a drop of water.

At this point all I had was my residual GCSE French, and *'Je voudrais une baguette'* wasn't going to get me too far in the real world. The woman taking my blood samples was speaking in rapid-fire French and when I said, *'Pardon, parlez-vous anglais?'* she replied with a simple, *'Non.'* I resolved then to learn French as a matter of priority.

Thankfully, the cardiologist spoke a bit of English and welcomed me more enthusiastically. 'Ah you're Welsh,' he exclaimed. 'We've had some really good Welsh signings over the years, like Halfpenny, he was amazing . . . and some not so good ones, like Jenkins and Webb.' I smiled wryly, declining to point out that Rhys had been my half-back partner for the best part of a decade.

There was a camera crew waiting for me when I eventually got to the training complex, and was introduced to Bernard Lemaître amid a scrum of journalists and flashing of bulbs.

He was as charismatic in real life as he'd been on Zoom, and chatted freely in heavily accented English as he led me to his office.

I glanced at my phone as he was outlining his plans to expand the brasserie, and noticed I'd missed fifteen calls. I was already feeling a little unmoored given the whirlwind events of the day.

This barrage of calls couldn't have been good news, and it was naturally very distracting.

I managed a quick scan of my messages while Lemaître's attention was elsewhere, and read one from the CEO at Northampton. There had been plenty of communication between the clubs about the etiquette surrounding the announcement, but it appeared something had been lost in translation, and the media guys – who can get quite territorial about this kind of stuff – had had some kind of quarrel.

It had been agreed that Northampton would announce my departure first, but Toulon had said they were going to post a video of my arrival. If that happened, Northampton had replied, the deal was off. No sooner had I read that message, than Bernard was engaging me in conversation again and I wasn't able to reply. I was nodding and smiling at the right moments, but my brain was whirring at the gravity of what I'd just read. It seemed like a trivial misunderstanding, but the words 'the deal will be off' were now imprinted on my troubled mind.

We moved to the boardroom to actually put pen to paper, when Tim appeared looking uncharacteristically flustered, and filled me in on events. Northampton, it seemed, weren't messing about, and we'd have to sort this quickly. We tentatively mentioned it to Bernard, desperate not to offend after we'd been shown such amazing hospitality. Could they please hold back on the announcement video until Northampton have done their bit? With typical French insouciance, he shrugged his shoulders and said, 'Yeah, no problem. The English are so bloody uptight!'

With that, he took his seat at the head of the boardroom table and placed my contract in front of him. Pulling a crumpled packet of Gauloises from his pocket he asked, 'Do you mind if I smoke?' I felt like saying, 'Crack on mate, you own the bloody place.'

He cast a cursory glance over the first few pages, before fixating on the last paragraph where there was a bonus clause in italics. He swivelled the contract towards me and prodded the clause in question.

It essentially said if you win a trophy, *any* trophy, you get a bonus.

He leaned in through a cloud of cigarette smoke and said, 'Trust me, I *really* want to pay you this bonus.'

The camera shutters began whirring again as I put pen to paper on the most lucrative contract of my career, and all I could think at that moment was, 'I've come a long way since signing my first contract on a used napkin in Mike Cuddy's office.'

There was a knock at the door, and Cheslin Kolbe appeared to say hello and hand over perhaps the best welcome present I could have received: a framed photo of him and me squaring up to one another in Pretoria with the inscription, 'Welcome my brother. Peace.'

It was a long day, and by the time we boarded the flight home, my knee was throbbing and swollen. I knew Prav would be annoyed. But once we were in the air, the co-pilot emerged from the cockpit and, in the most flamboyantly camp manner, said, 'I hear celebrations are in order?' popping the cork on what appeared to be a very expensive bottle of champagne.

As a professional sportsman, you often don't appreciate the glamour because you're so used to the grind. This was one of those rare occasions I allowed myself to bask in the moment. The Toulon deal was a culmination of all the hard work and dedication I'd put into my career, so I bloody well deserved to be sipping champagne on a private jet!

When I flew back in December to officially begin my Toulon career, I was on the red-eye from Cardiff to Amsterdam, followed by an easyJet flight to Marseille. The rain was coming down in rods when we landed, and the fog was so thick I couldn't even see the sea. For the first five days I lived in the Holiday Inn Express, like a lonely Alan Partridge.

The private jet was already a distant memory.

*

I'd love to have resumed the captaincy of Wales, but Gats never raised it with me. As the incumbent I'd like to have had a conversation at least; it's not as though he was a brand-new coach who didn't know me. That's never been his style, though, and the truth was I hadn't really expected him to change. Because it was effectively a new regime, it felt less like I was being stripped of the captaincy, and more that the slate was being wiped clean. I won't deny that I was disappointed, but I wasn't going to sulk about it.

Gats has always liked a forward as his captain, and there weren't too many contenders. Al wasn't guaranteed his place so Tips, Ken Owens and I were the only plausible options and he went with Ken.

One of Gats's first pronouncements after taking the job was that Wayne should have moved a few of the older players on earlier. He'd always been very unsentimental when it came to releasing senior players, and would probably have already despatched some of us to the discard pile if he'd been there all along. Just ask the likes of Bomb, Jamie and Phillsy. That's just how he is.

There was a corner of the dressing room to which the senior boys would gravitate – the rugby equivalent of the back of the bus. Most of the guys who got changed in that corner would be closing in on one hundred caps. Then someone joked that anybody who changed at the far end would be gone by the next campaign, and boys who'd never before shown any superstitious tendencies started avoiding that corner at all costs.

There were a few surprises in Warren's first squad, particularly at fly half. Rhys Patchell was back, having barely played for the Scarlets, and Owen Williams was picked off the back of four good games for the Ospreys. It's funny how things work; if Worcester Warriors rugby club hadn't folded in late 2022, he wouldn't even have been eligible. The press was rightly singing his praises, and my old insecurities returned as I imagined them waxing lyrical about another two contenders who should be picked ahead of me.

Rhys Webb was also back, having been excluded under Wayne.

He was still a classy player, but he and Wayne had rarely seen eye to eye. Whenever Wayne was questioned about his exclusion, he'd say he wasn't quick enough, but it went deeper than that. Rhys and Wayne are both headstrong characters, and there was a personality clash there that they just couldn't overcome.

Elsewhere, there were a lot of fresh faces representing the new generation, Jac Morgan, Joe Hawkins, Gareth Thomas and Teddy Williams among them.

It was interesting to clock their reaction to Gats when he strutted in on day one. They were probably feeling the way I did more than a decade earlier – slightly awestruck by this iconic figure who'd bestridden the rugby world for most of their lives. He still had that same air of intimidation about him, but to me he felt more approachable than when I'd first met him, which came across during his first squad meeting when he asked us what *our* expectations of the coaches were.

Not a lot of coaches would do that; it showed how comfortable in his own skin he'd become. It could have fatally undermined the authority of a younger coach, but Gats had no such concerns.

We all got into mini-groups and discussed our responses. I deliberately kept quiet to encourage the youngsters to seize the initiative. Most of them shuffled awkwardly in their seats, trying not to twitch or make eye contact, terrified that the slightest movement would mark them out as willing to speak.

Eventually the barriers wore down, though, and we started calling out suggestions. We talked about wanting absolute clarity, and for all the coaches to deliver a unified, coherent message.

The word 'honesty' came up a lot, and we spoke about what that actually meant, beyond being a clichéd buzz word. When we drilled down a bit further, we talked about the importance of honesty in selection, of not being bullshitted or gaslighted.

If someone gets picked ahead of me, for example, I want to know why. Basically we wanted to feel comfortable challenging the coaches. I'm not and never have been a nodding dog, and if I don't agree with something, I think it's important to be able to say so without fear of censure or being labelled a disruptor. It's not conflict for conflict's sake, but of opening people's eyes to a different way of thinking.

Gats was on board with that, admitting wryly that – despite appearances – he still didn't know *everything* about rugby. It eased some of the tension in the group that had undoubtedly ratcheted up since Wayne had left.

We had our team photo on the Tuesday, and as usual most of the senior players were seated either side of the captain in the front row. As we were lining up, I quipped that those of us in the front row should strike our best poses as this was surely our last Six Nations photo before Gats dumped us.

He gazed around, casting his eye across the front row, where Tips, Toby, Alun Wyn, Ken, Sanj, Pence and I were all sitting. He then glanced at the back row, where Alex Cuthbert was hiding among all the tall lads, and said drily, 'If Jaddsy and Cuthy swap, you're pretty much dead right, Bigs.'

We had to sacrifice a bit of the intensity we'd been used to in training so the new coaches – Alex King in attack, and Mike Forshaw in defence – could get their messages across. For ten years under Rob and Shaun the working patterns had been so familiar, the thought processes so aligned, we'd rarely needed to stop and talk.

Mike Forshaw was seriously impressive in his first meeting. Like all new arrivals, he had to stand up and introduce himself in thirty seconds.

He showed a couple of pictures, one of which was of him playing for Bradford in the 2003 Challenge Cup Final at what was then the Millennium Stadium. They beat Leeds in a pulsating match that he claimed was a career highlight. He spoke about how proud he was to now be coaching the team that played in that famous citadel of rugby.

There was something about his manner and choice of words that were immediately engaging. He referenced his old mate Shaun Edwards, and said if he could have 10 per cent of the impact Shaun had had, he'd consider it a success. It can be difficult coming into a hard-bitten environment like that – where bonds have been forged over time – and immediately ingratiate yourself, but he did so with ease.

I came first in the endurance test during the first week back, and felt inordinately pleased with myself. As a thirty-three-year-old who'd been living in France for a month, I'm sure Warren expected my fitness levels to have dropped. We'd seen it happen to other players who'd moved to France, where there was a more laissez-faire attitude to conditioning.

As I was lying sweating on the floor, gulping air into my lungs, Warren wandered past and muttered, 'Well done, you've managed to keep yourself here for another week.'

He used his subtle motivational techniques to massage a few bruised egos, namely those of back row Jac Morgan and Alun Wyn. He identified Jac – who'd had a stop-start international career to that point – as captain material, and brought him into the leadership group. Jac is quiet at the best of times, so Warren ended every meeting by handing him the floor and asking if he had anything to add. Every time, without fail, he'd shuffle nervously and say, 'No no, it's all been covered.'

He had a long chat with Alun Wyn, who was noticeably more relaxed than he'd been in ages. As someone who'd been a Welsh titan for more than a decade, he'd been unable to handle the drop in status he'd suffered when Wayne had started benching him. He'd become a little withdrawn – stalking silently around camp with his hood pulled up – but within a few weeks of Warren's return, he was the life and soul, joining us around the cards table, and even managing to laugh when some of the younger boys emptied his wallet. Whatever Gats said had had a transformative effect.

Slowly but surely, the self-belief was returning.

What we didn't realize, in among this cautious optimism, was that an almighty storm was brewing.

20

HURTLING TOWARDS THE ABYSS

We were dining in the opulent surrounds of the Parkgate in central Cardiff, the luxury WRU-financed hotel where couples come to spend romantic city-breaks in the Welsh capital. But the mood was far from romantic, or even cordial, as Martyn Williams and Ken Owens were engaged in a furious argument in the corridor near the toilets. The row was centred on what was about to unfold in the function room next door. We were at a sponsors' dinner, ten days before Wales were due to face England, and we were about to stage a mass walkout.

Despite the positive signs in the changing room, Warren Gatland's return had begun disastrously, with hammerings against Ireland and Scotland. Aside from the catastrophic on-field results, the legal agreement that binds the WRU and the regions had expired. The two sides were now at loggerheads over a new draft, with one Cardiff board member referring to the relationship between the union and the regions as that of 'master and slaves'. The arguments over funding were threatening players' livelihoods – dozens of professional players were in the final year of their contracts, and were being told extensions couldn't be discussed until an agreement had been reached.

Welsh rugby appeared to be hurtling towards the abyss.

Losing Six Nations games by huge margins was distressing enough, but nowhere near as alarming as losing your job and your income – a prospect that was becoming distressingly real for a good number of my colleagues.

The militant feeling had been bubbling beneath the surface for weeks, and with the WRU's most lucrative fixture about to take place, we were preparing to go on strike. Embarrassing the WRU by walking out of their sponsors' dinner would be just the beginning.

Two weeks earlier, we'd been humiliated by Ireland in front of our home fans as Gatland's second reign began in disastrous fashion. Any feel-good factor generated by his return was overshadowed completely by an incendiary BBC documentary, accusing the WRU of fostering a culture of sexism, misogyny and racism. It contained grim testimony from a number of former employees and dragged the image of Welsh rugby even further into the gutter.

My mood darkened considerably in the week that followed, and I let rip in the press conference before the Scotland game. They'd beaten England in round one, and it seemed the entire rugby world was queueing up to lavish praise on them. I was in a particularly combative mood, and bristled at the notion that they were suddenly favourites. It pissed me off that we'd been the most successful team in the tournament for the past decade, but were constantly being denigrated for our style of play or – in the case of 2021 – our 'lucky wins'. Scotland, meanwhile, had never finished in the top half during that period, but were being lauded for being supposedly world class.

'According to you guys, they're the best team around, aren't they?' I snapped, adding that there was barely any point in us catching the flight to Edinburgh if the hype was to be believed.

'Medals are important when you look back at your career,' I continued, 'and we have been lucky enough to fill the cabinet a few times.'

My annoyance was real, but it came from a place of insecurity too. I felt under pressure, and beneath it all I was questioning whether we were anywhere near the level we needed to be to compete. The Ireland defeat had been a rude awakening.

As it turned out, the Scotland game was equally horrendous. Finn Russell delivered one of his finest ever performances as they cut us to ribbons. Nothing went right for me personally, or for the team as a whole.

Needless to say, the Scottish fans took great pleasure in watching me eat my words. We still had quality individual players, but were blown out of the water by a Scotland side playing with a verve and swagger we couldn't match. Our penalty count soared through the roof, and by the time Matt Fagerson crossed for their fifth try, we were staring down the barrel of a grim 35–7 defeat. It was an ugly stain on Gats's coaching record, considering he'd never lost to Scotland before then.

I found out I was 'trending' on Twitter after the game following an altercation with one of my own players. Rio Dyer had thrown me a wayward pass when we were under pressure in our 22, and I gave him a rollicking for doing so. Predictably the Twittersphere exploded, with people accusing me of everything from petulance to unprofessionalism to outright bullying.

It was such bollocks. That's what happens in elite level sport. His being a newcomer was irrelevant; I'd have reacted in the same way if George North or Liam Williams had screwed up. Equally, and at his age, I'd been on the receiving end of some almighty bollockings from the likes of Gethin Jenkins and Martyn Williams, and I just had to suck it up, learn from it, and resolve not to make the same mistakes again.

The criticism from armchair pundits washed clean off me, but some of the comments from ex-professional players stuck in my craw. Mike Phillips, of all people, wrote a newspaper column decrying my reaction, claiming he 'would never have done that'.

He went on to say, 'I didn't like seeing that, Dyer's just come into the side and he's a young player with a few caps. I don't see the benefit of that. I think he'll be a bit disappointed with himself.'

For the record, I've seen Phillsy lay into dozens of people over the years, including me, and I've never had an issue with it. It drives standards and focuses minds.

The mood on the bus back from Murrayfield was among the most depressing I've witnessed in my career. Any optimism that Gatland's return had engendered had evaporated, and the bad vibes emanating from the WRU hung heavily over all of us. I glanced up the aisle at the rows of glum, scarred faces, all lit by the glow of their mobile phones, watching them sink into their digital worlds to find not solace, but further misery. The match had been broadcast to millions and our performance was now being dissected by thousands more in the frothing fury of social media.

The two defeats to Ireland and Scotland were not because of the off-field ructions, but they'd certainly been one hell of a distraction. Steve Phillips had been forced to resign over the sexism scandal and had been temporarily replaced by Nigel Walker. No progress had been made on the agreement between the Professional Rugby Board (representing the regions), and the WRU. Players were getting increasingly concerned about their futures. Not just those in the international camp, but *all* regional players, none of whom knew if they'd have an income beyond June. There weren't far off a hundred players who were now out of contract and stuck in limbo. Willis Halaholo was speaking for all his colleagues when he tweeted, 'Must be nice knowing u can still provide for your kids in about 4months.'

By the Wednesday after the Scotland game, we'd had enough, and formally called a meeting with Nigel Walker to let him know of our intention to strike. We were infuriated at the endless prevarication of the bureaucrats, and told Nigel that unless we'd seen positive progress by the following Wednesday, we'd be pulling out of the England game, depriving the Union of more than £10 million in revenue, a tenth of its annual income.

We had three specific demands: the scrapping of the sixty-cap rule, a players' representative on the PRB board, and the removal of the fixed-variable element of the proposed new contracts. The new contract structure being discussed was based on an 80–20 'fixed-variable' split, meaning 80 per cent of your salary was guaranteed, with the other 20 per cent only paid when certain targets were hit, namely victories on the field. So, out of, for example, a salary of £100,000, only £80,000 of it was guaranteed. The rest was made up of match fees, win bonuses, and other more nebulous stuff, including whether you started a game or came off the bench. It was farcical.

When budgets are squeezed and salaries reduced, squads naturally become less competitive. To deliberately weaken teams, and then tell players they'd only be paid in full if they kept winning was Kafka-esque in its lunacy.

The talk was of budgets being reduced to £4.5 million, which was £3 million below the Scarlets' wage bill at the time. How could you slash budgets that dramatically and still expect teams to be competitive, let alone successful?

As for the sixty-cap rule, it had run its course. If Wales could offer competitive salaries, then fair enough. But when players are being offered massive wage increases to move elsewhere, it's perverse to use the national shirt as a bargaining chip. Railing against market forces is like putting your finger in the dam. I disliked the policy in principle anyway; to me it smacked of small-minded parochialism. The benefits of playing in different countries and different leagues are manifold, and I speak from experience. My appetite for rugby was completely refreshed at Northampton, and my horizons have been immeasurably broadened by my move to Toulon.

I look at the younger generation, who have never experienced anything beyond the four walls of the academy system and feel resentful on their behalf that they're being held hostage by an administration using a sledgehammer to crack a nut.

Nigel was taken aback by the strength of feeling in the room, and appealed for more patience, saying we were at a pivotal juncture and couldn't afford to take a wrong turn. But plenty of the boys had already run out of patience. At least one was on anti-depressants, and another had been refused a mortgage because of uncertainty over his employment. Some players – grown men – were considering moving back in with their parents. This wasn't about numbers on a spreadsheet or abstract policies like the sixty-cap rule, but about real lives.

Sensing a lack of urgency, we told him we'd be boycotting the sponsors' dinner at the Parkgate that night. You could see the panic in his eyes, and he told us that if we didn't attend, the sponsors would walk and steer the game even closer to the cliff edge.

We reluctantly agreed to attend to show support for the coaches, but still intended to stage a walkout after the formal Q+A. There was an increased feeling of militancy after that meeting, and I was one of several players who didn't think we'd gone far enough. Someone questioned our appetite for the fight, saying if weren't prepared to boycott a sponsors' dinner, were we really prepared to boycott a Wales–England match in the Six Nations?

He had a point.

I'd envisaged the walkout to be a fairly theatrical affair, but the reality wasn't quite so dramatic. We'd stressed the need to be courteous to all the guests; our fight was with the WRU, not the sponsors, and we didn't want to come across as prima donnas. How we managed this would affect the way it played out in the press.

The plan was for all of us to stand up in unison and walk out once Ken had thanked the sponsors. Once he'd finished, some of us stood, while others hovered uncertainly, halfway between sitting and standing. Some of the coaches hadn't been told of our intentions, and looked baffled at what was going on. Leigh Halfpenny was on Jenks's table, and when he stood up, Jenks asked, 'Where the fuck are you going?'

Pence – one of the sketchiest and least confrontational blokes you'll ever meet – started mumbling awkwardly about 'needing to leave'. Rather than the choreographed, smooth exit we'd planned, it looked more like a bunch of startled meerkats poking their heads out of their burrows and scanning the room in alarm.

Eventually enough of us started leaving for the rest to follow, and we strode out without looking back. There were some shocked and confused faces as we left, but within twenty minutes I'd had several supportive messages from the sponsors who'd been told why we'd done what we'd done. It was reassuring to hear that, far from coming across as petty and ungrateful, our action had had its desired effect.

We held a players' meeting the following morning, and agreed that while striking was a last resort, it couldn't just be sabre-rattling: we *had* to be prepared to go through with it.

Nigel called another formal meeting, which began with him trying to negotiate a compromise. I quickly cut him off, though, telling him, 'This isn't a discussion Nige, it's an ultimatum. If those three things aren't delivered by Wednesday, the England game isn't happening.'

Nigel is a pretty calm and measured bloke, but that stoked his anger.

'If that match doesn't go ahead,' he replied, 'none of this will matter because the game will go bust.'

He was framing the strike as a naïve act of self-harm, and might have expected our resistance to crumble, but I snapped back, 'Well, it's an easy conversation to have, then.'

I wasn't without sympathy for Nigel; he'd inherited this mess from his predecessor and was trying to be as honest and transparent as possible, but there'd been so much accumulated rage, pain and misery, and he was just in the wrong place at the wrong time. The level of mistrust in the WRU had reached epidemic proportions, and he'd become the prime target.

Despite his apparent efforts at conciliation, I still sensed a lack of urgency. At one point, he said they would have to await the return of two board members before making any final decision. That summed up the attitude: the livelihood of dozens of players was at stake but we mustn't interrupt the board members' skiing holiday.

You might be wondering why I was so vocal in all of this, given that I was playing my club rugby in France. The answer is simple; these people are my friends, and I was determined to stand four-square behind them. Actually, the fact that I had no skin in the game was a benefit. I was able to be more bellicose because I had a lot less to lose.

Some of the boys pulled me up on it, asking if I was being too aggressive, but someone needed to be. It was harder for the likes of Ken, who was captain and still playing in the Welsh system. He had to be a little more diplomatic.

Consequently I found myself leading the negotiations, alongside Ken, Al, George, Scott Baldwin and Tomos Williams. Ken, Al and I caught up for a coffee afterwards and started reminiscing about the good old days. As much as we worked hard for our success, we'd been fortunate with our timing. We came into a Welsh team which was already successful, with that coterie of world-class coaches, and a number of senior pros who'd been around the block and won things.

The contracts we signed were generous and the money was good. We might not have realized it then, but those were halcyon days, compared to the experience the younger players were now going through. They had come into a team that had sunk into a trough amid a gloomy backdrop of financial collapse. The situations were starkly contrasting.

Rugby in Wales had long been reliant on generous benefactors who'd whip out the chequebook to cover the inevitable losses at the end of every financial year. When I started, you had the likes of Peter Thomas at Cardiff, and Mike Cuddy at the Ospreys, keeping their beloved clubs afloat, and it seemed like the game was only going to grow and flourish. Salaries were swelling, blockbuster overseas signings were plentiful, and the clubs were riding a wave of optimism.

Somehow that had all changed, though. Perhaps the WRU had

been too stingy, or the regions too profligate with the cash they received, but there was never any real attempt at collaboration. They always seemed to revel in the other party getting bad press.

I sometimes struggle to process how we've been so successful when the foundations are built on sand. As much as it pains me to say it the sun appeared to be setting on the golden generation, and there were only slate-grey skies on the horizon.

Gats had taken a back seat throughout much of this. His position as a full-time employee of the WRU put him in an awkward position, where he couldn't publicly back strike action, but he was offering us private support, insisting we could come to him for advice should we want to.

No one was willing to stick their head above the parapet and ask if *he* was willing to take a pay cut or go on a fixed-variable contract. It would have taken a brave man to do that, but there was definitely a feeling that the players were taking the brunt of the punishment while the coaches and executives were enjoying their usual bumper salaries and privileges. It would later emerge that Steve Phillips had received a pay-out of £480,000 after presiding over one of the most damaging episodes in WRU history. It all added to the growing sense of distrust between the players and the WRU.

There was a real edge to training that week, with tempers constantly bubbling over. It was actually a welcome opportunity to release our pent-up aggression. There were plenty of laughs too; every time Gats called a tough drill, someone would pipe up, 'Don't fancy that. Shall we strike for that one?'

When you have that many thoughts whirring through your mind, the only way you can truly empty it is to push yourselves to your physical limits. While the strike threat remained real, we were still prepping as though the match was going ahead. We were absolutely flogged by the end of the sessions.

We'd heard nothing back from the Union by Monday, and called a squad meeting to ensure everyone was on the same page. Striking was an easier decision for someone like me – missing one game wouldn't be the end of the world – but I was conscious that it was an entirely different dilemma if you were new to the squad, and had never before had the chance to play against England in Cardiff.

I explained that the decision had to be unanimous, and if anyone wasn't comfortable, they should make their feelings known. We'd fostered a strong sense of solidarity and were confident that people could express themselves regardless of status or seniority.

In fairness to all the youngsters desperate to play, they realized that this was way bigger than one match. This was going to shape their next ten years in the game. Everyone turned out to be fully on board, and some of the newest squad members were actually among the most vocal. I was impressed by Teddy Williams, who asked some searching questions, including some stuff we hadn't thought of.

He'd heard that the WRU had been considering lowering the sixty-cap rule anyway, so we should be wary of considering it a triumph if they did accede to that particular demand. It was a good point, and reaffirmed our belief that we should stick to our guns. Threatening strike action was the only thing that had spooked the bureaucrats into action.

As we were about to disperse, Tomos Williams yelled across to me, 'Are you sure you're not ramping up the drama here just so you've got a juicier chapter for your book?'

There was a ripple of laughter and, as I wandered towards the door, he shouted, 'I've got a title for it, by the way', pausing for maximum impact.

'A hundred caps and still shit!'

The feeling of unity cracked a little on Tuesday morning when we trundled into the 9.50 a.m. meeting where the team is traditionally announced. Gats looked sullen, and announced curtly that he wouldn't be selecting the team until later in the week.

Cryptically, he said there would be a debutant in it, and the five English-based players would all be playing.

His tone was difficult to read, and there was a strange atmosphere in the room. Streaming out of the meeting, we all turned to one another and said, 'What the fuck was that all about?'

I'm not sure what his intention had been, but it seemed like he was trying to dissuade us from going through with the strike. Giving that coded message to the English-based players and to the 'new cap' was a clear attempt to soften their stance towards it. Whether he was acting on his own or had been put up to it, he was clearly prodding at the more vulnerable flanks and aiming to spread doubt and confusion.

We went straight to training but discussed pulling out of the afternoon session. The whole squad huddled beneath the posts to discuss our options, while the coaches stood impatiently on the halfway line.

Gats figured out what was going on and announced he was cancelling it anyway; I'm not sure whether that was because he wanted to be seen to be in control or because he knew we weren't in the right state of mind. He told us to go home and come back on Thursday if a resolution had been reached.

There was a lot of anger among the boys that evening. We felt that Gats had shown us a lack of respect and was siding with the Union. We'd brought him a huge amount of success over the years, and the one time we needed his support, he'd withdrawn it. We were being treated like impetuous children rather than grown men standing on principle.

I wasn't the only one who was unimpressed. Leadership is about how you make people feel, and we felt pretty let down. It made me question whether his heart was really in the job the second time around.

I'm not sure Gats realized how deep a trough the Welsh game had slid into. I stewed on it that evening, and after a few hours my frustration and anger had curdled into disappointment. We were in an increasingly difficult situation, and in Gats we potentially had a massive, influential figure who could have thrown his weight behind us but hadn't. The longer I thought about it, the more it hurt.

It had blindsided us all.

If the move had been to separate the English-based players from the rest, it hadn't worked, as the likes of Louis Rees-Zammit and Nick Tompkins were still backing the strike action.

As the deadline loomed closer, it was actually some of the senior Welsh-based players who began to waver, spooked by the WRU's threat about the regions being liquidated if the game didn't go ahead. A new rumour had also surfaced that the WRU was secretly assembling a Barbarians-style 'Wales' team to fulfil the fixture if we went on strike.

I won't name names, but some were on the verge of losing their bottle. The narrative was slowly changing to one of damage limitation, as opposed to burning the whole thing to the ground.

Our case was being fought by Gareth Lewis, the head of the Welsh Rugby Players' Association, and his feedback was that the Union were budging but not capitulating. They were willing to reduce the sixty-cap rule to twenty-five, but not to scrap it altogether. We stuck to our guns, telling him we wanted it gone.

Reports were circulating in the press that Joe Hawkins, our talented young centre, who'd started against Ireland and Scotland, was signing for Exeter. It wasn't yet a done deal, but it might act as the canary in the coal mine. They were offering him a lot more money than the Ospreys could afford, and if he was to sign and our demands of scrapping the rule weren't met, his international career would come to a shuddering halt.

We owed it to guys like Joe to hold the line.

Wednesday dawned, and I didn't go to the meeting. I felt like my fight had been fought.

The outcome was hugely disappointing, with everything ending in a fudge. The sixty-cap rule was lowered to twenty-five, which helped a few players like Jaddsy, Ross Moriarty and Rhys Patchell, but not the rest.

The fixed-variable contracts weren't removed as we'd demanded. The WRU's counterproposal was that the player could *choose* between a fixed-variable or a fixed, but the base salaries on the fixed contracts were too low to be competitive. The only one of the three demands that was met was the one about having a player's representative on the PRB.

The WRU had put the frighteners on the boys and forced a climbdown.

I was absolutely gutted.

Several of them came into the team room virtually high-fiving one another at the outcome, having been duped by the WRU. They were claiming to have got everything we'd wanted, and it took a few of us hard-bitten cynics to point out that we'd actually achieved very little. A week earlier, we'd resolved to strike if our demands weren't met. They hadn't been, yet we'd rolled over and agreed to play. In hindsight, attending the sponsors' dinner had lost us a good deal of power, because they must have calculated then that we didn't have the courage of our convictions.

Ultimately, the players who went along with the compromises have got to live with their decisions. They blew their one chance to genuinely change things.

Tom Francis burst the balloon by telling the boys they were getting nothing out of it, and said he didn't want to hear another complaint coming out of anyone's mouths.

What could have been a paradigm shift ended up a damp squib.

A conspiracy theorist might speculate that I was dropped for the England game for my role as chief agitator; that it was an act of spite. I'm not sure that was the case, though.

Gats sat me down before the announcement and said he needed to find out a bit more about Owen Williams, who'd been going well for the Ospreys. Patch hadn't played much that season, and Chicken was still injured, so we were lacking a bit of depth and he wanted to give Owen a shot.

I couldn't disagree with that, and it didn't feel like I was being sidelined as a punishment. I was actually a touch relieved. The move to France with all the attendant worries about sorting visas, bank accounts, and removal vans had used up a lot of mental energy. Not to mention the arrival of a new baby, and all the emotional upheavals we'd experienced in camp.

To step away from the front line for a week or so felt like a blessing in disguise.

There was none of the usual excitement surrounding a massive Test match against England. We'd not really given the game a second thought, and suddenly it was less than twenty-four hours away.

Overnight, South Wales was shaken by its strongest earthquake in five years. It was an apt metaphor at a time when the very foundations of Welsh rugby were crumbling.

The pre-match mood was reflected in the match programme by the WRU president, Gerald Davies, where he wrote: 'This is a solemn time for Welsh rugby, which I must confess is putting it mildly. In the forefronts have been major complaints, recriminations, hostile censures and home truths. No sooner than one sore has been attended to than another blemish arises.'

There had been concerns that people would boycott the game, disillusioned by the off-field ructions, but the crowd was strong and delivered a passionate rendition of the anthem.

In the end, it was another disappointing defeat, which left us rooted to the bottom of the table. The 20–10 scoreline was an improvement on the thrashings we'd suffered against Ireland and Scotland, but we still looked bereft of ideas in attack, and were getting hit too frequently behind the gain line.

After so many years of success in the Six Nations, it felt as if it was all slipping away. The result saw us drop to an all-time low of tenth in the world rankings.

The off-field drama didn't recede during the build-up to the Italy game, with a bizarre story surfacing about a proposed merger between the Ospreys and English second-tier side, Ealing Trailfinders, which appeared to be genuine. The Ospreys–Scarlets merger, while hugely divisive, at least made economic and geographical sense, whereas this seemed completely bonkers.

The Ospreys boys – still reeling from the upheavals of the previous fortnight – now had a fresh set of worries. The Cardiff players, meanwhile, had been told the club still had twenty players to recruit for the following season, but only £400,000 left in their budget to do so.

There were some individuals earning that much alone, so you can imagine what sort of miserly wages were being proposed. Jarrod Evans had been offered an insulting pay cut and was left with no choice but to take a contract with Harlequins, rendering him ineligible for Wales. Other players were considering getting jobs as tradesmen and topping up their wages by playing semi-pro rugby. This included players who six months earlier had ambitions about rising through the ranks and becoming internationals. It was a potentially shameful waste of talent.

I was picking up a barbell in the gym the following Tuesday when Tomos Williams – arch-prankster that he is – sneaked up behind me and bellowed my name, Alan Partridge-style, at the top of his voice, 'DAN!' I jumped out of my skin, jarring my back in the process, and was pretty much ruled out of the Italy game there and then.

To assuage his guilt, he volunteered to be my gopher in Rome, buying me coffees, paying for Ubers, and generally sucking up to me.

Round the table with the boys, he was accusing me of milking it, claiming my poor lifting technique had been to blame, but privately he was quite remorseful.

Gats had already spoken about this being the last Six Nations for several of us, and I knew that applied to me.

I'd already been contemplating my international retirement, and I piled on the guilt, telling Tomos he'd ruined my big farewell.

Prav told me I wouldn't be able to train until the Friday, and Gats made the call to leave me out. If I had been a fresh-faced eighteen-year-old, I'd have understood, but I felt I had enough credit in the bank to be shown some faith.

With more than a hundred caps under my belt, I could have slotted in and done a job. Perhaps with hindsight it was the right call, especially given the importance of the game, but the disappointment I felt confirmed to me that the hunger still burned. The moment you feel indifferent at missing out on selection is the moment it's all over.

I had an emotional phone call with Alex afterwards, wondering if I'd played my last Six Nations game. If Owen Williams played a blinder and kept his place against France, I'd be going out with a whimper.

We beat Italy comfortably, exacting revenge for the previous year, and finally getting a win under Gatland's new regime.

In an echo of Gatland's previous tenure, we stayed on the continent, travelling to Nice ahead of the game against France. It was just the tonic we needed after the whirlwind of the previous month. After a victory and a few relaxing days on the Côte d'Azur, life didn't seem so bad.

When I pointed out that my new house was less than two hours' drive away, the boys masked their envy with sarcasm.

'Nice is all right,' said Tomos, 'but why would you want to live here when you could be training in the pissing rain in Llandarcy?'

Before he named the team to face France, Gats told the press there were eight of us who'd be playing their last Six Nations game. On the coach to training, I said, 'Stand up if you're one of the eight', and we all rose to our feet grinning. We'd worked out who he meant.

The boys were ripping the piss out of us, making the usual jokes about Zimmer frames and retirements. We told them if they couldn't win with us in the team, they'd have no hope when we all left en masse.

Some of the 'eight' were a bit down about it, but I took it as a positive. It focused my mind and helped me enjoy the build-up to what would undoubtedly be my last outing in this grand old tournament.

It wasn't a moment to get tight and worry about the outcome, but to revel in it, and enjoy my Six Nations swansong in an amazing country with great company.

If I wasn't to run out for my last Six Nations appearance in Cardiff, Paris would easily have been my second choice.

No one gave us a prayer of beating France, particularly after they'd battered England by a record score at Twickenham. The pressure was off, so we were given licence to go out and play. There was an element of coming full circle as I lined up outside Rhys Webb for the first time in five years.

We'd gone back a long way, first pairing up for Wales Under-16s in Dunvant, way back in 2005. Leigh Halfpenny had been in that team too, and he was alongside me again for this one. Two old friends who'd been through so much together, from those pre-dawn training sessions in Swansea College, all the way through to Wales and the Lions.

No offence to Nick Tompkins, who's a top bloke, but when he lined up next to me for the anthem, I had to politely tell him, 'Sorry mate, that's Leigh's spot.'

We started brilliantly, spurning kicks at goal in pursuit of the opening try which duly came for George North after seven minutes. But France turned up the heat after that, racing into an unassailable lead. They were simply better than us, but there were stirrings of our old selves as we battled back from 34–7 down to claim a four-try bonus point.

Some of the young players who came off the bench – Tommy Reffell and Dafydd Jenkins among them – added plenty of zip and energy, giving us some hope for the future.

Romain Ntamack was magisterial for France at fly half, and I was more than happy to oblige when he asked to swap shirts at full time.

Alex sent me a screengrab of his Instagram post showing him and me in each other's jerseys with the caption: 'Always an honour to play against you. One of my idols, huge respect #DanBiggar.'

I can't tell you how good that made me feel. It was a reminder of all that's great about rugby. You spend eighty minutes trying to undermine, outwit and hurt your opposite number, but at the end of it all you embrace, knowing that deep down you're just the same. For eighty minutes, that French emblem was a symbol of the enemy, yet within minutes of the final whistle, it was proudly adorning my chest.

Despite the loss, it felt as if we'd turned a corner. We'd fired a few shots and stumbled on a new way of playing. Perhaps that was the blueprint for the future, as opposed to the old way of strangling the life out of teams.

Gats said it was time to draw a line in the sand. He didn't think we were fit enough, and reckoned that was the root of the problem.

Overall, it had been our worst defensive performance in Six Nations history, and the irony wasn't lost on us that the guy who'd presided over our best was now installed in the opposition changing room singing 'La Marseillaise' in a Wigan accent.

Gats looked around the room and said, 'We're going to come in during the summer and I promise you, you'll become the world's fittest team again.'

Sitting there amid the detritus of our campaign, I thought he had a point. We'd probably all slackened off a bit without even realizing it. With the merest hint of a smile, he continued, 'If anyone thinks it's going to be too hard in the summer, that's no problem. Put your hand up now and we won't select you.'

I stole a few glances around the room and locked eyes with

Franny. He grinned and half-raised his hand in jest. The way my back was feeling, I nearly stuck both hands in the air. As much as the thought of another summer spent in Turkey and Switzerland filled me with dread, I knew Gats was right.

The old guard needed to fight for their places a bit more, and the new guys needed to be exposed to what *real* hard graft looked like.

I looked around at some of the youngsters and thought, *Buckle up boys, this isn't going to be some scenic trip to the Alps.*

He finished by praising our resilience against France, saying we showed real character. 'And on that evidence,' he said, 'we're going to surprise a few people in the World Cup.'

My season ended on a personal high as Toulon stormed to Challenge Cup victory, swatting Glasgow aside in a one-sided final in Dublin, to the noisy delight of our passionate supporters. After the misery and austerity of Wales, I had been transported back into a parallel universe where money was no object.

Bernard Lemaître hired a huge private plane to fly us to Dublin on the Tuesday, a full three days before the game. On arrival we all – players and coaches alike – piled into The Bridge bar in Ballsbridge where we gorged on a sumptuous dinner and saw off around eight pints of Guinness each. The bill was taken care of by the club, with no one having to put their hands in their pockets.

I couldn't help but feel guilty at such a conspicuous display of wealth at a time the game back home was in financial meltdown. London Irish would soon follow Worcester and Wasps into oblivion, and here we were, catching private jets, staying in luxury hotels and necking pints, all thanks to the club president's largesse. The whole week cost him a cool half-million quid, which seemed criminal when some of my mates in Cardiff were wondering if they'd get paid that month.

That Tuesday social set the tone for the week, giving us a sense of confidence that only grew. It was refreshing to see the coaches out with us, enjoying the vibe rather than being hunched over their laptops obsessing over every detail.

My contribution didn't last long as I suffered a head injury within the opening few minutes. Had I been twenty-one and hauled off that early, I'd have been gutted, but I'd been involved in our run to the final and felt I'd played my part. I'd joined Toulon to win trophies, and we won in style that day.

Remarkably, it was Toulon's fifth appearance in the Challenge Cup final, but the first time we'd won. I lived every moment of the match, urging my colleagues to pile the points on, and was as delighted as anyone at the final whistle, with the possible exception of Sergio Parisse, who spent the best part of an hour parading around the pitch with an Italian flag draped around his shoulders. It was his last ever game before retirement, and for a man who'd spent so much of his career on the losing side with Italy, it was fitting that he went out on a high.

It had been one of the most challenging seasons in my career. Rugby politics, financial collapses, sackings, scandals, threatened strikes and ugly defeats had all contributed to a toxic atmosphere that had seriously undermined my enjoyment of the game. As I returned to my new home on the Med, it was difficult to know how to gauge the future for Wales, with the World Cup looming large on the horizon.

21

EMERGING FROM
THE WRECKAGE

I was enjoying my Friday morning coffee on the terrace overlooking the Mediterranean when my phone buzzed. It was a message from Tips. 'Have you got two minutes?'

It sounded odd, like he had something to tell me.

I replied with a thumbs up, and he called immediately.

'I'm retiring, pal,' he announced, in his usual laconic way.

I thought he was taking the piss.

He'd been on fire and had finished the Six Nations as our first-choice open-side flanker.

'Why?' I asked bluntly.

He explained that he was struggling with a long-term toe problem and finding it increasingly harder to recover from injuries. His body, he claimed, was 'in bits', and he couldn't handle the thought of another summer being flogged to the point of exhaustion in Switzerland.

'Have you told Gats?' I asked.

'Yeah,' he replied, 'and he sounded a bit depressed, to be honest, because Al had just called him to say the same thing.'

'*What?*' I exclaimed. 'Al as well?'

In one fell swoop, we'd lost 250 caps' worth of experience. It was a lot to process.

'Anyway, I just wanted to let you know, pal,' he added, before mumbling his goodbye.

I laid down my phone, stared across at the shimmering sea and tried to get my head around it. Gats and Tips had never had a brilliant relationship. Although Tips had enjoyed an enormously successful career, he'd always been in Warby's shadow, and never felt like he was given the respect he deserved. So it's hard to know, but I wondered if he'd have stuck around if there was a different coach at the helm.

Once the news was made public, it sent social media into another whirl of conspiracy theories, with people speculating that Tips and Al had coordinated their announcements to inflict maximum damage on the WRU, or that their retirements were evidence of a wider unrest under the new regime.

The idea they were coordinated is nonsense. Al, in keeping with his personality, hadn't told *anyone*, so when he announced his retirement with a fairly prosaic Instagram post it was the first time any of his teammates knew about it.

The other theory doing the rounds was that they'd been told they were unlikely to make the final World Cup squad of thirty-three, so had jumped before they were pushed.

That might have been true of Al, who was that bit older and arguably past his prime, but Tips was still one of the first names on the team sheet.

I called Al and told him that while we'd had our ups and downs, one thing that remained constant was my respect for him and his phenomenal career. He was fairly guarded on the phone, but I hung up thinking it was probably the right move. He'll be remembered as one of our greatest ever players, and rightly so, but carrying on too long, when your body no longer responds to your mind's will, can be damaging. Knowing when to bow out is hard, but I think he's done so with his legacy intact.

The headline was that we'd lost two of our best players on the eve of the World Cup, but that wasn't strictly true. We'd lost two of our greatest ever, but at that point, Al was no longer first choice. Some players with that level of experience would still be an asset as a mentor or an auxiliary coach, but that's not in his character. He's all or nothing, and it's that singular focus that drove him to the very top. I think he would have struggled to come to terms with the fact he was no longer the main man. Fifteen years of being the undisputed number one, followed by two of being an also-ran was difficult to swallow.

He was never just a player; he was an institution. His aura was like a force-field, but it had faded in recent years, and it was the right time to exit the stage.

They couldn't have been more different, Tips and Al.

Often at breakfast, Al would sit on his own, hidden beneath his hoodie, happy in his own company. As I got older, I got to recognize his moods and knew when to steer clear. They were also a pretty reliable barometer for how training would go that day. The more distant he seemed, the further he'd drive standards out on the paddock.

Tips had no such emotional swings; he'd come in every morning whether he'd played or been dropped, whether he was fit or injured, and he was always the same. He and I came up through the ranks together, our careers running on parallel tracks, and there was no doubt I was going to miss him.

Warren's pre-World-Cup squad of fifty-four was the most bizarre I'd ever been involved in. Never before had such a large squad been assembled, leading to one of the boys joking, 'I didn't know we had fifty-four decent players in Wales.'

There were boys in it who were either not ready or not good enough. And when the squad is as bloated as that, any omissions appear even more glaring. Thomas Young was one of the form back-row forwards in Europe, scoring spectacular tries and winning turnovers for fun, yet he didn't make the cut.

I wondered what was going through Warren's mind. Was he doubting himself?

More negative press was to follow when Rhys Carré was very publicly ejected for failing to hit his fitness targets. The reasons were outlined in a press release and released via social media. I cannot fathom what the thinking was behind such a move, and to publicly shame him in that way seemed needlessly vindictive. With a squad that large, a cull was always going to be necessary, and he could have been cut then, along with several others, without all the ridicule he was forced to endure.

It left a bad taste in my mouth and amplified the feeling – with the team in disarray and the shock waves from the financial storm still being felt – that I was probably getting out at the right time.

Not long after, Gats claimed in an interview that he wouldn't have come back if he'd known the true scale of the problems facing Welsh rugby. That felt a little disingenuous, and was another negative swipe when we needed an injection of optimism. I considered myself really fortunate to have worked under him in his prime, but I wasn't convinced at that stage that he was the same coach he'd once been.

During the first session back in Fiesch, Switzerland, I looked across the line at all the boys doubled over, retching and gasping for air, and thought, 'What on earth am I doing here?'

It was even more brutal than I'd remembered. It wasn't even the end of the session, just the latest of an endless sequence of reps. I dug in through sheer mental willpower, but I do remember looking at the youngsters, marvelling at their energy and realizing that those days were behind me.

I didn't feel unfit necessarily, but I definitely felt four years older.

Selection felt really open, unlike four years earlier when we had a settled team. It was impossible for me not to compare this camp with that one, especially as we were in the same location.

The truth is, it was like night and day compared to 2019. Back then, we'd won the Grand Slam en route to topping the world rankings, and had enjoyed a record-breaking winning streak. Eight years earlier, when we were in the pool of death, Gats had walked into the gym early in the summer and written, 'We *will* beat England' on the whiteboard. At that point, there hadn't been one person in our squad who didn't believe it to be true.

Right now, we knew we were a long way behind the world's best. We couldn't just bluff our way to success.

By the time our first warm-up game against England rolled around, Gats was telling the media he had no idea who'd make our final squad of thirty-three. We beat England 20–9 in Cardiff on 5 August 2023, and looked comfortably the better side. We should have won the rematch in Twickenham too a week later, letting slip a 17–9 lead and failing to capitalize on their disciplinary implosion which saw them reduced to twelve men.

One of those given his marching orders was Owen Farrell, who saw red for a high tackle on Taine Basham. The following Monday I was walking through the car park at the Vale when a journalist beckoned me over and asked if I'd seen Gats's column in the *Telegraph*. I replied that I hadn't, and he raised an eyebrow suggesting I should check it out.

Fishing my phone out of my bag, I saw that Alex had already sent it to me. I began to scroll down and could feel my pulse quickening with anger. I couldn't believe what I was reading.

Once Gats had finished criticizing Owen's tackle technique, he started laying into me for confronting Faz on the field. 'Dan Biggar's reaction in confronting Owen after the tackle disappointed me,' he claimed. 'Dan is one of our most experienced players and in that moment, you wanted him to be calm and relaxed . . . But engaging and confronting Owen led to a bit of a scuffle [which] was the last thing we wanted. It would have sent mixed messages to our younger players. In big moments like that you want your most experienced players to show leadership and calmness.'

I had to stop myself from striding up to his office to have it out with him. My opposite number had been shown a deserved red card, and he'd chosen to bawl *me* out in a national newspaper column.

Alex must have read my mind, because a message popped up saying, 'Don't do anything you'll regret now.'

She was right – losing my rag with the head coach could easily put my World Cup place in jeopardy, and I wasn't about to do that.

To rewind a little, I didn't actually *know* why the ref had blown his whistle at the time. It wasn't until I saw Faz's tackle on the big screen that I reacted, instinctively saying, 'Fucking *hell.*'

Owen took umbrage, shouting back, 'Stop fucking complaining, Bigs.'

I told him to fuck off, and he marched over and yelled, 'What are you going to do about it, you soft cunt?'

That was the point at which it escalated, and I said, 'Who the hell do you think you are, going around cheap shotting people all the time?'

I told him just because his England mates didn't have the balls to stand up to him, it didn't mean I wouldn't.

It wasn't the most illuminating of exchanges, but he instigated it, not me. He was the one who put the high shot in, and he was the one who got up in my face.

I called the WRU press officer and vented, telling her what I'd wanted to tell Gats. *Is Owen in your team, or am I? Have I been part of the team that won you Grand Slams and Championships, and delivered you loads of money and kudos? Aren't I that guy?*

I have no problem in having confrontational conversations behind closed doors, but I don't expect my national coach to bad-mouth me in the press, especially when I'd done nothing wrong.

I'd been commissioned to write a newspaper column myself, but I'd given the WRU the right to veto anything they considered unsuitable. In fact, they'd asked me to remove a line referencing Faz where I'd said, 'He's not God', fearing it would be inflammatory. I wondered aloud whether Gats's column had been subject to the same degree of scrutiny, but inside I knew no one would have had the balls to challenge him.

There's also a question to be asked about how sensible it is to allow a head coach to write a column like that when he's in charge of a national team.

You may think I'm overreacting, but it would be disingenuous to pretend it didn't hurt. It resurrected the ghosts of 2015 when, for whatever reason, he couldn't find it within himself to praise me. It felt like a calculated move, but I didn't know what he was trying to achieve. It's not like I was some impetuous young kid who needed his wick trimming; I was one of the most experienced players he had, and I'd always worn my heart on my sleeve.

Though I allowed the rage to boil within, our relationship that week was entirely professional, which probably reflects a mutual stubbornness on both sides. Neither of us brought it up, and I gave my best impression of appearing unperturbed. There was clearly an elephant in the room whenever we sat down to talk tactics, but neither of us was willing to address it.

The recurrence of an old back injury ruled me out of the final warm-up game against South Africa, which bothered me for two reasons. One, it robbed me of the chance to run out in front of the home fans for the last time, and two, it denied me a final audition.

Given the unacknowledged tension between Gats and me, I couldn't take my World Cup place for granted. Sensing my nervousness, Prav told Warren that with a bit of management I could potentially play, but I wouldn't be 100 per cent. The three of us walked up to the barn together, and Gats said, 'Don't worry, we're not going to find out anything we don't already know, and it'll be a good chance for Sam Costelow to get more experience.'

While that sentence doesn't sound like much, it flooded me with reassurance. I interpreted it as, 'You're too important to risk in an ultimately meaningless game.'

He told me to relax, rest my knee and take the weight off my back. I couldn't help but reflect on his contradictory attitudes;

one day he's publicly bawling me out in a newspaper column, the next he's wrapping me in cotton wool. Nevertheless, it was the moment I knew I was in the World Cup squad, and that came as a huge relief. I'd genuinely begun to have doubts, particularly given Gats's past form in dropping big-name players, and his overtly critical column.

I was struck by a strange melancholy when I realized I'd played my last game at the Principality Stadium, and that I'd never run out into that glorious arena again and experience that magical ambience I'd grown to cherish. But it was counterbalanced by the knowledge that I'd done it my way.

My goal had been to reach the 2023 World Cup and retire from international rugby on my own terms. I'd seen so many great players either left stranded or limping on too long. I wanted to be in control of my own destiny, and I'd rather do it a year early than a year late.

Gats has given me a lot, and we've achieved so much together, but I didn't want him retiring me. I'm not saying the frostiness between us was unique – his management style was deliberately distant and aloof – but our relationship was always a functional rather than affectionate one.

And so, we travelled to France for the final chapter of my international career. After all the turmoil, the speculation and the preparation, it was finally time to enter the fray, and to see if we could emerge stronger from the rubble of a ruinous year.

We were in Pool C, alongside Fiji, Portugal, Australia and Georgia, and our first game was against Fiji on 10 September. They were a side who'd risen above us in the world rankings, and were considered by many to be dark horses for the tournament.

I wouldn't have said it publicly, but my opinion then was that it was coin toss: we had a 50-50 chance at best. Their squad was brimming with talent, they had an islands-based side in Super

Rugby and were on a steep upward trajectory. They also traditionally started strongly in World Cups.

Our attitude was nowhere near as bullish as it had been in 2019. The messages internally were all about working hard, improving, and hoping we could pull off a few shocks. So I'm not sure anyone imagined the game would be as dramatic and breathless as it turned out to be, delivering one of the most captivating spectacles in World Cup history. After the most horrendous nerve-jangling denouement, during which we spent ten minutes dangling from the edge of a cliff by our fingernails, we somehow emerged the victors.

At the final reckoning we'd made a shoulder-numbing 253 tackles, a tally virtually unheard of over eighty minutes of rugby. They'd enjoyed 65 per cent of possession, and at times had shredded our defence like a buzzsaw through plywood, but we'd held on.

By the end I was emotionally wrung out. For what seemed like an eternity, I stood with my hands on my head, just staring into the middle distance, trying to process what had happened. It may then surprise you to learn that – after overcoming the odds and delivering an epic bonus-point victory – my overwhelming emotion was anger.

I was furious at the negative coverage that followed our win; at the suggestions we'd been lucky, that the referee had been lenient, that we'd been 'sucked in' to playing the Fijian way. But most of all I was angry at the fevered dissection of my 'altercation' with George North.

The incident in question took place on the stroke of half-time and was utterly trivial in the scheme of things, but had been inevitably blown up into a 'story'. We were 18–14 ahead after a frenetic opening forty, and Nick Tompkins and George North decided to run from deep into the teeth of Fiji's aggressive defence. It was naïve and could easily have led to a turnover and a Fijian try. It was a tough enough game anyway, without us shooting ourselves in the foot, and I shouted at George to 'get the fucking ball off the park.'

That was it. Within thirty seconds George and I were in the changing room together calmly talking tactics. Yet if you read the papers and watched the coverage, you'd think I'd committed a capital offence. I guess if a newspaper can place me – or Owen, or Johnny for that matter – at the centre of the story, they'll get more clicks. You only have to look at what happened to Owen after the World Cup to see how it can grind you down. I hope we haven't seen the last of him in an England shirt, but it looks as if the constant carping and abuse might have forced him into premature retirement.

What hurt the most was that much of the criticism came from ex-colleagues; the guys who know me best and who I thought would have had my back. Some pundits also accused me of playing up to the camera. For the record, I've never done *anything* for the camera. When you're lost in the emotional maelstrom, gasping for breath, and wringing every last ounce of energy from your body, the presence of TV cameras doesn't even register.

Bottom line was, I thought my performance – and that of the team – deserved a bit more credit. As well as the nonsense about George and me, there were plenty of people peddling the theory that the referee had been biased in our favour. It seemed like the whole world had been desperate for Fiji to win, and it saddened me that so much of the coverage was about our supposed good fortune rather than our indomitable spirit. During one of Fiji's long raids on our line, we'd conceded multiple penalties but avoided a yellow card. When we eventually got back in their territory, they'd illegally collapsed a maul and had a player sent to the bin. Most pundits seemed to fixate on this as an example of favouritism. I agree, we might have been fortunate to have avoided a yellow, but their maul offence was a clear and obvious act of foul play.

As far as I was concerned, it was the game of the weekend. Our last-quarter wobble was as much down to Fijian brilliance as us freezing under pressure. It was the warrior spirit of a proud nation desperately trying to salvage something from the wreckage. When we'd built a 32–14 lead with fifteen minutes to play, we thought we were home and hosed. But Fiji surged back with menace and intent, taking advantage of a Corey Domachowski yellow card to roar back into the game. When Mesake Doge crashed over in the 78th minute it was 32–26, and we began to fear the worst.

I'd been subbed off, and my heart was thumping as I paced around the dugout, sweating relentlessly in the suffocating heat.

Five metres out, with eighty-one minutes on the clock, Fiji pulled the trigger. Our defence had narrowed alarmingly, and Semi Radradra – one of the deadliest finishers in the game – was out wide and in space. I could see it happening in slow motion. Teti Tela wound up the pass, floating it over the heads of his two centres, and towards Radradra who was accelerating towards it, unmarked. The past six months flashed before my eyes – the Six Nations, the training camps, the scandals, the uproar – a tumbling whirr of images that had led up to this point. We'd worked so hard, fought so desperately to pull Welsh rugby back from the brink, and it had all come down to this. There was no one in world rugby you'd trust more to catch that ball and finish it. But just this once, in a moment that will haunt him for evermore, Semi Radradra dropped it.

Never has a final whistle sounded more welcome.

The affection between the players was obvious, and several of us made an effort to console the Fijians, many of whom were splayed on the turf, consumed with disappointment and regret. Albert Tuisue, who I'd played against a lot, gave me a steel clamp of a hug and I told him, 'Albert, I'm so glad I'm retiring so I never have to deal with you running at me again.' He replied in a high-pitched giggle that belied his bear-like frame, 'You know I'm always gentle with you, Dan.'

I'd played against Fiji in three consecutive World Cups and was so relieved I'd never have to face them again. Dillon Lewis put it most succinctly; he said that for a team widely acknowledged to be the most skilful in world rugby, their biggest skill of all is making you think you're shit.

I lost five pounds in weight during the game what with all the excessive sweating, so I had no qualms about gorging on cheeseburgers and red wine until 2 a.m. If the nutritionist asks, I was just replacing calories.

The overwhelming feeling of relief was palpable when we sat down as a group in the hotel restaurant.

There was another reason I'd felt so tense, and why the carping had got under my skin: 10 September would have been Mum's birthday. I hadn't told anyone, but I'd met Rachel and Alex in the morning, and we'd reminisced over coffee and a croissant.

They could sense the tension in me, as I was a bit sharp with a fan who'd asked for a selfie. The significance of the date had had more of an effect than I'd realized, adding an extra layer of emotional pressure.

We caught our flight to Nice the following morning, having banked no more than a couple of hours' sleep. It was then that realization dawned about what we'd achieved.

The victory changed the entire complexion of the tournament. Had we lost, we'd have been plunged straight into knockout rugby, with another defeat being terminal. Winning meant we could now rotate our squad for our next match against Portugal and set our course for the group decider against our old foe, Australia.

Mike Forshaw looked like a different bloke during the review. His wrinkles had smoothed, his shoulders had slackened, and he looked altogether more relaxed. His entire body language had changed.

I was pleased for him, and equally pleased for Jac Morgan, who'd led us superbly during the week. He's not the most demonstrative of captains, but he has a quiet authority, and a maturity that belies his years. He was comfortable delegating, and would bring me, Sanj or Will Rowlands in when he needed another perspective. He's good at letting the right people speak at the right time. Whenever we had a huddle either before or during a game, I'd make sure he had the last word.

By the Tuesday, my anger had dissipated completely. I had one of those rare epiphanies where I realized that – actually – life was pretty good. There I was, hanging out on the French Riviera with some of my best mates, gorging on gourmet French cuisine as the sun slowly slid beneath the horizon, being paid to travel the world playing the sport I love. I told myself to surrender to the experience and rinse every last drop from it. I knew this was the last time I'd get to do it, and I couldn't afford to let these precious moments pass me by.

Gats made sweeping changes to the team to face Portugal and we delivered a disjointed, unconvincing performance. Critically, Toby scored a fourth try in the last play of the game to secure the bonus point. The 28–8 scoreline was less emphatic than we'd hoped, but it was another bonus point win, which meant we'd picked up ten points from ten in the opening two rounds.

Fiji – as we suspected they might – beat Australia in St Etienne, which kept the pressure firmly on us. Australian rugby was in the midst of its own soap opera. Despite their miraculous comeback against us in the autumn, they'd fired their coach Dave Rennie and rehired Eddie Jones, who'd been released by England.

Opinion was divided as to whether it was an inspired appointment or a desperate throw of the dice. Eddie had already set the cat among the pigeons by dropping long-term captain, Michael Hooper, and mercurial playmaker, Quade Cooper, from his squad, leaving it shorn of hard-bitten experience. They were an unknown quantity, and no one could confidently pick a favourite ahead of our clash in Lyon. So much had happened since we'd beaten them in the previous World Cup, it seemed pointless to try to draw comparisons.

Most fans were readying themselves for another night of high drama and tension, but it turned out to be one of the most one-sided matches in our long and tangled rivalry. After eighty minutes, we'd condemned the Wallabies to their heaviest ever World Cup defeat and stormed into the quarter-finals with a game to spare.

Two minutes in, we were awarded our first lineout on halfway and we called a strike move we'd conceived that week in training It couldn't have unfolded better. Ryan Elias to Aaron Wainwright in the middle, Cawdor with the precision pass, me to Nick Tompkins in the midfield, and then a perfectly timed incursion from Jac, who sliced through the Aussie defence. Cawdor was on Jac's shoulder to finish off the move.

The whole stadium erupted, with tens of thousands of Welsh fans leaping to their feet in unison. It was a rare moment when something we'd planned came gloriously to fruition.

Sadly, that was pretty much the end of my contribution.

Five minutes later, I lunged to tackle their big lock, Richie Arnold, and pulled a muscle in my chest.

It was my fault; I'd got ahead of the ball and ended up scrambling back which led to me over-stretching. In the heat of the moment, I insisted I could play on, but within minutes it had tensed up and spread to my shoulder. I was forced to summon the medics and admit defeat.

Gareth Anscombe came on and delivered a clinical, Man-of-the-Match performance, helping us to a commanding 40–6 victory. I was delighted for Chicken, who'd missed the last World Cup and spent so much of his time since sidelined with injury. He'd had a really tough time of it mentally, and would have wondered if he'd ever experience something like this again. Gutting as it was to have sat most of it out, I was thrilled for him.

By his own admission, he'd struggled against Portugal, worrying too much about the team and not enough about himself. His performance against Australia was the epitome of single-minded focus. We played precise, error-free rugby, scoring every time we got in range. Had he not missed the conversion for Jac Morgan's last-minute try, he'd have eclipsed my record of the most points scored by a Welshman in a World Cup game.

I was only too happy to point that out to him when we embraced at the final whistle!

I was equally pleased for the other Gareth – Cawdor, who'd been doing what he always seemed to do at World Cups; absolutely carving up. As he'd done in 2015 against England, and 2019 against Australia, he'd provided another defining moment in Welsh rugby history. His performance this time against the Wallabies was one of his very best; it had energized the entire team. His try broke the record for the most scored by a scrum half in World Cups. That's some accolade.

We suggested to Gats that he gives him three years off before reintroducing him in 2026 in time for the next tournament. There's something about World Cups that brings out the best in him. He was a far cry from the lonely figure he'd cut in South Africa the previous summer, where he didn't play a single minute on tour.

Jac Morgan had been imperious once again, and amid the euphoria that followed the win, it was easy to forget a crucial moment which might just have been the turning point. At 10–6 down, with twenty minutes on the clock, Australia had spurned a kickable penalty to go for the corner. They made a mess of the lineout, and Jac scooped up the loose ball, belting it seventy metres downfield with all the poise and precision of a Test fly half. It was a 50:22 as well, meaning we had the throw-in to the lineout, and within minutes we'd scored ourselves.

Before that result, we'd been riding more on hope more than expectation, but looking around at some of the faces in the changing room, there was a noticeable shift in mindset. Australia might have been in disarray themselves, but we'd shown them no mercy. It proved we had more to give, and that was the first time I genuinely believed we had a semi-final in us.

As much as we were encouraged to celebrate, the coaches also urged us to keep our feet on the ground. Someone mentioned

Ireland's quarter-final against Argentina in 2015, when Ireland had coasted through their group only to have their pants pulled down by the Pumas. With Argentina our likely quarter-final opponents, we couldn't allow ourselves to fall into the same trap.

There was a two-week gap before our final group game against Georgia, and we were all given a few days off. Several of the boys disappeared to Disneyland with their families, a few went to Biarritz to chill on the beach, and Zammo made a beeline for Cannes to update his Instagram reel. I headed home to Toulon where it was an agreeable 28 degrees and enjoyed a few days at the poolside with Alex and the boys. When we arrived back, Gats put photos of two hotels up on the overhead projector. If we topped the pool, we'd get to stay in an amazing luxury hotel down on the peninsula near Toulon. If we came second, we'd be in the Mercure at Marseilles Airport. That was all the motivation we needed.

The Food Committee – led by Franny – had a shocker that week, booking us into a dreadful Italian restaurant with a buffet that would been unacceptable at a kids' birthday party. Not only that, they'd also booked it to clash with Fiji v Georgia, Liverpool v Spurs and the last few holes of the Ryder Cup. The Entertainments Committee were furious, levying an immediate punishment, and forcing every member of the Food Committee to walk back to the hotel – a journey of around an hour on foot. Served them right.

I had to sit the Georgia game out as I recovered from my pectoral injury. Our victory was convincing enough, but tainted by the loss of Toby Faletau to a broken arm. There are few players as influential as Toby, and he'd been playing his way back into top form.

After that match, it hit me – I wasn't ready for it all to end. If we won our quarter-final, we'd be here for another fortnight, and I could prepare myself emotionally to exit the stage. But if we lost, the curtain would fall, and it would be over in an instant.

I was told on the Monday that I'd be starting. On Tuesday,

Tomos Williams ran into me at training and the pec flared up again. I could sense the trepidation in the medics as they were treating me.

Chicken was struggling with his groin, and they were contemplating a quarter-final without either of their first-choice fly halves. On Thursday the rather more considerable figure of Dewi Lake ran into me. It was only a glancing blow, but it hurt like hell.

I tried to project an air of confidence but I was thinking, if I can't absorb a glancing blow in training, how on earth am I going to fare in a full-blooded Test match against a pack of marauding Pumas?

For a few hours afterwards I felt really low, convincing myself that this was how my fifteen-year Test career was going to end; with a whimper. Gats pulled me out of any further contact work during the afternoon session, and for the sake of appearances I objected, but he shook his head and called me aside.

He turned to the rest of the boys and said, 'Bigs has just been sin-binned, you'll have to defend with fourteen for the rest of the session.'

It was a small but significant gesture; a tacit acknowledgement, from a man serially averse to giving praise, that I was too valuable to risk getting injured.

Warren was confrontational in his final press conference, tiring of questions about Wales being on the 'lucky' side of the draw and telling those moaning to 'just deal with it'.

There's no doubt the draw had been skewed by the decision to base the seedings on world rankings a year after the 2019 World Cup. We'd been fourth in the world then, but had slid down considerably in the intervening years, while the likes of Ireland and Scotland had moved in the other direction.

It meant we were on the opposite side of the draw to France, South Africa, Ireland and New Zealand – the four best teams in the world by some distance – and consequently had an easier route to the semis.

On Friday, the coaches finally allowed us to catch the ferry to

Toulon for our final walk-through. We'd been nagging them all week to let us do it, but they'd vetoed it on the grounds they didn't want us to feel 'on holiday'.

It felt fantastic, chewing the fat with the boys en route before docking and strolling through my new hometown towards the Stade Mayol. We'd been largely insulated by the excitement that had been building among the fans, but it began to filter through that week.

My mates were texting, asking about tickets, and loads of people were jumping on flights sensing something special might be about to happen. Argentina had rather stumbled through the tournament, failing to beat England despite having a one-man advantage for the entire game, and most observers considered us strong favourites.

I had to keep any optimism in check. Knowing my retirement was imminent didn't allow me to relax as you might think it would; it put me under more pressure to finish on a high.

We played some of our best rugby during the opening half an hour, but a malfunctioning lineout and general lack of precision prevented us from capitalizing. Three times we worked Louis Rees-Zammit into space, and three times we were snuffed out. We'd started at a fair lick and scored the opening try after some pleasing interlinking between forwards and backs that had bamboozled the Pumas' defence. Cawdor made the break that cut them open.

This time it happened to be me on his shoulder to take the scoring pass.

I nearly exploded with pride, saluting the crowd with a ferocious fist pump and hammering the hoardings with joy. I definitely wasn't ready to go home.

On the stroke of half-time, Josh Adams shoulder-checked Tomás Cubelli, sparking a mêlée in our 22. The resulting penalty allowed them to claw things back to 10–6, which seemed a poor return for our dominance. In addition to those spurned chances, I'd missed a penalty that I'd normally have kicked in my sleep. We were anxious about the fragility of that four-point buffer. It just didn't seem enough.

The last ten minutes had seen the pendulum swing towards them. We'd spoken before the game about not allowing them in our 22. Easier said than done, but a combination of good discipline and accurate kicking can keep the opposition away from the danger zone.

In those last ten minutes, we'd got sloppy and started conceding penalties around halfway, allowing them easy entries into our half. They're a team that can't hurt you too much from their half, but if you let them into your 22, they're much harder to stop.

The referee, Jaco Peyper, had withdrawn injured after fifteen minutes, and had been replaced by the Englishman, Karl Dickson. We'd prepared for Peyper and studied how he refereed crucial areas like breakdowns and scrums, so there was bound to be an element of disruption when Dickson came on, and there's no doubt the penalty count against us began to rise, too. But I won't claim that's the reason for the momentum swing. These things happen, and we should have been good enough to adapt.

We were still protecting a narrow lead as the game entered its final quarter, when the Pumas bulldozed their way back into our 22 and started pressuring our defence with a series of heavy-duty carries. As they were building momentum, Guido Petti, their enormous lock forward, hurled himself into a ruck, smashing into Nick Tompkins's jaw with his shoulder. It went unnoticed in the confusion of tangled limbs, but when the TMO drew Dickson's attention to it, we were all expecting him to brandish his red card.

To our utter astonishment, he not only left the card in his pocket, but declined to even give a penalty. It was a huge moment, and within minutes they'd regained the lead. Nick – already bewildered by Dickson's decision – was ordered from the field for an HIA. Insult to injury, literally.

The numbers on our jerseys had begun to peel off in the clammy Mediterranean heat, and there couldn't have been a more apt metaphor for our performance. Things were coming apart at the seams.

With five minutes to go, I was brought off. Sam Costelow replaced me, and around the same time Argentina brought on their thirty-four-year-old veteran, Nicolás Sánchez.

A changing of the guard for us, and a last hurrah for him.

We were two points down, and I didn't know whether that was it. Was this my final game for Wales? Would this be the last time I'd leave the field wearing that iconic jersey?

I had the answer within moments, as Sánchez – showing all his guile and experience – picked off Sam's pop pass to Tompkins and cantered all the way to the try line.

In those ten agonizing seconds our World Cup, and my international career, came to a shuddering end.

The scenes in the stands at the final whistle could not have been more contrasting. The Argentinian fans had whipped themselves into a frenzy, pulling off their shirts and spinning them above their heads, as the Welsh sank into their seats, heads in hands.

I was slumped in the dugout, physically spent and overwhelmed with emotion. It was all tumbling around inside me; the gut-wrenching reality of defeat and the stark realization that that was the final act.

After fifteen years of glorious euphoria, abject despair and everything in between, it had all ended on the sourest of notes. Rare is the sportsman who gets to go out on top, but this felt cruel and wrong.

At a time when I so desperately wanted to be revelling in triumph, I was slumped at the side of the pitch, exhausted and bereft. Argentina had thoroughly deserved their victory. Like us, they'd been written off, but had shown immense character to wrestle back control of that game.

Alex and the boys were sitting just above the dugout, and she passed James and Ollie down to join me on my final lap. I splintered off from the rest of the players, wanting to absorb as much of it as I could.

As much as I wanted to applaud the fans and thank them for their loyalty, I felt a bit of a fraud walking around after we'd lost.

Johnny Sexton had a similar moment with his kids later that night when Ireland were knocked out by New Zealand and the cameras picked up his son telling him, 'You're still the best, Dad.'

I wish I could tell you about an equally profound exchange between me and my boys, but Ollie wasn't speaking in full sentences, and all James wanted to do was look for my dad and our friends in the crowd.

I felt guilty that I hadn't given them and Alex a more worthy send-off.

Going down the tunnel, it hit me hard. It takes a lot to move me to tears, but I was pretty close on that occasion. Every step I took felt heavy with significance. It was the last time I'd ever walk into a changing room in a Welsh shirt again.

In my mind, I'd envisaged a triumphant one, full of laughter and high jinks. But this was like a funeral parlour. Everyone looked battered, defeated and drained of all vitality.

It's in those moments you notice the damage; the swollen knee joints, the bumps and bruises, the bleeding cuts and grazes. And beneath all that, beneath the discarded boots, the clumps of earth and the crushed water bottles, the silent howl of despair.

It never gets any easier.

This was my third World Cup, and I'd suffered three agonizing knockout defeats. Twice to South Africa, and now to Argentina.

You never get conditioned to that feeling of crushing disappointment. Every time, it feels fresh and raw.

With hindsight, I'd look back at the 2019 semi-final as the one that really got away. We could so easily have beaten the Springboks, and there wouldn't have been a single person in our squad who didn't think we could have beaten England in the final.

In 2023, once the dust had settled, there was an acceptance that perhaps a quarter-final had been the right time to leave the stage. Given the raging turmoil in Welsh rugby before the tournament, maybe we'd done as well as we could have expected. There would have been some in the squad, maybe even me, who thought play-ing New Zealand would have been a step too far.

Josh Adams and Gareth Davies were brilliant in those gut-wrenching moments after the final whistle, putting aside their personal disappointment to congratulate me on my career. They asked for photos, and that meant more to me than anything.

The respect of my teammates, with whom I'd travelled to some of the darkest places, was the most precious thing I could have asked for.

I was conscious that Prince William and his son George were hovering in the corner, and felt duty-bound to go over for a chat. He said, 'You're not really finished, are you?' I managed to crack half a smile, and said, 'I think I am.'

Twenty-four hours later, at Toulon harbour, at eight o'clock on a Sunday evening in mid-October, I found myself tumbling into the water. I say tumbled; pushed would be a more accurate descrip-tion. Tomas Francis, lubricated by several beers, thought it would be funny to bundle me in fully clothed. We were returning from a day on the sauce when Franny caught me off guard, shoving me unceremoniously off the jetty. The diners enjoying a quiet eve-ning meal didn't know what to think when a soaked Welshman hauled himself out of the harbour and staggered past their table, dripping wet and apologizing profusely.

I'd had my phone on me, full of photos from my last day in a Wales shirt and more than a hundred messages I'd not yet read. When I pulled it from my pocket it was – predictably – dead, and Franny had a sudden attack of conscience.

'Shit, sorry pal,' he muttered, as Mason Grady and Daf Jenkins wrestled him to the floor, stripped him to his pants and threw his clothes and flip-flops in the harbour.

He had no choice but to jump in and retrieve them. Now there were two sopping wet Welshmen trying to persuade a reluctant succession of taxi drivers to take them home.

With my phone dead, I had to rely on the charity of Kieran Hardy to order me an Uber and a bucket of KFC to soak up the booze.

I'd experienced glorious highs and devastating lows as a rugby player. I'd leapt for joy and wept in anguish. But I'd not experienced pathos like I did that following morning, when I woke in the hotel, ordered a taxi just for me and slipped quietly away.

An ex-international. A ghost in the night. There had been no emotional send-off, no opportunity to properly say goodbye. I'd seen a few people at breakfast, but most of the boys were either sleeping off their hangovers or packing to leave. The goodbyes I did have felt rushed and inadequate.

My eighteen-year professional relationship with Neil Jenkins ended with a brief hug next to the coffee machine.

It just didn't seem enough.

Jenks asked me to give Sam Costelow a pep talk, as he'd apparently been suffering terrible abuse on social media following the interception. I wandered over and sat with Costy for a few minutes, telling him the team was his now, and he needed to shape it in his image.

'Ignore the doubters,' I told him. 'Ignore the critics, and back yourself to the hilt.'

We shook hands and it felt like the final act; the handing over of the baton.

The glorious weather of the past few days had given way to dark skies and fine drizzle, which mirrored my mood as the taxi pulled away. It was the solitude that got me.

Through all the highs and lows of the previous fifteen years, we'd done it as a team. We'd won together and lost together. That brotherhood and sense of camaraderie would be impossible to replace in the real world.

I felt like I'd reached the end of a book, only to find the last chapter had been torn out. There was no weaving together of the strands, no satisfying resolution; just a silent taxi ride through the mist and mizzle.

The driver had attempted a bit of small talk when I'd clambered in, but soon realized I wasn't in the mood. My phone – much to Franny's relief – had come back to life, and I opened WhatsApp for the first time since Saturday morning.

Not only was it my last official day as a Welsh international, but also my thirty-fourth birthday. There was a smattering of birthday messages among the dozens of consoling texts. Most were from friends, colleagues and family, but there was one from the former South Africa coach, Alan Solomons, whom I'd never met. He'd tracked down my number just to pass on his commiserations, saying he was sorry my career had ended that way, but that I'd been a great servant to the game.

It was enormously touching that someone I didn't know had taken the time to do that. Tomos Williams messaged: 'Congratulations on an unbelievable career, one of the very best to have done it.'

It was simple and sweet but left a lump in my throat.

As I started to read more, the emotions came flooding to the surface. I wasn't in the right headspace to respond to any of them, and shoved my phone back in my pocket, preferring to be alone with my thoughts. All I could think about was how wrong it felt.

If we'd made it to the semis, I'd have had two weeks to soak it all up. A definitive period with an end point. I could have taken the whole squad out for a meal, and thanked everyone for the memories, for their support and their friendship. We could have reminisced, told stories and enjoyed one another's company, in my case, for one last time. It all felt horribly abrupt, like a door had been slammed shut.

Given how long I'd spent as a player and all I'd given to the jersey, I felt like I deserved more. In the final shakedown, that was far more disappointing than the result. I don't want or expect sympathy. Those were the cards I was dealt, and there's little I can complain about. If I'd still been playing in Wales, I might have had the same emotional send-off that Al, Leigh and Tips did a few weeks later when Wales played the Barbarians in Cardiff.

I'd made my bed by moving to France, and I had to lie in it, but seeing the outpouring of affection towards those three did make me feel a little envious.

Ultimately though, I have no regrets. Most rugby players give up when their bodies do. For me, it was more in the mind. As much as my limbs were beginning to creak and groan, it was the mental pressure that weighed the heaviest. That's unique to playing 10 in Wales. Whether you're the captain or not, you carry the biggest burden. You call the plays, you direct the players and you live and die by the performance of the team.

When I reflect on it all, I can say without any doubt that I gave it everything.

During that final game, with a plastic guard on my chest, and my knee heavily strapped, I harried and chased, I barked and cajoled, I kicked and tackled, and I leapt and tugged. I hurled my bruised and battered body into the path of every plundering Puma, emptying my tank until there was nothing left to give.

Most high-performance athletes retire in their thirties and have to confront the reality that their status is in perpetual decline. How do you recreate that adrenaline rush from behind a desk? How do you make connections as deep as those forged in the heat of battle? How do you maintain that superhuman aura? You can only marvel at the spoils of your victories for so long. They're an anchor to hold on to, a solid marker of achievement when the memory of success becomes illusory and difficult to grasp.

But there is also something daunting about winning a trophy and having to start with another blank page. There is an inner contentment in knowing I won't have to do that again.

My time is done, and I have a decent haul of medals to show the grandchildren.

It feels strangely comforting to have scaled that final mountain and not be gazing across at another series of jagged, unconquered peaks.

ACKNOWLEDGEMENTS

A professional sportsperson is only as good as his support network, and I've been blessed with one of the very best. There are many people who've played a huge role in my success, and I'd like to thank the following.

To Mum, Dad, Rachel, Mamo and Dado, thanks for always being there to 'mop up'. There'll always be people who want to share in the good times – the victories and the triumphs - but it's my family who've been there at *all* times. The ones I'd call in the car when I was frustrated, angry or upset. The ones who've listened without judgement and always given the best advice.

To Mandy, Paul and James, who are technically my in-laws, but are actually more like a second mum, dad and brother. They're genuinely lovely people with hearts of gold and personalities to match. I'm proud to call them family.

To Dean Mason, who believed in me at a young age, and remained one of my biggest supporters – not only when times were good, but when they were challenging, too. During some of the more difficult periods, he's invariably been the one to nudge me back onto the right path.

As we grow older and our lives become more complicated, we often drift apart from the friends of our youth. Thankfully, that's not been the case for me, and my friendship with the 'HOW' boys from Gowerton Comp has only strengthened over the years. We've lived together, holidayed together and been there for each other since we were kids. They've always been a massive support network for me, especially in those early days when I was a rugby obsessive. They may have teased me for refusing to drink, but there was no peer pressure, and they've always had my back. Rhys, Gwil, Ben, Damian, Aaron, Chris and Ciaran, I salute you!

I wouldn't have had the career I've had without Jenks. From those gloomy nights at the Gnoll working on my technique to lining up vital kicks in Grand Slam deciders and World Cup knockout matches, he's been my near-constant shadow, mentor and confidant. Never one to mince his words or stand on ceremony, his exacting standards have driven me to be the player I am. One of the all-time greats.

Likewise, Shaun Edwards. He set his standards so high and dragged everyone up to his level. I'm grateful that some of his traits – mental toughness, northern grit and a refusal to roll over – have rubbed off on me.

Thanks, too, to Rob Howley, for showing faith in me for all those years, often while taking flak for doing so. A fantastic coach and a great guy to have in your corner.

Warren Gatland and I are arguably two peas in a pod – stubborn, demanding and proud – and we didn't always see eye to eye, but there's no doubting his credentials and his influence on my career.

Prav, thanks for working miracles time and again, getting me fit for matches I had no right to be fit for. Without your magic hands, I'd have far fewer caps.

Caz, you were a second mum to everyone in that Welsh squad. Nothing was too much trouble, and you did far more than your job description gave you credit for. If they ever tried to get rid of you (as if they would), every last player would go on strike!

Sean Holley remains one of my closest friends in rugby. If he hadn't taken a punt and backed me ahead of more experienced players, I may not have ended up where I did. Likewise, if Tim Lopez hadn't phoned Mum when I was sixteen, who knows what might have happened. Our relationship is not just one of player and agent, but a genuine friendship.

ACKNOWLEDGEMENTS

To all of my teammates at Gorseinon, Swansea, the Ospreys, Northampton, Wales, the Lions and Toulon, thank you for the fellowship, the banter and the lifelong memories. I want to acknowledge each and every one of you, even James Haskell.

Thanks to Chris Boyd and Sam Vesty for transforming me as a player and pushing me to greater heights. Chris is the best head coach I've ever worked under. He cared about me as a person as much as a player, and created an environment that helped me flourish. Sam is the best technical coach I've had. His attention to detail helped me change and evolve my game; he made me better every single day.

Thank you to the team at Pan Macmillan. To Matthew Cole for commissioning the book in the first place, and to Sara Cywinski for taking on the project with such enthusiasm. Also to Rosa, Melissa, Jiri and Poppy for all their hard work behind the scenes.

Without Ross, clearly this book couldn't have happened. His talent for writing and ability to put me at ease helped make this process such an enjoyable one. Revisiting all these chapters of my life has been an invigorating and rewarding experience. I couldn't have chosen a better person to trust to tell my story. Our relationship began as one of writer and subject, but I now consider you a close friend. Thank you, mate, for your incredible contribution.

And, most importantly, my heartfelt thanks to Alex and the boys. You are literally everything to me. James and Ollie, you're the reason I play rugby – to provide for you and give you the best platform in life. I'm biased, but Alex is one of the finest human beings you'll ever meet. My beacon of sanity and the person who holds it all together behind the scenes. Quite simply, you're my best friend, my soulmate and someone I'm incredibly proud to call my wife.

PICTURE CREDITS